Routledge Revivals

A
TREATISE
OF
BOOK-KEEPING,
OR,
Merchants Accounts;

A
TREATISE
OF
BOOK-KEEPING,
OR,
Merchants Accounts;

IN THE
Italian METHOD of Debtor and Creditor.

Routledge
Taylor & Francis Group

First published in 1731 by J. Osborn and T. Longman

This edition first published in 2018 by Routledge
2 Park Square, Milton Park, Abingdon, Oxon, OX14 4RN
and by Routledge
52 Vanderbilt Avenue, New York, NY 10017, USA

Routledge is an imprint of the Taylor & Francis Group, an informa business

© 1731 by Taylor and Francis

Publisher's Note
The publisher has gone to great lengths to ensure the quality of this reprint but points out that some imperfections in the original copies may be apparent.

Disclaimer
The publisher has made every effort to trace copyright holders and welcomes correspondence from those they have been unable to contact.
A Library of Congress record exists under ISBN: 86029610

ISBN 13: 978-0-367-17535-1 (hbk)
ISBN 13: 978-0-429-05733-5 (ebk)

A treatise of book-keeping, or, merchants accounts; in the Italian method of debtor and creditor. ... By Alexander Malcolm, ...

Alexander Malcolm

ECCO

PRINT EDITIONS

Eighteenth Century
Collections Online
Print Editions

Gale ECCO Print Editions

Relive history with *Eighteenth Century Collections Online*, now available in print for the independent historian and collector. This series includes the most significant English-language and foreign-language works printed in Great Britain during the eighteenth century, and is organized in seven different subject areas including literature and language; medicine, science, and technology; and religion and philosophy. The collection also includes thousands of important works from the Americas.

The eighteenth century has been called "The Age of Enlightenment." It was a period of rapid advance in print culture and publishing, in world exploration, and in the rapid growth of science and technology – all of which had a profound impact on the political and cultural landscape. At the end of the century the American Revolution, French Revolution and Industrial Revolution, perhaps three of the most significant events in modern history, set in motion developments that eventually dominated world political, economic, and social life.

In a groundbreaking effort, Gale initiated a revolution of its own: digitization of epic proportions to preserve these invaluable works in the largest online archive of its kind. Contributions from major world libraries constitute over 175,000 original printed works. Scanned images of the actual pages, rather than transcriptions, recreate the works *as they first appeared.*

Now for the first time, these high-quality digital scans of original works are available via print-on-demand, making them readily accessible to libraries, students, independent scholars, and readers of all ages.

For our initial release we have created seven robust collections to form one the world's most comprehensive catalogs of 18th century works.

Initial Gale ECCO Print Editions collections include:

History and Geography
Rich in titles on English life and social history, this collection spans the world as it was known to eighteenth-century historians and explorers. Titles include a wealth of travel accounts and diaries, histories of nations from throughout the world, and maps and charts of a world that was still being discovered. Students of the War of American Independence will find fascinating accounts from the British side of conflict.

Social Science

Delve into what it was like to live during the eighteenth century by reading the first-hand accounts of everyday people, including city dwellers and farmers, businessmen and bankers, artisans and merchants, artists and their patrons, politicians and their constituents. Original texts make the American, French, and Industrial revolutions vividly contemporary.

Medicine, Science and Technology

Medical theory and practice of the 1700s developed rapidly, as is evidenced by the extensive collection, which includes descriptions of diseases, their conditions, and treatments. Books on science and technology, agriculture, military technology, natural philosophy, even cookbooks, are all contained here.

Literature and Language

Western literary study flows out of eighteenth-century works by Alexander Pope, Daniel Defoe, Henry Fielding, Frances Burney, Denis Diderot, Johann Gottfried Herder, Johann Wolfgang von Goethe, and others. Experience the birth of the modern novel, or compare the development of language using dictionaries and grammar discourses.

Religion and Philosophy

The Age of Enlightenment profoundly enriched religious and philosophical understanding and continues to influence present-day thinking. Works collected here include masterpieces by David Hume, Immanuel Kant, and Jean-Jacques Rousseau, as well as religious sermons and moral debates on the issues of the day, such as the slave trade. The Age of Reason saw conflict between Protestantism and Catholicism transformed into one between faith and logic -- a debate that continues in the twenty-first century.

Law and Reference

This collection reveals the history of English common law and Empire law in a vastly changing world of British expansion. Dominating the legal field is the *Commentaries of the Law of England* by Sir William Blackstone, which first appeared in 1765. Reference works such as almanacs and catalogues continue to educate us by revealing the day-to-day workings of society.

Fine Arts

The eighteenth-century fascination with Greek and Roman antiquity followed the systematic excavation of the ruins at Pompeii and Herculaneum in southern Italy; and after 1750 a neoclassical style dominated all artistic fields. The titles here trace developments in mostly English-language works on painting, sculpture, architecture, music, theater, and other disciplines. Instructional works on musical instruments, catalogs of art objects, comic operas, and more are also included.

The BiblioLife Network

This project was made possible in part by the BiblioLife Network (BLN), a project aimed at addressing some of the huge challenges facing book preservationists around the world. The BLN includes libraries, library networks, archives, subject matter experts, online communities and library service providers. We believe every book ever published should be available as a high-quality print reproduction; printed on-demand anywhere in the world. This insures the ongoing accessibility of the content and helps generate sustainable revenue for the libraries and organizations that work to preserve these important materials.

The following book is in the "public domain" and represents an authentic reproduction of the text as printed by the original publisher. While we have attempted to accurately maintain the integrity of the original work, there are sometimes problems with the original work or the micro-film from which the books were digitized. This can result in minor errors in reproduction. Possible imperfections include missing and blurred pages, poor pictures, markings and other reproduction issues beyond our control. Because this work is culturally important, we have made it available as part of our commitment to protecting, preserving, and promoting the world's literature.

GUIDE TO FOLD-OUTS MAPS and OVERSIZED IMAGES

The book you are reading was digitized from microfilm captured over the past thirty to forty years. Years after the creation of the original microfilm, the book was converted to digital files and made available in an online database.

In an online database, page images do not need to conform to the size restrictions found in a printed book. When converting these images back into a printed bound book, the page sizes are standardized in ways that maintain the detail of the original. For large images, such as fold-out maps, the original page image is split into two or more pages

Guidelines used to determine how to split the page image follows:

• Some images are split vertically; large images require vertical and horizontal splits.
• For horizontal splits, the content is split left to right.
• For vertical splits, the content is split from top to bottom.
• For both vertical and horizontal splits, the image is processed from top left to bottom right.

A TREATISE

OF

BOOK-KEEPING,

OR,

Merchants Accounts;

IN THE

Italian METHOD of *Debtor* and *Creditor*.

WHEREIN

The Fundamental Principles of that curious and approved
Method are clearly and fully explained and demonſtrated, from
the Nature and Reaſon of Things: From which again is deduced
a complete Syſtem of particular Rules, and Inſtructions for their
Application to a Merchant's Buſineſs, conſidered as acting either
for his own proper Account; or in Commiſſion, as Factor for
another; or, as concerned in Company. The whole illuſtrated
and exemplified with two Sets of Books, containing great Variety
of Practice in all thoſe Branches of Buſineſs.

To which are added,

Inſtructions for Gentlemen of Land Eſtates, and their Stewards or
Factors: With Directions alſo for Retailers, and other more private
Perſons.

By *ALEXANDER MALCOLM,* A. M.
Teacher of the Mathematicks at Aberdeen.

LONDON,
Printed for J. OSBORN *and* T. LONGMAN, *in* Pater-noſter-Row; F. FAYRAM
and E. SYMON, *at the* Royal Exchange. M.DCC.XXXI.

THE

PREFACE.

THE Neceſſity of a right *Method of Accounts* is ſo great; and the Perfection of the Method of *Debt* and *Credit* (called from the Inventors, the *Italian Method*) ſo well known, by long Experience, that I ſhould loſe all the Time and Pains beſtowed upon a more parti-cular Commendation of it. Yet, I cannot forbear quoting the Sentiments of the anonymous Author of a Book, cal-led, *The Gentleman-Accountant*; who is called in the Title Page, a *Perſon of Honour* : Speaking in Commendation of the Method of Accounts by *Debtor* and *Creditor*, he ſays, " Which Method is ſo comprehenſive, and perfect, as " makes it worthy to be put among the *Sciences* ; and to " be underſtood by all *Virtuoſi* ; whether they ever intend " to make Uſe of it or no ; even for pure Satisfaction " and Curioſity, or rather *Admiration* ; as happens, when, " with ſome Pains, we have attained the Knowledge of " any Art, or Skill, though leſs complex than this ; " which, through the Invention of Ages paſt, univerſal " Practice, and in Matters of Intereſt (the fierceſt En-" gagements of human Wit and Stratagem) is reduced, " as this is, to a conſummate Perfection, *&c.* Therefore " (*he thinks*) that, beſides the real Value of it in Life,

" every

" every *ingenious Gentleman* may have Reafon to know
" this Art, as a Sort of *human Learning.*

The Writers on this Subject are, indeed, very numerous, and as various in their Ways of Treating it; fo
that fome will be ready to think it is long ago exhaufted.
As my Bufinefs of Teaching has led me to examine very
narrowly into what others have done; fo, in Vindication
of the prefent Undertaking, I fhall only fay, that I have
not met with any Treatife that I could ufe for a Syftem of
Inftructions to Learners: And, as in a long Experience of
Teaching, I have applied my felf to find a plain and rational Way of delivering the Principles and Rules of this ufeful Art, fitted, as near as poffible, to every Capacity; fo
you have, in this Treatife, the Syftem or Courfe of Lef-
fons, which I have, for many Years, read to Students,
very fuccefsfully, with every Capacity that could learn at
all; and which I found my felf obliged to make publick,
for the Ufe of my own Scholars chiefly; though alfo very
willingly for the Sake of others.

As to any further Account of what I complain of in other
Treatifes, I have faid all that I thought neceffary, in the
Beginning of *Chapter* II. And for a more particular Account
of my own Plan, and the Contents of the following Work,
take it thus:

You have firft a *Treatife* of the *Principles* and *Rules* of
Book-keeping, divided into three *Chapters.* In the firft, I
have explain'd the *Fundamental General Principles* and *Rules*
of the Method, in fuch a Manner as to demonftrate the
true Reafon of every Step, from the Nature and Defign of
Accounts; fo that the Practice and Application may be a
Work of Judgment, and not merely of Memory. The
General Principles are but few, and thofe not very difficult:
                                                              Yet

Yet much depends upon a right Explication, to give a Learner a clear general Notion of them ; for if this is once got, particular Applications are very eafy.

In the fecond *Chapter*, I have explained the Application more particularly ; fhewing how a Courfe of Regular Accounts is begun and carried on ; in the Defcription of the various Accounts which are neceffary, or fufficient, to comprehend all the Parts of a Merchant's Bufinefs, in the moft diftinct and orderly Manner ; confidered particularly under thefe Heads, *viz.* What he does, or is done, for his own *proper Account* and *Behoof* : What he does in Commiffion, as a *Factor* for others ; and, What he is concerned in *Company*. And becaufe this laft has in it greater Intricacy, I have been the more particular upon it.

Now, the Inftructions of this Chapter being compared with the General Rules, you'll eafily underftand the full Ufe and Extent of thefe ; which is of the laft Importance in this Bufinefs : Becaufe hereby you'll fee how the General Rules comprehend the whole Art ; fo that you'll find, at laft, there is nothing elfe left to burden the Memory with ; and by this Means be capable of making Applications of this Art at Pleafure ; and contriving Schemes of Accounts, agreeable to different Defigns, and to the different Circumftances of any Bufinefs that can happen. For as this Method was invented and improved for the Sake of *Merchants Accounts* ; it was reafonable to make the firft Application to thofe ; which being well underftood, there can be nothing wanting but a diligent Attention to the General Principles, in order to make a right Application of them to any other Subject.

In the third *Chapter*, I have explained the Method of Clofing and Balancing of Accounts, in order to find the

total

total State of one's Affairs, or to make, out of all the particular Accounts, one General Account, or Inventory of
one's whole Effects and Debts ; upon which a new Courfe
of Accounts, or a new Set of Books, may be begun : And
upon this Part I have been the more particular ; becaufe it
is here, we fee the Accomplifhment of the whole Art.

Then follow two Sets of *Books* of *Accounts*, containing
a great Variety of the moft ufeful Examples of Merchants
Bufinefs, regularly ftated and formed into *Accounts*, according
to the preceding *Principles* and *Rules* ; the fecond Set being
begun upon the Balance of the firft ; in which you fee an
actual Application of the Art. I have not indeed made
Examples of every Thing that may be fuppofed ; for that
were infinite ; nor even of every Thing I have fpoken of in
the Inftructions of the Art : But I am confident I have
done what's fufficient (and, perhaps, more than enough)
to make one Mafter of any other Application, who underftands well what's in thefe Books, and has already a
clear Notion of the General Principles.

I have alfo added an *Appendix*, containing *Inftructions* for
the Application of the preceding Art, to the Bufinefs of
Retailers and *Private Concerns* ; more efpecially for *Gentlemen* of *Land-Eftates*, and their *Stewards* or *Factors*.

INDEX

INDEX *to the following* TREATISE.

CHAP. I.

Containing the fundamental Principles, and general Rules.

§. I. **O**F *the Nature and End of* Book-Keeping —————— Page 1
§. II. *Containing a more general Idea of the Method, in a Description,*
 1. *Of the* Waſte-Book ————————————— 3
2. *Of the* Leger ——————————————————— 6
§. III. *Explaining the* Leger *more particularly in its fundamental Rules:*
Rule I. ——————————————————————— 7
Rule II. ——————————————————————— 11
The Notion of Debtor *and* Creditor *explained* —————— 12
Further Directions, with Examples, for the Application of Rule II. —— 14
Rule III. ——————————————————————— 18
Rule IV. ——————————————————————— 19
Some Directions ſubſidiary to the Fourth Rule ————————— 22
§. IV. *General Reflections upon, and a brief Recapitulation of the preceding Rules*
 of the Leger, *&c.* ————————————————— 26
Of the Leger *Index* ————————————————— 27
Of the Journal ———————————————————— 28

CHAP. II.

Containing more particular Instructions for the Formation and Uſe of
Accounts in the Leger.

§. I. *Introduction, concerning the Method of thoſe Inſtructions, with ſome general*
 Directions ————————————————————— 33
§. II. *Accounts for* Proper Trade.
Article I. *How the* Leger *is opened or begun, in placing the Inventory* —— 37
Article II. *Proper* Domeſtick Trade ———————————— 39
Where, after the principal Tranſactions and Accounts are deſcribed, there are further
 Inſtructions relating to
Perſonal *Accounts* ———————————————————— 40
Real *Accounts* —————————————————————— 43
Imaginary *Accounts* ———————————————————— 44
The Caſh-Book ————————————————————— 54
The Book of Expences ——————————————————— ibid.
Of Living ———————————————————————— ibid.
And of Charges of Merchandiſe ——————————————— 55
Arti-

INDEX to the following *Treatise.*

Article III. *Accounts for Proper Foreign Trade* ——————— Page 55
§. III. *Accounts for Factorage* —————————————— 59
Of the Invoyce-Book ———————————————————— 62
Of the Factor-Book ————————————————————— 63
§ IV. Company Accounts ————————————————————— 64
Branch I. *When another Partner is Accountant and Manager, supposing,*
1. *The Company unfixed* ————————————————————— 65
2. *Supposing it fix'd* ——————————————————————— 66
Branch II. *When I am Accountant and Manager* ———————— 67
1. *In an unfixed Company* ——————————————————— *ibid.*
Of keeping these Accounts in separate Books ————————— 71
2. *In a fixed Company* ———————————————————— 74
Of Exchange in Company ———————————————————— 76

C H A P. III.

Of Closing and Balancing Accounts, and Correcting of Errors.

Introduction ———————————————————————————— 77
§. I. *Of the Discovery and Correction of Errors, especially in the* Leger ——— 78
Article I. *Of the general Proof of the Accounts* ———————— *ibid.*
Article II. *The Method of examining the Books ; of marking what's Right, and
   correcting what's wrong* —————————————————————— 79
1. *For the* Waste-Book ———————————————————————— *ibid.*
2. *For the* Journal —————————————————————————— 80
3. *For the* Leger ——————————————————————————— *ibid.*
§. II. *Of Closing and Balancing the* Leger —————————— 82
Article I. *General Reflections* ——————————————————— *ibid.*
Article II. *General Rule for Closing and Balancing* ——————— 83
Of the final Proof ———————————————————————————— 84
Article III. *Further Instructions for finding the State and Balance of particular
   Accounts* ——————————————————————————————— 88
1. *For Proper Domestick Accounts* ——————————————— *ibid.*
2. *For Proper Foreign Accounts* ————————————————— 91
3. *For Factors Accounts* ———————————————————————— 92
4. *For Company Accounts* ——————————————————————— 93
Branch I. ———————————————————————————————— *ibid.*
Branch II. ———————————————————————————————— *ibid.*
Exchange in Company —————————————————————————— 96
Conclusion —————————————————————————————————— 97

Likewise two Sets of Books, Waste-Book, Journal, *and* Leger.

With an Appendix, *containing Instructions for the Application of the preceding Art to
   the Business of* Retailers, *and private Concerns : More especially, for Gentlemen of* Land Estates, *and their Stewards or Factors.*

A

A TREATISE OF BOOK-KEEPING.

CHAP. I.

Containing the fundamental Principles, and general Rules.

SECT. I.

Of the Nature and End of Book-keeping.

DEFINITION.

BOOK-KEEPING *is the Art of keeping* Accounts [i. e. *recording the Transactions*] *of one's Affairs, in such a Manner, that the true* State *of any* Part, *or of the* Whole, *may be thereby known with the greatest Clearness and Dispatch.*

OBSERVE 1*st.* The Name *Book-keeping* is a compounded One, which yet of it self does very obscurely, if at all, express the Nature of the Art to which it is applied ; therefore we must take it in the Sense Men have imposed upon it, which is in general, *A Method of Accounts,* and may so far be applied to any Method. But though all Methods must propose the same End, since naturally there is but one End for which Men keep Accounts, yet one Method may

B   be

be more perfect than another; therefore, taking in the Whole of the preceding Definition, the Name is reftrained to that Method which is the moft perfect; as the Method hereafter explained moft certainly is.

2d. I have called Book-keeping an Art; and very juftly, becaufe, like other Arts, it has its Object, about which it treats; its End, to which it tends; and its Principles and Rules, by which the End is obtained. The Object is, in general, the Tranfactions of one's Affairs; and particularly, the making a regular *Account* or Hiftory of them, in order to this End, *viz.* the clear and ready Knowledge of the true *State* of any Part, or of the Whole. I fhall, in the remaining Part of this Section, explain the End more particularly; and the general Rules in the other two Sections of this Chapter.

The End of Book-keeping *further explained.*

As the Value of an Art can only be known by its End, fo the only Way to get a diftinct and clear Notion of the Art, and to underftand throughly its Principles and Rules, is to get firft a juft and complete Notion of the Defign and End of it; therefore I fhall here explain the End of Book-keeping more particularly, by which we fhall learn what is meant in the Definition, by the *State of any Part, or the Whole* of one's Affairs, as the End of Book-keeping is there more generally expreffed.

The Tranfactions of one's Affairs are diftinguifhable into two general Claffes, as they relate to two different Kinds of Subjects, *viz.*

The Tranfactions relating to

The
$\begin{cases} \textit{Perfons} \text{ with whom we deal, and} \\ \textit{Things} \text{ in which we deal; which are,} \end{cases}$

$\begin{cases} \textit{Money} \text{ (the principal Means of Commerce) and} \\ \textit{Goods}, \text{ comprehending all other real Effects.} \end{cases}$

Thefe then are the more general and effential *Parts* of one's Affairs; fo that if we have a Method whereby we can know the *State* of our Affairs, as they relate to every *Perfon* we deal with, and every Thing we deal in, we have what's propofed by keeping Accounts: But what is meant by that *State* of our Affairs, is yet to be further explained, and it is this, *viz.*

For
$\begin{cases} \textit{Perfons}; \text{ what every Perfon owes me, or I owe them.} \\ \textit{Things}; \text{ what Quantity (and Value) of every Kind is upon hand, with} \\ \quad \text{the Gain or Lofs upon that Subject, within the Time of the Account.} \end{cases}$

What is here expreffed, is what we call the final *State* of the Account (or of our Affairs) relating to Perfons and Things; for he who knows the Things mentioned, has an Anfwer to the laft and chief Demand that can be made relating to thefe Subjects; the knowing of which is therefore the chief End and Purpofe of Book-keeping, as to thefe Parts of one's Affairs. Then, as to the *State* of the *Whole*; fince the Whole is nothing but all the Parts taken together, the *State* of it can be known only by collecting the *States* of the feveral Parts into a complete Inventory, or Account of all one's Effects and Debts; the Difference of which is the final *State* of the Whole; fhewing what one's free *Eftate* is worth; or, what the Debts exceed the Effects.

There are other Queftions that may arife in the Courfe of Bufinefs, neceffary to be known for the Direction of our future Management, and for explaining the Reafon and Circumftances of the final State: Thefe are folved by what we may call the Current *State* of the Account, *i.e.* a View of all the Articles relating to every Subject, with all their Circumftances.

SECT. II.

Containing a more general Idea of the Method.

THE Art of *Book-keeping* is contained in the Ufe of feveral Books of Accounts; whereof the chief and neceffary Ones are called,

$$\text{The} \begin{cases} \textit{Wafte} \\ \text{and} \\ \textit{Leger} \end{cases} \textit{Book.}$$

Obferve, Among the principal Books, Merchants and Writers have commonly reckoned what they call the *Journal-Book*; but as it is only fubfervient to the Leger, I have limited the *principal* Books to Two; and fhall confider all others under the general Name of *fubfervient* Books; which are more or lefs neceffary, according to the Purpofes they ferve; the moft ufeful of which I fhall explain in their proper Places; and here proceed to the two principal Ones.

And that I may not be obliged to fay the fame Things oftner than once, you are to obferve, That the Name of the Book, with the Owner's Name and Place where he lives, are all written upon the firft Leaf, as you fee done in the following Books; and the Name of the Book alfo upon the Cover of it.

I. *Of the* WASTE-BOOK.

We may confider a Man either beginning to Trade; or beginning a regular and orderly Method of Accounts, and willing to follow the beft. The firft Step to be taken in either of thefe Cafes is, to make up a complete Account of the prefent State of his whole Affairs, *i.e.* An Inventory of all his Effects and Debts; after which, his Work is to make daily a diftinct and complete

Re-

Record of all the Tranfactions that occur in his Bufinefs; expreffing the whole Circumftances, *viz.* the Date; Names of Perfons; Times and Conditions of Payments; Names, Quantities, Qualities, and Prices of Goods; and every other Thing neceffary to make a complete Narration of what's tranfacted, or has happened in his Affairs. Let thefe be written in the Order of Time, *i. e.* Every Tranfaction and Event after another, in a continued Succeffion, according to their Dates; and all in a plain, familiar Stile, which makes a juft and diftinct Narration of *Matters of Fact.* The Book which contains fuch an Account, is what we call the *Wafte-Book*; whofe Ufe and Form being fo fimple, I fhall refer to the following Examples of a *Wafte-Book*, for further Particulars, as to the Manner of ruling and writing in it; and only obferve here, That the Dates may be placed either in marginal Columns (as you'll fee in the *Leger*) or as you fee it done in the following Books; where alfo, *obferve*, That though the Year, Month, and Day, are not all marked at every Article, when they are the fame with the preceding, or that laft marked; yet the Date ought to be completely marked to the Article that falls upon the Top of every Page; or, at leaft, one of every Opening, or two Pages; that we may hereby more readily find any Thing we would fee, by help of its Date.

Before I fay any Thing further as to this Book, I fhall fum up the preceding Defcription in this fhort

DEFINITION.

The WASTE-BOOK *begins with the Inventory of a Merchant's Effects, and Debts; and contains a complete Record of every Tranfaction of his Affairs, with all the Circumftances; in a plain Narration of Matter of Fact; every Tranfaction following another in the Order of their Dates.*

OBSERVE 1*ft.* This Book is plainly a *Day* or *Journal Book*; but that Name being applied to another, the Name *Wafte-Book* is applied here. What Relation the Word *Wafte* has to the Nature of this Book, is neither obvious, nor worth enquiring after; therefore I fhall only obferve, that we might more reafonably call it, *The Memorial Book* (as fome Authors do) becaufe in its principal Ufe and Defign, 'tis no more; as will prefently appear.

2*d.* As the End of *Book-keeping* is, to know the State of any Part of our Affairs, or of the Whole; fo, to come at this Knowledge, two Things are neceffarily required. 1. That we know what was the State of that Part at a certain Time, preceding the prefent Enquiry; And 2. That we know all that has happened, relative to that Part, fince that Time, whereby that preceding State has been in any ways changed. And for this Reafon it's manifeft, that regular Accompts muft begin with the prefent State of our Affairs, and be continued in a complete Hiftory of all that's tranfacted afterwards. But the great *Queftion* being, What Order, in the Account or Hiftory of thefe Things, does moft immediately anfwer the End of Book-keeping? I fhall next, by comparing that End with the Method of the *Wafte-Book*, fhew

what

what Defect in this makes another neceffary ; and alfo the real Ufe of this, as the firft Form in which Things muft appear ; which will be an ufeful Tranfition to the *Leger*, whereby the Connection and Dependance of the two principal Books will be clearly underftood.

3*d*. To know the State of any *Part* of our Affairs (*i. e.* of what relates to any *Perfon* or *Thing*) does (as we have above obferved) require, that we know all the Tranfactions relating to that Subject, after a certain known Beginning, or preceding State of it : But it is as plain, That unlefs that preceding State, and all thefe fucceeding Tranfactions are feen together in one View, the prefent State of the Account cannot be known ; becaufe, this being the Refult or Effect of all thefe Tranfactions, it can be difcovered only by a Comparifon of them among themfelves, and with that preceding State (as you will learn more particularly afterwards.) Wherefore, the *Wafte-Book*, tho' it contains a complete Hiftory of our Affairs, and in one Refpect, Simple and Regular, as it follows the natural Order of Time ; yet this very Order is the Defect of it, as to the more immediate anfwering the End of Book-keeping ; becaufe hereby *the Tranfactions, relating to every different Part or Subject, lie fcattered in it according to their Dates ; and fo are not feen all together in one View* ; as is required to our knowing the State of any Part, and confequently of the Whole, of our Affairs ; which is the End of Book-keeping. The Remedy of this Defect, and the more perfect Form of Accounts, we have in the *Leger*. But it remains that we confider the real Ufe and Neceffity of a Wafte-Book, as a previous Step to the other. Thus,

The *Leger Book* is the principal Book of Accounts, by which the End is more immediately anfwered, and in which the Art does moft eminently, appear · So that here lies the greateft Difficulty, and confequently the Accountant's greateft Skill and Care is to be imploy'd here , which will neceffarily require convenient Time and Place for doing it deliberately, and without Difturbance ; and therefore it cannot be expected that this Book fhould be filled up immediately, as foon as every Tranfaction is made : And therefore, that nothing be forgot or omitted, it's neceffary there be kept a daily Memorial of every Thing that's done, expreffing every Circumftance fully, fimply, and plainly , as the Materials of more perfect Accounts, to be made up out of thefe into the *Leger-Book* once a Week, or Month, or otherwife, at the Accountant's Pleafure ; who, having the Materials thus prepared, and laid up in the *Wafte-Book*, where nothing is omitted, can take his own Time to fill up the *Leger* Accounts, according to the Rules of Art.

This is the firft and great Ufe of the *Wafte-Book* ; to which add this other confiderable one , That, as the right placing of Things in the Leger is of the laft Importance in this Bufinefs , fo that firft and fimple Record is an ufeful Mean for our examining and proving that Things are right in the Leger, or difcovering the Errors thereof, by comparing the one Book with the other ; without which, we could not proceed with fuch Order and Certainty in this Examination ; as will afterwards appear.

II. *Of the* Leger-Book.

The Defect of the *Wafte-Book* points very naturally to the Remedy; and fhews us in general, what ought to be the Method of that Book, which contains the Hiftory of our Affairs in the moft perfect Form, and anfwers the End more immediately (the former being ftill confidered as the firft, and a neceffary Step in the Method.) The *General Method* of that Book (which we call the *Leger*) is therefore plainly this, *viz.* All Tranfactions that occur from Time to Time, muft be transferred from the Wafte-Book into the Leger, in fuch Order, that all belonging to one Subject (*i. e.* to one Perfon, or one Thing) be placed together; which is a Method directly oppofite to the Defect of the Wafte-Book, where they are fcattered according to their Dates; and is therefore a Remedy of it : Or, we may take the Definition of the Leger-Book, Thus :

D E F I N I T I O N.

The Leger-Book *contains all the Tranfactions of a Man's Affairs in fuch Order, that all belonging to every different Subject lie together in one Place ; making diftinct particular Accounts*

Observe, *1ft.* The Name, *Leger*, comes, very probably, from the *Latin* Word *Legere,* to *gather*; becaufe in it are gathered into diftinct Accounts, the Tranfactions relating to every *Subject*, which are fcattered in the Wafte-Book, according to their Dates. Some Authors write it *Ledger*, and derive it from an *Italian* Word, which fignifies *Sleight*, or *Art* ; becaufe that appears moft in this Book : But the Original of the Name is of fmall Importance.

2d It will be now ufeful, briefly to recollect the effential Forms and Difference, with the Connection and Dependance of thefe two Books : Thus ; The *Wafte-Book* is an univerfal and complete *Memorial* of all the Tranfactions and Events of Bufinefs, taken in the natural Order of Time ; whereby all Things of one Date, are placed together ; and is a Preparation for the *Leger-Book* ; into which they are all again transferred, upon diftinct particular Accounts, according to the Order and Diftinction of Subjects ; thefe particular Accounts following in Order, as they occur.

3d. Thus much I think fufficient for the general Idea of the Method of Book-keeping, propos'd in the Title of this Section. In the next I fhall more particularly explain the *fundamental Rules* of the *Leger* ; with the Principles and Reafons of each ; in fuch a Manner, that you may clearly underftand the Difference betwixt the natural and artificial Parts of this Method, *i. e.* fuch Parts as are effential, and flow immediately from the Nature and Defign of *Accounts*, and without which the End cannot be obtained ; and fuch as are contrived for an Improvement of the other, and the better anfwering of

the

the End. This being done, I shall, in the two following Chapters, make yet a more particular Application and Enlargement; shewing you how to begin, carry on, and finish the *Leger*.

SECT. III.

Explaining the Leger-Book *more particularly, in its fundamental Rules.*

RULE I.

FOR *every distinct* Subject, *with which you have an Account* [i. e. *for every* Person *with whom you deal upon mutual Trust and Credit, or who, by any Means becomes your* Debtor, *or you his*] *and for every* Thing *you deal in, there must be a certain separate* Space *or* Portion *allow'd; wherein are to be written all and only the Transactions relating to that* Subject; *whose Name is to be inscribed, or written upon the Head thereof; making thereby distinct particular Accounts.*

EXPLICATION.

1*st*. This Rule is the direct and immediate Consequence of the Definition of the *Leger-Book*; or it is, in Effect, only that Definition in another Form; founded upon this first and fundamental Principle of regular Accounting, *viz. That every distinct Part of a Man's Affairs ought to appear separately by it self, without which, there could be no distinct Knowledge of the State of any Part, nor of the Whole* (as has been already explained) And as we have hereby a general Idea of our Affairs, as distinguished into Parts, or particular Accounts, relating to different *Persons* or *Things*, so they make two different Classes or Kinds of Accounts, which may be distinguished by the general Names of *Personal* and *Real Accounts*. There is also a third Class, of which we shall hear afterwards.

2*d Personal Accounts* are limited to such with whom we deal upon mutual Trust and Credit; and do not extend to every Person with whom we have Dealing For the End of a *Personal Account* being to know what any Person owes to me, or I to him; therefore, to have an Account with any Person, supposes Debt betwixt us. For till a Transaction happen, by which the one of us owes, or is in Debt to the other, there can be no Account; because there is nothing that relates to the End of an Account. We may have Dealings together; but all these, in which there is mutual and equal giving and receiving betwixt us, or no remaining Obligation arising from the Transaction, can have no Relation to an Account betwixt us, since there is nothing due upon either Side.

3*d.* In the preceding Rule, 'tis faid, that only the Tranfactions, relating to that Subject, whofe Name is on the Head of the Account, are to be written there ; by which is not meant, that the Tranfactions can, or ought to have Relation to no other Subject ; but that no Tranfaction muft be entered into any Account, which has no Relation to that Subject (and fuch a Relation too as the particular Rules prefcribe :) For the fame Tranfaction may relate to different *Subjects* ; and muft, for that Reafon, be placed upon each of their Accounts, as far as it concerns each ; which I fhall explain by two Examples.

Exam. 1. I buy Goods from *A. B.* payable in a certain Time ; this Tranf-action relates to two Accounts, *viz.* The Account of thefe Goods, and an Account with *A. B.* tho' it is placed on each of them for a different Purpofe : In the firft, it is to fhew the Quantity of Goods I have purchafed ; in the other, to fhew what I owe to *A. B.* 'Tis true, that both thefe are ex-preffed in the Narration made upon each Account, by which, one of them may feem fuperfluous ; yet confider, that all the Tranfactions I make, con-cerning that Kind of Goods, will not alfo have a Relation to *A B*'s Ac-count, but to feveral others ; nor all the Tranfactions I have with *A. B.* be related to that Account of Goods : Therefore it is, that though the fame Fact is narrated in two different Accounts, becaufe of the Relation it has to them both, yet it is not fuperfluous ; the different Ends and Purpofes of every Account neceffarily requiring it ; without which, the Tranfactions relating to every diftinct *Subject*, would not be together in one Account.

2. Suppofe I buy Goods of *A. B.* paying the Value in Cafh ; this Tranf-action has no Relation to an Account with *A. B* becaufe there is no Debt here betwixt us, fince there is equal giving and receiving ; but it relates both to the Account of Goods, to fhew what I have received, and to the Account of Money or Cafh, to fhew what is given out of that.

Now, as this entering of Things, oftner than once, into the *Leger-Book,* is the neceffary Confequence of having diftinct particular Accounts ; fo it fhews us another very great Difference betwixt this and the *Wafte-Book,* wherein every Fact and Event is but once written.

Tranfition to the next Rule.

4*th.* After the firft great Principle of regular Accounting (*viz.* Having different Accounts for different Subjects) the next important and neceffary Confideration is, the Order and Form of thefe Accounts ; or, the Manner of placing together the Articles belonging to every Account, that beft anfwers the End, for any Method is not fufficient for this.

The moft fimple Way we can conceive is, to make one uniform and con-tinued Account, placing all the Articles belonging to it one after another in Order as they happen, for thus we have all belonging to every Subject toge-ther by themfelves ; which is all that the Definition, or the firft general Prin-ciple requires · But if we confider the Nature and End of thefe Accounts more particularly, we fhall eafily perceive that this Method does not fatisfy it.

1. For

1. For *Perfonal Accounts*, it has been already obferved, That the Founda tion of them is mutual Truft and Credit : So that an Account with any Perfon can never begin, till fuch a Tranfaction happens, in Confequence of which, that Perfon comes under an Obligation of Debt to me, or I to him ; and the Account being thus begun, the Reafon and End of it fhews, that all the Tranfactions that can afterwards belong to the Account, are in general, fuch only as make the one of us more or lefs in the other's Debt (for nothing elfe relates to the End of the Account) *i. e.* plainly new Debts, for which the one of us be comes engaged to the other ; or Payments of former Debts, which make the Payer lefs or nothing in the Receiver's Debt.   Suppofe now that all thefe Tranfactions, or Articles of mutual Debts and Payments, are written in the Account in Order as they happen ; then to know the State of the Account, or what the one of us, at laft, owes to the other, we fhould be obliged to take one of thefe two Methods, *viz.* either, (1.) To compare the firft and fecond Articles, and mark what Balance of Debt there is after the fecond Article ; then compare this Balance with the third Article, and fo on, through them all ; ftill comparing the laft Balance with the next Article.   Or, (2.) To fe parate and diftinguifh all the Articles ; thus, The Debts that each Party has come under to the other, upon different and independent Grounds (for fuch there will be in the Nature and Courfe of Bufinefs) gather thefe together in two Parts, by themfelves ; alfo the exprefs and formal Payments made by one Party to the other ; place thefe as if they were mutual oppofite Debts, owing by the Receiver ; and then it is manifeft, that the Balance or Difference of thefe two Parts of the Account, is the true State of it, and fhews the final and ftrict Debt owing by the one Party to the other : For, exprefs Payments being placed as mutual oppofite Debts, do balance and extinguifh them ; and confequently none of thefe Debts come into the final Balance or State of the Account ; which can therefore only be the Sum of fuch Debts, as are not paid exprefsly, or by a Compenfation of other mutual and oppofite Debts , and is therefore the true State of the Account

Now that this is a Method preferable to the other, is manifeft ; and there fore, that we may not have this Separation of the Articles to make at every Time we would know the State of a perfonal Account, it ought to be begun and carried on with this Diftinction of two Parts.

2. For *Real Accounts* ; The Defign of thefe being to know what's upon Hand at any Time, and what's gained or loft ; the Articles belonging to fuch Accounts, are plainly the particular Accounts of what Quantities and Value are from Time to Time received, and difpofed of, with the fubfequent Char ges ; and all the Returns that the Subject makes by the Ufe and Hire of it ; for fuch Articles relate to the State of the Gain or Lofs.   Now to find what's upon Hand, or what's gained or loft, it's not enough that we have all thefe Par ticulars together ; for if they are placed in Order as they happen, we fhould be obliged to transform the Account, and feparate the Particulars of what has been received with all the Coft and Charges, from thofe of the Difpofals and Returns ; becaufe the Comparifon of thefe two is the only, or, at leaft,

C   by by far the beſt Way of diſcovering the State of the Account ; which ought therefore to be begun and carried on with this Diſtinction of two Parts.

This Method, with ſome further Particulars, you have expreſſed in the following

RULE II.

1ſt. *Every* Account *is diſtinguiſhed into two Parts, taking for each an equal Portion (leſs or more, as you think fit) of right and left Pages, of one Folio or Open-ing ; the Name of the Subject being written on the Head of the Account, on both Sides ; which are diſtinguiſhed by the Words* Debtor *on the left Siae, and* Creditor *on the right ; for the Uſes following : To which the Columns explained below, are ſubſervient.*

2d. *A* Perſonal Account *muſt contain, on the* Debtor Side, *all the Articles which that Perſon owes to me, and the Payments I make of my Debts to him : And on the* Creditor Side, *all that I owe to him, and the Payments he makes of his Debts to me.*

Or, becauſe this Rule conſiders Payments under the Notion of mutual op-poſite Debts upon the Receiver, if this is once ſuppoſed, the Rule is briefly expreſſed thus:

Every Perſon *is* Debtor *for what he owes me, and* Creditor *for what I owe him.*

Fol. 6.				*l.*	*s.*	*d.*
A. B.		**Dr.**				
Tobacco.		**Dr.**	Hbds.			

3d. Real Accounts *must contain on the* Debtor *Side, the Quantity and Value of what was upon Hand at the Beginning of the Account, and all afterwards received, with all Coſt and Charges:* And on the Creditor *Side, the Quantity and Value of what is diſpoſed of, or any way taken away, or gone out of it, with all the Returns that Subject makes me.*

Or more briefly thus ;

It is Debtor *for all received, firſt Coſt and Charges* ; *and* Creditor *for all gone out of it, with the Returns.*

EXPLICATION.

1ſt. Since it will always be evident to common Senſe, from the Circumſtances of a Tranſaction, whether any Perſon is, by Vertue of it, my Debtor, or I his ; I have therefore not burdened the Rule with a tedious and ſuperfluous Detail of Caſes, or different Grounds and Cauſes of Debts.

2d. For the orderly placing of the Articles of an Account, the *Leger-Book* is ruled in this Manner : Upon the right Side of every Page, there are three Columns for Money, marked on the Top, *l. s. d.* Within theſe there is a ſmall Column, for an Uſe which will be explained afterwards, in a more proper Place. Alſo upon the left Side of every Page, are two Columns, for the Date ; the firſt for the Year and Month, and the other for the Day. And every Account of Goods has a Column on the right for the Quantities ; as in the following Specimens.

Fol. 6.					*l.*	*s.*	*d.*
	A. B.		Cr.				
	Tobacco.		Cr.	*Hhds.*			

For what Reafon the two Parts of the Account are taken upon oppofite Pages, and not upon the fame Page, will appear afterwards.

Obferve, That the common Method is to write the Titles of *Debtor* and *Creditor* along with the Name of every Account, as I have done in this Specimen: But it is better to write them only upon the Top of the two Pages of every Folio ; which fufficiently diftinguifhes the *Debtor* and *Creditor* Side of all the Accounts in that Folio ; as is done in the following Leger-Books. The Number of the Folio is alfo to be written on the Top of both Pages. Some write the Place of their Refidence upon the Top of the Folios ; but that is fuperfluous ; it is enough that it is written with the Titling of the Books along with the Owner's Name.

Again, If you make a Leger-Book ferve but one Year, then if you begin it with the Year, or 1ft Day of *January,* it will be fufficient to write the Year upon the Top of every Page ; or rather, only once for all, with the Title of the Book : Or, if it's not begun precifely with the Year, then write the Day and Month from which you begin ; as, if you begin *May* 1, 1730. write, *From* May 1, 1730. But if a Leger is defigned to ferve longer than one Year, the Year of every Article, in every Account, muft be exprefled. But to prevent fuperfluous writing ; it is enough that the Year of the firft Article, which falls upon each Side of the Account, be written ; and it need not be written in the following Articles of that Year. In the fame Manner let the next Year be marked with the firft Article only of that Year. Neither need the Month be written till a new Month comes.

The Notion of Debtor *and* Creditor *explained.*

3d. We have now feen the two great *Fundamental Principles* and *Rules* of the *Leger-Book* ; 1ft. Having diftinct Accounts for different Subjects (as in *Rule* I.) 2d. Having two diftinct Parts in each Account, fo oppofed to one another, that the Comparifon may fhew the State of the Account (as in this *Rule* II.) Thefe are the effential and neceffary Things in Accounts. For the Application of *Debtor* and *Creditor,* whereby the two Parts of an Account are diftinguifhed, that is the arbitrary and artificial Part of the Method, efpecially as to real Accounts, and all the other Confequences deduced from it for the Improvement of the Art ; as you'll learn in the following Rules What remains then to be further explained, as to the prefent Rule, is the Notion of *Debtor* and *Creditor :* The Senfe and Meaning of which, I fhall make clear and plain, by confidering its Application ; firft, to *Perfons,* and then to *Things ,* whereby all Obfcurity and Difficulty, in this Part, will be prevented or removed.

1. For *Perfonal Accounts. Debtor* and *Creditor* are Terms applicable only to Perfons in the ftrict and proper Senfe ; and what they fignify, when fo applied, is plain from their common Ufe. They are reciprocal Terms, the one always fuppofing the other : So that if any Perfon is Debtor to another, that other is the former's Creditor ; or, the one being fuppofed the other's Creditor, that other is Debtor to the former : And for this Reafon, what I

owe

owe to any Perſon is juſtly placed in his Account under the Title of *Creditor*, applied to him ; as his Debts to me are placed under the Title of *Debtor*. But that the Payment of a Debt ſhould be charged as a Debt on the Receiver (as the Rule preſcribes) will at firſt View ſeem to be abſurd, ſince what he receives is his own ; and yet, when the Senſe and Effect of it is underſtood there is nothing falſe or unreaſonable in it ; for the real Effect of it is no other than by balancing the former Debt with an oppoſite one, to ſhew that it is paid ; and though the Payment now made does not remain a Debt upon the Receiver in the ſame proper and ſtrict Senſe, that the Debt now paid was, before Payment, upon the other ; yet they are after this equally good Debts which balance and extinguiſh one another ; and in this general or improper Senſe only is the Payment entered as a Debt : And thus we have a very regular and orderly Account ; on the Debtor ſide of which ſtand all my Demands or Charge againſt him, and on the Creditor ſide all his Charge againſt me ; and theſe mutual Debts or Charges, ſo far as they are equal, are mutual Diſcharges of one another ; the Difference or Balance, if they are unequal, being the final State of the Account, and the only proper and ſtrict Debt betwixt us, in which ſtrict Senſe, tho' two Perſons cannot be Debtors to one another, yet they may be ſo in a more general Senſe, while the Articles of an Account are conſidered, each by it ſelf, as the Grounds of mutual Demands, in order to a more diſtinct and regular Compariſon, and ſtating the Account, to find the final and ſtrict Debt.

2. For *Real Accounts*. *Debtor* and *Creditor* are here applied in an artificial and improper Senſe, which is borrowed from Perſons. The Foundation of which is this, *viz*. That Money being contrived for a Medium of Commerce, by which all Things are valued, in order to a juſt and equal Exchange ; therefore we muſt in every other real Account mind not only the Quantity, but the Money Value (the Caſh Account we ſhall conſider by it ſelf afterwards.) And as theſe are really different Things, we may, under this Diſtinction, very eaſily apply the Notion of Debt and Credit to ſuch Accounts ; ſo that when any Thing becomes mine, I conſider it as a Subject which owes, or is accountable to me for ſuch a Sum of Money as it has coſt me, either in Specie, or other Effects, or I owe for it, or which I expect to make out of it (coſt what it will ;) for, in Effect, 'tis the ſame Thing to me, as if ſome Perſon owed me this Money, and ſo I charge it as my Debtor. Again, when it is given away, and ſome other Thing or Perſon is accountable to me in place of it ; it may eaſily be conceived to have hereby diſcharged ſo much of the former Charge ; and therefore we apply the Word *Creditor* to expreſs this, and to diſtinguiſh it from the other Side. If the Money Value is greater or leſſer than the Charge, it comes under the Notion of *Gain* or *Loſs*. And, *Laſtly*, Though no *Perſon* or *Thing* comes in place of it, yet ſo much being actually gone away, that Subject is no longer *chargeable* for it, becauſe it can never be made out of a Thing that is no more, and muſt therefore be made Creditor or diſcharged, to ſhew the true State of the Account ; and for the Caſh Account
it

it felf, we *charge* and *difcharge* it for what's received and given out, the fame Way as other real Accounts.

And here it's to be obferved, That the Word Cafh comes originally from the *Italian* Word, *Caffa,* which fignifies a Cheft ; for the Cheft in which the Money is kept was confidered by the Inventors as the Debtor and Creditor for what is received and given, to make the Subject charged and difcharged different from the Money, as in other real Accounts.

But now, in reality, all this does, in effect, anfwer no other Purpofe, than to fhew what I receive and give away feparately ; in order to know at all Times, by the Comparifon, what remains of the Quantity, and what I gain or lofe as to the Money Value : The Notion of Debt and Credit being (as already obferved) added as an Improvement ; for the fake of fome Confequences deduced from it, for the further perfecting of the Method ; as you'll learn in the following Rules.

Further Directions, with Examples for the Application of the preceding Rule.

3d. This fecond Rule being thus explained, there can be no difficulty in the Application of it ; *that is,* in finding how any Tranfaction is to be placed to the Accounts of the Perfons and Things mentioned in it : For if we confider carefully the Fact narrated, and compare it with this Rule, we fhall thereby eafily difcover, which of the Perfons and Things mentioned are to be made Debtors and Creditors, *i. e.* on which of their Accounts, and which fide of the Account, the Tranfaction, or any Article of it is to be written. And becaufe it's convenient, efpecially for Learners, to proceed in a certain Method, therefore I advife them to this, *viz.* *Firft,* Take the Perfons mentioned in the Tranfaction one by one, and enquire concerning each of them, what they owe to you, or you to them, by virtue of this Tranfaction ; then fee what Things are mentioned, and confider what's narrated concerning each of them, one by one, which will evidently fhew what's to be written on the Debtor or Creditor fide of each ; or if nothing at all, as fometimes happens. Having thus confider'd the Tranfaction, and difcovered what *Perfons* or *Things* are Debtors and Creditors, write out their Names, with their Titles of Debtor or Creditor (as you found they ought to be) which will be a fhort Hint of what's to be done in the Leger ; a particular good Ufe of which Method you'll fee afterwards.

Now, though there remain yet fome other Rules for filling up the *Leger-Book* ; yet that every Rule and Step of the Method may be diftinctly underftood, and you may be mafter of one before another, I fhall here make fome Applications of this fecond Rule, according to the Direction now given ; becaufe this Rule is indeed the chief and principal One.

Exam. 1. Borrowed and received of *A. B.* the Sum of 100 *l.* for which I have given my Bill, payable in two Months.

It's

It's plain here, that I owe *A. B.* 100 *l.* therefore he muſt have an Account, upon the Creditor ſide of which is to be written, that I owe

Cr *A. B.* £ 100
Dᴄ Caſh, 100

him 100 *l.* borrowed. Again, becauſe Caſh is mentioned as actually received, I muſt have an Account of Caſh, upon the Debtor ſide of which I write ſo much received; and ſo I mark them out, as in the Margin.

Obſerve, The Debtor and Creditor will be the ſame, if we ſuppoſe I receive this Money for Payment of a Debt, which *A. B.* owed me in his Account.

Exam. 2. Bought and received of *B. C.* 20 Hogſheads of Wine, at 8 *l. per* Hogſhead, which is 160 *l.* paid in ready Money.

Here *B. C.* is neither due to me, nor I to him; there being equal giving and receiving betwixt us. Then I conſider the Things mentioned, *Firſt,* There is Wine, which is ſaid to be actually received; therefore it muſt have an Account, on the Debtor ſide of which this Article is written: There is alſo Caſh mentioned as actually given away, it muſt therefore have an Account, and this

Dᴄ Wine, 20 Hogſheads, is £ 160
Cᴄ Caſh —————————— 160

Article be written on the Creditor ſide; which I briefly mark out as in the Margin.

Obſerve, If the Price is not paid, but payable in a certain Time, then would *B. C.* be Creditor; or, if I have paid it by Barter with ſome other real Thing, as *Raiſins,* then it is placed on the Creditor ſide of the Account of *Raiſins*; or, if by a Bill indorſed, or drawn on ſome other Perſon, as *A. B.* then is *A. B.* Creditor, for I do hereby owe him ſo much to balance what he is ſuppoſed to ſtand Debtor for to me in his Account; or, if I draw upon him without his being in my Debt, then this becomes a proper Debt upon me.

Exam. 3. Sold and delivered to *C. D.* 8 Hogſheads of Wine, at 13 *l. per* Hogſhead, is 104 *l.* whereof paid in Caſh 50 *l.* the remaining 54 *l.* payable in 6 Months.

Here *C. D.* owes me 54 *l.* for which he muſt have an Account, and be Creditor: And for the Things mentioned, there is Wine actually delivered, which I therefore write on the Creditor ſide of Wine Account, and Caſh actually received, 50 *l.* which I write on the Debtor ſide of

Dʳˢ { *C. D.* —— £ 54
{ Caſh —— 50
                ———
Cᴄ Wine —— 104

Caſh Account; all which I mark out briefly, as in the Margin. Or if the whole is unpaid, then is *C. D.* Debtor for the whole. Or we may ſuppoſe the Wine ſold to another, and *C. D.* become the Debtor for it, by a Bill indorſed or drawn on him.

Exam. 4. Paid to *B. D.* the Price of 50 Barrels of Raiſins, which I owed him; thus, in Caſh, 20 *l.* and a Bill on *J. H.* for 17 *l.* 10 *s.*

Here *B. D.* is due to me 37 *l.* 10 *s.* for the balancing my former Debt to him, for which he is already Creditor in this Account; then by this Bill upon

J.

Cᵣˢ $\begin{cases} \textit{J. H.} \text{——} £ \ 17 \ 10 \\ \text{Cash} \text{———} 20 \end{cases}$

Dʳ· *B. D.* ———— 37 10

J. H. which I have indorfed or drawn, I'm Debtor to him for 17*l.* 10*s.* (as before, in *Example* 2*d.*) therefore I place this to the Creditor fide of his Account. Again, Cafh is mentioned as actually given away 20*l.* which therefore I write on the Creditor fide of that Account, all which I mark out as in the Margin.

Obferve, That the Debtors and Creditors are the fame, if I fuppofe, that being Debtor to *B. D,* he draws upon me, payable to *J. H.* to whom, upon prefenting the Bill, I pay 20*l.* and am allowed a Time for paying the reft. Or, alfo it is the fame Thing, if I purchafe this Bill upon *B. D.* from *J. H.* paying 20*l.* of it, and am allowed Time for the reft. Or if *J. H.* being my Debtor 17*l.* 10*s.* I take this Bill for my Payment, giving him the Balance in Cafh.

Again, Obferve, That though *Raifins* are mentioned in the preceding *Example,* and are the Things for which this Payment is made, yet there is nothing to be written on that Account; becaufe they are not at this Time received; or, this is not the Place in which they are firft mentioned as received; therefore they muft be fuppofed to have been already entered into an Account, when it was firft faid they were received.

Laftly, Obferve, That though Cafh is mentioned in every Tranfaction, becaufe every Thing is reduced to Money value; yet, unlefs it be faid to be actually given or received, there is nothing to be written on that Account.

Thefe Examples will, I hope, fufficiently illuftrate the *Rule*; and in this Manner, by confidering carefully the Narrative of any Tranfaction, and comparing it with the preceding Rule, you'll find how to place it to the *Accounts* of the *Perfons* and *Things* mentioned, which you ought to examine and compare diftinctly one by one. And for your further Affiftance, compare the Examples that follow the *Inventory* in the following *Wafte-Book,* Nº I. as they are transferred into the Book called the *Journal,* and the firft Method of that Book.

Confequence to the preceding Rule, *and Tranfition to the next.*

4th. From the preceding Rules, and the Nature of Bufinefs, it plainly follows, That in the much greater Part, or Number of Tranfactions, there will be feveral Subjects concerned; fo as each of them muft have an Account, and the fame Tranfaction in whole or in part be written in each of thefe Accounts. So far was obferved already as a Confequence to the firft Rule. But now, by this fecond Rule, every Account having a Debtor and Creditor fide, that Confequence has this further in it, *viz.* That the fame Articles will be written not only on different Accounts, but particularly upon the oppofite Sides of thefe Accounts, [*i. e.* upon the Debtor Side of fome of them, and the Creditor Side of others] in fuch a Manner that there will be a Balance of Debt and Credit thereby entered in the *Leger*: What's entered in fome Accounts on the Debtor fide

being

being equal to what's put on the Creditor fide of others. The Foundation and Truth of which Confequence I fhall make plain. Thus,

1*ft*. When any *Perfon* is made Debtor, it's to be fuppofed, in the common Courfe of Bufinefs, to be either for fome real Thing given away by me, upon the Creditor fide of whofe Account the fame Tranfaction muft therefore be written, to fhew what's away (by *Rule 2d.* fee above, *Exam. 3d.*) Or the Tranfaction is fuch, that I'm accountable to fome other Perfon for the fame Article, who is therefore to be made Creditor for it. (See above, *Exam. 4th*) Or alfo, fuppofe a Perfon who is Debtor in my Books, gives me a Bill on another, and I take this Bill for Payment; then, as the Perfon, on whom the Bill is drawn, becomes my Debtor; fo the other, having hereby paid the Debt he owed me, muft be difcharged or made Creditor. Again, if any Perfon is made Creditor, it's fuppofed to be either for fome real Thing received by me, which muft therefore be made Debtor, to fhew what's received (*Rule 2d.* fee *Exam.* 1, 2.) Or the Tranfaction is fuch, that another Perfon is accountable to me for the fame Article; who is therefore to be made Debtor for it (the preceding *Examples* ferve alfo for this.)

2*d*. When any *Real Account* is made Debtor, it's to be fuppofed, in the common Courfe, that for what I enter here on the Debtor fide, fome other real Thing of equal Value is given away, upon the Creditor fide of whofe Account we muft therefore write what's given away (*Rule 2d.* fee *Exam. 2d.*) Or that the Value of it is owing to fome Perfon, who is therefore to be made Creditor (fee *Exam. 2d.*) Again, when a *Real Account* is made Creditor, it's fuppofed that for what I enter here, fome other real Thing is received, which is therefore to be made Debtor, to fhew what's received; or fome Perfon is become my Debtor for it (the preceding Examples ferve for this alfo.)

Obferve alfo, As to both *Perfonal* and *Real* Accounts, that the Debt or Credit placed upon one Account, may be balanced not only by an equal oppofite Credit or Debt upon another Account, but by the Sum of feveral Articles placed upon the oppofite Sides of feveral other Accounts; fo a Perfon may be my Debtor for fundry Things given away; or partly for Things given away, and partly for Bills drawn by me upon other Perfons, who are therefore to be made Creditors. See the *Examples* 3d and 4th, *Rule* 2d. and you may eafily conceive a Variety of fuch Cafes.

Now, as this Balance of Debt and Credit will be found in every Tranfaction almoft, in the common and ordinary Courfe of Bufinefs; fo if we fuppofe that it can never fail in any Tranfaction, the plain Confequence is, that there will always be a *General Balance* of Debt and Credit in the *Leger-Book*; that is, the Articles of Debt, upon all the Accounts through the whole *Leger*, being gathered into one Sum, and the Articles of Credit into another, thefe Sums will be equal to one another; the valuable Ufe of which would be, that by it we fhould have a Proof of the *Leger-Book*, and a more regular Method of bringing the whole Accounts to a Clofe, fo as from the State of all the Particulars to make a diftinct general Account of the whole, or a new Inventory of all our Effects and Debts.

But

But in the next Place, we muft *obferve*, That the Circumftances of all Tranf-actions, and every Event in Bufinefs, will not be fuch as to make a Balance of Debt and Credit, upon the *perfonal* and *real* Accounts concerned. One Example will fhew this : Suppofe I lend a Sum of Money upon Intereft, the Borrower is Debtor, and Cafh Creditor ; when this Money is paid with the In-tereft, the Borrower is difcharged, or made Creditor for the Sum lent, and Cafh Debtor · But Cafh is alfo Debtor for the Intereft received, yet there is no real Account Creditor, becaufe nothing is given away for it, nor any Perfon Credi-tor , for, I fuppofe this Intereft is not charged on the Debtor fide of the Bor-rower's Account ; and if we fuppofe it is, the fame Defect of a Balance will happen here, becaufe there is neither perfonal or real Account to be made Creditor for it   *Obferve alfo,* That there may be Tranfactions which ought to be entered in the *Leger-Book,* or at leaft it is ufeful and convenient that they fhould be entered ; and yet they cannot be placed with any Juftice or Proprie-ty upon any perfonal or real Account ; of which you'll find Examples in the following Chapter.

Now the Contrivers of this Art, confidering thefe Things, but efpecially the ufeful Confequence of a general Balance (which you'll find more particularly explained in *Chapter* III. and applied in the following *Leger-Books*) and the Defect of it in fome Cafes, even where perfonal and real Accounts are con-cerned, have brought into *Book-keeping* a third Clafs of Accounts, called *Ima-ginary Accounts,* which are alfo diftinguifhed into a Debtor and Creditor Side ; upon which the third general Rule of the *Leger-Book* is formed, *viz.*

RULE III.

Every Tranfaction muft be entered in the Leger-Book, *with a Balance of Debt and Credit,* i. e *fo that every Article be placed on the Debtor fide of one Account, and the Creditor fide of fome other, making thereby equal Debt and Credit in the* Leger ; *and where the perfonal and real Accounts, concerned in the Tranfaction, do not, in the Articles belonging to them, make this Balance (as they will in moft Cafes) then fome* Imaginary Account *muft be ufed to fupply the Defect.*

EXPLICATION.

I. This Rule is indeed no more than a general Principle, without fhew-ing us the particular *Imaginary Accounts* neceffary in the various Cafes where they are wanted. For this I fhall refer to the next Chapter ; and fhall here only defcribe one of thefe Accounts, which is the Chief of them all, and abfo-lutely indifpenfable in a regular Scheme : It is called,

Account of Profit and Lofs ; upon the Debtor fide of which are written all Loffes, and upon the Creditor fide all Gains.

Thus, in the preceding *Example,* Cafh being Debtor for the Money paid, Principal and Intereft ; the Borrower is Creditor for the Principal, and *Profit and Lofs* is made Creditor for the Intereft.   Or if the Intereft is charged on the

Bor-

Borrower's Account, *Profit* and *Loss* is Creditor for it ; and upon the Payment, the Borrower is Creditor for both Principal and Interest.

Take this other *Example* ; Suppose I make a Present of Money or Goods, or the like be made to me ; the Thing received or given away must be Debtor or Creditor ; but there is no personal or real Account to balance it ; and therefore we must find an imaginary one, which is, evidently, the Account of *Profit* and *Loss*. See what more is said of this Account in the next Chapter.

I shall here say but this one Thing more concerning *Imaginary Accounts*, which is, That besides their general Use in preserving the Balance of Debt and Credit, you'll find them also further useful, for giving a distinct View of certain Parts and Circumstances of your Affairs ; as you see here in the Account of *Profit* and *Loss*, whose particular Use is to shew the State of Gain and Loss in the Course of your Affairs.

A general Direction for the Application of this Rule.

II. As the Application of this Rule, comes in order, after the Second, because *Imaginary Accounts* are sought only in defect of *Personal* and *Real Ones* ; so in finding the Debtors and Creditors of any Transaction, first apply the second Rule ; by which having found what Persons and Things are Debtors or Creditors, if these balance one another, and bring in the whole Transaction, you have done ; otherwise an *Imaginary Account* is to be sought to make up the Balance ; and here you'll find the Conveniency of marking out the Debtors and Creditors in the Manner shown above.

Transition to the next Rule.

III. Having by the second and third Rules, (with what follows in the next Chapter) discovered the Debtors and Creditors of every Transaction, *i. e.* upon what Accounts, and upon what side of the Accounts, the whole or different Articles of any Transaction are to be entered in the *Leger-Book* (which must always be with a Balance ;) the last Consideration, is the Stile of the *Leger-Book*, or Manner of Writing the Articles into those Accounts. Now if we suppose every Article narrated in a plain common Stile, telling for what the Account is Debtor or Creditor, with all the Circumstances ; the Use and Design of the Account is answered : But there is another and better Method deduced from the Application of Debt and Credit to all Accounts ; as in the following Rule.

RULE IV.

Those Accounts, whose Articles of Debt and Credit in any Transaction, do balance one another, are, in the Leger, *connected together in the Stile of every Article, as mutual and correspondant Debtors and Creditors ; by writing in each of the corresponding Accounts the Name of the other, after the Particle*

To *in the Debtors Account, and* By *in the Creditors, which connects the two'; the Name of the Account, in which Articles are written, with its Quality of Debtor and Creditor, being underftood as joined to,* and *fo is read before, the Word* To *or* By *in every Article, (though it be written only once for all upon the Head of the Account.) Then, after the Name of the corresponding Creditor or Debtor, follows a brief Narration of the Fact; the Date and other Numbers being placed in their proper Columns. And now you find the Ufe of the Column that ftands within the Money Columns, which is this, viz. to write in it the Number of the Folio where ftands the corresponding Account, with which the Account, in which you write, is connected in every Article.*

EXPLICATION.

I The Debtors and Creditors being found, there can be no difficulty in making the Connection; for if the Balance is betwixt one Debtor and one Creditor, thefe are the connected Accounts. If there is one Debtor balanced by fundry Creditors, or contrarily, then that one is connected with each of thofe others; and each of thefe with that one. And if it happen (as you'll find fome Examples in the following Books) that there are fundry Debtors, and fundry Creditors, it will be neceffary to refolve it into two or more Parts, wherein there is a Balance and Connection of one Account with one, or one with fundry; but,

II. That you may clearly underftand this Rule, which finishes the Entry of every Tranfaction in the *Leger-Book,* I fhall here apply it to a few Examples, and put them in a Leger Form by themfelves; and then make fuch Obfervations upon the Senfe and Meaning of this Stile, and Connection, as may remove all Obfcurity or Difficulty.

Exam. 1. I have bought and received from *A. B.* 10 Hhds of Tobacco, at 6 *l.* ℔ Hd, is 60 *l.* payable in 3 Months.

Here *A. B.* is Creditor 60 *l.* and *Tobacco* Debtor 60 *l.* which is written in the *Leger-Book* thus, viz. in *A. B*'s Account it is, *A B.* Creditor, *By Tobacco;* and in the Account of Tobacco it is, *Tobacco* Debtor *To A. B.* [See how this ftands in the following Forms of thefe Accounts, which are at the End of this Section.]

Exam. 2. Sold and delivered to *M. N.* 6 Hhds of Tobacco, at 8 *l.* ℔ Hd. is 48 *l.* for which received in ready Money 30 *l.* for the reft an accepted Bill on *C. D.* 18 *l.* payable in 1 Month.

Cafh is Debtor 30 *l. C. D.* Debtor 18 *l.* and *Tobacco* Creditor 48 *l.* and in the *Leger* it is, *Tobacco* Creditor *By Cafh* 30 *l.* and *By C. D.* for 18 *l.* then *Cafh* Debtor *To Tobacco* 30 *l.* and *C. D.* Debtor *To Tobacco* 18 *l.* (fee the following Forms.)

Exam 3. Bought and received from *A. M.* 30 Barrels of *Salmon,* at 2 *l.* ℔ Barrel, is 60 *l.* whereof paid in *Cafh* 20 *l.* the Remainder 40 *l.* payable in 2 Months.

Salmon is Debtor 60 *l. Cafh* Creditor 20 *l.* and *A. M.* Creditor 40 *l.* which in the *Leger* is written thus, *Salmon* Debtor *To Cafh* 20 *l.* and *To A. M.*
40 *l.*

40*l.* then, *Cash* Creditor *By Salmon* 20*l.* and *A. M.* Creditor *By Salmon* 40*l.* (fee the Forms.)

Exam. 4. I have indorfed the accepted Bill I had upon *C. D.* for 18*l.* to *A. B.* in part of Payment of what I owe him.

Here *A. B.* is to be made Debtor for 18*l.* and *C. D.* Creditor 18*l.* and in the *Leger* it is, *A. B.* Debtor *To C. D.* and *C. D.* Creditor *By A. B.*

III. As to this Stile, whereby the feveral Accounts are connected, as correfponding Debtors and Creditors in every Tranfaction, obferve, That it is at the Bottom nothing but a mere Stile, which makes no Alteration in the Nature and Ufe of the Accounts; being contrived only for a neater and fhorter Narration of the Grounds of the *Debt* and *Credit* placed upon every Account; and for making a more diftinct Reference from one Account to another, which are concerned in the fame Tranfaction [and to the oppofite Sides of which the fame Article would be placed by *Rule* 2*d.* and 3*d.* without regard to this Stile] fo that the Connection is purely arbitrary and artificial. But to leave no Obfcurity, I fhall confider the Senfe of it a little more particularly; thus,

1. For *Perfonal Accounts* As Debtor and Creditor have their proper Application here, fo the Articles on a Perfonal Account in my *Leger* are underftood to be owing to or by me in the proper and legal Senfe; the other Subject with which the Account is connected, as its correfpondent Debtor or Creditor, being fo only as it is the Account, upon whofe oppofite Side the fame Article muft be written, by the Nature of the Tranfaction, and the preceding Rules; which happens for no other Reafon, with refpect to the Connection of perfonal Accounts with other perfonal Accounts, or real Ones, but that what is placed on the one Account is the Ground and Caufe (immediately or mediately) of what is placed upon the oppofite Side of the other.

For *Example*, If a Perfon is made Debtor to any Thing, or real Account, this Connection expreffes only, that the Debt arifes from that Thing, *i. e.* that it is for fome Quantity of that Thing (or for the Ufe of it) given either to this Perfon, or to fome other who gives me this Perfon Debtor for it. And if a Perfon is Creditor by a real Account, it expreffes that this Credit comes upon account of that Thing, which is received either from this Perfon, or from another to whom I am made Debtor for it, either by Bill drawn on me to him, or by me on him; or it may be an Article of Expenfes on that Thing due or payable to that Perfon; fo that *A. B.* Debtor to, or Creditor by *Cafh*, or *Wine*, is in Effect the fame Thing as Debtor or Creditor to me for *Cafh* or *Wine*. Again, if one Perfon is made Debtor to, or Creditor by another, it's not to be taken in the literal Senfe, as expreffing a Debt really and properly due by that one to the other; for, what have I to do with fuch a Thing in my Books? The Meaning is no more, than that the one Perfon is Debtor to me, and I Debtor for the fame Thing to the other (either in the more ftrict or more general Senfe) the one Debt being the Ground and Caufe of the other; as when one Perfon pays a Debt he owes me by a Bill upon another, or when I pay a Debt the fame way.

For

2. For *Real Accounts*. In what Senſe *Debt* and *Credit* are applied here, has been already ſufficiently explained; and for the Stile, it is to be taken in the general Senſe before mentioned, as ſignifying only that the Entry made upon each Account, is the Ground and Cauſe of what is made upon the other. For *Example*, When one Thing is received for another, the Thing received, is *Debtor*, and the other *Creditor*; and the Connection has no other Meaning, but that the one is exchanged for the other. And if a Real Account is Debtor to, or Creditor by a Perſon, it ſignifies that, that Perſon is Debtor to me, or I to him, for the Article enter'd upon this Real Account. (See what's before ſaid upon Perſonal Accounts.)

IV. *Some Directions ſubſidiary to the preceding Rule.*

1. Some conſider the *Leger-Book* as only an univerſal Index of a Man's Buſineſs; wherein, if all that belongs to each Account is fairly placed, though no more be written than the Name of the correſponding Accounts, and the Numbers in their proper Columns, the End, they think, is ſufficiently anſwered, becauſe the Balance or final State of the Account, will as eaſily appear as if there were more particular Narrations; and for the Circumſtances at large, they leave them to be ſought in the *Waſte-Book* (or *Journal* after deſcribed.) Others, though they do not make the Rule ſo narrow, yet they limit the Narration of every Article to one Line.

But theſe Rules are arbitrary, and at every one's Choice; the firſt, I think, makes the *Leger-Book* too ſhort and obſcure, and leaves us, in moſt Caſes, too troubleſome a Reference to the *Waſte* or *Journal-Book*, for underſtanding the Circumſtances of Articles written in the *Leger* Accounts. If the Page is broad (as *Leger-Books* commonly are upon very large Paper) one Line may contain all that's neceſſary to be narrated: Concerning which, I ſhall only ſay, that beſides the Date, the Name of the correſponding Account, with the Reference Number, and the Sums of Money, which are neceſſary in all Accounts, and the Quantity in an Account of Goods; as much more ought to be narrated, as is neceſſary to bring to his Memory, who is the Keeper or Owner of the Books, the other particular Circumſtances.

In a *Real* Account, the Things mentioned will be generally ſufficient; and for the *Caſh* Account, there needs no Narration, but the Name of the correſponding Account; nor in the *Profit* and *Loſs* Account; that being ſufficient to anſwer their End. For a *Perſonal* Account, the Term of Payment is a proper Circumſtance to be mentioned in it: And as a *Perſon* may be Debtor to, or Creditor by, a *Real* Account which is not the immediate Ground of his Debt or Credit, as when this comes by a Bill drawn on him, it will be fit, in theſe Caſes, to add the Words, *By Bill*, which will explain the Reaſon of the Connection; and where this is not ſaid, it's to be underſtood, that the Thing connected with the Perſon's Account, was received from or given to him, or otherwiſe immediately the Ground of his Debt or Credit. In the next Chapter I ſhall remark what is further neceſſary, in the ſeveral particular Accounts there deſcribed.

2.

2. When one Account is balanced by sundry, *i. e.* when one is Debtor or Creditor for a Sum, and sundry Accounts Creditors or Debtors for the Parts of that Sum, there are several Ways of writing in the *Leger* upon that one Account : The Writing in these particular Accounts, connected with that one, being still the same, according to the general Rule. (1.) One is, to place each of the Articles in a separate Line, as I have done in the preceding Examples, and in the following *Leger-Book*, Number I. (2.) Another common Method is, to write only *To* or *By sundry Accounts*, drawing out the whole Sum, without distinguishing the particular corresponding Accounts, leaving these to be known from the *Journal.* This Method is, in my Opinion, too short. Instead of it, (3.) I'd rather name the particular corresponding Accounts, one after another, in a Line, without distinguishing their particular Sums, and draw out the total Sum. (4.) There is still another Method founded upon this, That all the Accounts in the *Leger-Book* are numbered from the Beginning, in Order, 1, 2, 3, 4, *&c.* Then when one Account is balanced by sundry, write *To* or *By Sundry*; and after this write in Order, the Numbers of the particular Accounts ; and so they are easily found without Help of the *Journal.*

Observe, That in all these Methods, except the first, the Use of the Reference Column is lost for such Cases. In the second Method you may, after the Words, *Sundry Accounts*, write, in Order, the Number of the Folios where the corresponding Accounts stand , and though this will not direct particularly to the Account, when it stands in the same Folio with other Accounts ; yet, by the Date of the Article, and the opposite Reference on that Account, it will be soon discovered. In the third Method, let the Number of the Folios where the particular Accounts stand, be written after each of their Names. In the fourth Method, the Number of the Account will easily direct to it , but it will be more easily found, if we also write the Number of the Folio where it stands ; and to do this most conveniently, write the Number of the Folio over the Number of the Account, or one after another.

Observe *in the last Place*, That a Column for the References is not necessary in any Method , for the only Reason of gathering Numbers into Columns, is when they are to be added into one Sum ; which is not the Case with these Numbers . And therefore, that Column needs not be made in the *Leger*, but the Reference Number written after the Name of the Account to which it refers ; and if all the Accounts are number'd, you may write also the Number of the Account under the other Number, or before or after it.

The following *Leger-Book*, N°. I. is filled up after the first Method, with a Reference Column. The *Leger-Book*, N°. II. is filled up according to the fourth Method, without a Reference Column.

					l.	*s.*	*d.*

| 1729.
May | 10 | **A. B.** To *C. D.* for Bill on *C. D.* indorfed to him——— | **Dr.** | | 18 | | |

| 1729.
May | 4 | **Tobacco.** To *A. B.*   at 6 *l. per* Hogfh. | **Dr.** | *Hbds.*
10 | 60 | | |

| 1729.
May | 6 | **Cafh.** To *Tobacco* —— —— —— —— | **Dr.** | | 30 | | |

| 1729.
May | 6 | **C. D.** To *Tobacco, per* Bill of *M. N.* payable in 1 Month | **Dr.** | | 18 | | |

| 1729.
May | 7 | **Salmons** To *Cafh,* ⎱
To *A. M.* ⎰ at 2 *l. per* Barrel —— ——
    Or Thus,
To *Sundry* (N^{rs}.   ) at 2 *l. per* Barrel | **Dr.** | *Barrels*

30

30 | 20
40

60 | | |

| 1729.
May | | **A. M.** | **Dr.** | | | | |

			l.	s.	d.
1729. *May*	4	**A. B.** **Cr.** By *Tobacco,* payable in 3 Months —— ——	60		
1729. *May*	6	**Tobacco.** **Cr.** | Hbds. By *Cash,* ⎱ at 8 *l. per* Hogshead — — 6 By *C. D.* ⎰ *Or Thus,* By *Sundry,* (N^{rs}.) at 8 *l. per* Hhd. 6	30 18 48		
1729. *May*	7	**Cash.** **Cr.** By *Salmons* ————————	20		
1729. *May*	10	**C. D.** **Cr.** By *A. B.* for his Bill indorsed to *A. B.* ——	18		
		Salmons **Cr.** | Barrels			
1729 *May*	7	**A. M.** **Cr.** By *Salmons,* payable in 2 Months —— ——	40		

E

SECT. IV.

Containing fome general Reflections *upon, and a brief Recapitulation of the preceding* Rules *of the* Leger *; with a Defcription of two chief fubfervient Books.*

WE have now feen all the general and fundamental Rules of the *Leger-Book* ; and, perhaps, it will not be ufelefs to make thefe general Reflections upon, and brief Recapitulation of them.

1. The firft Rule expreffes the firft general Principle of Accounts, *viz.* having diftinct Accounts for particular Subjects ; but gives us no Direction for particular Cafes or Queftions in Bufinefs.

2. The fecond Rule comprehends the firft ; and carries it further, by fhewing us the Form of Accounts, in the Diftinction of two Parts, under the Notion of Debtor and Creditor ; fo that the Comparifon of thefe different Parts fhews the State of the Account, and is a particular Direction for the Ufe or Way of making up *Perfonal* and *Real Accounts* ; teaching us to know in every Tranfaction, how it is to be placed to the Accounts of the Perfons and Things mentioned : For the Application of which, it's fit that a Learner proceed orderly, by confidering, firft the *Perfons* mentioned, and then the *Things*, one by one ; and comparing the Fact narrated with the Rule ; which will fhew him what's to be done.

3. The third Rule carries the Method further, by requiring a Balance of Debt and Credit, for every Article enter'd in the *Leger-Book* (for the fake of the ufeful Confequences of fuch a Balance.) The general Application of which, in the Difcovery of the Debtors and Creditors of every Tranfaction, is this, *viz.* Having difcovered the *Perfonal* and *Real* Debtors and Creditors, by *Rule* II. if they comprehend the whole Cafe, and contain a Balance of Debt and Credit, there is no more to be done : Otherwife, fome *Imaginary Account* is to be ufed, for fupplying the Defect. And of all thefe, the moft univerfally ufeful is the Account of *Profit* and *Lofs* ; which is Debtor for all Loffes, and Creditor for all Gains. Other *Imaginary Accounts*, with further Directions concerning *Perfonal* and *Real Accounts*, you'll find in the next Chapter.

4. Having difcovered the Debtors and Creditors, *i. e.* the feveral Accounts, and the Sides of them, upon which the Tranfaction is to be placed in the *Leger*, in writing them there;

The fourth Rule is this, *viz.* To connect thefe, in the Stile, as correfponding Debtors and Creditors, which are found Debtors and Creditors for the fame Article in every Account ; expreffing briefly the Circumftances that relate to the End of that Account. And when an Article on one Account is balanced by the Articles of feveral other Accounts, follow any of the Methods already explained.

5. It is now, after all, evident, that the great Difficulty of the Application lies in difcovering the Debtors and Creditors of any Tranfaction, *i. e.* finding upon what Accounts, and what Sides of the Accounts, the Tranfaction, or any Article of it, is to be enter'd; for which, the preceding *Rule* II. is the principal one; as it is a complete general Rule for the Accounts of *Perfons* and *Things*; which are the true and effential Subjects of Bufinefs. What further Inftructions are neceffary for the Invention and forming of Accounts, fhall be delivered in the next Chapter.

6. The laft *Reflection* I fhall make, is, That in however eafy a Senfe the Notion of Debt and Credit is transferred from *Perfons* to *Things*, yet as it is not effentially imply'd in the Nature and Defign of thefe Accounts, the Application is ftill to be confidered as Artificial. And becaufe the Money (which is the *Medium*, by which all Things are valued, and, as it were, the final Subject of all Accounts) is, in the Courfe of Bufinefs, continually paffing from one Subject to another, according as they come in Place of one another, by a mutual Exchange of Things, or by Perfons becoming Debtors or Creditors for them, or in Place of other Perfons; hence, I judge, has been taken the firft Hint of the Application of Debt and Credit to other Subjects than Perfons, and of the Stile and Connection of all Accounts, as correfponding Debtors and Creditors, according as they come in Place of one another; this Stile and Connection being the Confequence of the Application of Debt and Credit to all Accounts; as that Application has alfo been contrived for the fake of this Connection, and the mutual Charge and Difcharge of Accounts: For the Notion of Debt and Credit (as explained in *Rule* II.) is applied to all Accounts, fo as to refpect me as the correfponding Debtor or Creditor, in the *primary* Senfe; yet in a *fecondary* Senfe, they have a mutual Refpect to one another; as what is placed upon one Account, on the Debtor or Creditor Side, is the Ground and Caufe of what is placed upon another, upon the oppofite Side (according to the *primary* Senfe of their Debt and Credit) and fo is the Foundation of this Connection; which being univerfally preferved, by the Balance of Debt and Credit, by Means of *imaginary* Accounts, affords a curious Proof of the Whole; as you'll learn in *Chapter* III.

Of the Leger Index.

This is a Book divided Alphabetically, *i. e.* fo many Pages as you think fit, are affigned to every Letter of the Alphabet, which is marked at the Beginning of the Divifion: And under each Letter are written the Names of the *Accounts*, in the *Leger*, in Order as they are begun or opened; each in the Space belonging to that Letter with which the Name of the Account begins; and commonly it is the Letter of a *Man's* Sirname, and of the proper Name of a Thing. For *Example*, *John Gordon* is put at G. and *Claret Wine* at C. unlefs all Kinds of Wine be comprehended in one Account; and then we take the Letter of the common Name, *W.* for *Wine*. And the Number of the Leger *Folio*, where the Account ftands (or begins) is marked here with its Name;

the

the Ufe of which is, that we may readily find where any Account ftands in the *Leger*. But this *Index* muft alfo be contrived fo as we can readily find where every Letter ftands; which is very conveniently done thus: Cut away the Breadth of a Capital Letter from the firft Leaf, length-wife, and upon the external Edge of the next Leaf write the Letter *A*, and affign the two Pages of the firft Opening, to that Letter: Or you may write two or more Letters upon the fecond Leaf; and divide the Folio into as many Parts to ferve all thefe Letters. Then, from the Leaf upon which the firft Letters are written, cut off as much below them, and upon the next Leaf write as many Letters, and divide the next Folio for thefe Letters; and fo on till you have all the Letters: And by this Means, without opening the Book, you'll fee where each Letter is to be found.

Now more particularly, for the right ufing of the *Index*, take this *Direction*: When any Tranfaction is to be entered in the *Leger*, confult the *Index*, to know where the Accounts that are Debtors and Creditors ftand; if thefe Accounts are already opened, then enter the Tranfaction on the proper Side of each · But if any of thefe Debtors and Creditors have no Account yet opened (as it happens particularly at the Beginning or firft Opening of the *Leger*) then turn to the firft empty Place of the *Leger*, and open Accounts for fuch of thofe Debtors and Creditors as yet have none; *that is*, feparate a certain Space from the reft, beginning where the laft Account in the *Leger* ends, and make it as large as you think fit; upon the Head of it write the Name of the Account, both on Debtor and Creditor Sides: As foon as this is done, enter it in the *Index*, as already explained; this will direct you to it when you have Ufe for it again: Then enter your Tranfaction. And be fure that you go not backwards to open an Account upon a Part of the Space that has been already affigned to another Account; for this breeds Confufion, and may be fufpected: But let Accounts, in the *Leger*, follow each other in Order, as they occur in the *Journal*, uninterruptedly. The fame Subject muft never have two Spaces or Accounts open at once; to prevent which, and for finding the Accounts readily, the *Index* is defigned.

Of the JOURNAL.

It has been already obferved, That the *Wafte-Book* is plainly a *Journal*, *i. e.* a *Day-Book*: But to diftinguifh two Books, which agree in this Refpect, that they are both properly *Day-Books*; the one is called the *Wafte-Book*, and the other the *Journal*; which, in as far as it differs from the *Wafte-Book*, is only a Book of *Aid* to the *Leger*. I fhall here explain two different Methods of a *Journal*; (1.) That which has been hitherto more commonly ufed, and was the firft Invention. And, (2.) A new *Method*, which I have found practifed by fome eminent Traders; and which, in my Opinion, is the preferable One; as the Comparifon and Reafons following will fhew.

Firſt Method.

This firſt *Method* is a complete Tranſcript of the *Waſte-Book*, in the ſame Order of Time, but in a different Stile : For the *Waſte-Book* expreſſes every Tranſaction in a ſimple Narration of what's done ; but the *Journal* diſtinguiſhes the Debtors and Creditors, as a Preparation for the *Leger* ; thus, When any Tranſaction is to be tranſported from the *Waſte-Book* into the *Journal-Book*, we examine it, by the Rules of the *Leger*, as if it were to be entered immediately there ; and finding the Debtors and Creditors to which it belongs, theſe are diſtinctly marked by their Denominations of Debtor and Creditor, in the Stile of the *Journal* ; at leaſt, the Accounts that are Debtors, are expreſsly ſo named , and by their being directly connected Debtor to ſome other Accounts, theſe are ſufficiently determined to be the Creditors, though the Word *Creditor* is not written.

Three Examples will completely ſhew the Practice of this Method : For there is either but one Debtor and one Creditor, or one Debtor or Creditor balanced by ſundry Creditors or Debtors ; which will comprehend all the Variety in the Manner of writing in this Book.

Waſte-Book.	*l.*	*s.*	*d.*		*Journal-Book.*	*l.*	*s.*	*d*
Exam. 1. Bought and Received of *A. B.* 10 Hhds. of *Claret Wine*, payable in 3 Months ————	90			²⁄₁	*Claret Wine*, Debtor to *A. B.* for 10 Hhds. Bought and Received of him, payable in 3 Months ————	90		
Exam. 2. Bought and Received of *L. M.* 10 Pieces of *Broad Cloth*, containing 40 Yds. each, at 12 *s. per* Yd. is 240 *l.* whereof Paid in Caſh ——— 100 *l.* The Remainder payable in 6 Months— 140 ____ 240	240			7	*Broad Cloth*, Debtor to *Sundry Accounts* for 10 Pcs. 40 Yds. each, at 12 *s.* is 240 *l.* Bought and Received of *L. M. viz.*			
				1 Cⁿ.	Caſh, ————— 100 *l*			
				4	L. M. (in 6 Mᵒ.) 140 ____ 240	240		
Exam 3. Sold and Deliver'd to *B. C.* 6 Hhds. *Claret Wine*, at 13 *l. per* Hhd. is 78 *l.* whereof Paid in Caſh ——— 28 *l.* The Remainder payable in 2 Months — 50 __ 78	78			2	*Sundry Accounts*, are Drs. to *Claret Wine*, for 6 Hhds. at 13 *l. per* Hhd. is 78 *l.* Sold and Deliver'd to *B. C. viz.*			
				1	Caſh, ——— 28 *l.*			
				2 Dʳˢ.	B. C. payble in 2 Months — 50 __ 78	78		

The

The Debtors and Creditors being thus marked in the *Journal,* the Tranf-actions are transferred from this into the *Leger,* upon the feveral Accounts marked Debtors and Creditors in the *Journal,* according to the Connection there expreffed; and upon the Margin of this Book are marked the Numbers of the *Leger* Folio, where the feveral Accounts ftand; each Number in the fame Line with the Name of the Account it belongs to; and if there is but one Debtor and one Creditor, which are therefore always in one Line, write the Debtor's Number above the Creditor's (thus you are to underftand the Figures on the *Journal* Margin of the preceding Examples.) And this is ufeful for comparing the *Journal* and *Leger,* that we need not be troubled to ufe the *Index* (which is defigned only to find an Account in the *Leger,* when we have no Bu-finefs with the *Journal.*) And then it ferves to fhew us how far the *Journal* is transferred into the *Leger,* by marking thefe Numbers as foon as every Tranfaction is transferred.

The Defign of this Book is to prevent Errors in the *Leger,* and to be a Help for the more eafy proving, that what's entered in the *Leger* is right; or difcover-ing and correcting the Errors of it. For, the *Leger* being the principal Book, muft be filled up with the greateft Care and Attention, and therefore it has been thought neceffary firft to mark the Debtors and Creditors in a *Journal;* and then by transferring from this Book into the *Leger,* there is an Occafion of confidering the Thing once more, before it enter the *Leger;* wherefore be-fore it be transferred, we ought again to examine whether the Debtors and Creditors are right in the *Journal.*

Again, by having the Debtors and Creditors marked, and diftinguifhed in the *Journal,* we can more eafily examine the *Leger,* and be fatisfied of what's right, or difcover what's wrong in it; as the Practice will make evident. For fuppofe you have only a *Wafte-Book,* from which Things are transferred imme-diately into the *Leger,* it's plain, that when you come afterwards to examine and prove the *Leger,* you muft firft confider the Tranfaction as it is narrated in the *Wafte-Book,* and fee what the Debtors and Creditors ought to be (as you did at firft when you transferred it into the *Leger*) then compare the *Leger* with thefe Debtors and Creditors; and if this muft be done in examining of every Tranfaction, it is thought the better Way to do it all together in a *Jour-nal.*

Now obferve, that to anfwer this End, it feems plainly fufficient, to mark out the Debtors and Creditors, without repeating the whole Narration; which is the Foundation of the fecond Method of the *Journal.*

Second Method of the Journal.

Make a complete Tranfcript of the *Wafte-Book,* without any Alteration, leaving upon the left Side of every Page a large Margin, about a third Part of the Page; upon which Margin, againft every Tranfaction, write the Names of the Debtors and Creditors of that Tranfaction, with their Titles of Debtor and Creditor, and Sums of Money; and obferve, that where there are

fundry

fundry Debtors or Creditors to one Creditor or Debtor, you muft write the Names of thefe fundry next each other, and the Name of the one correfponding Debtor or Creditor againft the Total of the other Sums, and fo the Balance and Connection appears at fight. Then, when the Tranfaction is transferred to the *Leger*, write upon this Margin the Numbers of the Folios where the Accounts ftand in the *Leger* ; for the fame Purpofes mentioned already in explaining the other Method of a *Journal*.

This Book you may call either the *Wafte-Book* or *Journal*, becaufe, indeed, it is both ; not only as every *Wafte-Book* is really a *Journal* ; but as there is here alfo all that diftinguifhes a *Wafte-Book* and *Journal*.

The preceding Examples, put in this Form, will fufficiently fhew it ; where obferve, that the Figures fet on the left of each Name, are the Numbers of the Folio's of the *Leger* where thefe Accounts are fuppofed to ftand.

		l.	s.	d.		l.	s.	d.
2	Dr. *Claret Wine* ⎱	90			*Exam.* 1. Bought and received of *A. B.* 10 Hds of *Claret Wine*, payable in 3 Months	90		
1	Cr. *A. B.* ⎰							
1	Drs. ⎰ *Cafh,*	28			*Exam.* 2. Sold and delivered to *B. C.* 6 Hds *Claret Wine*, at 13 l. ℔ Hd, is 78 l. whereof			
2	⎱ *B. C.*	50			Paid in Cafh ——— 28 l.			
2	Cr. *Claret Wine*	78			The Remainder payable in 2 Months-- 50			
					78	78		
1	Crs ⎰ *Cafh,*	100			*Exam.* 3. Bought and Received of *L. M.* 10 Pieces of *Broad-Cloth*, containing 40 Yards each, at 12 s. is 240 l. whereof			
4	⎱ *L. M.*	140			Paid in Cafh ——— 100 l.			
7	Dr. *Broad-Cloth*	240			The Remainder payable in 6 Months- 140			
					240	240		

It has been already faid, that when a Tranfaction is fo Complex as to have fundry Debtors, and fundry Creditors, it muft be refolved into two or more Parts, in each of which the Balance is betwixt one Debtor and one Creditor, or one Debtor or Creditor and fundry Creditors or Debtors. Accordingly, thefe different Connections and Balances of Debtor and Creditor muft be diftinctly marked on the Margin. Examples of this you'll find in the following *Wafte-Book* or *Journal,* N°. II.

Again obferve, That if the Name of an Account is long, it may be contracted on this Margin (though it muft be at length in the *Leger*) as you find done in the following *Journal,* N°. II.

Now the Reafons why I think this Method preferable, are thefe.

1*ft* If the Copy of the *Wafte-Book,* or *Memorial,* that is firft written, is made fo fair and clean, as there be no need of making another Copy, then it's plain that, as the marking of the Debtors and Creditors on the Margin anfwers the fame Purpofe as the firft Method of a *Journal,* fo it is very much fhorter; unlefs inftead of the *Wafte-Book* you would make a *Journal* (in the firft Method) your firft and only *Memorial Book*; but this would by no Means be convenient, becaufe the Difcovery of the true Debtors and Creditors being the great Difficulty, muft not be done in a Hurry; as this Method would often occafion. Or if, to prevent this Effect, the *Journal* is filled up more flowly, then there is danger of forgetting, and therefore it's necefary that a plain and fimple *Memorial* be taken Day by Day, and as foon after every Tranfaction is finifhed as poffible; and confequently the *Marginal Journal,* as it is the fhorteft, and ferves the fame Purpofe equally, is preferable.

2*d. Again obferve,* That where there is a great deal of Bufinefs, and feveral Perfons employed about it, the firft Copy that's made of the *Wafte* or *Memorial Book,* will be filled up by different Hands, every one writing in it as different Accidents call them to it. In this Cafe 'tis indifpenfable that there be a fair and clean Copy of this Book written with one Hand.

Now in tranfcribing this Book, you may either chufe to form it at once into a *Journal,* according to the firft Method; (for to copy the *Wafte-Book* fimply, and then make a feparate *Journal,* are not both neceffary) or make a fimple Copy of the *Wafte-Book,* with a Margin for the Debtors and Creditors. As to thefe Methods, obferve, that there will be lefs writing in the firft (where you do not take a fimple Copy of the *Wafte-Book,* and a feparate *Journal* too.) Yet I would prefer the laft for thefe Reafons, that the firft does in many Cafes occafion an unavoidable Confufion in the Narration; whereas in the other Method you have the Tranfaction narrated in the fimple and natural Manner, without any Art, fo as it is obvious to every one who can read it, which the other is not.

Again, as any Body who writes fair and correct, is capable to make a right Copy of the *Wafte-Book,* who yet could not make up the *Journal;* the Bookkeeper, whofe Principal Tafk is the *Journal* (in fo far as it differs from the *Wafte Book*) and the *Leger,* may be faved the Trouble of writing the *Wafte-Book,* where you have others that can conveniently do it; by which means

he

he will have more Time and Leifure for filling up the *Leger*, and the Debtors and Creditors on the Margin of the *Waſte-Book*; which is alſo to be left upon him.

Obſerve alſo, That though a Copy of the *Waſte-Book*, and a ſeparate *Journal*,
are not both of abſolute Neceſſity, yet the Convenience of having a fair Record in the ſimple narrative Stile, has made Merchants generally chuſe, when
the firſt Copy of the *Memorial* is not fair and clean, to make both ſuch a Copy
of it ſimply, and a ſeparate *Journal*; but it's manifeſt that a ſimple Copy of
the *Waſte-Book*, with the Debtors and Creditors marked on the Margin, is here
alſo preferable, as before when we ſuppoſed but one Copy of the *Waſte-Book*
neceſſary.

C H A P. II.

Containing more particular Inſtructions for the Formation and Uſe of Accounts in the Leger.

S E C T. I.

Introduction, concerning the Method of theſe Inſtructions; with ſome general Directions.

THE preceding Chapter contains the fundamental Principles, and
Rules of the *Leger*; which are never to be tranſgreſſed, but in every Caſe to be applied, either in a more general or particular Man-
ner: You muſt therefore take care to remember, and have them always in
View. But then as to the complete Application of them, there remain ſeveral
Things to be yet explained; and that we may have firſt a general Idea of what's
further neceſſary, conſider, that all *Accounts* belong to one of theſe three Claſſes,
Perſonal, Real, or *Imaginary*; and accordingly all the further Inſtruction that
needs, or can be added, for finding the Debtors and Creditors (*i. e.* where any
Tranſaction is to be placed in the *Leger-Book*) relates to theſe two Parts, *viz.*
1. The Invention of *Imaginary* Accounts for ſatisfying the third general Rule.
2. Particular Accommodations of the ſecond general Rule for *Perſonal* and
Real Accounts to ſome particular Caſes; either in the limiting of them to particular Conditions, or extending them ſo as to comprehend ſeveral like Subjects

F

under

under a common Name; and sometimes by a Mixture of both, in different Respects. The Consequence of which you'll see in what follows.

Before I proceed further in those particular Instructions, I shall here make a short Reflection upon the Method of Instruction as to the *Leger-Book*, which has hitherto universally obtained, among our *English* Writers on this Subject; that the Difference of that, and what I have chosen, may more clearly appear. Their Method is this.

After such a very general Description of the *Leger-Book*, and of the Notion of Debt and Credit, as I could never think sufficient to give the Learner a clear and perfect Idea of the Principles, and Reason of this Method; they reduce all their other particular Instructions and Rules to certain Heads, and Branches of Business (which is so far right:) And then, in the Way of Question and Answer, they shew what Accounts are to be made Debtors, and what Creditors, in the various Cases and Transactions that most commonly occur under each of those Heads.

Now, though this Method seems to be very plain, and adapted to Learners, yet that it is both unreasonably tedious and obscure, will easily appear, when we consider, that a very few general Rules comprehend all those Cases, in such a Manner as to make the Sense and Reason of what's to be done much more clear and obvious. Thus, for Example, one general Rule for the Use of *Personal* and *Real Accounts*, is a complete Instruction, for finding which of the *Persons* and *Things* concerned in any Transaction, are Debtors and Creditors. And though the corresponding opposite Debtors and Creditors (which make the Balance) are not expressed directly in that Rule, yet they are found by the Application of it, in all Cases where the *Personal* and *Real Accounts* concerned are Debtors or Creditors for the same Articles; and so this one Rule comprehends a great many Cases; and (after the Explication of the fundamental Principles and Reasons of this Method, given in the preceding Chapter) is a complete and plain Instruction for them all; which saves the Memory the Burden of so many particular Rules. If these particular Cases were only brought as Examples, and Applications of a general Rule, which is first completely explained, the Method were more tolerable: But without this it's not only tedious but obscure; because the Reason of all those particular Rules is contained, and must be sought in the general Principles and Use of the several Kinds of Accounts. For as the Work of the *Leger* is the forming of Accounts for different Subjects; so till one has a distinct Idea of the different Kinds of Accounts, he can find nothing but Obscurity and Confusion, in a Multitude of particular Questions, answered in this Manner; whereas, after a clear, general Notion of the Nature and End of Accounts, and a distinct Description of the Use of the several Kinds of Accounts, as they are applicable in general, and also in different Parts and Branches of Business, such a Detail of Cases and Applications is altogether superfluous: And as every Thing ought to be done with a sufficient Reason, so I shall here once for all

OBSERVE, *That the Reason of making any Account, in any Case, Debtor or Creditor, is, that that particular Case or Article, falls within the Use of that Account,*

accord-

according to the Description of it ; and again, the Reasonableness of forming such an Account, is to be sought in its answering the Design of Book-keeping, by representing such a particular Part of our Affairs in a clear and distinct State.

Therefore as I have in the preceding Chapter laid the Foundation of a perfect Knowledge of this Art, in a complete Explication of the general Principles and Rules; the Method I am to take in what's further necessary, is, to give you, under distinct proper Heads, a general View of Transactions of Trade; and shew what Accounts, for recording those Transactions, are to be opened in the *Leger*; and how they are to be used, *i. e.* what they ought to shew on the Debtor, and what on the Creditor side; by which means you'll have a short, easy, and distinct Scheme of Accounts under every separate Branch of Business; and can with Ease and Understanding, find, in any particular Case, under those Heads, the true Debtors and Creditors, *i. e.* the Accounts, and side of the Accounts to which that Case relates; and the Connection of the Accounts follows of course, according to what has been explained in the preceding Chapter.

Such particular *Notes* and *Directions*, and even particular Cases, as may be proper to make the Nature and Use of some *Accounts* more plain, shall be added in their Places; but the Names and Uses of the several *Accounts* are to be well remembred as *general Rules*.

If, after all that I have said in Vindication of the Plan I have chosen, there may be some who would wish to be instructed in the *Catechetical* Way; I must say this to them, that if they mean to fall to work, without laying any Foundation of general Principles, they propose a very unreasonable Thing; but if they'll first study these, as they are explained in the first Chapter, then they may go on to the Comparison of the Books of Accounts, and as there is a great Variety of Examples of Business in the two *Waste-Books*, they may consider those as so many *Questions* proposed, in order to find the Debtors and Creditors; (which is the Purpose of all the tedious Instructions given in the Way of Question and Answer) and in the *Journal* they have the Solutions. But to put them in a better Way with this, I have after the second *Leger-Book* added a *Table* of all the Variety of Cases contained in the preceding *Waste-Books*, digested under distinct Heads, with the Dates, where Examples of these Cases may be found in the *Waste-Book*. But, if they'll take my Advice, the more rational and effectual Way will be, to read the Instructions of this Chapter, and compare the Books along with them, according to the following Directions.

Some may, perhaps, say, I have complained of the tedious Instructions of other Authors, and yet have made a larger Treatise than most others. To which I answer, That I have complained of their saying Little in a very tedious Method; while, at the same Time, they have neglected the more solid and rational Part of the Instruction, and are also deficient in many useful Particulars. I have, indeed, made a pretty large Treatise, larger, perhaps, than those of some others of whom I complain; but then I hope it will be found, that I have done much more in the same Bulk; and in a Way more

pro-

proper to bring a Learner to a clear, exact, and comprehenfive Judgment of the whole Art.

The General Divifion *of Bufinefs is into thefe three Branches:*.

I. *Proper Trade*, which is for a Man's own proper Account, and Behoof; and this again is diftinguifhed into *Domeftick*, which is managed by himfelf or his Domeftick Servants; and *Foreign*, which is managed by *Factors*, who ferve him in Commiffion.

II. *Factorage*; which a Man manages as Factor for another.

Observe, Though the Materials of proper Foreign and Factorage Accounts, are the fame, yet they muft be feparately confidered, as they ftand in the Employers and Factors Books.

III. *Company* or *Partnerfhip*; which is for the joint Account of feveral Partners.

As all Tranfactions belong to one of thefe Heads; fo, under each of them, you'll find, in what follows, all the Inftructions which, with the preceding general Rules, are neceffary, for placing every particular Tranfaction in the *Leger-Book*. And for the Learner's more diftinct and ready Application of them, let him take thefe

General Directions.

1. Carefully read over what's explained under every Head, with the Defcription of the feveral *Accounts*, fo as to fix in your Memory, at leaft the Titles and Denominations of thefe *Accounts*; by which Means you'll readily know where to feek any particular Inftruction you want. And it will ftill be better, if you can alfo remember the Defcriptions and Ufes of the *Accounts*; but this will come by Degrees through Practice and Experience. And as I now fuppofe a Learner, after having read and underftood the general Rules in the former Chapter, fet down to examine, and find the Debtors and Creditors in the following *Wafte-Books*, in order to transfer them to the *Leger*; that he may apply what is in this fecond Chapter more eafily and effectually, let him firft read over what relates to proper *Domeftick Trade*, then begin his Work, and go on till he meets with fomething relating to proper *Foreign Trade*; then read over what's explained under that Head, and go on till he meets with fomething relating to *Factorage*; and after that to *Partnerfhip*, for in that Order I have gradually brought in Things in the following Books.

2. Confider carefully the precife Matter of Fact of every Tranfaction; or, the Thing narrated as then done (*viz.* at the Date of the Tranfaction) or then firft mentioned as done, or advifed of by your Doers and Correfpondents; for this is the Thing to be now entered in the *Leger*; and if any Thing which was formerly done or advifed of, is mentioned in any Tranfaction, becaufe of its Connection with the prefent Fact or Advice, then to be fure it was (or ought to have been) entered when it was firft mentioned or advifed of. And, to have done, as it is neceffary to have in your View at once, all the *Accounts* belonging to any particular Branch of Bufinefs; fo it's fit always to confider the laft

Step

Step or Tranfaction enter'd in thofe *Accounts* ; becaufe to know how the laft Entry was made, will frequently be ufeful for difcovering what is next to be done ; fo that as the State of Affairs changes, and *Accounts* come in Place of one another, they may be mutually *charged* and *difcharged*.

As to the Connection of the *Accounts*, or the Debtors and Creditors, after they are feparately difcovered, enough has been faid already.

SECT. II.

Accounts for Proper Trade.

ARTICLE I. *How the* Leger *is opened or begun in placing the* Inventory.

THE firft Thing that occurs in a Merchant's *Wafte-Book*, is his *Inventory* ; which confifts of thefe two diftinct Parts, *viz.* His *Effects*, including the Debts owing to him ; then the Debts owing by him. By the *General Rules* we know that each *Perfon*, in the *Inventory*, muft have an *Account*, in which he is Debtor for what he owes me, or Creditor for what I owe him ; and every Thing in it muft have an *Account*, and muft be made Debtor for what is now on Hand ; but the Queftion is, *What is the correfponding Debtor and Creditor* to keep the Balance ? for here I don't confider the Grounds of thefe *Debts* and *Credits* ; and mind only, that fuch Effects belong to me ; and that there are fuch Articles of *Debt* and *Credit* betwixt thofe Perfons and me, which are to be vouched by proper Documents ; or they are, perhaps, the Balance of a former *Account* ; therefore we are to form fome *Imaginary Account*, for prefervng the Balance of the *Leger* ; and this we call *Stock-Account*, to be ufed according to this Defcription.

Stock-Account, is,

DEBTOR, *for all that I owe by the Inventory*.

CREDITOR, *for all my Effects on Hand, and the Debts owing to me, by the Inventory*.

The correfponding Creditors and Debtors are the feveral Subjects that compofe the *Inventory*.

This *Account* may be conceived as reprefenting the Owner of the Books, as in its Nature it really does, and is therefore oppofite to all other *Accounts* ; for the Articles on the Debtor Side are owing by him, and thofe on the Creditor are owing to him. But in every other Account the Articles on the Debtor Side are owing to him, and thofe on the Creditor owing by him, or what the Subject has yielded him.

The

The Ufe of this *Stock-Account* is chiefly to preferve the Balance of the *Leger*. And if you enter the feveral Articles particularly on it, then your *Inventory* will appear fully in this *Account*: But this being already in the *Wafte Book* and *Journal*, you may rather make the *Stock* Debtor to, and Creditor by *Sundry Accounts* for the Total Sum; and refer to the *Wafte* or *Journal* for the Particulars: But ftill be fure that every Article be entered feparately on the feveral particular Accounts to which they relate; and make them Debtors to, or Creditors by *Stock*.

This being done, the *Leger* is fairly begun; what new *Accounts* occur in the Courfe of your Bufinefs being opened gradually as they happen. And thus you have an Idea of the Opening and Spreading of a Regular *Account*; for the Whole is but one *Account*, as it relates to the Owner, whofe feveral Members make particular *Accounts*, as they relate to the different Subjects of his Trade and Correfpondence.

The Definition given, is fufficient to fhew the Ufe of the *Stock-Account*. And as for the various Denominations of *Accounts*, under which the different Articles of a Man's *Inventory* may beft be brought, thefe you'll learn from the particular Accounts after defcribed. In the *Inventory* of the following *Wafte-Book*, N°. I. I have made no Articles that require any *Accounts*; but fimply the *Perfons* and *Things* mentioned; but in the fecond *Inventory* you fee other *Accounts* that arife out of the Balance of the firft *Leger*.

I have only one Reflection to make relating to the *Stock-Account*, which is, that it may be confidered as a *Root* or *Trunk* to which all the other *Accounts* in the *Leger-Book*, do, in fome Senfe, belong, as Branches. As to thofe that originally belong to it in the *Inventory*, the Notion is plain enough; and for others that arife in the Courfe of Bufinefs; they may be faid to grow upon it in this Refpect, that in all the Tranfactions of our Trade, whether there is Increafe or Decreafe, or fimply a Changing of Things of equal Value, or putting one Account in the Place of another, the Capital-Stock is always affected, being either raifed or diminifhed in its Value, or fimply changed in its conftituent Parts; fome of the old Branches remaining, but altered in their State; fome, as it were, lopt off, by being finifhed and cleared, and new ones grown up. Now whatever Alterations happen in the State of the Capital *Account*, either in the Value of the Whole, or the Qualities and Denominations of its conftituent Parts; thefe are to be known, not by the *Stock-Account* it felf, in which we write nothing but the *Inventory*, as it is at the Beginning of the prefent Courfe of *Accounts*; but by the State of the feveral Accounts that ftand in the *Leger*, as they are collected into one general Account, called the *Account* of *Balances*; as you'll learn in the third Chapter.

The *Leger* being thus begun, by the entering of the *Inventory*; the daily Tranfactions of Bufinefs are next to be transferred from the *Wafte-Book*, gradually, as they happen.

ARTICLE II. *Proper Domeſtick Trade.*

A General View of the Tranſactions that occur under this Head.

The moſt ordinary and material *Tranſactions* belonging to this Head, are, 1ſt. *Buying.* 2d. *Selling.* 3d. *Bartering.* 4th. *Receiving, and making Payments of Debts.* 5th. *Borrowing and Lending.* In *Buying* or *Selling* we give or receive for Goods, either *Caſh, Bills,* (or *Aſſignments*) on a third Perſon; or there is an Obligation for Payment on the *Buyer;* which is called *Buying* and *Selling* on *Time.* In *Barter* one Thing is given for ano her; and ſometimes there is a Surplus of *Caſh,* preſently paid or owing: This may be called a mix'd *Bartering;* becauſe, as far as the Surplus reaches, it comes under the former Head; and indeed, *Bartering* is but *Buying* and *Selling;* though theſe Names are differently applied for Diſtinction ſake: *Debts* are pay'd by *Caſh, Bills,* or *Goods;* and ſometimes there is an Abatement made to the Payer. Money is borrowed or lent upon *Bill* or *Bond* (or without any Security; which does not alter the Nature of the Tranſaction) payable with Intereſt, or, perhaps, without it.

What other Tranſactions of Importance belong to this Head, which are leſs common, I ſhall conſider by themſelves; and for theſe Things now mentioned, it is to be obſerved, That though out of them might be formed a Variety of different Caſes, yet the ſecond *General Rule,* for *Perſonal* and *Real Accounts,* with the *Profit and Loſs Account,* is a complete Inſtruction for the Whole I might therefore refer to the Deſcription already given of theſe Accounts: But I ſhall briefly repeat them here, that this Part, according to the Method propoſed, may contain a Definition of all the Accounts belonging to the *Leger;* and then add ſome further Inſtructions concerning the Uſe of them.

A Perſon's Account, is,

DEBTOR for what he owes to me, or I pay to him.
CREDITOR for what I owe him, or he pays to me.

An Account of Goods, is,

DEBTOR for the Value of all received, firſt Coſt and Charges.
CREDITOR for the Value of all that goes away, with the Returns.

Caſh, is,

DEBTOR for what's received. CREDITOR for what goes out.

Profit and Loſs, is,

DEBTOR for all *Loſſes.*　CREDITOR for all *Gains.*

Further Inſtructions *concerning the Uſe of thoſe* Accounts : *Which I divide into three* Parts, *as they relate to Perſons, Things, or Gain and Loſs.*

PART I. *Of Perſonal Accounts.*

What I have to ſay further concerning *Perſonal Accounts,* under this Head of *Proper Domeſtick Trade,* relates in general to the reducing of ſeveral Accounts into one ; applied more particularly to theſe three Caſes, *viz.* the entring of *Bills* ; Money lent upon *Bottomree* ; and of ſuch *Debts* as belong to the *Charges* and *Expence* of *Trade* or *Living.* But I ſhall ſpeak,

ıſt. *Of a General Account for Sundry Perſons.*

Though the *General Rules* ſpeak of particular Accounts for every particular Perſon ; yet it may be convenient, in many Caſes, to comprehend ſeveral Perſons in one general Account. Accordingly ſome Authors propoſe the keeping of one general Account for ſundry Perſons with whom you have little Dealings, under the Title of,

Account for Sundry Perſons.

Which is to be uſed the ſame Way as a particular *Perſonal Account* ; naming the particular Debtor or Creditor in the Narration of every Article.

OBSERVE, Some propoſe to make two General Accounts ; one for the Perſons whoſe Account begins with a *Debt* they owe you ; and another for ſuch whoſe Account begins with a *Debt* you owe them ; diſtinguiſhed thus,

Account for Sundry Perſons, $\begin{cases} \text{who owe to me (}\textit{for the one.}\text{)} \\ \text{and} \\ \text{to whom I owe (}\textit{for the other.}\text{)} \end{cases}$

By which it appears, that the *Perſons* for whom theſe General Accounts are deſigned, are ſuch, as have no Articles of an Account but *Debts* which they contract to me, and their expreſs Payments ; or *Debts* I contract to them, and their Payments. And that theſe *Debts* and *Payments* may not be ſo confuſ'd as they would be upon one *General Account* ; They think it neceſſary to make two Accounts ; but one may ſerve as well, if you'll form it thus, *viz.* Upon each Side make two Sets of Money Columns ; in the Innermoſt, on the Debtor

Side place the *Debt*, contracted to you ; and your Payments in the Innermoft on the Creditor Side ; and begin the Narrative of the Article clofe by the Column for the Date. In the outermoft Column, on the Creditor Side, place the Debts you owe, and their Payments in the fame Column on the Debtor Side ; and begin the Narrative about an Inch within the other Articles : And thus the Comparifon of the two Sides, or the feveral *Debts* and their *Payments*, can be made with eafe ; efpecially if you'll alfo number the feveral Articles. Thus, mark the firft Debt, either owing by or to you, with the Number 1, at the Beginning of the Line ; mark the fecond Debt with 2, and fo on. Then, when the Payments of the Debts are enter'd on the oppofite Side, mark them with the fame Numbers.

Obferve again, That if any *Perfon*, who owes to you, or you to him, a *Debt* enter'd in this *General Account*, happens, before this *Debt* is cleared, to have more Dealings with you, fo that there be a Profpect of a greater Correfpondence, and a larger Account ; then, give him a particular Account, and transfer the *Debt* he owes to you, or you to him, from the General Account to the Particulars, by making the one Debtor to the other, as the Cafe directs.

I come next to fome more particular Cafes, where a *General Account* may be ufeful.

2d. *Of the Entering of* Bills.

To fay any Thing here of the Nature or Diftinctions of *Bills*, would be foreign to my Purpofe, which relates only to the Manner of entering them in the *Leger-Book* ; concerning which, the firft Thing neceffary to be obferved, is, That when I receive a *Bill*, payable to me, which is to be prefented for Acceptance ; then, if the Perfon, on whom it is drawn, lives in the fame Place, or fo near that I can know in a very fhort Time, whether he accepts or not ; I would make no Entry of it till it were accepted ; and if it is refufed, or accepted and not immediately paid, the Cafe will eafily fhew to whofe Account it is to be charged. But if it's fent far off for Acceptance, I would immediately charge it to his Account on whom it is drawn, or the *General Account*, after defcribed. If it is return'd, the Account formerly charged, muft be difcharged ; and the Drawer or Indorfer charged for the Contents, with the Charges, *&c.*

The fecond Thing to be confider'd here is the entering of thefe Bills (when it is to be done) in the *Leger* ; and as to this, obferve, That if the Debtor or Creditor, in a Bill, is one who has no current Account already in my Books, nor like to have any ; it will be convenient to enter all fuch *Bills* upon two *General Accounts*, viz.

Account of Bills owing to me. And,
Account of Bills owing by me.

G The

The firſt repreſents *Perſons* who owe *Bills* to me ; and is made **Debtor** when I receive the Bill, or when it is accepted ; and Creditor upon Payment, or when the Account is to be diſcharged.

The other repreſents Perſons to whom I owe *Bills.* It is Creditor upon my Acceptance, and Debtor when I pay it.

But *obſerve* again, That one *General Account* of *Bills* may ſerve, if you form it with two Sets of Money Columns, as the *General Account* already deſcribed.

You may alſo apply here what I ſaid above, in Caſe any Perſon, who is Debtor or Creditor for a *Bill* enter'd in theſe *General Accounts,* has Buſineſs with you, that requires a particular Account, before theſe *Bills* are clear'd.

There is another Thing worth obſerving here, eſpecially for thoſe who have much to do with *Bills,* viz. That if they have Correſpondence with different Places, and many *Bills* payable, either by or to them, in theſe Places ; the Debtor or Creditor of the *Bills* having no current Account with them ; it will be convenient in theſe Caſes to have a different Account of *Bills* for each of theſe Places. And you may make one *General Account* for each, diſtinguiſh'd by the Name of the Place ; as, *London* Account of Bills. *Amſterdam* Account. of Bills ; or for every Place two Accounts, *viz.* An Account of *Draughts* , and an Account of *Remittances.*

Which way ſoever you keep theſe *General Accounts,* it will be convenient to number the *Bills* when you enter them, and when they are pay'd. You'll find afterwards, in a Deſcription of the Book called the *Month-Book,* ſomething of further Uſe to one who deals much in *Money.*

3d. *Of Money Lent upon* Bottomree.

Bottomree is the lending Money upon the *Bottom* of a Ship, bound to a certain Place ; upon Condition, that if the Ship is loſt, the Debt is diſcharged : But if ſhe arrives ſafe in the Terms of the Contract, the Money lent, with the Intereſt agreed upon, becomes a real Debt, to be paid to me or my Factor, where the Ship arrives ; and till the Payment be actually made, it is a Debt upon the Ship.

For the Entry of ſuch Tranſactions in the *Leger,* we muſt conſider them ſeparately, with Reſpect to the Borrower or Lender upon *Bottomree.*

1. For the *Lender.* To follow the General Rules ; the *Borrower* has a particular Account, in which he is made Debtor for the Money lent, and Intereſt, and Creditor when it is paid, or the Ship loſt. But if you deal much this Way, it will be convenient to bring in all your Buſineſs of this Kind, into one General Account, repreſenting all Perſons who borrow from you upon *Bottomree* ; which you may Title thus,

Account of *Borrowers* upon *Bottomree* ; or ſimply,
Bottomree Account.

It is to be ufed the fame Way as the *Borrowers* particular Account would be ; remembring to name the Perfon concerned in every Article.

OBSERVE, The Intereft needs not be entered till it be paid ; though in fome refpect (as you'll fee below) it is better to do it when the Principal is enter'd

Again, Thofe who make particular Accounts for the *Borrowers*, make a general Account for the *Intereft*, which they call *Bottomree* Account, or *Profit* and *Lofs* by *Bottomree*, which is *Debtor* for what is loft, and *Creditor* for what is gain'd : The Defign of this is to fee all the Gain and Lofs by *Bottomree*, feparate from other Gains and Loffes. But this Purpofe is fufficiently anfwered by the general *Account* for the *Borrowers*, by charging the Intereft with the Principal ; which fhews the Method of a general Account to be in all Refpects preferable.

2. For the *Borrower*. He muft make an *Account* of *Lenders* upon *Bottomree*; to be made Creditor for Principal borrowed with the Intereft, and Debtor for the Payment, or upon the Lofs of the Ship.

OBSERVE, Tho' Ship Mafters are moft commonly the *Borrowers* upon *Bottomree*; yet a Merchant, the Owner of the Ship, may *Borrow* upon *Bottomree*; and if fuch a Perfon is concerned both in Lending and Borrowing, he muft have two Accounts, one for the *Borrowers*, and one for the *Lenders*; or one general *Account* of *Bottomree*, with double Money Columns; the one for the *Borrowers*, the other for the *Lenders*.

4th. *Of* Debts *which belong to the* Charges *and* Expences *of* Trade *and* Living.

Of this Kind are *Houfe-Rents*; *Duties* owing to the Publick, for the Payment of which a Time is allowed ; Accounts running with Shop-Keepers, and Mechanicks ; and the daily out-giving of Cafh, *&c.*

Such *Debts*, when the Creditor has no current Account with you, may be placed to the general Account of *fundry Perfons*, above defcribed ; or into a more limited, though ftill general Account, under the Title of

Account of Out-ftanding Charges.

Which is to be made Creditor when the *Debt* is contracted, or to be entred ; and Debtor when it is paid ; naming the particular Perfon in every Article.

The correfponding Debtor for the Credit of this Account, is either the particular Subject for which the *Debt* is contracted, or it is the Account of *Profit* and *Lofs*, as in all the Expences of *Living*. But you'll fee more of this in what's faid afterwards upon the *Profit* and *Lofs Account*.

PART II. *Of Real Accounts.*

What I have to fay upon this Head, relates either to the forming of General *Accounts*, or fome particular Directions for filling up the Articles either in general

neral

neral or particular *Accounts* ; and of other Things relating to some particular Subjects and Circumstances of *Trade.*

1st. *Of General Accounts.*

Accounts of Goods may be more general, or more particular ; because, of Goods of the same Name, there may be several Species and Distinctions, each of which may be brought into a separate particular Account, or they may be all put into one Account.

For *Example,* There may be a general Account of *Wine* ; or a particular Account of *Red Wines,* and another of *White Wines* ; or they may be distinguished by the Country, as, Accounts of *French Wines,* and Accounts of *Spanish Wines.*

Again, *Linen Cloth* has many Species, as *Muslin, Cambrick,* and what is particularly called *Linen* ; which of the *Dutch* kind we call *Holland* ; the *Linen Cloth* of different Countries may also have different Accounts ; and, if they have different Species, be also subdivided.

Woollen Cloaths have also a Variety of Species, as what is more particularly called *Cloth, Druggets, Serges, Camblets, Crapes,* &c. Here may be formed a general Account for all the Kinds you deal in ; or one for each : Or to avoid too general an Account, or too many particular Accounts, class two or more (as you think fit) together ; and either name them all in the Title, as Account of *Cloths* and *Druggets* ; or *Cloths Druggets* and *Serges* ; or distinguish the several Classes by Numbers, and so the Titles of the Accounts will be, *Woollen Cloths* first Class, or second Class. How the Species belonging to each Class are to be distinguished in the Account, you'll see immediately.

These Species are again subdivisible, thus, *Cloths* into *Broad* and *Narrow,* or into *Cloths* of one Colour, and mix'd : Or *Broad* and *Narrow,* may be each distinguished as the Colours are simple or mix'd : Or *Cloth* of simple and mix'd Colours into *Broad* and *Narrow.* Thus you may make a Variety of Accounts particular or general

Again, the Manufactures of particular Places may be brought all into one Account, especially such as are made of the same Materials, as *Wooll, Flax, Iron.* Thus (for *Example*) *Norwich Woollen Manufactures, Manchester Linen Manufactures,* &c. and these may be subdivided into Classes, or Assortments, as before mentioned.

The like Distinctions and Subdivisions you may conceive in most other Things. And as to the forming of Accounts for them, I must first say in general, that it depends upon the Circumstances of one's Dealings in these Things, whether it will be most convenient to make the Accounts general or particular, and how many Species to take into one Account ; for which he must apply in the most judicious Way he can, this *Maxim, viz.* That too many particular Accounts, or too general Accounts, are equally opposite to that Clearness and Readiness, with which the State of our Affairs ought to appear in our Books.

If you make a general Account for two or more Species; then, that the State of the Account may be diſtinctly and readily found, by the Compariſon of the two Sides, it is neceſſary to make a Quantity Column for every Species, and ſet its Name on each Side on the Head of it. And if you alſo make Subdiviſions of theſe, ſo muſt the Columns be ſubdivided; as in this Specimen, repreſenting either the Debtor or Creditor ſide of an Account of Wine.

	Hds.	*l.*	*s.*	*d.*
Account of Wine. Here there is no Diſtinction of Countries or Colours.				
In this Form the Colours are diſtinguiſhed; and other neceſſary Diſtinctions left to the Narration, or to the Journal. — Red Hds. / White Hds.				
Account of French (*or* Spaniſh) *Wine.* This repreſents an Account for a particular Country, with a Diſtinction of Colours. — Red Hds. / White Hds.				
Account of Red (*or* White) *Wine.* This is an Account for a particular Colour; with a Diſtinction of Countries. — *French* Hds. / *Span.* Hds.				
Account of Wine. Here is a general Account, in which both the Countries and Colours are diſtinguiſhed. — *French* Red | White / *Spaniſh* Red | White				

From this you'll eaſily conceive how to make Columns for the Diviſions of any other general Account · Thus, where ſeveral general Accounts of the ſame Name are diſtinguiſhed by Claſſes, as *Woollen Manufactures* firſt Claſs, there muſt be a Column for every Species of that Claſs.

2d. *Of the Diſtinction of* Parcels *in* particular Accounts; *or the* Parts *of* general Accounts.

There is ſcarcely any Subject where there is not a Diſtinction of Fine and Coarſe, and conſequently of greater and leſſer Value, in the ſame Quantities, or Individuals of the ſame Name; and an Account comprehending Things which

which are diftinguifhable no other Way, I call a *particular Account.* Thus, an Account of *Claret Wine* is a particular Account; for it's a particular *Red French Wine,* of which there is ftronger and weaker, and confequently dearer and cheaper. But I muft *obferve* that, in refpect of the Parcels of different Prices, fuch Accounts may alfo be called *General,* as indeed all Accounts are *General* or *Particular* in different Refpects, or in Comparifon of others, which are more or lefs fo; unlefs we would limit an Account to Things of the fame Name, Quantity and Value in all refpects, which would be a particular Account in the moft ftrict Senfe; but fuch a Limitation would, in moft Cafes, be very inconvenient.

Now, for *particular Accounts,* it is necefary that the Parcels of different Prices be diftinguifhed, which may be done by different Marks or Numbers, applying Number 1ft to all of one Price, Number 2d to another, and fo on. And for each of thefe Numbers you may make a particular Column on each fide; in each of which are to be written the particular Quantities received and given away of that Kind, whofe Number is fet on the Head of the Column. Or if fo many Columns take up too much Room in the Account, it will be well enough if you only mark the Number of each Parcel both on Debtor and Creditor fide, placing them at the End of the Line of the Narration, next to the general Quantity Column. And obferve, If Quantities of different Numbers are entered in one total Sum (as belonging to one Tranfaction) mark all their Numbers, and either leave the particular Quantities of each to be found in the *Journal*; or mark them each after its Number; which, unlefs they are very many, will be no Inconvenience, and fave much Trouble afterwards, in examining the State of the Account (as you'll fee in *Chapter* III)

Again, the fame Method of diftinguifhing by Numbers is alfo to be applied to the feveral Parts or Species of general Accounts, which are otherwife diftinguifhed than by different Prices; or if fuch a general Account, which comprehends Species otherwife diftinguifhable than by different Prices, is not actually diftinguifhed, and fubdivided into its Species; it will be the more necefary to diftinguifh the Parcels by Numbers, according to their Prices, which in many Cafes will be fufficient.

3d. *Of the* Inlack *of* Goods.

If Goods Inlack of the Weight or Meafure, and more is bought to make it up, the Value of what is fo bought is charged in the Account, but the Quantity muft not be placed in the Column with the reft, becaufe it's only to make up an Inlack; and fo if it were added to the reft, then the fame Quantity would be twice enter'd.

If the Inlack is not fupplied, you'll learn how it is to be fet down at the Balancing of the Account, where I fhall alfo confider the Cafe of *Out-Come* in Weights and Meafures.

4th. *Of* Houfes *and* Ships.

(1.) For *Houfes*, which are let out; you may give to each a particular Account; or make a general Account for them all: Debtor for the prime Coft or Value, with all the Expence of *Reparations, Taxations,* and *Improvements:* And Creditor for the Rents received or owing for them, and the Price of them when fold.

Obferve, The Rents may be entered as they fall due, or not till they be paid; but this is not convenient in cafe they ftand long unpaid, and therefore the firft is the better general Rule. And for the *Tenents,* it will be convenient to give them one general Account, which may be called, *Poffeffors of Houfes,* naming the Perfon in every Article, as you enter the Rent due on the Debtor fide, or difcharge it on the Creditor fide.

I have allotted a Place by it felf afterwards, to fpeak at large of the Way of making Accounts for *Farms* and *Land Eftates.*

(2.) For *Ships;* you may either have a general Account of *Ships,* for all that you are concerned in; or a particular Account for each; *Debtor* for the Value it coft you, and *Creditor* for the Price when fold. As for the Charges and Profits arifing from it, I fhall confider that in two Cafes. 1. If you employ her only in Freight, the Account is Debtor for all the Charges of *Reparations* and *Navigation,* and Creditor for the Freights paid or owing. Or after Stating the Account of her *Charges* and *Freight,* enter on the *Ships* Account only the Difference; for moft commonly thefe Accounts are ftated and given up by the *Ship-Mafter,* fo that the Owner has no more to do but *Receive* or *Pay* the *Balance.* 2. If you employ your Ship in Trade; then to keep a clear and feparate Account of the Gain and Lofs by your Ship, and by your Merchandize, charge your Goods (or the *Voyage Account.* See the next Section) with the Freight, as you would pay to a Stranger; and place all the Charges of *Reparations* and *Navigations* to the Debt of the Ships Account, and the *Freights* to the Credit.

5th. *Of* Goods *Bought or Sold to be* delivered *fome Time afterwards.*

Thefe are by fome called *forehand Bargains,* where Goods are bought or fold to be delivered at a certain Time afterwards, either with a Penalty, or not; and Money, or other Effects, given *per* Advance of the Price; as is common in fuch Cafes.

Now, becaufe the Nature of thefe Bargains is fuch, that there is an Obligation on either Party to fulfil it, the other being willing for his Part; therefore not only muft the Advancement be ftated to Account, but it is fit that the whole Tranfaction appear in the *Leger.* As to the Method of doing which, confider, the Goods not being actually delivered cannot be placed to their proper *Account;* for to make an Account of *Goods* Debtor or Creditor, fuppofes an actual Receipt or Delivery of them; and therefore it is fitteft, in this Cafe, to ufe an imaginary or qualified *Account*, reprefenting the *Goods* till they be actually delivered ; and for thefe, we may chufe to make particular Accounts for every particular Tranfaction of this kind ; or one general Account for all you buy, and another for all you fell ; or one general Account for both. Thus,

1. If you chufe a particular Account for every Tranfaction, call it,

$$\text{Account of } \textit{Wine} \text{ (for Exam.) } \begin{cases} \text{Bought} \\ \text{or} \\ \text{Sold} \end{cases} \text{ upon } \textit{Delivery}.$$

The firft is *Debtor* for what I buy ; and *Creditor* for what is delivered, or not to be delivered.

The other is *Creditor* for what I fell, and *Debtor* for what is delivered, or not to be delivered.

The corresponding *Creditors* and *Debtors*, in all Cafes, are obvious ; for they are the *Things* advanced ; the *Seller* or *Buyer* ; and the Goods actually delivered.

2. If you make a *General Account* for what you buy, and another for what you fell, which is the far better way, name them thus,

$$\text{Account of } \textit{Goods} \begin{cases} \text{Bought} \\ \text{or} \\ \text{Sold} \end{cases} \text{ upon } \textit{Delivery}.$$

Or you may call them, as fome do,

$$\textit{Delivery Account} \text{ of } \begin{cases} \textit{Buying} \\ \text{or} \\ \textit{Selling} \end{cases}$$

Thefe Accounts are to be ufed the fame Way as the particular Accounts; *obferving* carefully to name the Goods and Quantity in the Narration of each Tranfaction　And thus you'll have upon the Debtor fide of one, and the Creditor fide of the other, all your Bargains of this kind ; and the oppofite fide will fhew what Bargains are fulfilled, and what not.

3. You may make one general Account for all, and call it

Goods Bought *and* Sold *upon Delivery*,
or fimply,
Goods to be delivered.

Which is to be ufed as you would do the feparate Account for Buying and Selling ; and to make the Account more diftinct, make it with two Sets of Money Columns; over the one write *Bought*, and over the other *Sold* ; and accordingly write the Value of the Goods bought in the one ; and of thofe fold in

the

the other; by which means the State of the Account will appear with little trouble.

OBSERVE, Some Authors confidering the Debt contracted in fuch Tranf-actions as conditional till Delivery, think fit not to place any Credit or Debt on the Seller's, or Buyer's Account, till the Delivery (if it is not then actually paid) but propofe to make another Account for thefe *Perfons*, which they call, *A. B. his Account of Delivery*; and this they ufe till the Delivery; and then if the Price is not paid, they place it upon the Perfon's proper Account; and the oppofite Side of the preceding Account to balance it. But that is needlefs trouble; fince the Narration of thefe Articles qualifies the Debt: Or, if you will have a qualified Account, it is better to make a general one, and call it,

Perfonal Account of Delivery;

which may ferve both for Seller and Buyer, with double Money Columns.

PART III. *Of* Profit *and* Lofs.

Every Thing given away, or Debt contracted, for which there is no real Thing received, nor Obligation for it upon any Perfon, is reckoned in this Method, Gain or Lofs; though in Effect it may be neither Lofs nor Gain. Thus, if I give or receive Money or Goods in Gift, it's a real Lofs or Gain; as it is alfo when I buy or fell at different Prices. But other Things will of Ne-ceffity come to the Profit and Lofs Account, which in Effect are neither Gain nor Lofs; as Intereft paid or received for the Loan of Money; for though there is no other Account to carry this to, yet there may be more gained by the Ufe of the Money borrowed, than the Intereft; which Gain will fall upon the Account to which the Money was applied, and from this be car-ried at laft to the Profit and Lofs Account (as is explained in *Chapter* III.) where all Gains and Loffes are balanced againft one another; fo that if Things are enter'd as Gain or Lofs, which in Effect are not fo, they are ba-lanced by others of an oppofite Kind.

Again, it's to be obferved, That every Article belonging to the *Profit* and *Lofs* Account is not immediately, as foon as it happens, carried to that Ac-count; for upon *Accounts* of *Goods* there is no neceffity, and it would be alfo very inconvenient, to feparate and ftate the Gain or Lofs upon every Article bought and fold; that being better left to be ftated all together, when the Account is finifhed, or when you make a general State and Balance of the whole Accounts. (See *Chapter* III.)

To this Account belong particularly *Difcounts* made in *Payments of Debts*, *Intereft* of *Money*, *Expences* of *Living*, and fome other Things; for which, mind the following Directions.

 1. *Of*

1. *Of the* Discounts *or* Rebatements *made upon Payments.*

The Payer must be discharged of the whole Debt; and for the *Discount,* it may, in all Cases, be carried to the *Account* of *Profit* and *Loss.* But if the Discount is made for Defect in Goods, for which that Debt is paid; it may be as proper to state it to the *Account* of *Goods,* to take off so much of the Price formerly stated: For by this Discount the Price is really less or more than it was at first stated; and thus the true Gain or Loss upon the Account appears more justly, than when the Discount is stated to the *Profit* and *Loss Account.*

But if the Discount is for advancing the Money before the Term agreed on at selling the Goods, the same Reason is not equally good; however you may chuse either way.

A *certain Author* speaking of this Case, says the *Discount* ought to be placed to the *Account* of *Goods,* because hereby Goods that were formerly sold on Time, become now, as it were, sold for ready Money, and so much less. And for the same Reason, if it were not paid till after the Term agreed upon, and Interest paid for the Forbearance, I say, that *Interest* should be placed to the Account of *Goods*; because Goods formerly sold to be paid for at a certain Time, become now, as it were, sold payable at a longer Time, and so much dearer. But there is no positive Reason for it in either Case, and it's no matter whether you place the *Discount* or *Interest* to the Account of *Goods,* or *Profit* and *Loss.*

2. *Of* Interest *for the* Loan, *or* Forbearance *of Money*

When Money is borrowed upon Interest, the Principal goes to the *Borrower* or *Lender's* Account, and the Account of Cash; and the Interest to the *Profit* and *Loss* Account. But in Stating the Interest there is this Variety, *viz.*

You may charge the *Interest* on the Account of the Borrower or Lender before it falls due; thus, upon your Lending or Borrowing, state the Interest which will be due at the Term of Payment; and after that, state every Term's Interest at the beginning of the Quarter, half Year, or Year, according as it is payable: And if Principal and Interest be paid before the Term to which Interest is charged, there will be so much to be taken out of the Account again, by an opposite Entry. Or,

You may charge the Interest only from Term to Term, as it falls due. Or, *Lastly,* Enter it only as it is paid: And in this Case it needs not be placed to the Person's Account, unless it be to prevent Mistakes, or to let you see by the Account, what Interest is due. For by first placing it to the Account, and then discharging the Payment, it will be understood, that all the Interest, from the Time of last stating of Interest, is due: Remembering, both in this and the Method of the preceding Article, that when the State of that

Per-

Perfon's Account is demanded, all the Intereft then due, is to be placed to the Account.

If any Thing befides the legal Intereft is paid for the Loan of Money, it has nothing to do with the Perfon's Account.

Obferve, That fome propofe to keep an Account of Intereft as a Branch of the *Profit* and *Lofs Account;* where your whole Concern in Intereft may appear diftinctly. But as this Account, unlefs one deals both in Borrowing and Lending, will be all Debt, or all Credit, it is not convenient.

3d. *Of Infurance.*

1. If I pay for the Infurance of any Thing, the *Præmium* is an Article of Expence to be charged upon that Thing.

2. If I infure any Thing to another, then both the *Præmium* received, and what I pay for the Thing infured, when it is loft, belongs to the *Profit* and *Lofs Account.* But if I deal much this Way, it will be convenient to keep a particular Account of my *Gain* and *Lofs* by Infurance, under the Title of,

Infurance Account.

Which is to be made *Debtor* for what I pay of infured Goods which are loft; and *Creditor* for the *Præmiums.*

OBSERVE, As the Infurer has a Right to the Thing loft; if any Thing be recovered, all he lays out upon the recovering of it, muft go to the Debtor Side; and what he recovers, to the Creditor Side of *Infurance Account.*

4th. *Of Wagering.*

The Tranfactions under this Head, are, in General, the Engagement in the Wager, and the Decifion of it: Alfo in the Engagement we either confign, or come under a verbal Obligation [called *Wagering upon Parole.*] Thefe Tranfactions will be duly recorded, by Means of thefe two *Imaginary Accounts.*

Wager's Account, is,

Debtor for what I confign or ingage for in a Wager, and for what I lofe when it was upon *Parole.*

Creditor for what I lofe, which was configned (to fhew the Decifion) and for what I receive upon the Gaining of any *Wager.*

And *obferve,* That, on Decifion of a Wager upon Parole, whether I gain or lofe, befides entering the Gain or Lofs, this Account muft alfo be Creditor: The Reafon of which, and the correfponding Debtor, you'll fee in the following Account.

Hazard Account, is,

Creditor [by *Wager's Account*] for my Engagement, upon Parole ; and *Debtor* [to *Wager's Account*] upon Decifion of the Wager, whether I gain or lofe : To undo what was formerly done, and fhew that the Wager is decided.

It is manifeft that the State of your Affairs relating to *Wagers*, will clearly appear upon thofe Accounts ; efpecially the *Wagers Account* ; the other being contrived merely to get Wagers upon Parole, entered in the *Leger* ; which they ought to be, becaufe of the mutual Obligations.

Obferve, Some Authors confider the *Wager's Account*, as a Branch of the *Profit* and *Lofs Account* : And therefore, upon the lofing a *Wager* confign'd, they would make no Entry of that Decifion ; becaufe, fay they, the Lofs will appear upon the final State or Balancing of the *Accounts* ; but in Cafe of Gaining, or upon Decifion of Wagers upon Parole, whether I gain or lofe, what's receiv'd or paid makes an Entry neceffary.

But againft this Account's being confider'd as a mere *Profit* and *Lofs Account*, there is this manifeft Objection, *viz.* That it is not true, that what is either confign'd or engag'd for in a *Wager*, is a Lofs at the Time of the Engagement, any more than that Goods are loft when they are fhipped, becaufe they may be loft in the Voyage. And, for the fame Reafon, fuch *Wagers* as are not decided, are Articles that would belong to a new Stock or Inventory, if we were to make up one before they were decided ; whereas a mere *Profit* and *Lofs Account*, contains no Article that belongs to an *Inventory* ; it has therefore fomething more in it than a *Profit* and *Lofs Account* ; being in its Nature an *Imaginary Account*, intermediate betwixt the *Profit* and *Lofs Account*, and other Accounts, till the Decifion make it either *Gain* or *Lofs*.

Again, As to the Cafe of lofing what was configned ; this muft be obferved, That unlefs there be an Entry made of it, or fome Mark or other Thing written in the Account upon the lofing of thofe Wagers, to fhew that they are loft ; the Account will not fhew the State of your Bufinefs, in Wagering, as it ought to do ; and if the Decifion of Wagers muft appear as well as the Engagement, I'd chufe rather to do it in Form, by making *Wager's Account* Creditor, as the preceding Rule directs (*Profit* and *Lofs* being the Debtor.)

To have done ; I muft obferve, That as to the Balance of *Gain* or *Lofs* upon the *Wagers* decided, it will be found a little more readily, if the Loffes upon Wagers decided, are not ftated in Form. But of this I fhall fpeak more particularly in Chapter III.

5th. *Of Defperate Debts*.

When a Debt becomes loft by the Circumftances of the Debtor, I would not any longer encumber my *Leger* with that Perfon's Account ; but difcharge it by *Profit* and *Lofs*. Or if I do not actually difcharge the Debtor ; and look on the Debt only as defperate for the Time, but which may afterwards

possibly

poffibly be recovered ; I would not difcharge the Account abfolutely, but only transfer it from the Debtor's *Particular Account* to a *General Account* of *Defperate Debts* ; and there let it ftand, till it's either recovered, or till I look upon
it as irrecoverable ; and then it's difcharged out of this Account.

6th. *Of Conditional Promifes.*

This is a Subject fcarce worth many Words ; yet becaufe feveral Authors
have confidered it, I will not omit it.

If I come under an Obligation to pay a Sum of Money or the Value in
other Effects ; or, if I have the like Obligation upon another, upon certain
Conditions, to be performed to or by me, there is no real Debt till Performance ; yet we muft confider, whether the Promifer is under pofitive Obligation to the other upon his performing ; if he is not (or when the Promife is
altogether gratuitous, revocable at Pleafure) there is no Reafon to make
any *Leger* Entry of this ; but when the Condition is performed, let the Thing
promifed, and now given or received, be ftated to the *Account* of *Profit*, &c.
For *obferve*, it is not fuppofed, that any real Thing which can be again difpofed of, is to accrue to the Promifer by the Performance ; which would' bring
it under the Notion rather of *Delivery-Account* ; efpecially if there be a pofitive Obligation on the Promifer ; but we fuppofe here no fuch real Thing to
be expected by the Performance ; yet may the Promifer be obliged to the
other ; becaufe of the Trouble and Expences he has been put to in accomplifh-
ing the Conditions : In this Cafe there may be a better Reafon alledged why
there ought to be a *Leger* Entry made, becaufe of the Obligation on the one
Party ; tho' a *Pocket-Book Memorandum* may ferve till Performance ; efpecially
when that is expected to be foon, or not at all : But if in Profecution of the Method of *Book-keeping*, it be required to ftate thefe conditional Obligations ;
which is the more neceffary, when a confiderable Time muft be allow'd for
performing the Conditions ; it may be done under the *Imaginary Accounts,
Promife* and *Conditional Accounts* ; thus, *Promife Account* is Debtor to *Conditional Account*, for my Promifes ; and Creditor by *Conditional Account*, when
the Performance is made, and Promife fulfilled. Again, *Promife Account* is
Creditor by *Conditional Account*, for Promifes made to me ; and Debtor to
Conditional Account, upon Performance and Promife fulfilled, or Advice as
aforefaid ; or upon Advice that the Conditions cannot be fulfilled. *Obferve*
too, that there be two Sets of Columns in each Account, for the Promifes
made by me and to me.

Thus will you always find, by thefe Accounts, the true State of fuch Parts
of your Affairs, *i. e.* what Promifes you have made, or others to you ; and
which of them remain ftill in Force, or are extinguifhed by actual Performance,
or otherwife ; and mind that the Things given out or received, go to *Profit*
and *Lofs*.

Note, Some would have fore-hand Bargains come under the Directions of
Promife Accounts, but what's already deliver'd upon this Head, is much
preferable.   P ART

PART IV. *Of fome Accounts whofe Particulars are kept in feparate Books, for eafing the* Leger.

1ft. *Of the* Cafh-Book.

In Bufinefs where *Cafh* happens to be an Account that has numerous Articles, it is convenient to keep the more particular Account of all the Articles in a feparate Account from the *Leger*; which is for that Reafon called the *Cafh-Book*. It is formed in all Refpects, like the Cafh Account in the *Leger*, with a Debtor and Creditor Side; in which, all the Cafh received, and given out is enter'd; either in a fimple Stile, or in that of the *Leger*: But which Way foever the Narration is made, every Article muft be duly entered on the oppofite Side of the correfponding Account in the *Leger*; with a Reference to the *Leger Account* of *Cafh*: For fuch an Account there muft alfo be, in which the Sums of the Debtor and Creditor Sides of the feparate particular Account muft be transferred once a Week or Month, as you think fit; thus, in the *Cafh-Book*, the Sums being written down, againft them write *Transferred to the Leger*, and mark the Folio: And in the *Leger Account*, enter the Sum, with the Date of the Tranference, Debtor *To*, and Creditor *By* fundry Accounts, as *per* the *Cafh-Book*. The *Cafh Account* in the *Leger*, is necefary for the Balance of the Whole; and the Convenience of the feparate Account of all the Particulars, is, that we have them all together, in one continued Account: Whereas, the Rule of the *Leger* being not to allow more than one Folio for one Account, till that be filled up, the Account might hereby lie in feveral different Folios.

Some propofe to diftinguifh the feveral Species of Money in the *Cafh-Book*, but to make this of any Ufe, it will require a Column for every Species, befides the Columns of *l. s. d.* in which the total Value is fet down.

2d. *Of the Book of Expences of Living.*

This is a feparate and continued Account of all the Expence of Living, which ferves to keep both the *Profit* and *Lofs Account*, and alfo the *Cafh-Book* more diftinct. The greater and more confiderable Articles are to be placed here particularly: But there are many fmall Articles, of daily Difburfments, that muft come in Totals; but under what Denominations, and how general or particular the Articles of this Book are to be made, muft be left to every one's Choice. What I have to do here, is only to *obferve*, That all the *Cafh* paid out upon this Account, muft be carefully entered here; and then once a Week or Month, be transferred to the *Cafh-Book*, and to the *Profit* and *Lofs Account* in the *Leger*; which is Debtor to *Cafh* for it. By this Means both the *Cafh-Book* will be more diftinct, and the Expence of Living, which otherwife would be fcattered upon the *Profit* and *Lofs Account*, will be here feen all at once.

once. But if any Articles are paid otherwife than by *Cafh*, they muft go to the Account to which they are placed.

It will anfwer the Purpofe fufficiently, though no Articles are placed here till they are actually paid. Yet if any confiderable Debts are contracted upon this Account, it is fit a Memorial of them be taken in a feparate Part of this Book ; and as they are paid, enter them among the other Articles paid ; marking them alfo paid where they were entered Outftanding ; which may be conveniently done by double Money Columns, drawing the Sum into the outer Columns, as they are paid. But if you think fit you may ftate thefe Debts in the *Leger* to the Creditor's *Particular Account*, if he has one ; or to the *General Account* of *Out-ftanding Charges*, (*Profit* and *Lofs* being Debtors) And when paid, they are difcharged in the Account that was Creditor. But the Payment muft not be placed in the Book of Expences, among the Articles paid and transferred to the *Cafh Account* ; becaufe, *Profit* and *Lofs* being Debtor for all thefe, it would be twice Debtor for the fame Thing : Yet you may mark it paid in that Part of the Book where it was enter'd as owing.

Thus, you have, in this Book, a complete Account of all your Expences of Living ; both what's paid and what's owing, which is already known and adjufted.

Of Charges of Merchandife.

What's faid here concerning Expence of Living, is applicable to a feparate Account of thofe Articles of Charges of Merchandife, which are not ftated to the particular Accounts for which the Charges happen ; as there are a great many Articles that belong, in common, to feveral Things, and efpecially petty Charges, which are all more conveniently carried to the *Profit* and *Lofs Account*.

ARTICLE III. *Accounts for proper Foreign Trade.*

All the Tranfactions that occur upon this Branch may be comprehended under thefe general Heads, *viz.* The Shipping of my Goods, the Advices concerning the Voyage, as whether they are loft, or come fafe to my Factor's Hands ; my Factor's Advices concerning the Difpofal of the fame ; his buying Goods for my Account ; and the mutual Draughts and Remittances betwixt us for my Account. Thefe and what elfe may occur in the Way of Foreign Trade, by fettled Correfpondence, you'll have very diftinctly recorded by the following Accounts.

Voyage to———— *in the Ship*——— A. B. *Mafter, is*

Debter for the Value (including all Charges till on Board) fhipped for my Account ; alfo for the *Salvage*, *Ranfom*, and other Expence that may happen afterwards upon the Voyage.

Creditor

Creditor upon Advice of their being loft, or fafe at their Port, to difcharge this Account [the correfponding Debtor is *Profit* and *Lofs*, or my Factor's Account, as below; or the Infurer; if they were infured.]

OBSERVE, 1. It will make the Account more diftinct, to place each Quantity of different Goods fhipped, in a feparate Column.

2. You may chufe either one general *Account* of *Voyages*, or an *Account* of *Voyages* for every particular Place; or more particularly, an Account for every *Cargo* and *Voyage*, diftinguifhed by the Name of the Ship, the Mafter, and Place to which the Ship is bound.

3. If Goods are bought immediately before they are fhipped, and in order to it; it's needlefs to put them into their proper and particular Accounts, tho' you have already fuch an Account; but charge them to the *Voyage Account*: For if you place them to their proper Account, you'll have that to difcharge immediately, and the *Voyage* to make Debtor; and it makes no Error if you open an Account of *Voyage*, even before the Goods are actually fhipped, which will be in fome Circumftances convenient, that the Goods bought may not be long unenter'd in the *Leger*.

4. If part of the Cargo is loft, you may either charge *Profit* and *Lofs* Debtor to the *Voyage* for it; or put the Value of the whole upon what is faved, unlefs it be infured, in which Cafe the *Infurer* is Debtor.

5. Goods fhipped upon my Account at another Place, to come homewards, or to any other Place, are to be charged upon an *Account* of *Voyage* from —— to ——, or homewards, &c.

6. If a *Voyage* is committed to a *Supra-Cargo*, and not confined to a Factor, the *Voyage* to —, &c. ftands Debtor till the Ship returns, or till the *Supra-Cargo* advifes of the Sale of the Goods and remits the Value, or configns them when he cannot fell them. Or if he advifes of Goods loaded in return, you may make an Account of *Voyage* from —— &c. Debtor, and difcharge the *Voyage* outwards.

7. When a *Cargo* is confined, you will have ufe for the following Accounts with your Factor, *viz.*

A. B. of *Amfterdam* (for Ex.) my *Account of Goods ♈ Ship* —— A. B. *Mafter.*
Or thus,
Account of Goods ♈ Ship, in the Hands of A. B.

Debtor for the Value of Goods confined to him, upon Advice that he has received, but not yet difpofed of them.

Creditor upon Advice that they are difpofed of, or out of his Hands. The correfponding Debtor is according to the Advice. See the following Accounts.

OBSERVE, Every diftinct *Cargo* and Confinement ought to have a diftinct Account: If there is but one Species of Goods, name it in the Account, as *Account* of *Stockings*. If there are more, either name each of them in the Title, or call it in general, *Account of Goods*, diftinguifhing the Particulars in the Narration; and either way it's fit to make Columns for the different Species.

A. B.

A. B. of ———— *My Account of Sales on Time* [*or Out-ftanding Debts.*]

Debtor for the Value of Goods he advifes me are fold upon Time (and which is not remitted.)

Creditor for the Payment he receives of thofe Debts.

OBSERVE, If there is a Difference of the Species of Money in my Factor's Country and mine, this Account ought to have a particular Column for the Money of my Factor's Country, becaufe he accounts with me by that ; yet I muft have *Englifh*-Money Columns, in which the Value of the *Foreign*-Money is put, according to the current Rate of Exchange.

A. B. of ———— *My Account Current.*

Debtor for all the Money received by him for my Goods ; his Draughts upon me, or my Remittances to him : In fhort, for all he owes, or is accountable for to me as my Factor (for which the preceding Accounts do not ftand charged.)

Creditor for the Returns or Payments he makes of my Money in his Hands, by my Draughts on him, or his Remittances to me ; and for Goods he buys and fends off by my Order : In fhort, for all I owe or am accountable for to him, as my Factor. There muft be a Foreign-Money Column here, as in the former Account.

OBSERVE, 1. So many Accounts with my Factor are very ufeful and convenient, to fhew diftinctly the different Pofture and State of Affairs ; (and therefore I cannot approve of their Method who never difcharge the *Voyage* till the Factor advifes that the Goods are difpofed of) but the *Account Current* is the moft general Account, and called *Current*, with refpect to the other two, whofe Ufe is more limited, and may be clofed or finifhed, while this one is ftill open ; which is alfo a Recipient for the firft two (as you fee by comparing their Ufes) unlefs what is due upon them, be immediately remitted.

2. It is plain, thefe Accounts come all in Place of one another, *i. e.* are Debtors and Creditors one to another, as the State and Circumftances change. And to know which is Debtor and which is Creditor in any Cafe, you need only to compare their Ufes. But I fhall ftate the common Cafes briefly. 1. Upon Advice that he has received my Goods : This Account is Debtor, and the *Voyage* Creditor : Unlefs he advifes alfo, that they are fold ; for then one of the other Accounts is *Debtor* for what is fold, or the Cafh received, or Perfons on whom I have Bills for the Value remitted, with Advice of the Sales. 2. The Goods having been upon hand fome Time, when he advifes of the Sales, then is *Account* of *Goods* Creditor, and one of the two other Accounts Debtor, or Cafh, or Perfons on whom I have Bills for the Value. 3. When he advifes me of Out-ftanding Debts paid, the *Account of Sales* is *Creditor*, and *my Account Current* Debtor, or *Cafh, &c.* if he remits it. And *obferve*, If it is not remitted, to ftate the Exchange at the fame Rate it

I   was

was before (though it were now altered) for before you draw for it, it may alter again; and it's sufficient to mark the Rate of Exchange which happens when you draw, or it is remitted to you.

3. *A. B.* may act as my Factor in negotiating Bills of Exchange, though I never consign any Goods to him; and then the only Account to be used is *My Account Current.*

4. *My Account* of *Sales,* may be said to represent the Persons that buy my Goods from my Factor; but these Persons knowing nothing of me, and my Factor being accountable, as having the Direction; therefore this Account bears his Name, and represents him in a particular Circumstance, *viz,* as accountable for these Debts, when he receives Payment thereof; for this Account supposes, what is the most ordinary Way, *viz.* That my Factor is liable to me for the Buyers, no further than it can be prov'd he sold my Goods to reputed Bankrupts, or neglected the necessary Course for recovering the Debts. But there is another Supposition to be made, *viz.* That my Factor for a greater Allowance, obliges himself to make good all the Sales he shall make of my Goods; then the *Account* of *Sales* is needless, and the *Account Current* is to be charged for all the Sales; and because even then we may suppose the Factor not bound for Payment of those Sales, till the Term of Payment come, at which they are payable by the *Buyers;* therefore, let that Term be narrated in the Article, according to the Advice. And if this Contract for insuring your Debts, is entred into after the *Account of Sales* is opened, and some Articles standing upon it, I would immediately balance it, *viz.* make it *Creditor* by *Profit* and *Loss,* or *my Account* of *Goods,* for the additional Provision allowed for the Insurance, and by *My Account Current* for the neat Balance of the Debts, when this is deducted.

And indeed you may save this *Account of Sales,* and use *Account Current* in it's stead, upon any Supposition; because the Narration will sufficiently qualify the Article; or when the Debts are not insured, you may let the Sum stand not carry'd into the Money Columns, until your Factor advises you that he hath received Payment; or if you carry it in at first, then when he advises you that he hath received Payment, make a Mark on the Article, to signify this; and when he remits the Money, discharge the Account, or use double Money Columns.

5. My Factor, in advising me of the Sales of my Goods, may either send his *Account* of the neat Produce, (*i. e.* deducting Charges and Commission) or he may send the total Amount of each Sale; and when all are sold, he gives in his Account of Expences and Provision; in which Case I make *Profit,* &c. or my *Account* of *Goods* Debtor to my *Account Current* for those Charges, and also for what Abatements he makes to the *Buyers* for defect in the *Goods,* or by my Order for whatever Cause.

6. If my Factor advances Money for me, he will be sure to charge me with the Interest; and so I must charge *Profit,* &c. Debtor to my *Account Current,* for the same. Some talk of an *Account on Time,* different from the foresaid *Account of Sales;* upon which they enter all Bills drawn at long Usance, in order to know

how

how much your Factor is in Advance for you; and when the Time of Payment comes, they carry it into the *Account Current:* But this is needle[s], the Narrative of the Article upon this *Account* being [s]ufficient.

SECT. III.

Accounts for Factorage.

WHEN I act in Commi[s]ion as Factor for another, the Tran[s]actions will be comprehended under the[s]e general Heads, *viz.* my receiving Effects of his to di[s]po[s]e for his *Account,* with the Account of the Charges and Expences, and Provi[s]ion thereupon; my di[s]po[s]ing thereof; my buying up Goods, and [s]ending them el[s]ewhere by his Order, and for his *Account;* or [s]ending away his con[s]igned *Goods* in my hands; our mutual Draughts and Remittances for his Account. The[s]e, and what el[s]e concern, or relate to my Management as Factor for another, you'll have orderly and di[s]tinctly recorded upon the following Accounts.

We may [s]uppo[s]e that a Factor has it in his Commi[s]ion to make no Sales upon Time, but all for ready Money; or he may [s]ell upon Time; and in this Ca[s]e, either he is not accountable for tho[s]e Debts till he receives Payment; or no further than common Ju[s]tice (according to the known Rules and Laws in [s]uch Matters) can oblige him for his Mi[s]managements; or he is bound by Agreement for Security and Payment of the Debts. I [s]hall explain the Accounts with a View to the[s]e Circum[s]tances.

With your Employer keep the[s]e Accounts, *viz.*

A. B. of ——— *his Account of Goods,* ⅌ *Ship* ——— D. M. *Ma[s]ter.*

Debtor for all the Charges they co[s]t while under my Care, and for the Commi[s]ion due to me.
Creditor for the Value of the Sales.
OB[s]ERVE, There ought to be a di[s]tinct Account for every Con[s]ignment, and if there is but one Species, name it.

A. B. of ——— *his Account Current.*

Debtor for whatever he owes, or is accountable for to me as his Factor, which does not [s]tand charged on the preceding Account.
Creditor for whatever I owe, or am accountable for to him as his Factor.

OBSERVE, 1. His Account of *Goods* is diſtinct for every Conſignment. If there is but one Kind, let the Title bear it, and make Columns for the Species and Quantities.

2. The Buyers on Time muſt have particular Accounts ; but to make a parallel betwixt theſe and proper *Foreign Accounts*, you may uſe this *General Account* for all the Buyers, *viz. A. B.* his *Account of Out-ſtanding Debts* ; though the ſame Reaſon does not hold here, becauſe the Buyers know only you ; and when they have already an Account in your Books, it is more proper to charge it there . Or, if you think this general Account of any good Uſe, you may uſe it for all thoſe Buyers ; and upon their particular Account, who have ſuch already in the Books, make ſome Mark whereby to know that they are Debtor on this Account ; that nothing be forgot when you clear Accounts with them.

3. You may charge your Proviſion upon every Sale for the Value, and at every Sale for ready Money, deduct all Charges and Proviſion owing ; and for the Balance of that Money, make *his Account of Goods Debtor to his Account Current.* (See *Article* VI.) And the Debts owing remain upon the Creditor ſide unbalanced till they are paid ; and then do the ſame ; but ordinarily the *Account of Goods* is not balanced till all are diſpoſed of ; or, that your Employer demands his Account, and then charge the *Account of Goods*, Debtor to *Caſh* and to *Profit*, &c. for all Expences and Proviſion due to you, and to his *Account Current* for the Balance of ready Money received for the Sales of his Goods ; your Charges and Proviſion being paid ; and give him up alſo an Account of his *Out-ſtanding Debts* ; but the Account is not to be balanced for thoſe, unleſs he now takes the Goods out of your Hands ; in which Caſe, make his *Account* of *Goods* Debtor to the Buyers ; and aſſign him to the Debt ; and his *Account Current* will ſhew the true State of Affairs betwixt you, beſides what *Goods* remain in your Hands.

4. When Abatement is made to the Buyers at Payment, my Employer is bound to allow it, if it is made for defect in his Goods ; or by order for Advancement of Money to anſwer his Bills ; and then his *Account* of *Goods*, or *Account Current*, is made Debtor for the ſame · In other Caſes it may fall upon me as Factor, as when I have taken up his Money upon Abatement before due, to ſerve my ſelf, or, when having inſured the Sales, I make Compoſition with the Debtors altogether for my own Account, then *Profit* and *Loſs* is Debtor for thoſe Abatements.

5. If by Order I ſend away any of his Goods conſigned to me, I make his *Account* of *Goods* Debtor for the Charges ; and alſo put on the Creditor ſide in the Quantity Column, ſo much ſent away by Order ; but without any Debtor, becauſe the Hazard of the Voyage is my Employers ; and I put the Quantity there only for a *Memorandum* to my ſelf ; but nothing in the Money Columns ; and ſo the Balance of the *Leger* is ſafe. And if there was no Sale of his *Goods*, but the whole were now ſent away by his Order, I then balance the *Account* of *Goods*, by marking his *Account Current* Debtor to it for the whole Charge, on the Debtor ſide ; and with that Sum ſet down the Quantity on the Creditor-ſide of the *Account* of *Goods*.

6. If

6. If I oblige my felf for the Sales on Time, then, when the Goods are all difpofed of (or at any Time, when I would make a Balance) I carry the whole Balance of his *Account* of *Goods*, to his *Account Current*; becaufe it is all abfolute Debt upon me, only I may diftinguifh the Articles that are not yet due: Or in this Cafe, becaufe all the Sales are unconditional Debts upon me, I need keep but one Account, viz. his *Account Current*, and make it Debtor for whatever he owes me as his Factor, and Creditor for what I owe or am accountable to him for his Account: And this will do well, efpecially with the Ufe of a *Factor-Book*; which fee defcribed below. If that Agreement for the Sales is made after Part of the Goods are fold, make the *Account* of *Goods* Debtor for the *Præmium* or additional Provifion on the Sales already made on Time, and for all that follows; or balance the Account now, and make no more Ufe of it, but of the *Account Current*.

N. B. Some ufe fuch an Account, as *A. B.* his *Account* on *Time*, to which they make the *Account* of *Goods* Debtor for the *Outftanding Debts*; but it is unneceffary, fince thefe may as well ftand upon the *Account of Goods*, till they are paid, and then the Balance goes to the *Account Current*.

7. When my Employer's Goods are all fold, I make the *Account* of *Goods* Debtor for the Provifion due to me, and for what Charges are not already enter'd; and then I balance this *Account* by making it Debtor to his *Account Current* for the Difference, which is the neat Product of his *Account of Goods*; and in this State, a Copy of his Accounts is to be fent him. And *obferve,* That this is not commonly done till the Out-ftanding Debts are all paid, unlefs the Factor take thefe Debts upon himfelf.

8. If I return any of my Employer's Goods, by his Order; or fend them off to another of his Factors, who is accountable to himfelf immediately; I have nothing more to do, but to ftate what is due to me, and balance the Account, as in the laft Article.

Of Factorage by Means of other Factors.

We may fuppofe one Factor to ferve by Means of other Factors, whofe immediate Correfpondence is with that one, and not with his Employer: Which yet cannot be done without his Employer's Order. I fhall therefore fuppofe, that by my Employer's Order I fend his Goods to another Market; all the Rifque and Hazard being his; Then, 1. If the Goods fent off were formerly configned to me, I now charge the Account with the Expence at fhipping or fending them off; and fo the Account ftands, till the Factor, to whom they are configned, advifes me of the Receipt of them. Then I keep with this Factor three different Accounts, as in *proper Foreign Trade* Thus,

A. B. of —— my *Account of Goods*, for the *Account* of *D. M.* And fo of the other *Accounts*, for the fame Ufes as thofe in proper Trade.

If the Goods now fent off, were not configned to me, but bought by Order for that Purpofe, my Employer's *Account Current* is Debtor for them. And when the Factor, to whom they are fent, advifes of the Receipt of them, he is Debtor upon one of the *Accounts* kept with him, according as the Advice is ; and for the Creditor, you may either make it *my Employer's Account Current* [the Narration qualifying the Debt] or rather make a particular qualified *Account*, and call it, *A. B.* his *Account*, at —— And when the Returns of this Adventure come into my Hands, besides stating them in the *Factor's* Account, according to the Advices, I state them in my Employer's Account, making, *his Account* at—— Debtor to his *Account Current.*

It will be easy to know what to do in every particular Case of this Kind of *Factorage,* if the Nature of these Accounts are well consider'd: Therefore I shall say no more.

Company Accounts come next in Order ; but there are some particular Books that relate to the preceding Branches, fit to be described in this Place.

1st. *Of the Invoyce Book.*

This Book contains an Account (called the *Invoyce*) of all the Goods which I ship off, either for my own Account, or for others in Commission, according to the Bills of Lading ; with the whole Charges till on Board ; every *Invoyce* following after another, in Order as they happen. It's nothing but a Copy of what is written in the *Waste-Book* in these Cases: Examples of which you'll find in the following *Waste-Books* ; and therefore it's needless to make any particular Example of the Form of it here. I shall only say in general, that after the Date the Narration is to begin thus, —— *Shipped Aboard the Ship* —— *A. B. Master ; bound for—— the following Goods ; consigned to——for my Account, or by Order, and for the Account of* ——. Or, the Narration may be begun, thus, —— *Invoyce of Goods Shipped Aboard*—&c.

The Design of this Book is for the more ready finding out these *Invoyces,* than can be done in the *Waste-Book* ; but, in my Opinion, there is little in this. For the *Index* directs us very readily to the *Account* of the Voyage in the *Leger,* if it's for our own Account, or to the Employer's Account, if it's for another ; and these Accounts will as readily direct us, by the Date, to the *Invoyce,* as it stands in the *Waste-Book.* Some propose the entering of these *Invoyces,* both in this separate Book, and also in the Grand Memorial or *Waste-Book* ; where, they think, every Thing ought to be, to make a complete Memorial of all our Business together, in Order of Time. But this Method would be double the Work, to no Purpose ; because, either the *Waste-Book* or *Invoyce Book* is sufficient. And if it's thought more convenient to put all *Invoyces* together, you may chuse a separate Place in the *Waste-Book* for them ; though it's of no Importance whether they are thus placed, or in a Book quite distinct from the Memorial of all other Transactions.

Again

Again *obferve*, That fome who ufe thefe *Invoyce-Books* have an equal Space on the oppofite Page, againft the *Invoyce* of *Goods* fhipped for their own Account; in which they enter all the Advices from their Factor, concerning the Difpofal of thofe Goods; by which the whole State of thefe Affairs is feen at once. But your Factor's Accounts, in the *Leger*, are fufficient for this.

Of the Factor-Book.

This Book is an Account of what I receive to fell in Commiffion for others, and of the Difpofal thereof. It is number'd and diftinguifh'd into Folios, like the *Leger*; upon the left Side is written, in a plain narrative Stile, *An Account of the Goods received, with all Charges*: And on the other Side is written, *An Account of all the Sales and Difpofal of thofe Goods.* So that it is plainly a Copy of your Employer's *Account of Goods* in the *Leger* (formerly defcribed) in the Stile of the *Wafte-Book*.

If you do little in Commiffion, a feparate Book is needlefs; but otherwife it may be more convenient. For though the Leger Accounts with your Employer are ftill neceffary, yet they will, by this Means, be contracted. For I would take this Method, *viz*. The Charges paid upon his Goods being entered in this *Factor-Book*, from Time to Time, I would not enter them in the *Leger* till the Goods were all fold, or out of my Hands, or the Account otherwife brought to a Conclufion; then place the Charges and Commiffion due, to *your* Employer's *Account of Goods*; (the Creditors being *Cafh*, and *Profit*, &c.) and give it Credit alfo for all the Sales in one Sum. [And *obferve* that where Sales were made on Time, I would place them to the Debtors Account as foon as they are fold] but if all the Sales are for ready Money, you may enter the Charges and Sales upon his *Account Current*. Or rather, in this Cafe, enter only the Balance of the Charges and Sales to his Account, and that of *Cafh*; and at the fame Time make his *Account Current* Debtor to *Profit* and *Lofs*, for your Commiffion. When you fend your Employer his Accounts, he muft have a Copy of his *Account of Goods*, at large, from the *Factor-Book*.

As to the placing the Contents of this Account, both in the *Wafte-Book* and *Factor-Book*, it is certainly fuperfluous, one of them being fufficient. But all other Tranfactions, relating to my Employer's Affairs; as Bills drawn or remitted, *&c.* muft go into the *Wafte-Book*. Alfo, when *Out-ftanding Debts* are paid, befides the Entry of them in the *Wafte* and *Leger*, you may mark them paid in the *Factor-Book*.

There

There is another fubfervient Book, which may be very ufeful to thofe who receive or make many Payments, though it makes no Alteration in the other Books. It is called,

The Month-Book.

It is numbered in Folios like the *Leger,* and divided into Spaces, on the Top of each of which are the Names of the 12 Months of the Year ; *January, February,* &c. allowing a whole Folio, or what you pleafe, to each Month ; and a different Set of 12 Spaces for every different Year, On the left Page enter the Payments to be made to you, in that Month : And on the right Page the Payments you are to make. Make a Column on the left Hand of every Page ; in which, write the Day of Payment. After which, write the Name of the Debtor or Creditor ; and draw the Sum into the Money Columns : Then, when the Payment is made, either mark it by the Word *paid,* on the Margin ; or, if you make double Money Columns, enter the Debt in the Inner ; and when paid, draw it out to the outer Columns. In Cafe of partial Payments, you may fhew it in the *Month-Book,* by fome particular Mark ; and when the Whole is paid, draw it out.

SECT. IV.

Company Accounts.

THERE may be a great Variety here, according to the Nature and Conftitution of Companies ; and the Conditions upon which Men enter into Partnerfhip. I do not take it for my Bufinefs to infift upon every Suppofition that might be made ; my chief Defign, in all this Treatife, being to give a true and univerfal Notion of the Method of *Debtor* and *Creditor,* by explaining the general Principles, and making as much Application as may fufficiently illuftrate them. For the whole Knowledge of *Book-keeping* is comprehended in a few fundamental Rules and Notions ; fo that the Defign or End, and the Method in general, being well confidered, and diftinctly apprehended, there is no Neceffity for a vaft Variety of Applications : A few Cafes well chofen (efpecially if you fee practical Examples thereof, duly ftated in Form, as is done in the following *Wafte,* &c. *Books*) will fix the Notion of the Method, and open all the Nature of it, fo as to put one who has duly confidered the effential Parts, which are few and general, in a Capacity to apply them to any Subject and form fuch arbitrary Schemes (ftill within the Limits of the general Rules) as fhall exactly anfwer the End of

Book-keeping : Therefore I have thought it fufficient, upon the Head of *Company Accounts,* to make the Application in a few Inftances of more *private Partnerfhip :* And for the greater Diftinctnefs, I divide them into two Branches, and upon each Branch make two Suppofitions, concerning the Conftitution of the *Company.*

BRANCH I. When I am concerned in a Company, where the Accounts and chief Management are under the Direction of another Partner.

BRANCH II. When I am Accountant and chief Manager.

Again, As to the Nature of the *Company,* I make thefe Suppofitions :

1. I fuppofe a very fimple Kind of Society, which I call an *Unfix'd Company ;* becaufe they have no ftanding and fixed Stock, but (for Example) buy, from Time to Time, Parcels of this or the other Kind of Goods, to be difpofed of in domeftick or foreign Trade ; and withdraw their Shares of the Value fold, when they pleafe ; by which Means their Stocks or Effects in Company, perpetually vary, according to the Value of thofe different Tranfactions : And fuch Partnerfhips may be enter'd into for one fingle Parcel of Goods, or Voyage ; or they may continue for fome Courfe of Trade.

2. I fuppofe a fix'd Capital Stock, of which every Partner furnifhes his Share ; and this to be the fubject Matter of all the fubfequent Tranfactions of Trade.

Company Accounts.

Branch I. When another Partner is Accountant and Manager.

Suppofition I. When the Company is unfix'd.

In this Cafe the Manager (*A. B.*) is obliged, at all Times, to exhibit fair and diftinct Accounts of the State of Affairs to his Partners : I have no more to do but to keep plain Accounts of what I give, or owe to the Company, and what I receive ; which I do under thefe Titles, *viz.*

1. A. B. *My Account with him,* &c. *in Company* ½ (or ⅓, *containing every Share*) is

Debtor for all that I give out, or owe to the Company, as my Share of the Stock, and Charges ; *that is,* of the firft Stock, or any fubfequent Purchafe ; and all Charges which I am accountable for a Share of.

Creditor for all that I receive on Account of my Concerns in Company, or allow for the fame (See the 2d *Obfervation* below) and for my Share of Loffes.

Obferve, 1. The Partners may have Accounts in my Books, as other Men have ; and even the Partner *Truftee* may have another Account ; becaufe,

K   that

that defcribed is the Account of a mere Truft; and muft be diftinguifhed from the real and abfolute Debts betwixt us, upon other particular Dealings: Befides which, there may be abfolute Debts betwixt us, relating to the Company's Concerns; as when he pays or ftands bound for the whole, or part of my Share and Effects purchafed for *Company Account*; or I the like for him; as, if he fhould draw a Bill on me for Payment of more than my Share. This other Account I call,

A. B. *His proper Account.*

Debtor and *Creditor* for what we mutually owe, and pay upon other particular Dealings, or what he ftands bound for, or pays for me, or I for him, of our Shares of the Effects purchafed for the Company.

OBSERVE, 2. When *A. B.* advifes of Money received for Effects of the Company fold, unlefs I immediately draw my Share from him, I make his *proper Account* Debtor *to my Account in Company*, for the fame, that I may more readily know what Money is in his Hands; but efpecially, this is ufeful, when I was owing him a Debt, particularly for *Company Account*, which he now pays himfelf out of the Money come into his Hands; and if he charges Intereft for what he has advanced for me, I give his *proper Account* Credit for the fame.

3. When the Partners come to a Reckoning with their *Truftee*, he will charge them with his *Provifion* or Allowance as Manager, and other petty Charges, and Intereft for Advance of Money, which have not yet been charged to Account, for my Share of all which I make *my Account* in *Company* Debtor to his *proper Account*. And now, for what *A. B.* gives for clearing of his Truft, let it be charged to the Accounts according to their Ufes; and then the *Account in Company* will fhew what I have gained by the Partnerfhip; and *A. B's proper Account* will fhew what other real Debts are betwixt us. See more concerning this, in *Chapter* III.

Company Accounts.

Branch I. When another is Manager.

Suppofition II. Of a fix'd Company.

My Account in Company with A. B. &c.

Debtor for my Share, ftocked in, or owing; and this Account I never touch more, till the *Company Accounts* are examined and balanced with the Managers; and then if I withdraw my Stock, this Account is Creditor for it: What Gain or Lofs falls to my Share, I ftate to the Account of *Profit and Lofs*; and if the Company think fit either to encreafe or diminifh their Stocks, I make this Account Creditor for the Part leffened, or Debtor for the Addition.

In

In this Cafe I give alfo the Partners *particular Accounts* in my Books; and for the Partner, who by being chief Manager, gives his Name to the Company, upon his particular Account I place every Thing (except what is already faid to belong to the former Account) which I give or receive from him upon *Company Account.*

Company Accounts.

Branch II. When I am Accountant and Manager.

Suppofition I. Of an unfix'd Company.

Every Partner keeps *Accounts* for himfelf by the former Directions; and I am bound to keep Accounts for them all (becaufe their Effects are in my Cuftody, and under my Management) which I may do either in my own Books, if their Affairs are but fimple; or I may do it in feparate and diftinct Books, if the Value and Circumftances of their Affairs require it. I fhall take the moft fimple Cafe firft, *viz.* That I record the Company's Tranfactions in my own Books; which is done upon thefe Accounts.

1. *Account of Goods in Company with* ———

Ufe this Account the fame Way as if the Goods were all your own, *i. e.* make it Debtor for all that's brought in, or purchafed for the Company's Account, with all Coft and Charges; and Creditor for what's difpofed of out of the fame.

Observe, You may ufe a general *Account*, or a particular one, for every kind of Goods, as you think convenient; alfo, you may name all the Partners, and their Shares, in the Title; or fay only, ——— with *A. B.* and *Partners*, if there are any more; or give it any other Diftinction you pleafe, whereby it may be known to what Company the Goods belong.

For every Partner there muft be an Account, and perhaps two; which are thefe,

2. A. B. *His Account in Company with* ———

Creditor for his Share of all the Goods (or Stock) of the Company, ftocked in at firft, or brought into it afterwards; and of all Charges and Expences, and of the neat Gains.

Debtor for what I pay my Partner on Account of his Concerns in Company, or give out of his Effects in my Hands, either in Bills, Goods, or Money given out for his Account, or what elfe he ought to allow for the fame, as his Share of all Loffes.

This is an Account of a mere Truft; and therefore the following Account will alfo be neceffary.

3. A. B.

3. A. B. *His proper (or particular) Account.*

Debtor and *Creditor* (as any other Perfon's Account in proper Trade) for what we mutually owe, and pay, upon other particular Dealings ; and even Things relative to the Company's Affairs, which fall not within the Ufe of the former Account: Particularly, it is Debtor to me for what I advance or am bound for, of his fhare of Goods or Charges that belong to the Company ; and Creditor for his Payment of this, or what he advances, or is engaged for of my Share ; and when I draw a Bill upon him for more than his own Share, which he accepts for my Account: But if he accepts for the Account of another Partner, I give him Credit for no more than his Part, and give that Other Credit, as if I had drawn on him.

If the Ufes of thefe Accounts be carefully confidered, the *Debtors* and *Creditors* in all Tranfactions of domeftick Trade in Company, will be eafily difcovered : But to make the Application as plain as I can, I fhall fubjoin a few Cafes, which when you have well confidered, and compared with the Defcription of the Accounts, you'll fee that this is all that's neceffary to be known or remember'd, for thefe, or any other Cafes ; provided alfo we take along with us the general Rules for other Accounts that may be concerned ; which are never to be tranfgreffed ; for 'tis plain, every Tranfaction of Company Trade muft be recorded the fame way as the like Tranfactions of proper Trade, (with the bare change of fome Titles) the only Thing that's new here, being, the Record I muft make for my Partner's Shares due to them, and by them.

Cafe 1. If my Partners give me *Cafh* to be laid out for their Account, in buying Goods, I make *Cafh* Debtor to their *Account in Company*, for their Share, or make *Cafh Debtor* to my *Partner's proper Account*, for what he gives; and when that is laid out, make this *Account Debtor* to his *Account in Company*: Both Ways are equal upon the Matter ; but the firft is fhorteft. When the Goods are bought, they are *Debtor* to *Cafh*; but if they ftock in Goods, or pay the Money at the Buying, or I draw upon them for their Shares ; I make the *Account of Goods Debtor* to their *Account in Company* for their Share, and to what I put in for my Share.

2. If I buy Goods for the Company from a Stranger, or fell them out of my private Effects, either I have Money in my Hands that belongs to the Partners, or not ; in both Cafes I firft charge the *Goods in Company Debtor* to *Partner's Account in Company*, for his Share, and to what I have given, or the Perfons to whom I owe my Share ; then I make Partner's *Account in Company Debtor* to *Cafh*, for fo much of his Share as I have laid out at this Time ; becaufe this is a real Payment to him of that Money in my Hands ; and for what I have advanced or ftand engaged for on his Account, I make *his particular Account Debtor* to *Cafh*, &c. If the Partners pay in their Shares at the Buying, or ftand perfonally obliged for the fame (when bought of a Stranger) or when I draw Bills on them immediately for their Shares ; the Seller has Credit for nothing but what I owe him for my Share ; and there is no more to be

done

done than what is firſt ſaid. But if I draw on any Partner for more than his Share, *his proper Account* muſt be *Creditor* for that. If I pay for thoſe Goods by a Bill on one who owes the Company, the Goods are *Debtor*, as before, to *Partners Account in Company*, to ſhew their Share ; but becauſe it is paid by their Share of this Debt, make thier *Account in Company Debtor* (to diſcharge me) to the Perſon, on whom the Aſſighment or Bill is drawn.

3. If I pay a Debt owing by the Company to my ſelf, or to another, out of their Money in my Hands, or by a Bill on one who owes to the Company, their *Accounts in Company* (whoſe Money I pay it with) are *Debtors* to their *particular Accounts* (for the ſame Reaſon as in the laſt Caſe.) If the Debt is paid to my ſelf, there is no more to be done ; if to another, I charge him *Debtor* to the Account that pays him, to balance his Account. If the Debt is more than Partners Share of Caſh in my Hands amounts to, yet there is no more to be done ; for their particular Accounts ſtand *Debtors* ever ſince the Debt was contracted.

4. If my Partner for Payment of a Debt, which he owes me by his particular Account, aſſigns to me his Share of a Debt owing to the Company, which I accept of as Payment, His *Account in Company* is *Debtor* to his *particular Account*, for the Value of that Share ; for it is ſo much of his Concerns received of me.

5. If by Order, or Conſent of the Company, I take Goods for Payment of a Debt owing to the Company —— *Goods in Company* (received) are *Debtors* to the Perſon who gives them ; or if they are received in *Barter*, they are Debtor to the Goods given out ; and for theſe nothing need be put on the *Creditor-ſide* of the Partners *Account in Company* ; becauſe they are received only in return for other Value of the Company's, which is already on the *Creditor-ſide* of their Account. But to ſhew every Step, I may make the Goods received *Debtor* to Partner's *Account in Company* for his Share thereof, and at the ſame Time make this Account *Debtor* (to diſcharge my ſelf of what's given out) to the *Account* of Goods given out in the one Caſe, and to the Perſon who now pays the Debt in the other Caſe. And if there is more received than given out, or than the Debt which was due, the Surplus paid or owing, muſt be conſidered as a new Purchaſe, and ſtated as above, in *Caſe* II.

OBSERVE *alſo*, If I take theſe Goods for my own Account, then I'm become abſolutely *Debtor* to the Company for their Shares of the Debt now paid ; and if we ſuppoſe the *Debtor* would have paid the Debt in Money, then I'm accountable for it as if it were Money paid.

6. If I give Goods of the Company's, for Payment of a Debt contracted for their Account, the Receiver is Debtor to the *Account of Goods* ; and Partner's *Account in Company* is *Debtor* (to diſcharge me) to his *particular Account* for his Share thereof, which alſo diſcharges him, if he is ſtill owing his Part of that Debt ; and if not, gives him Credit , for which he may draw upon me.

7. If any Buyer of the Company's Goods draw a Bill on any Partner for the Price, that Partner's *proper Account* is *Debtor* ; and if I was owing that Partner by his *proper Account*, an equal Sum, become due at this Time, and which he de-

demands, the one balances the other, and this Sale is as ready Money to the Company; if that Partner be *Creditor* for nothing, and by Agreement with me, takes this Bill as Payment of his Money in my Hands, I make his *proper Account Debtor* as before; and at the same Time make his *Account in Company Debtor* to his *proper Account* for the same, at least so much thereof as goes to that Payment; thus his *proper Account* is balanced, and I have paid him so much of his Concerns. But it must be considered, that this Way the Bill becomes also as ready Money to the rest of the Partners for their Shares.

8. If one Partner assign his Concerns in Company to another; make his *Account in Company Debtor* to that other's *Account in Company*; but if it be an Assignment for the Share of the ready Money in my Hands, the Assignees *proper Account* is *Creditor*.

9. If any Partner sell of the Company's Goods, and receive Payment, his *proper Account* is Debtor: If I owe him, or he takes this to Account of his ready Money in my Hands, do as above in *Case* 7.

10. If I draw a Bill upon one Partner payable to another, the Assignees *proper Account*, or *Account in Company*, is *Debtor* (the first, if it's for Payment of what I owe him by that Account; the second, if it's for his Concerns in Company) to the other's *proper Account*.

11. For small Sales made on Time, of the Company's Goods, to Persons who have no other Account with you, use this Account, *viz. Retail Account of Sales in Company*, to represent such *Debtors*.

12. When I lay out Money for the Company, and have none of theirs in my Hands, I ought to have Interest allowed me till the Time I receive Payment thereof; when I receive Money of theirs, I charge their *proper Accounts Debtors* to *Profit* and *Loss*, for the Interest owing, and then paying my self out of their Money, I make their *Accounts in Company* Debtor (because this Money is so much of their Concerns) to their *proper Account*, which discharges them; but if they pay this Debt and Interest any other Way, I make the Account by which they pay, Debtor to *Profit* and *Loss*, and to their *proper Accounts*.

OBSERVE, Some propose to make Partner's *Account in Company Debtor* to his *proper Account*, for his Share of the ready Money received by me for the Company's Effects, that it may be seen at all Times what Money of the Partners is in my Hands; and his *proper Account* is made *Debtor*, when that Money is given out by me. But this is needless Labour, especially in such simple Societies. The other Accounts belonging to the Company will shew what Money is in my Hands; and then let their *Account in Company* be charged for what I give out, as above directed. When the Company's Affairs are more considerable, I have shewn you a little above what you may do.

OBSERVE, The petty Charges and Provision due to me as Manager for the Company, may either be stated to the Account of Goods in Company; or I may erect an Account of *Profit* and *Loss* for every Company, and make it *Debtor* and *Creditor* for all Gains and Losses, which belong to the whole Company,

upon

upon the fame Occurrences as in proper Trade. See more of this in *Chapter* III.

For Foreign Trade *in Company.*

There are the fame Accounts to be kept here, as in proper Foreign Trade, only in the Titles change *My* into *Our,* and let it be known what Company the Account belongs to, thus ; *viz.* (1.) *Voyage,* &c. *for the Account in Company with* ——— &c. (2.) *A. B.* (*Factor*) *our Account of Goods in Company,* &c. (3.) *Our Account of Sales in Company,* &c. And, (4.) *Our Account Current in Company,* &c. Thefe Accounts are to be ufed the fame Way as in proper Trade, in like Circumftances ; and there can be no Difficulty, if you underftand and remember the true Defign and Ufe of the two Accounts above directed to be kept for every Partner ; and therefore I fhall not infift upon any Particulars.

And now when I have done with thefe Inftructions for keeping *Company Accounts* in my own private Books, if you afk me where my own Share ftands, I tell you it ftands upon every Account which is either *Debtor* or *Creditor* upon *Company Accounts* ; for my Partner's Share being juftly placed to his Account, the Remainder is my Share, and in my own Hands with the common Stock.

Of Keeping *Company Accounts in feparate Books from my other private Affairs.*

If we fuppofe the Company is ftill unfix'd, and their Affairs to be of that Confequence, that it is neceffary their Accounts be kept in diftinct and feparate *Books,* from my other private Affairs ; then I would choofe this Method.

1. Let there be a feparate *Wafte-Book,* wherein every Thing is recorded that concerns the Company.

2. For the *Company's Leger,* let it contain thefe Accounts, *viz.*

(1.) Every Partner an *Account in Company,* and a *particular Account,* for the Ufes abovementioned.

(2.) I would give my felf, (by my Name) two Accounts of the fame Kind, and for the fame Ufes, *viz. My Account in Company,* to fhew on the *Creditor-fide* my Share of all Goods, *&c.* like the other Partners ; on the *Debtor-fide,* what Goods or Money of the Company's I take to Account of my Concerns · *My particular Account,* to fhew on the *Creditor-fide,* what the Company (or any one Partner) owes me for Goods paid for them, out of my private Cafh or Effects, or any other Thing paid for them, as they are Partners of the Company ; or what I am engaged for them on my private Credit : On the *Debtor-fide,* what Payment is made to me of thofe Debts ; and alfo my Share of Goods bought for the Company, and Charges on them, owing on their Credit ; or Money borrowed on the Company's Credit, for which *my Account in Company* is to be Creditor, as above directed.

(3)

(3.) There muſt be an Account *Caſh in Company* ; *Debtor* for every Article I receive from others, or bring from my private Caſh any manner of way, for the Company's Uſe, or receive from any Partner, if it relates to his Concerns in Company ; and *Creditor* for all I give out of that which is before put on the *Debtor-ſide.*

Though all the Company's Effects are in my Hands, yet it is neceſſary I ſhould have Accounts in the Company's Books (titled with my Name) the ſame as the other Partners have ; for theſe Reaſons, *viz.* that there be no Tranſaction in which the Debtor and Creditor be, the one in my private Books, and the other in the Company's, which would be abſurd ; for then neither of thoſe Books could be brought to a Balance, unleſs the other were balanced too , which is contrary to the Deſign of keeping ſeparate Books. This is remedied in the Company-Books by the Uſe of my Accounts in it ; but then as to my private *Leger,* there muſt neceſſarily be kept in it ſuch an *Account* as, *My Account with Company,* &c. whoſe Uſe is to contain on the *Debtor-ſide,* all the Articles of Money, Goods, Bills, *&c.* which go from my private Effects to the Company for my Share, or what my private Credit is engaged for upon the Company's Account ; and it is *Creditor* for whatever I receive or transfer from the Company to my private Concerns, either on account of my particular Share in the Company, or for payment of what was due to me by the Partners ; ſo that the Uſe of this Account in my private *Leger,* is for keeping up the Balance thereof, upon the transferring of any Thing from my private Concerns into the Company, or from this to that. The more diſtinct State of my Concerns in the Company you'll find in this new *Leger.*

By this Means my private Books may be balanced when I pleaſe, without touching the Company's Books ; as you'll better underſtand in *Chapter* III. Every one who deals with the Company on their Credit, has an Account in their Books , the ſame Perſon may alſo have an Account in my private Books for his dealing with me, as may alſo thoſe who are my Partners in Company.

Now with reſpect to this way of keeping Company Accounts, I'm convinced I need not make a Multitude of Examples ; for whoever underſtands the ſimple Scheme of *Company-Accounts* kept in my Books, needs to have nothing added to the Deſcription I have now given of this Method, in the Uſe of the ſeveral Accounts . But that I may leave no Obſcurity, and yet not be tedious, I ſhall add a few Things.

1. If you remember that nothing is put to any Partners *particular Account*, or *Account in Company,* or *Goods in Company,* &c. but what would have gone to the ſame Accounts, if they had been kept in my private *Leger,* every Thing will be eaſy ; for I have nothing to do, peculiar to this Method, but to charge my Share of every Thing to *my Account in Company,* and my *particular Account* in theſe ſeparate Books, as I do with the other Partners ; and then to take care, that what is transferred from my Property to the Company's, or what from this to that, be duly entered, both in my Books and the Company's, according to the Uſe of the Accounts already deſcribed. But more particularly,

2. When

2. When I give in Goods or Money of my own to the Company, I firſt make *My Account with Company* — &c. *Debtor* for it, in my private Books; then it becomes the Company's, therefore in their Books I make *Caſh in Company,* or *Account* of *Goods in Company Debtor* to *My Account in Company,* for my Share, and to the *Partners Accounts in Company* for their reſpective Shares, which they give in, or I for them; but then I muſt conſider their Debt to me, and make their *particular Accounts* Debtors to my *particular Account* for their Shares owing me; and when they pay me, I diſcharge their *particular Account,* and make mine Debtor, and transfer the Thing received into my private Accounts, by means of the Title, *My Account with* ———— &c. in my own Books.

3. If I buy Goods for the Company, and pay for them with Caſh of theirs in my Hands; I make the *Goods in Company* Debtor to each of our *Accounts in Company* for the Shares, and then make the ſame *Accounts in Company Debtor* to *Caſh in Company,* for each one's Share of that *Caſh* given out; and thus Things are in a diſtinct Balance. If there is any Thing given out of my private Concerns at this Time; as, if I pay the whole or part out of my own Caſh, or the Goods be ſold out of my private Effects to the Company; then, beſides recording it in my *Leger,* the Partners *particular Accounts* are *Debtors* to my *particular Account* in their Books for the ſame. When they pay me, do as laſt directed.

4. If Goods are bought for the Company *on Time,* either they are bought on the Company's Credit, and then the Seller has Credit in their Books by each Partner's (and my own) *particular Account,* each for his Share; or they are bought on my private Credit, and then the Seller has Credit in my Books, by *my Account with* ——— &c. The *Account of Goods in Company,* in their Books is Debtor to each *Account in Company* for the Shares, in both Caſes; and, for what the Partners owe me in the laſt Caſe, make their *particular Accounts Debtor* to my *particular Account.*

5. If I take any Partner's Share of the Company's *Caſh,* come into my Hands, for Payment of what he owes me upon *Company Account,* or if he pays me any other way, in both Caſes *my particular Account* is *Debtor* to his, to diſcharge him; and alſo in the firſt Caſe, his *Account in Company, Debtor* to *Caſh in Company,* to diſcharge me; then I carry the Thing received into my private *Leger,* as above directed. If this Debt was paid to another who had Credit in the Company's Books, the Receiver is Debtor to *mine,* and to each Partner's *particular Account* (who owes) for his Share of this Caſh paid; and our *Accounts in Company* are *Debtors* to *Caſh in Company.* If the Debt I pay is more than this *Caſh in Company* amounts to, ſo that I advance any Thing out of my private Effects; or when I pay the whole Debt with private Effects; the Partners *particular Accounts* ſtand *Debtors,* ſince the firſt contracting the Debt, and the Receiver is made *Debtor* to my *particular Account* for what I ſo pay out of my private Effects; and let it be ſtated in my private *Leger,* as above. If the Perſon who is now paid off this Debt, had Credit for the ſame in my private *Leger,* he is made *Debtor* there to *my Account in Company,* &c. and in the Company's *Leger,* each Partner's (and my own) *Account in Company Debtor* to *Caſh in*

L

Com-

Company, for our Shares of what is paid out of that: And becaufe my *particular Account* was Creditor for the whole Debt, being contracted on my Credit; therefore my *particular Account* is Debtor to their *particular Accounts,* for their Shares of the Debt paid with their Money; and if the Whole, or Part, is paid with my private Effects, there is nothing to be done for that in the Company's *Leger;* the Partners *particular Accounts* ftanding already Debtor for their Shares of the Debt now paid.

6. For what I take out of the Company's Effects on Account of my particular Concerns; *my Account in Company* is Debtor for it (as the other Partners for what they receive) and then it becomes private Effects, and to be ftated in my own *Leger.*

Laftly, I fhall *obferve,* That it is rare if unfix'd Companies need to have feparate Books; however, to compare thefe Inftructions with the Defign of *Book-keeping,* and the more general Notions thereof, may prove very helpful to the forming a more comprehenfive and univerfal Idea of this Art.

Company Accounts.

Branch II. When I am Manager.

Suppofition II. Of a fix'd Company,

The Affairs of this Kind of Society, efpecially thofe of a more publick Nature, muft be recorded in diftinct and feparate Books; the Method whereof is very eafy: Thus,

1ft There muft be a diftinct *Wafte-Book,* and *Journal* too, if you pleafe.

2d. A *Leger;* in which all the *real* Subjects, that is, *Cafh,* and *Goods,* belonging to the Company, muft have Accounts, and every Man who deals with the Company upon its Credit. There muft alfo be *Foreign Accounts* with the Company's Factors; and other Accounts, as in proper Trade, for the fame Ufes. *Laftly,* Every Partner (and my felf) muft have two Accounts, *viz.* an *Account in Company,* and a *Particular Account,* for thefe Ufes:

Every one's *Account in Company* is made Creditor for his Share of the Stock, and it ftands fo; for there goes no other Thing to that Account, except the Company increafe or diminifh their Stock, or at balancing of their Accounts; of which we fhall treat below.

The *Particular Accounts* are made Debtors for what any of us receives out of the Company's Effects, and Creditors for whatever any of us gives out of his private Concerns, to the Company, (excepting the Capital Stock) either Money lent to the Company, or Goods fold to it, or bought on our private Credit, or Bills payable to the Company, or to thofe to whom they are Debtors, &c. and all fuch Debts or Credits are underftood to be owing to, or by the whole Company

It muft be remembred alfo, that what goes from my private Property to the Company's, is to be enter'd both in my Books and the Company's; which is
done

done in my Books, by an Account, which, as in the former Scheme, I call, *My Account with* ——, or, *in such a Company*, naming it. Now this being carefully remember'd, all the Transactions belonging to the Company's Affairs are recorded in their *Leger*, the same way as in proper Trade, *i. e.* by the general Rules for the Use of *Personal* and *Real Accounts*, &c. the Partners *Particular Accounts* being charged and discharged, as any indifferent Person's Account, who is Debtor to, or Creditor by the Company. So that, in short, the Capital Stock being enter'd upon the Creditor Side of the Partners *Account in Company*, and the Debtor Side of *Cash in Company*, &c. or of those Partners *Particular Accounts*, who have not yet paid in their Share ; all the following Transactions of their Affairs are enter'd as in proper Trade : Every Partner's *Particular Account* being used afterwards, as any other Person's Account who deals with the Company, *i. e.* It is Debtor for what he receives from, or otherwise owes to the Company ; and Creditor for what the Company receives from, or otherwise owes him. The same is true of my own *Particular Account*, (remembring carefully the Entry, necessary to be made in my private Books) for I consider my self in a double Capacity ; *1st.* As *Book-keeper* to the Company, I do every Thing as if I were not a Partner. But, 2. As I am one, I must give my self Accounts in their *Leger*, as I do to the rest of the Company ; and if at any Time the Company require to ballance their Books, I am accountable for all the Balance of Money or Goods found to be in my Hands, by these Accounts : And what I am Debtor for, on my *Particular Account*, or any other Partner or Person whatever, 'tis all understood to be Effects belonging to the whole Company ; and what I or any other Partner (or any other Person) is Creditor for, on our *Particular Accounts*, or our Accounts in Company, is a Debt due by the whole Company ; to be clear'd out of the foresaid Effects : And thus I keep a distinct State of their Affairs ; and can make up my Accounts with Ease.

But lest any Difficulty should remain, I shall add these few Particulars :

1 When the Company give in their Stocks, I make *my Account with Company*, &c. (in my private Books) Debtor to what I stock in ; then in the Company's Books make *Cash in Company*, such Goods or other Effects, as are stocked in, Debtors to each of our Accounts in Company, for our Shares. If afterwards they increase or diminish their Stock, it's plain what we must do.

2. But if you would have an Account, on which all the Shares of the Stock should be seen at all Times, and no other Thing ; then make *Cash in Company* (or other Things stocked in) Debtors to *Stock in Company* for the Shares ; but immediately balance this Account of Stock, and make it Debtor to the Partners *Accounts in Company*.

3. If any Partner does not immediately give in his Stock, then, because I must begin the Company's Books upon its first Existence, I state the Things actually given in ; and for the Partner who has not paid, make his *Particular Account* Debtor to *Stock* ; and that Debtor to his Account in Company : If no Stock Account is kept, make his *Particular Account* Debtor to his Ac-

count

count in Company; and when he pays it, his *Particular Account* is difcharged.

N. B. If you do not extend thefe Shares unpaid, upon the Stock Account,
it will appear at a Glance, what is paid, and what not. When they are paid,
draw them out, and difcharge his *Particular Account*, who owed, and has now
paid.

4. If I or any Partner, take a certain Time to pay in our Stock; for which
we are to give the Company Interest; let that Partner's *Particular Account*
be made Debtor to *Interest Account*, or *Profit* and *Lofs in Company*, for the fame,
as well as to his *Account in Company* for his Stock.

5. If any Partner fell his Share, or any Part thereof, the Perfon to whom
he fells, muft have an Account in the Company's Books; and his *Account in
Company*, be Creditor by the Seller's *Account in Company*, for the Value. Or,
if there is a *Stock Account*, make the Partner (who transfers) *His Account in Company*, Debtor to Stock, and this, Debtor to the new Partner's *Account in Company*. Alfo *obferve*, That if he who transfers, owes that, or any Part of it,
to the Company, then, the Company having confented to this Transfer, make
the new Partner's Account Debtor to the others *Particular Account* for what is
owing to the Company; and if the Company take in one or more Partners
afterwards, making hereby an Addition to the Capital, enter thefe Partners
Shares as the former were; and if thefe pay or owe any Thing to the Company, more than their Stock, for being taken in; it goes to the *Profit* and
Lofs Account.

6. If a Perfon, who owes me in my private *Leger*, fells Goods to the Company, or becomes their Creditor otherwife; if he and I agree that the one
Debt fhall difcharge the other (for fo much) I give him Credit in my Books,
by *my Account in Company*, &c. and fuppofing he was already Creditor in the
Company's Books, make him Debtor there to my *Particular Account*.

7 If I buy Goods for the Company, or fell them out of my private Effects, having no Money of theirs to pay for them, or having given nothing of
theirs for them; in my private Books, *my Account with*, &c. is Debtor for what
I pay and give out of my Effects for the Company, or what I am perfonally
engaged for; and in the Company's Books, the Goods are Debtor to *my Particular Account*, but being paid out of their Effects, the Thing received is
Debtor to the Thing deliver'd, for the Value of what's deliver'd, or if the
Seller gives Credit to the Company, then the Goods are Debtor to him, in the
Company's Books.

Of Exchange in Company.

This is a Kind of Trade, wherein two Perfons living in different Places, remit to one another certain Sums, to be employ'd for both their Accounts, in
mutual Exchange, *i. e.* they anfwer one the other's Bills; the Gains made by
the Exchange are equally divided, becaufe the Stocks are fo. This is, in
Effect, a Kind of *Proper Trade*; for both keep the fame Kind of Accounts

for what they give out or receive, which I would call, *A. B. at* ⸺ *our Account of Exchange in Company*, Debtor for all the Bills I remit to him, or he draws on me ; Creditor for all he remits to me, or I draw on him.

This Account muſt have an inner Column for the Foreign Money of the Bills ; and ſo the outer Column of the Debtor Side, ſhews what Money, of my own Country, I have given out ; and the inner Column ſhews what Value, of his Country Money my Partner has received : On the Creditor Side it is contrary ; and what is outer-Column on the Debtor Side of my Book, is inner-Column on the Creditor Side of my Partner's ; and my inner, his outer Column of oppoſite Sides, the ſame Way.

Obſerve, 1. You may have Uſe for another Account with your Correſpondent ; as, **A. B.** *his Particular* or *Current Account* ; in Caſe of other Dealings betwixt you, or in Caſe his Bills are refuſed and proteſted ; then this Account is Debtor for the Charges, and Creditor for the Charges of my Bills proteſted. *See more of the Uſe of this Account in the next Chapter.*

2. For Bills drawn at long Uſance, ſome make Uſe of *our Account on Time* ; and when the Bills fall due, carry them from this to the other Account : But the firſt is ſufficient to ſhew the whole State and Circumſtance, by the Narration.

CHAP. III.

Of the Cloſing *and* Balancing *of Accounts ; with the Method of comparing the Books, and correcting of Errors.*

INTRODUCTION.

WE are now come to the laſt *Stage* of this Work, *viz.* the *Cloſing* and *Balancing* of the *Leger*.

The firſt Chapter ſhews the general and fundamental Principles of this Art. The ſecond ſhews more particularly, beſides the Uſe of ſome ſubſervient Books, how the *Leger* is begun, and carried on, in the Uſe of various particular Accounts. And this Chapter ſhall finiſh the Inſtructions of this Art ; by ſhewing you how the whole Accounts are cloſed, and terminated in one *General Account* or *Inventory*, of the preſent total State of your Affairs ; upon which a new *Leger*, and Courſe of Accounts, may be begun. But before we begin this Work, two Things are ſuppoſed to be done.

ſt.

1*ft.* That every Thing be duly transferred from the fubfidiary Books, into the *Leger, viz.* from the *Cafh-Book, Book of Expence of Living,* and *Charges of Merchandize,* &c. not only Articles already paid, but alfo what are owing, if they are known and adjufted.

Any particular Note that may be neceffary for fome particular Accounts, fhall be afterwards added to the Inftructions for balancing thofe Accounts.

2*d.* That all Errors committed in the Books be corrected; for till thefe are difcover'd and corrected, or that you find fome probable Argument that there are no Errors, you ought not to begin this Work of making a general State of your Affairs; becaufe you'll ftill want a reafonable Probability for the Truth and Juftice of your Accounts.

SECT. I.

Of the Difcovery *and* Correction *of Errors, especially in the* Leger.

ARTICLE I. *I fhall here, in the firft Place, take Notice of the* General Proof *of the* Accounts, *arifing from the Rule of a* Balance *of Debt and Credit, in every Article entered in the* Leger.

THE Confequence of that Rule, being an Equality of the total Debt and Credit; therefore, if the total Debts of all the *Accounts* are gathered into one total Sum, and alfo the Credits, thefe two Sums will be equal, if all is right; fo that if they are not equal, it's a certain Proof that there are Errors, or Omiffions, in fome Account or other. But then it muft be *obferved,* That though this Balance be good, it's no certain abfolute Proof that there are no Errors; becaufe fomething may be quite omitted, or there may be like Errors, *i. e.* Exceffes or Defects, in the Debt and Credit of the *Leger;* which being equal to one another, will ftill preferve the General Balance. Yet again, this muft be *obferved,* That there's a very great Chance againft this Circumftance of Errors; for there muft be, at leaft, two Errors, which muft alfo be like, equal, and upon oppofite Sides. And if there are more than two; then if one or more of them are Defects or Exceffes, others muft be of the fame Kind, and upon oppofite Sides, and muft alfo be equal. Now if we confider the great Chance againft fuch a Circumftance of Errors, we may reckon the General Balance a very probable Argument that there are no Errors. But then fuppofing we have made Trial of the General Balance, and found it to fail, we are ftill where we were, as to the Difcovery of the particular Errors; which can be made no other Way than by a diligent and careful Comparifon of all the Books with one another, from the Beginning: And this indeed will be a troublefome Work; yet not to be avoided, if you
would

would have a regular and juft Proof; unlefs by fome lucky Accident, or Memory, you make a Difcovery which reftores the Balance.

Again *obferve,* To prevent having all this troublefome Comparifon to make at once, it ought to be done gradually, as the Accounts go on. For *Example,* Once a Month, or Week, as you think fit, for if there's a Multitude of Bufinefs, it will require to be oftner done; fo that when you come to the Work of making a General State of your Affairs, you have nothing to examine but the laft Week or Month.

Obferve alfo, That though all the Books are fuppofed to be filled up with great Care; yet, as there's no Infallibility; fo, by a fecond Examination, at fome Diftance of Time, we may difcover Errors not difcovered the firft Time; or prove the Work to be right; at leaft, there will be a great babality of it.

Now all Things being thus carefully examin'd, and all Errors correct the General Balance will certainly be good; and fo by both thefe Means you have the greater Probability againft Errors.

But if you have taken this Method of comparing your Books gradually, you need not take the Trouble of making any further Proof by the Balance, till you have made up your General State, (in the Manner after explain'd) becaufe if that Balance fhould fail, I know not what elfe can be done to correct it; and you muft make the beft you can of the Accounts, but as there's a great Probability that all is right, you'll have the laft Proof of it, after the General State is made up, from the fame Rule of the General Balance.

ARTICLE II. *I fhall next confider more particularly, the Method of examining the Books; of marking what's right, and correcting what's wrong.*

1ft. *For the* Wafte-Book.

As the *Wafte-Book* is the Ground-Work of the Accounts, here the Examination muft begin: And,

1 If any Tranfaction or Circumftance of a Tranfaction is quite omitted; then, becaufe this is the firft Record made of it, you can have no Affiftance from a Comparifon with other Books; therefore the Difcovery of this will entirely depend upon the Accident of remembring it, which fometimes may be owing to the reading over other Tranfactions, that happened in the fame Day Such Omiffions, when they are difcover'd, ought to be enter'd in a feparate Place alotted for that Purpofe; with a Reference to it, from the Place where it is omitted

2. If the Error be a wrong Number, or Name, or any other Word; you may correct it by razing out what's wrong, and filling up the right If a Number or Word is wanting, interline it, or if it's too much, cancel it with your

your Pen But here I muſt *obſerve* the extreme Delicacy and Exactneſs that ſome Authors propoſe, *viz.* That if the leaſt Word or Figure is wrong, or omitted, they would have the whole Tranſaction written again, among the *Corrections* ; and if a Number or Word is diſcover'd to be wrong, immediately after it's written, or before the whole Sentence is finiſhed, they preſently write over all, from ſuch wrong Word or Number, with the Words, *I ſay,* prefix'd *Thus* , if inſtead of the Word *Deliver'd,* you have written *Receiv'd,* which you immediately diſcover, before any Thing more is written ; then they would have you write thus ; *Deliver'd, I ſay, Receiv'd·* Or, if more is written after the wrong Word, write it all over thus ; *Deliver'd to* A. B. *&c. I ſay, Receiv'd from* A. B. *&c.*

2d. *For the* Journal-Book, *or* Journal, *as it is moſt commonly call'd.*

If it is diſtinct from the *Waſte-Book,* after the firſt Method deſcrib'd in *Chapter* I. compare every Tranſaction with the *Waſte-Book.* So far as it is a Tranſcript of the *Waſte-Book,* it will probably have the ſame Errors, at leaſt, as to greater Omiſſions ; or it may have others, which will be diſcover'd by the Compariſon : But as it is different from the *Waſte-Book,* in diſtinguiſhing the *Debtors* and *Creditors,* in Order to the *Leger-Book* ; there may alſo be Errors in this Part, when there is none in the *Waſte-Book.* Such Errors are to be diſcover'd by a careful Conſideration of the Tranſaction, and examining anew, what are the true Debtors and Creditors ; whereby, if there was no Error, you prove it to be right ; and if there was, you correct it ; either where it ſtands, by razing out what's wrong, and filling up the right ; or by tranſcribing the Whole in a ſeparate Place alotted for the Purpoſe. *Obſerve,* That this Direction ſerves alſo for the *Marginal* Journal.

3d. *For the* Leger.

The *Journal* being found right, and corrected, the *Leger* is to be compar'd with it, to prove if every Article is right placed to the Accounts of the ſeveral Debtors and Creditors, as they are found in the *Journal.* As to the Method of making this Compariſon, there is no Difficulty. You find in the *Journal,* ſuch and ſuch Accounts, named Debtors and Creditors, in every Tranſaction , therefore turn to thoſe Accounts one by one, and ſee if the Articles are accordingly right placed : If they are right, then to ſhew that they are examin'd and right, mark them in the *Leger* with a Point (.) ſet in the Margin, in the Column with the Day of the Month, in every Article ; but if there's any Error, that muſt firſt be corrected, and then mark the Article. *Obſerve* alſo, That as ſoon as the *Leger* is compared and marked, you muſt mark the *Journal* with a Point ſet by the Figure, which refers to the *Leger.* And by this you'll know how far the Compariſon of the *Leger* and *Journal* is carried.

It

It remains now to explain the Method of correcting the Errors found in the *Leger* ; which I fhall reduce to three Cafes.

1. When an Article is quite omitted upon an Account, it is to be corrected, by writing it on the proper Side of the Account ; but do not crowd it in betwixt two Articles, where it fhould have ftood ; write it after the laft Article : And though it will thus ftand out of its Place, as the Date will fhew, that will be underftood to have happened by an Omiffion.

2. When an Article is placed upon an Account, to which it does not belong. This is to be corrected, by placing the fame Article upon the oppofite Side ; which may be narrated thus, *viz. For correcting the Article* To *or* By ——— (naming the Account to which it is made Debtor or Creditor on the other Side, and the Date) *wrong on the other Side.* Or, upon the oppofite Side, make it *Debtor To*———, or *Creditor By* ——— *(that other Account.)* For extinguifhing the Article (of fuch a Date) wrong on the other Side.

3. When an Article is placed upon the right Account, but upon the wrong Side : This is corrected by entering it twice upon the oppofite Side ; once to place what ought to be on that Side ; and again, to balance or extinguifh what's wrong upon the other Side ; which is to be narrated as above, in *Cafe* 2. And *obferve,* That if, befides the Article's being upon the wrong Side, there is alfo an Error in the Sum, it's corrected the fame Way ; writing the fame Numbers in the Article that corrects it, and the true Number in the other Article, that places what's right on the oppofite Side. Again, If there is a Miftake in the Name of the Account with which it is connected on the wrong Side, or in any other Part of the Narration ; write the fame in the correcting Article, on the oppofite Side, making the other Article as it ought to be.

4. If an Article is placed upon the right Account, and alfo the right Side, but fome Miftake committed, either in the Numbers or Name of the correfponding Account, or other Part of the Narration ; you may correct it, by razing out what's wrong, and putting what's right in its Place. But if you will be more fcrupulous, then write it again as it ought to be, upon the fame Side ; and alfo write it on the oppofite Side, with the fame Numbers and Names, *&c.* as it was firft written, to extinguifh that : But this Method is not of any great Neceffity, and is (I think) rather too great a Nicety than very ufeful ; efpecially if the Error be not in the Sum of Money, or Quantities drawn out into the Columns, or in proper Names ; nor even in fuch like Cafes, if it's right entered in the correfponding Account, or in the Journal. I proceed now to explain the Method.

SECT. II.

Of Clofing and Balancing the Leger.

ARTICLE I. *General Reflections.*

IN Order to what's propos'd, let us reflect, That as the End of *Book-keep-ing* is daily obtained in that diftinct and ready Knowledge which is to be had thereby, of the true State of the feveral Parts of ones Affairs, as thefe are diftinguifhed and divided into particular Accounts ; and as the Whole is nothing elfe but all the Parts ; fo the total State is the neceffary Refult of the States of all the particular Accounts, collected into one *General Account* or *Inventory* ; which is the laft great End of *Book-keeping* ; and, as it were, the *Accomplifhment* of the Whole. Again *obferve,* That as the doing of this Work aright, is of great Importance, with Refpect to the End of it ; fo is it alfo to a Learner, as it gives Occafion to, and requires an exact Reflection upon all the Principles and Rules of the Method, and the Ufes of all the different Accounts that are in the *Leger.* For,

If we would know the State of any particular Account, we muft confider the Nature and Ufe of it ; or what Articles it contains on the Debtor, and what on the Creditor Side ; by which it will be obvious what is meant by the *Final State* of the *Account* ; or, what it is we would know, by enquiring what the *Final State* is : And we fhall by this alfo know eafily how to find it by a Comparifon of the Debtor and Creditor Sides : As to which, I firft make this *General* Reflection, *viz.* That the Refult of this Comparifon in every Account, will be the Difcovery either of a *Balance of Debt,* which that Account owes to me, or I to it ; or of *Gain,* or *Lofs,* made by that Subject ; or there may be from one Account, both a *Balance of Debt* and of *Gain* or *Lofs.*

Now, thefe *Balances* of Debt (whether upon *Perfonal, Real* or *Imaginary Accounts*) are the Articles of the new *Inventory* or *Stock-Account* fought : And for the Articles of *Gain* and *Lofs,* though they belong not to the *Inventory,* yet it's neceffary that they be now all gathered into the *Profit* and *Lofs Account* ; becaufe the final Balance, or Difference of the Gain and Lofs muft anfwer to the Increafe or Decreafe of the Neat Stock ; or more generally, to the Alteration that has happened with Refpect to the Difference of your Debts and Effects ; fince there can be no other Reafon for any Alteration but what arifes from your Gains and Loffes ; and fo the *Profit* and *Lofs Account* becomes the Proof of the new Inventory, and gives you the Satisfaction of knowing the Reafon of the Alteration.

Thefe general Things being rightly underftood, I fhall more particularly explain the Method of making up the *Inventory,* and *Profit* and *Lofs Account* ; and of clofing the Accounts in the Leger, in Order to begin a new Set of

Books :

Books : In which you'll also see what's neceffary to be done, when at any Time, for the Satisfaction of knowing the State of your Affairs, you would make up an Inventory without defigning new Books. Here alfo you'll find the laft Proof of the whole Work, and of the Beauty and Excellence of this Method of Accounts.

Thefe Inftructions I fhall deliver in this Method, *viz.* 1. Suppofing you know how to find the Balances of Debt, and of Gain and Lofs, that belong to every Account [which indeed has no Difficulty in it, if the Nature and Contents of every Account are well confidered] I fhall explain the regular Method of collecting them, and of clofing the Accounts in the Leger ; with the Proof we have hereby of the whole *Accounts*. Then I fhall give more particular Directions for finding the Balances of Debt, and of Gain or Lofs, belonging to every Account.

ARTICLE II. *General Rule for* Clofing *and* Balancing *the* Leger *and making out of all the Accounts one* General Account, *or* Inventory, *of the prefent Total State of your Affairs ; with the final Proof of the Whole.*

1. Make an *Account* of *Balances* [or rather call it fimply *Balance*] with a Debtor and Creditor-fide, as other Accounts have ; then paffing the *Stock*, and *Profit* and *Lofs Accounts*, examine and compare the Debtor and Creditor-fides of every Account ; by which, according to the Nature of it, you'll find whether there is any Balance of Debt owing to you by that Account, or by you to it : Place this Balance upon the leaft Side, in the Stile of the Leger ; thus, Debtor *To*, or Creditor *By* Balance ; and carry it to the oppofite Side of that Account : Then, if there is no Gain or Lofs belonging to the Account (or which is not already placed upon it, as there will be in fome Cafes) the Account is balanced, *i.e.* the Sum of the Debt and Credit will be equal. But if there is any Gain or Lofs, make the Account Debtor to *Profit* and *Lofs*, for the Gain ; or Creditor by it for the Lofs ; and carry the Article to the oppofite Side of that Account ; and then the Account is balanced. Again, if the Account has only a Balance of Gain or Lofs, but no Debt, then the Gain or Lofs being duly placed, the Account is alfo balanced. *Laftly*, If there is neither any Balance of Debt, nor of Gain or Lofs, then the Account is already balanced in courfe.

2. In all thefe Cafes, write down the equal Sums upon the Foot of the Account (as you fee done in the following Books) and fo the *Account* is *balanced* and *clofed*. It is *balanced* becaufe of the Equality of the Sums ; and it is faid to be *clofed*, becaufe the Sums being fet down, no more is to be written in that Account in that Leger ; a new Leger, and new Accounts for all thofe Subjects that have remaining Balances of Debt, being to be begun upon the Inventory now made from the former Accounts.

Which

Which *Inventory* you have in the *Account of Balances*; the Debtor-side whereof contains all the Articles of the Debts, Personal, Real, or Imaginary, due to you [*i. e.* the positive and absolute Debts owing by every Person, the Effects in Cash or Goods remaining undisposed of; and the Debts and Effects standing upon *Imaginary Accounts*, as Money consigned in *Wagers* undecided, &c.] for it is manifest, that if any Account owes to you, the Debtor-side must be greatest; and so the Balance is placed upon the Creditor-side, and consequently comes upon the Debtor-side of the *Balance Account*. Again, the Creditor-side contains all the Debts that you owe, absolutely or conditionally; for if you owe to an *Account*, the Creditor-side is greatest, and so the Balance is placed upon the Debtor-side, and consequently upon the Creditor-side of the *Balance Account*.

3. The *Profit* and *Loss* being now also completely filled up, the last Step of the Work is, to close this *Account*, and the Accounts of *Balance* and *Stock*; which finishes the whole Work, and affords the last Proof of all the Accounts. Thus,

Take the Difference of the Debt and Credit of the *Account of Balance*; set it upon the least side, Debtor *To*, or Creditor *By Stock*, and carry it to the opposite Side of the *Stock Account*. Do the same with the *Account* of *Profit* and *Loss*. And as these Accounts are thus closed and balanced, so the *Stock Account* will, by this Means, be also balanced, because of the universal Balance of Debt and Credit that has been from the beginning preserved in every Entry made in the Leger. If this Consequence is not clear enough, I demonstrate it thus,

All the Accounts, excepting the *Stock*, having their particular Sums of Debt and Credit equal, or now made so; and the Articles which balanced them (in this artificial Balancing) being carried to the opposite Sides of the *Accounts of Balance*, and *Profit* and *Loss*, these two Accounts being also closed, and their Balances carried to the opposite Side of the *Stock Account*; the two Sides of this Account must necessarily be equal: For as all the other Accounts, besides it, have their Debt and Credit equal, so the total Sum of their particular Sums of Debt, and of Credit, must be equal; wherefore if the Debt and Credit of the *Stock* is not now also equal, the total Debt and Credit in the Leger is not equal; as it is supposed to be, according to the general Rule of making equal Debt and Credit for every Article entered. Hence, if this Rule has been always observed, as we suppose, the *Stock Account* must now necessarily be balanced.

Of the Final Proof.

4. The Conclusion of all is, That if the Balance of the Stock fails, there is some Error in the Book, committed either in the balancing Work, or before this, and not corrected: As upon the other hand, if this Balance is found, it is a very probable Argument that all is right.

But again, *observe*, That as the Rule of a perpetual Balance makes the Balance of the *Stock Account* necessary [after all the other Accounts are balanced in the manner directed] so from hence we have a more immediate Proof that the *Inventory*, or present State of all the Accounts, is right; for it demonstrates a Thing which is a proper and natural Proof of this, and must necessarily be true, if all is right, *viz.* The Equality betwixt the Balance of Gain and Loss, and the Increase or Decrease of your Neat Stock; or, more generally, betwixt the Balance of Gain and Loss, and the Alteration made in the State of the Stock Account, as to the Difference betwixt the Sums of your Debts and Effects; comparing that Difference upon the Stock Account at the beginning, with what it is now upon the Balance Account.

As to which I shall first observe, That you may prove it to be actually so, by taking the Difference of the Gain and Loss, and comparing it with the Differences of the Debt and Credit of the *Stock* Account, and of the *Balance* Account: But the Proof of it is more curious and artful, which we have by the Balance of the *Stock* Account, which Proof being once demonstrated to be a certain Consequence from this Balance, we need not afterwards seek any other Proof of it.

Now to make this *Demonstration*, I shall, *First*, Suppose that there was a Real Stock in the beginning of these Accounts, and is also now in the Balances: And as the present Neat Stock may be either greater or lesser than the last, I shall,

(1.) Suppose it greater; then, as from the Nature of the Thing it's obvious, that there must be a Balance of Gain equal to the Increase of the Neat Stock; so I shall demonstrate from the Balance of the *Stock Account* that it actually is so. Thus,

The Debtor-side of the Stock Account (as it stands now closed) contains these two Articles, *viz.* the Total of your Debts at the beginning, and the present Neat Stock (brought from the Account of Balances) The Creditor-side contains these Articles, *viz.* The Sum of your whole Effects at the beginning, and the Neat Gain made since (brought from the *Profit* and *Loss* Account) But the Sum of your Effects is equal to the Sum of your Neat Stock and the Sum of the Debts; wherefore the Sum on the Creditor-side is composed of these three Articles, *viz.* the Neat Stock, Sum of the Debts at the beginning, and Neat Gain made since. Now, the Sums on the Debtor and Creditor-side of the Stock, being equal, if out of each you take the same Article, *viz.* the Sum of the Debts at the beginning, what's left on each Side will necessarily be equal; but these Remainders are, on the Debtor-side the present Neat Stock, and on the Creditor-side the Sum of the Neat Stock at the beginning, and the Neat Gain made since; whose Equality is therefore hereby proved.

(2.) If there be more Loss than Gain, the Difference will come upon the Debtor-side of the Stock Account; and so there will be upon this Side these three Articles, *viz.* the Sum of the Debts at the beginning, the present Neat Stock, and the present Neat Loss. On the Creditor-side there is only the Sum of the Effects at the beginning, equal to the Sum of the Debts, and of the Neat Stock; and taking out of each Side the Sum of the Debts, there remains on the Creditor-side the Neat Stock at the beginning, and on the Debtor-side fide the prefent Neat Stock, and Neat Lofs incurred fince ; which Remainders are therefore equal, as they ought to be.

OBSERVE, There are various other Circumftances to be fuppofed, as to the State of the *Stock Account* at the beginning, and of the prefent Account of *Balances* ; for in each of them the Debts may be equal to, or be greater or leffer than the Effects ; and the various Combinations of thofe Circumftances in thefe two Accounts, make nine different Cafes ; in each of which the Difference of the Gain and Lofs muft neceffarily be equal to the Alteration that has happened in the final State of the Stock ; and the Balance of the *Stock Account* will prove it to be actually fo in every Cafe, as you may eafily demonftrate after the fame Manner as I have done in the preceding Cafe of a Neat or Free Stock, both at the beginning and at the balancing. About which, all I fhall do further (leaving the reft to your own Exercife) is to point out what is the *Equality* to be proved in thofe feveral Cafes, which I fhall alfo reduce to three *Generals* (comprehending the former.)

1. If there was a Free or Neat Stock at the beginning ; then *either* there is one now alfo, and then there is a Balance of Gain or Lofs, which is equal to the Increafe or Decreafe of your Neat or Free Stock : Or, there is now no Neat Stock, the Debts and Effects being equal ; and then there is a Neat Lofs, equal to the former Neat Stock : Or, the prefent Debts exceed the Effects, and then the Neat Lofs is equal to the Sum of that Excefs, and of the former Neat Stock.

2. If there was no Neat Stock at the beginning, the Debts and Effects being equal ; then *either* there is now a Neat Stock, which is therefore equal to the Neat Gain ; *or*, the prefent Debts exceed the Effects, and then the Excefs is equal to the Neat Lofs ; *or*, there is no remaining Free or Neat Stock (Debts and Effects being equal) and then there is no Balance of Gain or Lofs.

3. If the Debts exceeded the Effects at the beginning ; then *either* they are now equal, and fo there muft be a Neat Gain equal to that Excefs : Or there is now a Neat Stock, and then there is a Neat Gain equal to the Sum of the prefent Neat Stock, and what the Debts exceeded the Effects at the beginning : Or, the Debts do now alfo exceed the Effects ; and then, if thofe Exceffes are equal, the Gain and Lofs is equal ; but as the prefent Excefs is leaft or greateft, fo there is a neat Gain or Lofs equal to the Difference of thofe Exceffes.

As the natural Reafon of thefe Equalities is plain and obvious, fo the Balance of the *Stock Account* will prove it to be actually fo in every Cafe.

Before I give the Inftructions promifed, for finding the *States* of the particular *Accounts*, I fhall add the following

General Obfervations *to the preceding General* Rule.

1. As we have in the foregoing Method left the *Stock Account* laft open to receive the Balances of the Accounts of *Profit* and *Lofs*, and *Balance* ; we may inftead of that, carry the Balances of the Accounts of *Stock*, and *Profit* and *Lofs*, into the *Balance* Account, or of the *Stock* and *Balance* into the *Profit* and *Lofs* Account ;

count, and either way the Account laſt open will be thus balanced, for the ſame Reaſon as was explained in the firſt Method ; and the ſame Conſequence will hold from this Balance to the Equality of the neat Gain or Loſs, with the Alteration of the Stock.

2. The *Account* of *Balances* ought firſt to be made up upon a looſe Sheet ; and alſo the *Profit* and *Loſs* Account (carrying into it the Sums of the Articles that ſtand already in the Account) till all is finiſhed and proved. For the ſame Reaſon alſo, write the Balances of Debts, and of Gain or Loſs, in theſe looſe Accounts, without writing them upon the Accounts to which they belong in the Leger, till the Proof is made. By this Means, if any Errors are committed in the balancing Work, they may be corrected, before the Balances are filled up in the Leger. Then after all is finiſhed and proved [which will alſo require the transferring of the *Stock Account* upon the looſe Sheet ; at leaſt in the total Sums of the Debt and Credit ; for there is no more neceſſary] cloſe the Accounts in the Leger, by filling up the Balances of Debt, and of Gain and Loſs, belonging to each, from the *Accounts of Balance*, and of *Profit* and *Loſs* ; and tranſcribe thoſe Accounts into the Leger, marking in them the Folio where the ſeveral Accounts with which they are connected, ſtand ; and alſo in theſe ſeveral Accounts mark where the Accounts of *Balance*, and *Profit* and *Loſs* ſtand.

Again, *Obſerve*, That in tranſcribing the *Profit* and *Loſs* Account, you may fill up as many of the new Articles into the old Account as it will hold, till one of the Sides, or both, will hold no more ; then transfer the Sums into a new Space, and there fill up the reſt of the Articles, and the cloſing of the Account. Or you may transfer the Sums of the former Articles into the new Space, and place all the new Articles together in that Space.

3. If you keep a complete *Journal*, diſtinct from the *Waſte-Book*, the Particulars of the *Account of Balance*, and of *Profit* and *Loſs* are commonly entered in the Journal ; and then you need only enter the Totals in the Leger, making them Debtor *to*, or Creditor *by*, ſundry Accounts (as ℞ *Journal*.) Or you may enter them at large in the *Leger*, and not at all in the *Journal*. Either of theſe Methods you may alſo uſe with a *Marginal Journal*.

Observe *alſo*, That though the Balance of ſome *Accounts* will be the Sum of ſeveral Articles that muſt be diſtinguiſhed, yet you need not make this Diſtinction of the Particulars, in filling up the *Account of Balance* in the *Leger* ; but take the Total, and mark the Particulars ſeparately, in tranſcribing it as the *Inventory* of the new *Waſte-Book* ; or if you tranſcribe it into the *Journal*, do the ſame.

4. If you propoſe to make an Inventory for the Satisfaction of knowing the State of your Affairs, without deſigning a new *Leger* ; then make up your *Balance*, and *Profit* and *Loſs*, upon a looſe Sheet, as before directed, without writing any Thing in the *Leger* ; leaving the Accounts as they were, unleſs any of the Accounts are balanced in courſe, for then you may cloſe them, or not, as you pleaſe.

ARTICLE III. *Further* Inftructions *for finding the* State *and* Balance *of particular* Accounts.

1. *For proper Accounts Domeftick.*

I. In a *Perfon's Account*, the Difference of the Debtor and Creditor fides is the final Balance, owing by that Perfon to you, or by you to him.

OBSERVE, If there is any Intereft of Money due at this Time by either of you to the other, not yet placed to the Account, it ought now to be ftated. *Again,* If it happens that there are Articles of Debt and Credit upon various Dealings, which you would not have confounded; for Example, a Perfon owes me a Sum of Money upon Bond, which I leave in his Hands for Intereft, and has alfo a Current Account with me upon other common Dealings; I would clofe the Account, *thus:* Firft, State the Money lent with its Intereft, as a Balance upon the oppofite Side; then what Difference or Balance there is of the two Sides of the Account, after this firft Balance is ftated, it is the Balance of the other Debts betwixt us, which I place on the leaft Side; and fo the Account is balanced. By this you'll underftand what to do with any other different Balances, that you would have diftinguifhed from one another.

II. In the *Account of accepted Bills*, and *Bottomree Account*, (which are general Accounts for Perfons) the Difference of the two Sides is a Balance, due by you, if they comprehend only Bills due by you, and Money lent or borrowed by you on Bottomree; but if they comprehend Bills both payable to you and by you, and Debts due to and by you upon Bottomree; then as thofe different Kinds of Articles are diftinguifhed in each Account, by the double Money-Columns, each of them muft be balanced feparately in their different Columns, as they were different Accounts.

Account of Out-ftanding Charges, &c. and all other general perfonal Accounts, are balanced the fame Way.

OBSERVE *alfo,* That the particular Debts that make up the Balance muft be diftinguifhed in the new Inventory.

III. In the Account of *Cafh*, the Difference of Debt and Credit is the Balance due to you by that Account; for the Creditor-fide cannot exceed the Debtor-fide.

IV. In an Account of *Goods* there are three Cafes, (1.) If there is no Part difpofed of, then the whole on the Debtor-fide is a Balance due to you. (2.) If all is difpofed of, the Quantity Columns are equal, and the Difference of the Money Columns is Gain or Lofs, to be fet on the leaft Side, which will balance the Account. (3.) If part is difpofed of, and part remaining, then take the Difference of the Quantities on both Sides, and having calculated the Value as it ftands you, it is the Balance which the Account owes you, to be placed on the Creditor-fide. After this is ftated, the Difference of the Money Columns is the Gain or Lofs upon the Part difpofed of; for the Part undifpofed of being ftated on both Sides at the fame Value, the Difference of the Money

can

can have no relation to that Part, and so muſt be the Gain or Loſs on the other ; which therefore is to be placed on the leaſt Side, *To* or *By Profit* and *Loſs*, and so the Account is completely balanced.

OBSERVE, 1. Though there is but one general Quantity Column, yet if the Parcels entered on the Debtor-ſide are of different Kinds and Value, they are diſtinguiſhed by Marks or Numbers ; and to find the Value of the Balance, you muſt collect the Quantities of every Mark or Number on both Sides, to find the Balances of each Kind, whoſe Sum is the total Balance, and the Sum of the Values of each Part, taken according to the Prices at which they are entered, with a Proportion of the greater Articles of common Charges, makes the Value of the total Balance. Thus, in the *Account* of *Wine*, in the following *Leger*, N°. 1. the Quantity of *Claret*, entered on the *Debtor* and *Creditor* ſides, as they are diſtinguiſhed by Numbers, with their Balances and Values, are as I have here collected them,

Claret D'. N'. 1—Hds, 6. C'.—Hds, 5. Bal.—Hds, 1. value £ 8

2	4	4	0		
3	10	8	2	20	
4	7	0	7	45	16 8
	27	17	10	73	16 8

If there are different Quantity Columns for different Species, the Balances of each are to be taken ſeparately ; and if there is a Subdiviſion by Numbers in any of theſe, you muſt take the ſame Method as before.

2. As to the making a Cloſe and Balance of your Leger, you may value the Balances of Goods as they coſt you, or according to the current Rates : Yet it ſeems more reaſonable to value them as they coſt you ; for otherwiſe you bring in Gain and Loſs into your Accounts, which has not yet actually happened, and may, perhaps, not happen ; becauſe you may not diſpoſe of them at thoſe Rates. But if your Accounts are balanced, in order that your Effects may be diſpoſed of to your Creditors for Payment of your Debts, it ſeems juſt that they be valued at the current Rates ; or with ſuch Allowances as Merchants have from one another.

3. If there happens to be *Inlack*, that is ſhort Meaſure, or a Deficiency of the Quantity of *Wine*, &c. which was not filled up, then if all is diſpoſed of, the Creditor-ſide will be leſs than the Debtor, and to balance the Account the Difference of the Money is Gain or Loſs ; and when that is ſtated, to make the Quantity Columns equal, ſet down the Deficiency on the Creditor-ſide, writing before it, *Deficient* in *Meaſure* [or *Quantity* ;] but this has nothing to do with the Balance Account. Again, if there be a Deficiency diſcovered, while there is at the ſame Time any remaining Quantity , then after Stating this Quantity as a Balance due to you, ſtate the Gain or Loſs, and the Quantity deficient, as before.

N 4. If

4. If there is *Out-come* (*Over-meafure* or *Excefs*) in *Weight* or *Meafure* in the Quantity, this will be known by the Creditor-fide exceeding the Debtor, when all is difpofed of; in this Cafe, the Difference of the Money is Gain or Lofs; and to balance the Quantities, fet the *Over-meafure* on the Debtor-fide, writing before it, *Over-meafure*; but this goes to no Account. *Again*, if there is an *Over-meafure* or *Excefs*, which you have difcovered, and yet all is not difpofed of, then firft ftate the Whole that remains (which will include that *Over-meafure*) as a Balance due to you; then ftate the Gain or Lofs, and at laft fet the *Over-meafure* on the Debtor-fide, as before, to make the Quantities equal.

V. For *Accounts* of *Houfes* and *Ships:* You may value them at the firft Coft; and when that is ftated on the Creditor-fide, the Difference of the Debt and Credit is Gain or Lofs, arifing from the Difference of the Reparations, *&c.* and the Rents or Freights. Or you may take the Difference of the two Sides, and ftate as the Balance due to you; by which means the Value of the Thing will appear lefs and lefs at every balancing, till it's nothing. And then in a new Inventory you enter it again, at what Value you think proper; and fometimes alfo you may appear to be a Lofer, which muft go to *Profit* and *Lofs*; but the firft Method I think the beft: And though thefe Subjects do not really keep up their Value, yet I would continue them at the firft Value till they were difpofed of, or loft; or you may chufe to ftate them at another Value from Time to Time, as you think they are then really worth.

VI. In *Delivery Accounts* of *Buying* and *Selling*, the Difference of the Debt and Credit is the Sum of the Bargains that remain to be delivered (all other Bargains being balanced in the Account) therefore it is to be fet on the leaft Side, and goes to the Account of *Balance*, as what that Account owes you. And take Notice, by comparing the two Sides, what thofe particular Bargains are, that they may be diftinguifhed, and the *Perfons* and *Things* particularly mentioned in the Inventory.

OBSERVE, If you have made a general Account of *Delivery* both for *Buying* and *Selling*; then, as the Numbers of each are put in feparate Columns, they muft be balanced feparately, as they were two different Accounts.

VII. In *Wagers Account* you muft compare the two Sides, and find what Wagers are undecided, for which make the Account Creditor by *Balance*, as a Debt to you (diftinguifhing them particularly in the Inventory) then the Difference of the Money goes to *Profit* and *Lofs*, to balance the Account.

OBSERVE, If you have loft Wagers upon which there were Confignments, and thefe Loffes are already ftated in the Account, then what is now ftated as Gain or Lofs, will not be the whole Gain or Lofs made up in the *Wagers Account*; and indeed the prefent Balance may be Lofs, when there is real Gain in the Total. And the Way to know that real Balance of Gain or Lofs, is, to compare all the Wagers decided, and collect the Gains or Loffes feparately. But if, when Wagers were loft upon which Confignment was made, you only made fome Mark in the Account, to fhew that the Wager was decided and loft; then the prefent Balance of Gain or Lofs, is the Total upon the whole Account.

Account. If you confider the Account a little, and how Things are placed upon it, the Reafon of all this will be manifeft.

For *Hazard Account.* The Difference of the Debt and Credit is the Wagers upon Parole not decided, which muft be confidered and ftated as a Balance I owe ; and this will anfwer an equal Balance, ftated as owing to me upon the Wagers Account.

VIII. If you have fuch Accounts as *Promife* and *Conditional Accounts*, the Difference of Debt and Credit of the correfpondent Columns, *i. e.* which relate to the Promifes made to you, or to thofe made by you, are the Sums of the Engagements remaining to be fulfilled ; and muft be ftated as Debts owing *To* or *By* you.

But, Observe, That what will thus appear as a Debt owing to, or by you on the one Account, will on the other appear contrarily a Debt owing *By* or *To* you ; and fo they will balance one another in the Inventory, and therefore have no Influence on the total State of that ; and fo be of no further Ufe there, than to preferve in your Accounts a Record of thefe Conditional Obligations till they are performed.

IX. *Infurance Account*, is a mere Account of *Profit* and *Lofs*; therefore in this, and all of the fame Kind if there is any other, (as *Intereft Account*) the Difference of their Debt and Credit is Gain or Lofs.

2. *Proper Accounts Foreign.*

I. *Voyage.* The Value of what Goods are ftill at Sea, and not yet delivered into the Hands of my Factor, is a Balance due to me by this Account ; and if they are all unloaded, the Account is either equal on both Sides, or the Difference is *Gain* or *Lofs*.

II. *A. B. of —— My Account of Goods*, is clofed the fame Way as any other Account of Goods.

III. *A. B. of —— My Account of Sales.* If there is foreign Money, that muft be firft balanced ; *thus:* The Account is Creditor by Balance for the Difference (for the Debtor-fide muft be greateft if there is a Difference, becaufe the Account contains the Debts owing for my Goods) ftating the Value in *Englifh* Money, according to the Current Exchange : Then if there is any Difference in the Debt and Credit of the *Englifh* Money, it is the Gain or Lofs upon the Exchange, which arifes from the different Rates of Exchange at which thofe Debts were at firft entered, and afterwards difcharged in this Account.

A. B. of —— My Account Current, is balanced the fame Way, as directed in the laft Account, *i. e.* the Foreign Money firft, which goes to the Account of *Balances* ; and then the *Englifh* Money, which goes to the *Profit* and *Lofs*.

3. *Factors Accounts.*

When I would make a General State of my own Affairs, there is a Necef-fity to clofe alfo the Accounts of thofe who employ me as a Factor, that the Debts betwixt us may be duly ftated. Thefe Accounts are;

A. B. of —— *His Account of Goods.* What Charges and Commiffion are owing for his Account of Goods, not yet ftated, let them be now ftated. Then carry the Sales that are yet unpaid to the Account of *Balance* ; and the Difference of the other Articles on Debtor and Creditor Sides, into his *Account Current*, if this is not done already ; as the Account will fhew.

A. B. of —— *his Account Current.* It is clofed with Balance for the Diffe-rence of the two Sides, as any other *Perfonal Account.*

OBSERVE, 1. If you have *Accounts* with another Factor for the Account of your Employer ; clofe thofe Accounts by carrying the Gain or Lofs that happens upon any of them into your Employer's *Account Current :* Then clofe all the Accounts by *Balance.*

2. This Method of clofing your Employer's Accounts and others that re-late to his Bufinefs, will bring equal Articles into both Sides of your In-ventory, which do not belong to the State of your Affairs, any further than as you are the Manager, and accountable : But becaufe they are equal, they can make no Error in the final State or Balance of your Inventory ; and the Narration will diftinguifh them : Or you may feparate them from the Articles that are properly your own. And *obferve*, That when there is Out-ftanding Debt ; if the Debtor has an Account of other Dealings with you, you may take the Balance of what is properly betwixt you and him, fe-parately from what he owes for your Employer.

3. Your Employer's Goods remaining undifpos'd of, have nothing to do with the *Balance* Account ; only you may mark the Quantity upon the Creditor Side, with the Word *Undifpofed* fet before it ; fo that when you open the Account in the *New Leger*, as will be to do, if there was any Ba-lance carried to the Account of *Balance* ; then fet the Quantities in their Columns on the Debtor Side, writing before them *Undifpofed of in the laft Ac-count.* And if there was no Article to the Account of *Balance*, then this Ac-count will not be opened again, till fome new Tranfaction happen relating to thofe Goods.

4. You may choofe to clofe your Employer's Accounts by a double Balan-cing, *viz.* Set the Sum of each Side upon the other, *To* and *By Balance :* And thus, the Accounts will appear, in the new Books, in the fame State as they were in the Old, except that you have the Sums in Place of the Particulars

5. If you clofe the Accounts after the former Method, then you ought to fend your Employer a Copy of them fo clofed.

4. *Company Accounts.*

Branch I.

Suppofition I. (1.) If the Effects of the Company are all difpofed of, and the Accounts already adjufted and finifhed, with the Manager ; then clofe, A. B *my Account with him,* &c. with *Profit* and *Lofs,* for the Difference of the two Sides ; which is the Gain or Lofs upon that Partnerfhip. And at the fame Time, if the Partner Manager has a particular Account, clofe it with *Balance,* if there is any Difference.

(2.) If the Bufinefs of the Partnerfhip is unfinifh'd ; then clofe, A. B. *My Account with him,* &c. and *His particular Account,* with *Balance* ; or clofe the former with a double Balance (as mentioned upon Factor's Accounts.) Thus your Books will be brought to a Balance : Yet the precife State of your Affairs, in this Part, will not appear ; becaufe you neither know what Effects you have in that Company, nor what you have gained or loft.

Suppofition II. If it is a fix'd Company, clofe your *Account in the Company,* By *Balance* for your *Stock* : And what Difference there is after this, is the Gain or Lofs made fince laft balancing of the Company's Books. And here alfo *obferve,* That if they have not been balanced immediately before, you cannot know the precife State of this Part of your Affairs.

Branch II.

Suppofition I. The Company's Accounts being kept in my Books, it is in my Power to know the precife State of this Part of my Affairs (fo far as they are immediately under my Direction ; for there may be fome Part in the Hands of Factors) and this muft be examin'd and ftated ; without which, I cannot bring my Leger to a Balance, fo as that the true State of this Part may appear. The Method is this :

1. See what petty Charges are due to you (not ftated) For thefe and the Commiffion due to you, upon the preceding Negotiations, make the *Account of Goods in Company,* Debtor ; or, *Profit* and *Lofs in Company* [if you have fuch an Account ; and if there is not fuch already, it will be neceffary now, in Cafe there be feveral Accounts belonging to the Company, upon which Gain or Lofs may happen.] The Creditors are *Cafb,* and *Profit* and *Lofs.*

Obferve, Some would charge every Partner's *particular Account,* Debtor to his *Account in Company,* for his Share of thefe Charges and Commiffion ; but this is needlefs. It appears neceffary only in this Cafe, *viz.* If fo much of the Company's Effects fhould happen to be loft after this, that there is not fo much as will pay me thefe Articles. But if fuch a Thing happens, you may then charge the Partners particular Accounts Debtor to *Profit* and *Lofs* for their Shares of this Debt. And *obferve* alfo, That if after this you pay your felf thefe Debts, out of the firft of their Money that comes into your Hands, then all is fived, and for this you have no particular Entry to make.

2. Go through all the Accounts, *Domeftick* and *Foreign*, belonging to the Company ; and clofe them with *Balance* for the remaining Effects and Debts owing to or by the Company, and *Profit* and *Lofs in Company*, for the Gain or Lofs. But *obferve*, If there is no Account of *Profit* and *Lofs in Company*, then make the Account upon which the Gain or Lofs happens, Debtor *To*, or Creditor *By* each Partner's *Account in Company*, for his Share, and *Profit* and *Lofs* for your own Share.

3. If you have an Account of *Profit* and *Lofs in Company* ; then all the Articles being gathered into it, take the Balance, and having found every Partner's Share, make the Account Debtor to, or Creditor by each Partner's *Account in Company* for his Share, and *Profit* and *Lofs* for your own Share.

4. The Partners *Accounts in Company*, and particular Accounts, are to be clofed with Balance ; or the firft with a double Balance, in Cafe the Company's Affairs are ftill in Motion.

Obferve, The Confequence of clofing the Company's Accounts, with Balance, will be this ; It will make Effects, which belong partly to others, and partly to you, come into your Inventory, as if all were your own : But then for your Partners Shares, there are equivalent Articles, which will come in among your Debts, from their Accounts in Company ; and therefore, your neat Stock, which is the Difference of the Debtor and Creditor Sides of Balance, is ftill the fame as it would be without thefe : And if any Body is Creditor upon the Company's Account, the Partners proper Accounts ftand Debtor for their Shares ; and thefe balance one another for the faid Shares.

When the Partners demand an Account of the State of their Affairs, you ought to give them a fair Copy of the fame, clofed in the Manner directed, upon that feparate Copy ; but not yet touched in your *Leger*, till you fee what's refolv'd about their Affairs. What they receive from you, on Account of their Concerns, place to the Accounts, by the former Inftructions ; and if they owe you, upon their *particular Accounts*, as much as you owe them, by the Balance of their *Accounts in Company*, then make their *Accounts in Company* Debtor to their *particular Accounts* for the fame. *Laftly*, If the Company diffolve, and they withdraw their whole Effects, each Partner receiving his Share of the Money, or Goods remaining, and Affignments for his Share of the Out-ftanding Debts ; then, after all Things are duly ftated, the whole Accounts will be balanced (except, perhaps, their *particular Accounts* ; becaufe you or they may remain in fome real Debt to one another ; unlefs alfo clear'd at this Time.) If the Society breaks not up, then the Accounts will ftand open as they were ; except fo far as the collecting the Articles of Gain and Lofs, into the *Account of Profit* and *Lofs* ; alfo the Divifion, and clofing of that, and the Stating of what is given or received, makes a Difference.

When the Company's Accounts are kept in feparate Books.

At making up the General Balance of my proper Affairs, I clofe that Account, *viz. My Account with*, &c. as directed under the firft Branch ; and then

my

my *Leger* will come to a Balance; becaufe, every Thing paffed betwixt my private Concerns and the Company, is duly fet down on this Account; the chief Ufe whereof is, the preferving the Balance of my private Leger. But (as I faid upon the firft Branch) the true and complete State of my Affairs will not appear, unlefs the Company's Accounts are already finifh'd; yet I may fatisfy my felf in this, by making a State of the Company's Affairs, feparately, thus; Going through all the Accounts, I collect the Articles of Gain and Lofs in the Manner already mentioned; and charging the *Account Profit* and *Lofs in Company*, for my Provifion, the neat Gains being alfo divided according to every Partner's Share, and my Part added to the Creditor Side of my Account in Company; the Balance of it will fhew the true Value of my Concerns in the Company, according to the prefent State of their Accounts.

If the Company demand the State of their Affairs, their *Leger* fhews them that; but firft do this, *viz.* Go through all the Accounts, and collect the Articles gained or loft, into the Account of *Profit* and *Lofs in Company*; then charging this Account Debtor to your *particular Account*; for your Commiffion, make a Dividend of the neat Gain or Lofs, and clofe the Account Debtor *To*, or Creditor *By* each Partner's and your own *Account in Company*. If the Society breaks up, the Accounts will be entirely finifh'd at this Time, in the *Leger*; becaufe there will be a Dividend of the remaining Effects of the Company's; the Debts owing to the Company will be alfo affigned to the Partners; and for thofe owing by the Company upon their Credit, there will be Order taken for the Payment of them: When all this is done, your own Share, which returns to your private Accounts, is to be transferred there in the Manner already directed. Every Thing that can occur here, you'll foon find how to order, by diligently confidering the Matter in hand, and the Nature of each Account; and fo I leave you to make what Cafes you pleafe, and anfwer them when you have done. If you would have an Abftract of the State of the Company's Affairs; then upon a feparate Paper make an Account of Balances, and bring here, from every Account in the *Leger*, what Articles belong properly to fuch an Account (the Articles of Gain and Lofs are already fpoken off) but touch not the Accounts to write any Thing in the *Leger*, till you fee what they do about their Affairs, when this is done, the *Balance* Account will be equal on both Sides, for the Debtor Side contains all the remaining Effects, and Debts owing to the Company by the Partners, as well as others; and on the Creditor Side is, what the Company owes, particularly to the Partners for their Shares, and the neat Gain or Lofs being already added to their Accounts, and confequently now brought to the *Balance Account*; this muft be equal, becaufe there is nothing in the Nature of the Thing to make any Inequality, but the neat Gain or Lofs not being added. But if the Society continue, their Accounts will ftand open; unlefs you propofe to clofe them in the Spaces where they now ftand, and transfer them to new ones; and then clofe them with Balance: And to enter them in the new Spaces, you have nothing to fay, but Debtor *To*, or Creditor *By Balance* (transferred from the former Account) and though the Word *Balance* is mentioned, yet it is the old and new Account that are properly the reciprocal Debtors and Creditors, for that Article of Balance ; but you may put in that *Balance Account* in the Book, betwixt the two Sets of Accounts ; and it will equally refpect them both, and be, as it were, the Capital Account, whence the new Set flows ; which makes, in a Manner, a new *Leger* ; in the fame Manner as you'll find below the Balance Account of my private Affairs, to ftand betwixt the Accounts of the old *Leger*, and the Stock Account of the new.

Suppofition II. If the *Leger* of a ftanding Company is propofed to be balanced ; then as to the collecting the Gain and Lofs, and making the Dividend, it is done the fame Way as in the former Cafe. And if you would tranfer the Accounts into new Books, clofe them all with an *Account of Balance in Company*. But if this Balancing be made upon the Company's Demand, let the Articles of Balance be collected in a feparate Paper, and touch not the Accounts : Then, if the Partners withdraw their Shares of the neat Gain, make their *Accounts in Company* Debtors to the Things given ; thus, their *Accounts in Company* will remain Creditor for no more than the firft Stock.

If they leave any of the Gain for augmenting their Stock, it will remain upon the Credit of the Account. If there be Lofs upon the Accounts, their Stocks will be diminifhed, which if they make up, or if they add any Thing elfe to the Stock, then *Cafh* is Debtor to their *Accounts in Company* for what they add, or their *proper Accounts*, Debtor, if it's not prefently paid in. After all this is over, you may proceed to clofe the Accounts with *Balance* ; and then the Balance Account will be equal on both Sides, for the Reafons fhown in the former Cafe ; and its Articles compofe the *Stock* Account for the new Books : The Debtor Side is what is owing to the Company, either of Effects remaining, or Debts, whether by the Partners or others ; the Creditor Side is the Debts owing by the Company to the Partners, or others. But *obferve*, the *Stock Account*, made from this Balance, will contain other Things than the *Stock Account*, made at the Beginning of this Partnerfhip , becaufe there may now be feveral Articles owing to the Partners upon their *proper Accounts*, or to other Perfons who deal with the Company ; yet ftill the new Account of *Stock* is equal on both Sides, as the former was ; becaufe it is the Tranfcript of the forementioned *Balance Account*, which is equal ; and to know upon this Account, what the Stock is, you muft confider the Articles for which it is Debtor to the Partners *Accounts in Company*; for thefe contain the Stock of the Company.

Of an Account of Exchange in Company.

Take the Balance of the Foreign Money, and calculate the Value of it according to the current Exchange ; for which, make *A. B. Our Account of Exchange*, Debtor *To*, or Creditor *By*, *His Account Current* : [Thus the Ac-

Account is balanced for the Foreign Money ; and put in the fame State as if that Balance were remitted to or by him : But becaufe it is not actually fo, it's therefore placed to his *Account Current*] Then what Difference there is of the *Englifh* Money, is Gain or Lofs ; for which the Account muft be made Debtor *To*, or Creditor *By* A. B. *His Account Current*, and *Profit* and *Lofs*, each for a Half.

This is the proper, and indeed the only Way of Balancing the Account, when the Correfpondence is broken up betwixt you. But if it continues, and you want only to bring your *Leger* to a Balance ; then you may clofe the Account of Exchange with a double Balance : Though by this Way you make no State of the Gain or Lofs hitherto made by this Account.

A. B. *His Account Current*, is clofed like any other *Perfonal Account*.

CONCLUSION.

I Now prefume, That whoever underftands the *Rules* and *Principles* of the Method above explain'd, with their Application in the following Books, is fully fatisfied of its Excellence ; feeing it anfwers all the Purpofes of Accounts, in the moft diftinct and eafy Manner. With what beautiful Regularity and Connection are Accounts begun, carried on, and finifhed ? For, as all Accounts do, in a Manner, arife out of the *Stock Account*, or have a Relation to it ; fo all of them, which are not in Courfe extinguifhed, do, at laft, terminate in the *Account* of *Balances* ; which may therefore be called the *Metamorphofis* (or *Transformation*) of the *Stock Account* ; fhewing all the Alterations that have happened to it, either in the Total, or in the conftituent Parts ; and is accordingly the *Stock Account* of the new *Leger*, though in a contrary Form ; the Debt and Credit of the one being contrarily the Credit and Debt of the other ; as the Nature of thofe Accounts plainly fhews.

We fee now clearly the valuable Ufe of the mutual Connection of Accounts, and the univerfal Balance of Debt and Credit ; which, befides the Neatnefs of Stile, and the diftinct Reference it makes betwixt one Account and another concerned in the fame Tranfaction, affords a curious Proof of the whole Work : So that if there is the leaft Defect in this Balance, we muft conclude there are Errors in the Accounts ; and if it holds, there is a very probable Argument, and, indeed, the beft we can have, that all is right.

O

WASTE-

WASTE-BOOK,

NUMBER I.

OF ME,

A. M. Merchant in *Aberdeen.*

From the Firſt of *May,* 1729.

WASTE-BOOK,

NUMBER I.

Aberdeen, May 1, 1729.

INVENTORY *of the whole Effects and Debts of me A. M.*
Merchant in Aberdeen.

		l.	*s.*	*d.*
IMprimis, I have in Ready Money, the Sum of ———		800	o	o
I have 20 Hhds. of Claret Wine, of Numbers and Prices following:				
	l.			
N°. 1. 6 Hhds. at 8 *l. per* Hhd. ———————— 48				
2. 4 Hhds. at 10 *l.* ———————— 40				
3. 10 Hhds. at 12 *l.* 10 *s.* ——————— 125				
213		213	o	o
I have 18 Hhds. of *Virginia Tobacco,* Neat Weight of each 600 lb. at 11 *l.* 3 *s. per* Hhd. ——— ——— ———		200	14	o
I have 30 Barrels of *Raisins,* marked N°. 1. at 1 *l.* 12 *s. per* Barrel ——— ——— ——— ———		48	o	o
I have 14 Pieces of *Broad Cloth,* of Numbers and Prices following:				
	l. *s.*			
N°. 1. 8 Pieces, each 20 Yds. at 16 *s. per* Yd. —— 128 0				
2. 6 Pieces, each 18 Yds. at 14 *s.* ——— —— 75 12				
203 12		203	12	o

There

	l.	*s.*	*d.*

There is due to me by ſeveral Perſons, as follows:
By Mr. *William Wallace,* by Bond, dated the 1ſt of *Febru-ary* laſt, payable at *Martinmas* next;

                                         l.   *s.*

Principal Sum —————————————— 100   0
Intereſt due at the Term of Payment, at *5 per Cent.*   3   15

                                           103   15

	103	15	0

By Mr. *Andrew Hunter,* as the Balance of an Account ad-juſted betwixt us, payable on Demand —————   80   0   0
By Mr. *Andrew Cochran,* payable on Demand ———   140   0   0
My Moveables and Houſhold Furniture (as *per* particular *Inventory* thereof) are Worth ——————————   200   0   0

I owe to ſundry Perſons as follows:
To Mr. *David Johnſtone,* payable the 1ſt of *November* next —   120   0   0
To Mr. *James Truſtwell, per* Account, payable on Demand   60   0   0

Here follow my daily Tranſactions in Trade.

May 2d.

Sold and delivered to *Alexander Paygood,* 4 Hhds. *Claret Wine* (Nº. 1.) at 12 *l. per* Hhd. for Ready Money receiv'd, is—   48   0   0

Sold and deliver'd to *William Smith,* 2 Pieces of *Broad Cloath* (Nº. 2.) meaſuring 18 Yards each, at 17*s.* 6*d. per* Yard, payable in 2 Months, is ——— ——— ———   31   10   0

4th.

Bought and received of *Peter Chapman,* 18 Bales of *French Paper* (Nº. 1.) at 4 *l. per* Bale, payable in 1 Month, is —   72   0   0

6th.

Sold and delivered to Mr. *John Paton,* Bookſeller, in *Edin-burgh,* 5 Bales of *French Paper* (Nº. 1.) at 5 *l. per* Bale, is 25 *l.* of which
Receiv'd in Caſh —————————————— *l.* 10
The Remainder payable in 20 Days by his Note —— 15

                                   25

	25	0	0

May

	l.	*s.*	*d.*

———————— *May 6th.* ————————

Bought and received of *David Watfon*, 32 Casks of *Brandy*, at 3 *l. per* Cask (N°. 1.) is 96 *l.* of which,

Paid in Cafh ——————————————————— *l.* 16

Given him a Bill upon Mr. *Andrew Hunter*, for ——— 80

———
96 | 96 | 0 | 0 |

———————— *7th.* ————————

Sold and delivered to *Elias Freeman*, 3 Hhds. *Claret Wine* (2, of N°. 2. and 1, of N°. 1.) at 12 *l.* 10 *s. per* Hhd. is 37 *l.* 10 *s.* for which I have an accepted Bill on Mr. *Daniel Trader*, payable on Demand ———————————————

| | 37 | 10 | 0 |

———————— *8th.* ————————

Sold and deliver'd to Mr. *John Houfton*, 10 Barrels of *Raifins* (N°. 1.) at 2 *l. per* Barrel, is 20 *l.* whereof

Received in Cafh ——————————————— *l.* 8

An accepted Bill on Mr. *John Hutchefon*, payable in 10 Days ———————————————————— 6

The Remainder payable by him in 2 Months ——— 6

———
20 | 20 | 0 | 0 |

Bought and received of Mr. *John Fergufon*, 24 Cafks of *Brandy* (N°. 2.) at 2 *l.* 10 *s. per* Cafk, paid in Ready Money— | 60 | 0 | 0 |

Bought and received of *Alexander Black*, 1000 Stone Weight of Iron (N°. 1.) at 3 *s. per* Stone, is 150 *l.* whereof

Paid by Bill on Mr. *Andrew Cochran* ——————— *l.* 100

The Remainder payable by me in 3 Months ———— 50

———
150 | 150 | 0 | 0 |

———————— *11th.* ————————

Sold and delivered in Barter with *Thomas Jamefon*, 6 Pieces of *Broad Cloath* (N°. 1.) containing 20 Yards each, at 17 *s.* 4 *d. per* Yard, in all 104 *l.* for which

Received 12 Pieces of Holland, 25 Yards each, in all 300 Yards, at 4 *s. per* Yard, is———————— *l.* 60

In Cafh ———————————————————— 44

———
104 | 104 | 0 | 0 |

May

	l.	*s.*	*d.*

———————— *May* 11th. ————————

Sold and delivered in Barter with *Robert White*, 15 Barrels
of *Raisins* (N°. 1.) at 1 *l.* 16 *s. per* Barrel, in all 27 *l.* for
which I have received 12 Barrels of *Salmon* (N°. 1.) cured
with *Spanish* Salt, at 2 *l.* 5 *s. per* Barrel ——————— | 27 | 0 | 0 |

Sold and delivered to *Abraham Fairholm*, 4 Pieces of *Holland* (N°. 1.) 25 Yards each, is 100 Yards, at 5 *s.* 3 *d. per*
Yard, payable in 5 Months ————————————— | 26 | 5 | 0 |

———————————— 14th. ————————————

Bought and received of Mr. *James Montgomery*, 8 Lasts
of *Salmons*, cured with *Spanish* Salt, at 2 *l.* 5 *s. per* Barrel, is
216 *l.* whereof
Paid in Cash ————————————— *l.* 60
Given, a Bill on Mr. *Andrew Cochran* ———— 40
The Remainder, payable by me on Demand———— 116

                                                                 216 | 216 | 0 | 0 |

Sold to a Stranger for Ready Money, 3 Hhds. *Tobacco*, at
4 *l.* 14 *s. per* Hhd. in all———————————— | 14 | 2 | 0 |

———————————— 20th. ————————————

Delivered this Day in Barter, 2 Hhds. *Tobacco*, at 4 *l. per*
Hhd. is 8 *l.* for which I have received, *viz.*
In Cash ————————————————— *l.* 2
4 Barrels of Figs, at 1 *l.* 10 *s. per* Barrel ——————— 6

                                                                   8 | 8 | | |

The 4 Barrels of Figs I have immediately sold, and deliver'd
to *John Houston*, at 1 *l.* 18 *s.* payable on Demand 7 *l.* 12 *s.* | 7 | 12 | 0 |

Bartered with *Ninian Nicolson*, 200 Stone of Iron (N°. 1.)
for 3 *s.* 6 *d. per* Stone, is 35 *l.* which I have instantly delivered, and 15 *l.* overplus; for which received 750 Yards of *Scotch
Linen Cloth*, at 16 *d. per* Yard, is ——— —————— | 50 | 0 | 0 |

                                                                   May

	l.	*s.*	*d.*

——————— *May 24th.* ———————

Paid in Caſh to *James Truſtwell,* in Part of what I ow'd him—— | 40 | o | o |

Received in Caſh from *Daniel Trader,* in Part of what he owes me——————————————— | 20 | o | o |

——————— 28th. ———————

Received this Day from *John Paton,* for Payment of what he owes me, an Aſſignment on *Alexander Black,* for 15 *l.* payable on Demand, which *Ditto Black* accepts, to diſcount from what I owe him ; which not being payable till the 8th of *Auguſt,* I charge him with Diſcount till then, *viz.* 2 *s.* 8 *d.* Total—— | 15 | 2 | 8 |

——————— 30th. ———————

Bought and received for ready Money, 16 Barrels of Figs (N°. 1.) at 2 *l* 4 *s. per* Barrel—————————— | 35 | 4 | o |

Sold and delivered for Ready Money, 300 Stone of Iron (N°. 1.) at 4 *s. per* Stone ————————— | 60 | o | o |

Paid to *James Montgomery,* what I ow'd him for Salmons, in the Manner following, *viz.*

		l.	*s.*			
Given in Caſh ———————————		108	8			
An Aſſignment on *John Houſton*———————		7	12			
		116	0	116	o	o

——————— *June 3d.* ———————

Bought and received from *Daniel Trader,* 300 Stone of Iron, at 3 *s.* 4 *d. per* Stone, is 50 *l.* whereof I have paid him 32 *l.* 10 *s.* the Remainder, 17 *l.* 10 *s.* he owes me by his Account. Total ——————————————— | 50 | o | o |

Bought upon 'forehand Baigain, from Mr. *Andrew Cochran,* to be delivered to me the 1ſt of *July* next, 24 Barrels of Raiſins, at 1 *l.* 10 *s. per* Barrel, is 36 *l.* whereof

		l.			
Advanced him on the Bargain, in Caſh ———————		16			
The Remainder payable at Delivery, is———————		20			
		36	36	o	o

P

June

	l.	*s.*	*d.*

——————— *June* 6th. ———————

Paid to Mr. *David Johnſtone* what I owed him, in manner following, *viz.*

Given in Caſh ———————————————— *l.* 117
Allowed me Diſcount for 5 Months Advance ———— 3

	120			

	120	o	o

——————— 7th. ———————

Sold and delivered to *John Paton* 10 Bales of *French* Paper, (N°. 1.) at 4 *l.* 18 *s.* ℔ Bale, payable in 10 Months; by his Bill, is ————————————————————

	49	o	o

Sold upon 'forehand Bargain to *John Houſton*, 13 Barrels of Raiſins, at 1 *l.* 15 *s.* 8 *d.* ℔ Barrel, is 23 *l.* 3 *s.* 8 *d.* to be delivered on the 10th of *July* next.

	l.	*s.*	*d.*

Advanced me on the Bargain, in Caſh ————— 13　3　8
The Remainder payable in 20 Days after Delivery ——————————————— 10　0　0

	23	3	8

	23	3	8

Received from *John Hutcheſon*, for what he owes me upon *John Hauſton*'s Aſſignment, in Caſh ——————

	6	o	o

——————— 10th. ———————

Paid to *Peter Chapman* what I ow'd him, thus: Given him,
2 Pieces *Broad-Cloth*, N°. 1. qt. 20 Yds. each, at 18 *s* is *l.* 36
2 Pieces *Ditto*, N°. 2. qt. 18 Yds. each, at 15 *s.* is ——27
Caſh ———————————————————— 9

	72			

	72	o	o

——————— 12th. ———————

Bought on 'forehand Bargain from Mr. *William Wallace*, 20 Bales of *French* Paper, at 3 *l.* 16 *s.* ℔ Bale, to be delivered the 1ſt of *Auguſt.*

Given him ℔ Advance, 100 Yds. of *Holland*, at 4 *s.* ℔ Yd. *l.* 20
The Remainder payable at *Martinmas* next, is ———56

	76			

	76	o	o

June

	l.	*s.*	*d.*

——————— *June* 12*th.* ———————

Received of *William Smith,* for Payment of what he owes me, *viz.*

	l.	*s.*
8 Barrels of Figs, at 2 *l.* 10 *s.* ℔ Barrel ———	20	0
The reſt in Caſh, is ———	11	10
	31	10

| | 31 | 10 | 0 |

——————— 15*th.* ———————

Sold on 'forehand Bargain to *William Smith,* 8 Bales of *French* Paper, at 4 *l.* ℔ Bale, to be delivered the 5th of *Auguſt* next.

		l.	
Given me *per* Advance a Bill on *Daniel Trader,* payable on Demand, for ———	*l.*	18	
The reſt payable at Delivery ———		14	
		32	

| | 32 | 0 | 0 |

Sold and delivered to *Peter Chapman,* 18 Barrels of Figs, *viz.* 16 of Nᵣ. 1. and 2 of Nᵣ. 2. at 2 *l.* 17 *s. per* Barrel, is 51 *l.* 6 *s.* in Manner following, *viz.*

	l.	*s*
Received in Caſh ———	15	0
An Aſſignment on Mr. *James Truſtwell,* payable on Demand ———	20	0
The Remainder payable by himſelf in 20 Days———	16	6
	51	6

| | 51 | 6 | 0 |

——————— 18*th.* ———————

Lent to Mr. *Andrew Hunter* upon his Bond, payable at *Martinmas* next.

	l.	*s*	*d.*
The principal Sum in Caſh given, is ———	100	0	0
Intereſt till *Martinmas* at 6 *per Cent.* is ———	2	11	5
	102	11	5

| | 102 | 11 | 5 |

This Day ſhipped on Board the *Hind* of *Montroſe,* in the Harbour of *Aberdeen, James Mariner* Maſter, for *London,* 56 Caſks of *Brandy,* conſigned to Mr. *John Blackwood,* my Factor there, to be diſpoſed of for my Accompt.

P 2　　　　　　　　Value

	l.	*s.*	*l.*	*s.*	*d.*
Value of the 56 Caſks, as they coſt me	156	0			
Paid Charges at Shipping	2	16			
Advanced of the Freight in Caſh	9	0			
	167	16	167	16	0

I have inſured the ſaid Cargo in the Hands of *Alexander Truſty,* at 7 ½ *per Cent.* Premium paid him, is — 11 | 5 | 0

———————— *June* 21ſt. ————————

Bought of *Richard Dick* 2 Butts of Sack, at 15 *l. per* Butt, is 30*l.* paid him in ready Money. The ſame I have alſo ſold to Mr. *David Johnſtone* (who receives it from *Ditto Dick*) at 17 *l. per* Butt, payable in 5 Months, is — 34 | 0 | 0

Ship'd on Board the *Swan* of *Peter-head*, *David Fortune* Maſter, the following Goods for *Rochel*, conſigned to *Daniel Stratton*, my Factor there, to be diſpoſed of for my Account, *viz.*

	l.	*s.*	*d.*
96 Barrels of *Salmons*, coſt	216	0	0
240 Yards of white *Plaidin*, bought (and received) this Day of *Alexander Brigs*, for ready Money	7	0	0
40 Barrels of *Beef* bought this Day of *James Montgomery*, payable in one Month	60	0	0
	283	0	0
Charges at Shipping paid, is	4	16	8
	287	16	8

287 | 16 | 8

———————— 22*d.* ————————

I have lent to *Thomas Speedwell* on Bottomree of his Ship, the *Mary* of *Borrowſtouneſs*, 50*l.* to be paid at her Arrival at *Liſbon* to *Cornelius Mandoli*, my Factor there, with 24 *l.* of Intereſt for my Riſque. Total — 74 | 0 | 0

I have wagered with *John Ramſay*, that the *Britiſh* Parliament will not be adjourned until the firſt of *July* next: (if then) Both of us have conſigned our Money in the Hands of *John Blackadder*. My Conſignment is — 5 | 0 | 0

June

	l.	s.	d.

—————————————— *June 25th*· ——————————————

Bought of Mr. *James Truſtwell* 4 Packs of *Wooll*, Number and Weight as follows, *viz.*

	Stone	℔
Nʳ. 1. containing	18	00
Nʳ. 2. containing	22	14
Nʳ. 3. containing	30	00
Nʳ. 4. containing	25	10

N.B. *In* Scotland *the Stone con-ſiſts of* 16 ℔

Total Groſs ———96 08
Allowed for Tare-- 3
which is near ½℔ ℔ *St.*

93 08 neat Weight, at 10 *s.* 7 *d. per Stone*, is 49 *l.* 9 *s.* 6 *d.* ½, whereof

	l.	s.	d.
Paid in *Caſh*———————	19	9	6½
Given him 6 Barrels of *Figs* (Nʳ. 2.) at 3*l. per* Barrel	18	0	0
The Remainder payable the firſt of *Auguſt* ——	12	0	0
	49	9	6½

	49	9	6½

I have lent to *Hercules Handy* 40 *l.* on Bottomree of his Ship, the *Owner's Good-will*, bound for *Stockholm*, to be paid to me at her ſafe Return to *Aberdeen*, with 10 *l.* Intereſt ———·——— — 50 0 0

Wagered againſt *Thomas Murray* 10 *l.* upon a private Circumſtance, to be determined by Mr. *Mathew St. Clare*, upon the 12th of *July* next, in whoſe Hands we have conſigned each — 10 0 0

—————————— *28th.* ——————————

I have inſured upon the *Grey-hound* of *Leith*, bound for *Virginia*, the Value of 300*l.* belonging to Mr. *James Dickſon*, and have received the Premium, being at 15 *per Cent.* —— —— — 45 0 0

Bought for ready Money 20 Packs of *Sheep Skins*, at 2 *l.* 13 *s.* 4 *d. per* Pack, is——————————— — 53 6 8

July

	l.	*s.*	*d.*

——————— *July* 2*d.* ———————

Received of Mr. *Andrew Cochran*, in Performance of our forehand Bargain, 24 Barrels of *Raiſins*, at 1 *l.* 10 *s.* (marked Nʳ. 2) ——— ——— ——— ——— ——— | 36 | 0 | 0

Paid him the Remainder of the Price in Caſh ——— ——— | 20 | 0 | 0

Bought upon 'fore-hand Bargain from *Daniel Trader*, 100 Yards of *Holland*, at 5 *s. per* Yard, to be delivered to me on the 20th inſtant, under the Penalty of 5 *l.* ——— ——— ——— | 25 | 0 | 0

He owes me already by an Aſſignment, which diſcompts
ſo much of the Price——— ——— ——— ———*l.*18
The Remainder payable at Delivery——— ——— ——— 7
                                                                                   ———
                                                                                   25

——————— *4th.* ———————

Shipped on Board the *Succeſs* of *Aberdeen*, *John Kennedy* Maſter, the following Goods, entruſted to the Management of Mr. *Quintin Malcolm*, as Super-Cargo, bound in the firſt Place for *Bourdeaux*, with a Power to him to carry them to any other Port of *France*, where he can make the beſt Market.

                                                                 l.   *s.*   *d.*
Shipped 12 Barrels of *Salmons* (Nʳ. 1.) at 2 *l.* 5 *s.*
   per Barrel——— ——— ———   ——— ——— 27   0   0
4 Packs of *Wooll*, neat Weight 93 *Stone* 8 ℔ ——— 49 09 6½
                                                                          ————————
                                                                          76 09 6½
Paid Charges at Shipping ——— ——— ——— ——— 2 08 0
                                                                          ————————
                                                                          78 17 6½ | 78 | 17 | 6½

This Day I have received certain Advice that the *Owner's Good-will*, belonging to *Hercules Handy*, is loſt on her Way to *Stockholm*, on Bottomree of which I had lent Money

Principal and Intereſt is ——— ——— ——— ——— | 50 | 0 | 0

——————— *10th.* ———————

Shipped on Board the *Wild-Cat* of *Aberdeen*, *G. S.* Maſter, for *Amſterdam*, 20 Packs of *Sheep Skins*, conſigned to *Herman Van Rimer*, Factor there, to ſell for my Account

                                                                                          The|

	l.	*s.*	*d.*	*l.*	*s.*	*d.*
The Value of the Skins	53	6	8			
Charges at Shipping paid	3	0	0			
	56	6	8	56	6	8

July 10*th.*

I have Inſured on the *Unicorn* of *Pittenweem, David Lyon*
Maſter, bound for *Leghorn,* the Value of 100 *l.* belonging to
Archibald Cockburn.
Received the Premium in *Caſh* — — — — — — — — 12 | 0 | 0

12*th.*

Delivered to *John Houſton,* in Performance of a 'fore-hand
Bargain, 13 Barrels of *Raiſins,* (N.̃ 2.) at 1 *l.* 15*s.* 8*d. per*
Barrel — — — — — — — — — 23 | 3 | 8
I have ſold and delivered him 6 Barrels more (N.̃ 2.) at the
ſame Price, payable the ſecond of *Auguſt* — — — 10 | 14 | 0

I have loſt the Wager with *Thomas Murray,* this Day deter-
mined againſt me by Mr. *Matthew St. Clare.* My Loſs is — 10 | 0 | 0

This Day I gained and received 15 *l.* by wagering upon a
Horſe Race — — — — — — — — — 15 | 0 | 0

I have Advice from *John Blackwood,* my Factor at *London,*
that he has received from on Board the *Hind* of *Aberdeen,* my
56 Caſks of *Brandy,* value — — — — — — — 179 | 1 | 0

15*th.*

This Day I received of *John Blackader* 10 *l.* having gained the
Wager againſt *John Ramſay,* the Parliament not being adjourned 10 | 0 | 0

16*th.*

I have inſured upon the *Speedwell* of *Leith, Nicholas Armſtrong*
Maſter, bound for *Aleppo,* the Value of 600 *l.* at 15 *l. per Cent.*
Premium is 90 *l.* for which I have an accepted Bill on *Jeremy*
Thomſon, payable in three Months — — — — — — 90 | 0 | 0

July

	l.	*s.*	*d.*

——————————— *July* 16*th.* ———————————

Received Advice from *Cornelius Mandoli*, Factor at *Liſbon*, that he has received from *Thomas Speedwell*, Maſter of the Ship, the *Mary* of *Stonebive*, 74 *l.* which I had lent on Bottomree, being 222 *Milrees*, at 6 *s.* 8 *d. per Milree* —————— **74** | **0** | **0**

——————————————— 20*th.* ———————————————

Sold to *James Stevenſon* two Pieces of *Broad-Cloath*, (N^r. 2.) meaſuring 18 Yards each, at 16 *s. per* Yard, for which I have an Aſſignment on *Gideon Keith*, payable in two Months——— **28** | **16** | **0**

——————————————— 22*d.* ———————————————

I have this Day required *Daniel Trader* to deliver me the 100 Yards of *Holland* formerly bought, which he cannot perform, therefore I charge him for the Value, 25 *l.* and Penalty, 5 *l.* Total ——————————————————————— **30** | **0** | **0**

Received Advice from *John Blackwood*, my Factor at *London*, that he hath ſold 20 Caſks of my *Brandy* for 6 *l. per* Caſk, and received ready Money, neat Proceeds, deducting Charges——— **120** | **0** | **0**

——————————————— 25*th.* ———————————————

I have taken of *Peter Chapman*, for Payment of 16 *l.* 6 *s.* which he owes me, 18 *French Louis d'Ors.*——————— **16** | **6** | **0**

I have wagered againſt *Simeon Wilful*, that there will be no Peace concluded between *Britain* and *Spain* before the 10th of *Auguſt* next ; each has engaged on Parole, for——————— **6** | **0** | **0**

——————————————— 28*th.* ———————————————

I have diſpoſed of the 18 *Louis d' Ors* which I took of *Peter Chapman* for 16 *l* 6 *s.* and have received for them ————— **17** | **11** | **0**

——————————————— 30*th.* ———————————————

I have certain Advice, that the *Unicorn* of *Pittenweem* is caſt away, and the Cargo loſt, in her Way to *Leghorn*, on which I had inſured the Value of 100 *l.* whereupon I have this Day paid to *Archibald Cockburn* 80 *l.* and he has diſcharged me ——— **80** | **0** | **0**

Auguſt

	l.	*s.*	*d.*
―――――― *Auguſt* 1ſt. ――――――			
Sold for Ready Money 10 Hhds of *Claret Wine*, viz. 2 of Nᵣ. 2. at 10 *l. per* Hhd, and 8 of Nᵣ. 3. at 14 *l. per* Hhd. Total	132	0	0
Bought 4 Hhds of *White Wine*, at 9 *l. per* Hhd, paid in Caſh―	36	0	0

Bought of Mr. *David Johnſtone* 3 Pieces of *Broad Cloth*, viz.

		l.	*s.*			
Nᵣ. 1. contains 25 Yds. at 14 *s.* is ―――――	17	10			
Nᵣ. 2. 30 Yds. at 16 *s.* 8 *d.* is ―――	25	0			
Nᵣ. 3. 18 Yds. at 12 *s.* is ―――――	10	16			

73 Value――53 6	53	6	0

For which I have given him a Bill payable the 1ſt of *October* next.

――――――――― 3*d.* ―――――――――

	l.	*s.*	*d.*
This Day Mr. *William Wallace* has delivered to me 20 Bales of *French Paper* formerly bought ――― ―――― ―――	76	0	0
For Payment of part he has taken my Aſſignment on *William Smith*, payable on Demand ―― ――― ―――	6	0	0

Delivered to *William Smith* 6 Bales of *Paper* formerly ſold, both being content that the 6 Bales make good the Bargain which was for 8 Bales.

The 6 Bales delivered worth ――― ――*l.* 24		
The 2 Bales retained by me ――― ――― 8		

	l.	*s.*	*d.*
32	32	0	0

Received Advice from Mr. *Quintin Malcolm*, Super-Cargo on Board the *Succeſs* of *Aberdeen*, that he has got Safe to *Bourdeaux*, and ſold for Ready Money, my 12 Barrels of *Salmons*, the neat Proceeds whereof, (all Charges, with 10 *l.* Freight paid) amounts to 160 Crowns, at 56 *d. per* Crown, is 37 *l.* 6 *s.* 8 *d.* for which he has ſhipp'd, by my Order, 7 Hhds *Claret Wine*, to be brought home ――― ――― ――― ―――

	l.	*s.*	*d.*
	37	6	8

Q *Auguſt*

	l.	*s.*	*d.*

————————— *Auguſt* 5th. —————————

Drawn upon *John Blackwood*, my Factor at *London*, 100 *l.*
payable to *Chriſtopher Higgins*, or Order, upon Sight, for which
I have received Ready Money, with 2 *l.* for the Exchange; in
all ———— ———— ———— ———— ———— ———— | 102 | 0 | 0 |

————————— 8th. —————————

Received of *John Houſton* 20 *Carolus's* of Gold, which I have
taken at 23 *s.* a Piece, in all 23 *l.* on account of what he ow'd
me for *Raiſins* ———— ———— ———— ———— | 23 | 0 | 0 |

I have delivered the 20 *Carolus's* of Gold, which I took of *John
Houſton* at 23 *s.* to *Alexander Black*, in part of my Debt, for
22 *s.* 6 *d.* is 22 *l.* 10 *s.* ———— ———— ———— | 22 | 10 | 0 |

I have Advice from *Herman Van Rymer*, my Factor at
Amſterdam, that he hath received from on Board the *Wild Cat*,
of *Aberdeen*, 18 Packs of *Sheep Skins* for my Account (the remaining 2 Packs of the 20 which I ſhipp'd being loſt at Sea)
and that he hath alſo ſold 10 Packs thereof for Ready Money,
which, by his Account, deducting Charges, Proviſion, and
Freight paid, amounts to 436 $\frac{4}{11}$ Guilders, at 22 *d.* per Guilder,
is 40 *l.*
  The total Charge of the Voyage is ———— *l.* 56 6 8 | 56 | 6 | 8 |
  The Amount of the 10 Packs ſold, is ———— ———— | 40 | 0 | 0 |

————————— 10th. —————————

Received Advice from *Daniel Stratton*, my Factor at *Rochel*,
that he hath received from on Board the *Swan*, of *Peterhead*,
my Goods conſigned to him, all in good Order, *viz.*

	l	*s.*	*d.*
8 Laſts of *Salmons* ———— ————	216	0	0
40 Barrels of *Beef* ———— ————	60	0	0
280 Yards of *White Plaiden* ————	7	0	0
The Charges of the Voyage ſtated to that Account,			
is ———— ———— ———— ————	4	16	8

287 16 8 | 287 | 16 | 8 |

Received Advice from *Cornelius Mandoli*, my Factor at *Liſbon*,
that he hath ſhipp'd by my Order, and for my Account, 50
Barrels of *Raiſins*, on Board the *Red Lion* of *Montroſe*, *M. S.*
Maſter; which, with all Charges and his Proviſion, are worth
222 *Millrees*, at 6 *s.* 8 *d.* ———— ———— | 74 | 0 | 0 |

Auguſt

	l.	*s.*	*d.*
─────── *Auguſt* 13*th.* ───────			
I have wagered on Parole againſt Mr. *John Juſtice,* upon a private Affair, to be determined by Mr. *John Mein*; the Hazard is	10	0	0
I have lent to *Laurence Lovemoney,* upon Bottomree of his Ship, the *Faulcon* of *Aberdeen,* bound from thence to *Genoa,* 60 *l.* to be repaid to me at his ſafe Return, with 20*l.* for my Riſque ─────	80	0	0
────────── 14*th.* ──────────			
I have paid Mr. *James Truſtwell* what I owed him for *Wool*; thus: I have given him 100 Yards of *Holland* (N'. 1.) at 3 *s.* 6 *d. per* Yd. is 18 *l.* 6 *s.* 8 *d.* and he has given me in the Surplus, *viz.*			

	l.	*s.*	*d.*
My Debt due to him, is ───────────	12	0	0
The Surplus received, is ─────────	6	6	8
	18	6	8

	l.	*s.*	*d.*
(carried out)	18	6	8
Received of *Gideon Keith,* Payment of *James Stevenſon*'s Bill on him, in Ready Money ───────────	28	16	0
I have Advice from *John Blackwood,* my Factor at *London,* that he hath ſold the Remainder of my *Brandy, viz.* 56 Caſks for Ready Money; the neat Proceeds whereof, deducting all Charges and Proviſion, as by his Account, amounts to────	200	0	0
────────── 15*th.* ──────────			
Received Advice from *Herman Van Rymer,* Factor at *Amſterdam,* that he hath ſold for Ready Money, for my Account, 8 Packs of *Sheep Skins,* the neat Proceeds of which, by his Account, amounts to 400 *Guilders,* at 22 ½ *d. per Guilder,* is ─────	37	10	0
Drawn by me upon *John Blackwood,* Factor at *London,* for my Account, 20*l.* payable to *J. R.* which he has paid ─────	20	0	0
────────── 16*th.* ──────────			
Received from on Board the *Leopard* of *Aberdeen,* the following Goods, conſigned to me by *Hero Moy* at *Amſterdam,* to ſell for his Account, *viz.*			

Q 2   Received

Received	Charges paid				*l.*	*s.*	*d.*
		l.	*s.*	*d.*			
8 Packs of *Flanders Flax*	Petty Cuſtoms————	2	10	0			
40 Dozen of *Wooll-Cards*	Shore Dues ————	0	18	0			
50 ℔ Weight of *Bohea Tea*	Carriage ————	0	6	8			
		3	14	8	3	14	8

———— *Auguſt* 16th. ————

Drawn upon *Herman Van Rymer*, my Factor at *Amſterdam*, 436 *Guilders*, payable to *John Beaver*, or Order, upon Sight, for which I have received Ready Money, at 22 ¼ *d. per Guilder* — 40 | 8 | 5

———— 19th. ————

I have loſt the Wager (which was on Parole) with Mr. *John Juſtice*, this Day, determined againſt me by Mr. *John Mein*, and have given him in Caſh ———— 10 | 0 | 0

I have gained the Wager (which was on Parole) againſt *Simeon Wilful*, there being no Peace concluded between *Britain* and *Spain* , received in Caſh———— 6 | 0 | 0

———— 20th. ————

Sold for Ready Money, for the Account of *Hero Moy*, 8 Packs of *Flanders Flax*, at 4 *l. per* Pack, is———— 32 | 0 | 0

Remitted to *Hero Moy*, for his Account, 20 *l.* in the Bills of *John Duncanſon*, on *Maurice Moliere*, payable at 10 Days ſight, which I have paid to ditto *Duncanſon*, being 208⅖ *Guilders*, at 23 *d. per Guilder.* ———— 20 | 0 | 0

Received this Day from on Board a Bark of *Inverneſs*, from *London*, the following Goods, with the Bill of Loading incloſed in his firſt Letter of Advice come with them, which *John Blackwood*, my Factor there, hath ſent me, by my Order, and in return for my Account of *Brandy*, ſold by him, *viz.*

		l.	*s.*			
6 Pieces of *Muſlin*, 40 Yards each, at 5 *s. per* Yard —		120	0			
His Charges and Proviſion ————		3	10			
		123	10		123	10	0

Paid Freight and Charges here ———— | | | 15

Auguſt

	l.	*s.*	*d.*

--------- *Auguſt* 22d. ---------

Received Advice from *Daniel Stratton*, my Factor at *Rochel*, that he hath ſold on Time, for my Account, to ſundry Perſons, 8 Laſts of *Salmon*, the Neat Proceeds of which (deducting all Charges, with the Freight upon the whole Cargo cleared by him) amounts to 1500 Crowns, at 4 *s. per* Crown, is —— | 300 | 0 | 0 |

Bought upon 'forehand Bargain, from *Thomas Dalziel*, 100 Bolls of *Wheat*, to be deliver'd me the firſt of *November* next, at 1 *l.* 10 *s per* Boll, is 150 *l.*

Advanced him on the Bargain ——————— *l.* 10			
The Remainder payable at *Martinmas*——————— 140			
150	150	0	0

Drawn upon *Herman Van Rymer*, my Factor at *Amſterdam*, 400 Guilders, at 22 ½ *d. per* Guilder, is 37 *l.* 10 *s.* payable to Mr. *Andrew Cochran*, or Order, at ſingle Uſance, for the Value to be paid by him to me in one Month——————— | 37 | 10 | 0 |

--------- 23d. ---------

Sold for the Account of *Hero Moy*, 40 Dozen of *Wooll Cards*, at 16 *s. per* Dozen, to *Peter Chapman*, payable in 20 Days —— | 32 | 0 | 0 |

Received Advice from Mr. *Quintin Malcolm*, my Super-Cargo on board the *Succeſs*, of *Burnt-Iſland*, that having left *Bourdeaux*, he is ſafe at *Rochel* ; and that he has conſign'd my 4 Packs of Wool, in the Hands of *Daniel Stratton*, my Factor there ; being ready himſelf to ſail homewards : Value of the Wool, as formerly charged, with a Part of the Freight and Expences, is—— | 55 | 9 | 6½ |

--------- 24th. ---------

I have certain Advice that the *Red Lion* of *Leith*, is loſt, with her whole Cargo ; on board of which I had 50 Barrels of *Raiſins*, from *Lisbon* ; Value ——————— | 74 | 0 | 0 |

--------- 26th. ---------

Having received a Letter from *Charles Chareu*, at *Bourdeaux*, adviſing me that he is content to embrace my Propoſal of keeping an Account of Exchange betwixt us, each for ¼, I have in Purſuance thereof, remitted to him this Day, a Bill, the Draught of *Peter Stewart*, upon *Elias Morgan*, for 400 Crowns, payable upon Sight, to *Ditto Chareu* ; the Value whereof I have paid in Caſh to *Ditto Stewart*, at 56 *d. per* Crown, is ——————— | 93 | 6 | 8 |

Auguſt

	l.	*s.*	*d.*

─────── *Auguſt 26th.* ───────

I have this Day bought a Houſe in *Caſtle-Street*, for 300 *l.* to be paid to Mr. *John Campbel*, in 1 Year : And I am to pay beſides, an Annuity of 3 *l.* payable quarterly to the ſaid *John Campbel*, during the Life of his Mother, and for her behoof ; the firſt Quarter's Payment being due at *Martinmas* next.

		l.	*s.*
Price of the Houſe ───────────		300	0
Firſt Quarter's Payment of the Annuity, due at *Martinmas* next────────────		0	15
		300	15

	300	15	0

The ſaid Houſe is, at preſent, poſſeſs'd by *William Davidſon*, who took it at *Whit-Sunday* laſt, for one Year, for 20 *l.* payable at the two Terms of *Martinmas* and *Whit-Sunday*, by equal Portions ────────────   10   0   0

─────── 29*th.* ───────

I have this Day, by the Death of *D. M.* my Uncle, got a Legacy of an Houſe, in *Broad-Street*, worth 200 *l.* (after the following Legacy is paid) which has ſtood empty ſince *Whit-Sunday* laſt ───────────   200   0   0

But I am, by the ſaid Will, to pay a Legacy of 30 *l.* to Mr. *Thomas Richman*, at *Martinmas* next ────────   30   0   0

I have bought ⅓ of the Ship the *Dragon*, of *Aberdeen*, of *Thomas Dalziel*, for 100 *l.* payable at *Candlemas* next ────   100   0   0

─────── 30*th.* ───────

I have this Day enter'd into Partnerſhip with *Benjamin Barclay*, for an Inland Trade, to be manag'd by him for both our Accounts, each ½, and he to be allow'd 10 *per Cent.* for his Commiſſion, in Purſuance whereof I have given him in Caſh──   20   0   0

Remitted to me by *John Blackwood*, my Factor at *London*, 76 *l.* 10 *s* in his own Bill on Mr *Alexander Gordon*, Merchant in *Aberdeen*, payable in one Month ; accepted ────   76   10   0

	l.	*s.*	*d.*

———————————————*September* 2d. ——————

I have this Day ſhipp'd on board the *Roſe*, of *Kinghorn*, *J. C.* Maſter, bound for *Amſterdam*, the following Goods, by Order of *Hero Moy*, at *Amſterdam*, and for his Account, *viz.*

		l.	*s.*			
4 Packs of Sheep-ſkins, for which I have this Day paid in Caſh ————————		12	0			
Charges at buying and ſhipping paid ————		2	15			
My Proviſion ————————		0	15			
		15	10	15	10	0

By the Death of a Friend, I have got a Legacy of 50 *l.* payable in 3 Months, by Mr. *Andrew Cochran*, Executor to the Deceaſed ———————— | 50 | 0 | 0 |

I have taken *John Brown*, Son to Mr. *Adam Brown*, for my Apprentice for 3 Years; for which I have 70 *l.* for his Maintenance and Education, whereof there is,

		l.			
Now paid ————————		20			
The reſt payable in one Year ————————		50			
		70	70	0	0

———————————————— 5th. ————————————

Remitted to me by *Charles Chareu*, for our Account of Exchange, 200 Crowns, at 58 *d.* is 48 *l.* 6 *s.* 8 *d.* the Draught of *Allan Bruyere* on *Andrew Dick*, payable on Sight; which being this Day preſented, I have received Payment ——— | 48 | 6 | 8 |

———————————————— 6th. ————————————

Received from on board the *Succeſs* of *Aberdeen*, arrived from *Bourdeaux*, 7 Hhds. *Claret Wine* (Nº. 4) which Mr. *Quintin Malcolm*, my Super-Cargo for that Voyage, loaded for me at *Bourdeaux*, in Return of my *Salmon* ſold by him there.

		l.	*s.*	*d.*		
The 7 Hhds. charged to the Voyage from *Bourdeaux*, is ————————		37	6	8		
I have paid of Duty and Charges here ———		5	10	0		
		42	16	8	42	16	8

	l.	*s.*	*d.*

———————— *September 7th.* ————————

This Day I have ſhipp'd on board the *Proſperity*, bound for *London*, 50 lb. Weight *Bohea Tea*, belonging to *Hero Moy*, by his Order, conſign'd to *Evander L'Eſtrange*, his Factor at *London*.

	l.	*s.*	*d.*
Paid by me of Charges, ſince his Goods have been in my Cuſtody, beſides what was paid at firſt—	4	14	8
My Proviſion on his whole Account of Goods—	12	0	0
	16	14	8

	l.	*s.*	*d.*
	16	14	8

Paid for 15 Gallons of *Wine*, to fill up the 7 Hhds. of *Claret* from *Bourdeaux* ———— ———— ————

	3	0	0

I have this Day bought and received for the Account of *Chriſtianus Marbach*, at *Rotterdam*, and by his Order, the following Goods, to be ſent to him by the firſt Opportunity, *viz.*

	l.	*s.*
200 Pair of *Stockins*, from *Andrew Cochran*, payable in 4 Months ———— ————	50	0
700 Yards of *Plaiden*, whereof paid————	7	10
The reſt due to *Thomas Richman*, in two Months ———— ————	10	0
Paid Charges ———— ————	0	18
My Proviſion ———— ————	4	0
	72	8

	l.	*s.*	*d.*
	72	8	0

———————— *10th.* ————————

Drawn upon *Charles Chareu*, at *Bourdeaux*, for our Account of Exchange, 500 Crowns, at 57 *d. per* Crown, is 119 *l.* 15 *s.* 10 *d.* payable at ſingle Uſance, to *Anthony Van Helm*, or Order ; the Value whereof I am to receive in one Month, from *Thomas Richman, per* his Bill ———— ———— ————

	119	15	10

I have Advice from *Daniel Stratton*, at *Rochel*, that he hath received Payment of the Debts due for my Salmon, and deſires me to draw for it when I pleaſe, being 1500 Crowns, ſtated at 4 *s.* is ———— ———— ————

	300	0	0

September

	l.	*s.*	*d.*

—————————*September* 11*th.*—————————

Received Advice from *Herman Van Rymer,* my Factor at
Amſterdam, that he hath, by my Order, and for my Account,
bought and ſhipp'd on Board the *Lamb* of *Aberdeen* (then at
Amſterdam) the following Goods, *viz.*

	l.	*s.*	*d.*			
400 Pound Weight of *Coffee* ——— ——— ———	40	0	0			
4 Packs of *Flax,* 18 *Stone* each Pack ———	37	0	0			
His Charges and Proviſion *per* Account ———	8	16	9			
Being 981 Guilders, at 21 *d. per* Guilder ———	85	16	9	85	16	9

—————————13*th.*—————————

Received of *Peter Chapman,* Payment of what he ow'd
for *Hero Moy*'s Account of Goods ; in Caſh ——— ———— | 32 | 0 | 0 |
Hero Moy's Goods being all diſpoſed of, and the Outſtand-
ing Debts pay'd, the Balance of his Account of Goods is ——— | 43 | 10 | 8 |

This Day ſhipp'd on Board the *Mermaid,* *Magnus Black*
Maſter, the *Stockins* and *Linen* bought the 7th of this Month,
for the Account of *Chriſtianus Marbach,* upon which I have ad-
vanced of the Freight to the Owners, and other Charges——— | 6 | 0 | 0 |

I have wager'd againſt *Thomas Arrowſmith,* 10*l.* conſign'd
in the Hands of Mr. *Gabriel Bowman,* that the Ship the
Crocodile of *Aberdeen,* now at *Virginia,* will not be home be-
fore the firſt of *November*——————————— | 10 | 0 | 0 |

—————————15*th.*—————————

Received Payment of Mr. *Alexander Gordon,* of the Bill
Mr. *John Blackwood* remitted me on him, by an Aſſignment
on Mr. *David Johnſton,* payable on Demand ——————— | 76 | 10 | 0 |

Paid to *James Montgomery,* what I ow'd him for *Beef,* in the
Manner following, *viz.*

| Given him 500 *Stone* of *Iron* (N°. 1.) at 3 *s. per St.* is — *l.* 75 | 75 | 0 | 0 |
| He has given me the Surplus of the Price in Caſh ——— 15 | | | |

Difference I ow'd him ——— ——————— 60

	l.	*s.*	*d.*

——————————————*September* 18*th.*——————————————

Benjamin Barclay advifes me that he has bought for the Account in Company, betwixt us, feveral Goods, to the Value of 60 *l.* whereof my ½ is 30 *l.* of which he has already 20 *l.* and for the other 10 *l.* he has drawn a Bill on me, payable to *Alexander Black,* in two Months, which I have accepted ——— | 10 | 0 | 0 |

Received Advice from *Daniel Stratton,* Factor at *Rochel,* that he hath fold for ready Money, my 40 Barrels of *Beef,* the Neat Proceeds whereof, as *per* Account, is 336 Crowns, at 57 *d.* ——— | 79 | 16 | 0 |

Received further Advice from *Daniel Stratton,* that according to my laft Advice, he has fhipp'd on Board the *Fortune* of *St. Martin's, Pierre Petite* Mafter, bound for *Amfterdam,* confign'd to *Herman Van Rymer,* my 4 Packs of *Wool,* lying in his Hands.

	l.	*s.*	*d.*
The Value, as they ftand already charged ———	55	9	6½
He has paid of Charges, with his Provifion, 6 Crowns, which, at the prefent Exchange of 57 *d.* is ———————	1	8	6
	56	18	0½

Right column: | 56 | 18 | 0½ |

Received of *John Houfton,* in Payment of his Account, in Cafh ——————————————— | 3 | 14 | 0 |

————————————— 22*d.* —————————————

Drawn upon me by *Charles Chareu,* for our Account of Exchange, 300 Crowns, at 57 *d. per* Crown, is 71 *l.* 5 *s.* payable to Mr. *Robert Blackwood,* at fingle Ufance ——————— | 71 | 5 | 0 |

Arrived here, the *Lamb* of *Aberdeen,* from *Amfterdam,* from on Board of which I have received the following Goods fent me by *Herman Van Rymer,* for my Account, *viz.*

	l.	s.	d.		l.	s.	d.
400 *lb.* of *Coffee*, prime Coſt in *Holland*	40	0	0				
74 *Stone* of *Flax* (N^r. 1.)	37	0	0				
Charges and Proviſion	8	16	9				
Total Charge of the Voyage	85	16	9				
I have paid of Freight, and other Expences here	5	0	0				
	90	16	9		90	16	9

I have this Day ſold and delivered the 400 *lb.* weight of *Coffee* to Mr. *Adam Brown*, at 3 *s. per* Pound, payable in 6 Months by his Bill, is ——— | 60 | 0 | 0

——————— *September 25th.* ———————

Received Advice from *Herman Van Rymer*, my Factor at *Amſterdam*, that he hath drawn for my Account upon *Daniel Stratton*, my Factor at *Rochel*, 180 Crowns, which at 56 *d. per* Crown, is 458 2/11 *Guilders*, at 22 *d. per* Guilder ; the Value of each Species in *Engliſh* Money being ——— | 42 | 0 | 0

Drawn upon *Daniel Stratton*, Factor at *Rochel*, for my Account, 100 Crowns, at 57 *d. per Crown*, is 23 *l.* 13 *s.* 4 *d.* payable on Sight, to *David Bromfield*, or Order, for which I have received, *viz.*

	l.	s.	d.				
2 Pieces of *Broad Cloath*, containing 16 Yds. each, at 10 *s. per* Yard, is	16	0	0				
The Reſt in Money	7	13	4				
	23	13	4		23	13	4

Benjamin Barclay has ſold off the Goods in Partnerſhip betwixt us, for 80 *l.* Ready Money, and for my Share he has given me, *viz.*

			l.				
In Caſh			25				
For the reſt, 100 Stone weight of Iron, at 3 *s. per* Stone			15				
			40		40	0	0

——————— *28th.* ———————

Drawn upon me by *Hero Moy* of *Amſterdam*, for his Account, 8 *l.* 8 *d.* payable to Mr. *Robert Clark*, (which I have accepted) at ſingle Uſance ——— | 8 | 0 | 8

October

	l.	*s.*	*d.*
	10	00	

——————————*October 5th.*——————————

Received this Day (with the firſt Advice concerning the ſame) from on Board a *Dutch* Brigantine, the following Goods, which *Chriſtianus Marbach* at *Rotterdam*, by my Order, has ſent me, in return for what, by his Account Current, he ow'd me, *viz.*

	l.	*s.*	*d.*			
4 Pieces of *Holland*, 25 Yds. each, coſt with Charges———	20	0	0			
4 Packs of *Flax*, containing 18 *St.* each ———	36	0	0			
Remitted me a Bill of his own Draught on *George Gordon*, payable in 2 Months, which he has accepted for ———	22	8	0			
	78	8	0			
I have paid of Charges here on the Goods ———	4	12	0			
	83	0	0	83	0	0

Abraham Fairholm has paid what he owed me for *Holland*, in the Manner following, *viz.*

	l.	*s.*	*d.*
I have received in Caſh———	24	0	0
I have rebated him, becauſe he complains he had bad Markets in ſelling it———	2	5	0
	26	5	0

By my Book of Charges of Merchandize, I have paid out ſince the 1ſt of *May* laſt, beſide what is charged to particular Accounts ———	20	0	0
By my Book of Houſhold Expences, I have laid out ſince the 1ſt of *May* laſt ———	30	0	0
There is due, by particular Accounts ſtanding in the Book of Houſhold Expences ———	15	0	0

——————————*7th.*——————————

There is due by me, and payable at *Martinmas* next, to *J. S.* ½ Year's Rent of 2 Cellars———	2	0	0

JOURNAL-

JOURNAL BOOK,

Number 1.

Of me *A. M.* Merchant in *Aberdeen:*

From the Firſt of *May,* 1729.

JOURNAL BOOK.

Number 1.

		l.	*s.*	*d*
	——————*Aberdeen, May* 1, 1729——————			
1	*Sundry Accounts* are *Debtors* to *Stock*, for my whole Effects, and the Debts owing to me, *per* Inventory, *viz.*			
1	*Cash.* ——— ——— ——— ———	800	00	00

						2	*Wine*, for 20 Hogsheads of Claret, of N°. and Prices following, *viz*						

Wine, for 20 Hogsheads of Claret, of N°. and Prices following, *viz*

N°.		*l.*	*s*	*d.*			
1 —— 6 Hogsheads, at 8 *l.* per Hogshead		48	00	00			
2 —— 4 Ditto, at 10 *l.* ——— ——		40	00	00			
3 —— 10 Ditto, at 12 *l.* 10 *s.* —— ——		125	00	00			
		213	00	00	213	00	00

2	*Tobacco*, for 18 Hogsheads of *Virginia*, neat Weight of each 600 ℔. at 11 *l.* 3 *s. per* Hogshead. —— ——	200	14	00
2	*Raisins*, For 30 Barrels, marked N . 1. at 1 *l.* 10 *s. per* Barrel. —— —— —— —— ——	48	00	00

2 | *Broad Cloath*, for 14 Pieces N°. and Prices following.

N°.		*l.*	*s.*	*d*			
1 —— 8 Pieces, 20 Yards each, at 16 *s.* -		128	00	00			
2 —— 6 Pieces, 18 Yards each, at 14 *s.* -		75	12	00			
		203	12	00	203	12	00

3 | Mr *William Wallace*, by Bond, dated the 1*st* of *Feb.* last, payable at *Martinmas* next.

		l.	*s.*	*d.*			
Principal Sum ——— —— ——		100	00	00			
Interest due at *Martinmas* ——— ——		3	5	00			
		103	5	00	103	5	00

3	Mr *Andrew Hunter*, by Ballance of an Account. ———	80	00	00
3	Mr *Andrew Cochran*, by Ballance of Account. —— ——	140	00	00
3	*Moveables* and *Houshold Furniture*, as *per* particular Inventory thereof. ——— ——	200	00	00

May

		l.	*s.*	*d.*

————————— *May 1.* —————————

Stock is *Debtor* to *Sundry Accounts*, for the Debts owing by
me, *viz* To

| 4 | Mr. *David Johnston*, payable the 1st of *Nov.* next. —— —— | 120 | 00 | 00 |
| 4 | Mr *James Trustwell*, on Demand. —— —— | 60 | 00 | 00 |

————————— 2 —————————

| 1/2 | *Cash Debtor* to *Wine*, for 4 Hogsheads of Claret (N°. 1) Sold and delivered to *Alexander Paygood*, at 12 *l* per Hogshead - | 48 | 00 | 00 |

| 4/2 | *William Smith*, *Debtor* to *Broad Cloath*, for 2 Peices (N°. 2) 18 Yards each. Sold and delivered to him, at 17 *s*. 6 *d*. per Yard, payable in 2 Months. —— | 31 | 10 | 00 |

————————— 4. —————————

| 4/5 | *Paper Debtor* to *Peter Chapman*, for 18 Bales (N° 1.) bought and received of him, at 4 *l.* per Bale, payable in 1 Month. - | 72 | 00 | 00 |

————————— 6. —————————

| 4 | *Sundry Accounts Debtors* to *Paper*, for 5 Bales (N°. 1) at 5 *l.* per Bale, is 25 *l.* Sold and delivered to Mr. *John Paton,* *viz.* | | | |

		l.	*s.*	*d*
1	Drs. { *Cash* received —— ——	10	00	00
5	{ *Jo. Paton*, payable in 20 Days —— ——	15	00	00
		25	00	00

| | | 25 | 00 | 00 |

| 5 | *Brandy Debtor* to *Sundry Accounts*, for 32 Casks (N°. 1.) at 3 *l.* per Cask, is 96 *l.* Bought and received from *David Watson, viz.* | | | |

		l.	*s*	*d*
3	Crs { *Cash* paid —— —— ——	16	00	00
1	{ Mr. *Andrew Hunter*, by my Bill ——	80	00	00
		96	00	00

| | | 96 | 00 | 00 |

	l.	*s.*	*d.*

------------------ *May 7.* ------------------

5
2   *Daniel Trader Debtor* to *Wine*, for 3 Hogsheads of Claret, viz. 2 Hogsheads of (N°. 2) and 1 Hogshead (N°. 1.) Sold and delivered to *Elias Freeman*, at 12 *l.* 10 *s.* per Hogshead, for we have an accepted Bill on *Ditto Trader,* payable on Demand. —— —— —— | 37 | 10 | 00 |

------------------ 8 ------------------

2   *Sundry Accounts Debtors* to *Raisins*, for 10 Barrels, (N°. 1.) at 2 *l. per* Barrel, is 20 *l.* Sold and delivered to Mr. *John Houston,* viz

		l.	*s.*	*d.*
1	*Cash* received. —— ——	8	00	00
5	Drs. { *Account of Bills* payable to me, for Bills on Mr *John Hutcheson,* payable in 10 Days ——	6	00	00
5	*John Houston,* payable in 2 Months. —	6	00	00
		20	00	00

| | 20 | 00 | 00 |

5
1   *Brandy Debtor* to *Cash*, for 24 Casks (N°. 2) at 2 *l.* 10 *s.* per Cask   Bought and received of *Jo. Fergusson*. —— | 60 | 00 | 00 |

6   *Iron Debtor* to *Sundry Accounts*, for 1000 Stone (N°. 7) at 3 *s. per* Stone, is 150 *l*   Bought and received of *Alexander Black,* viz.

		l.	*s.*	*d*
3	Crs. { Mr *Andrew Cochran*, by my Bill on him.	100	00	00
6	*Alexander Black*, payable in 3 Months.	50	00	00
		150	00	00

| | 150 | 00 | 00 |

------------------ 11 ------------------

2   *Sundry Accounts Debtors* to *Broad Cloth*, for 6 Pieces (N° 1.) of 20 Yards each, at 17 *s.* 4 *d. per* Yard, is 104 *l.* Sold and delivered to *Thomas Jameson, viz.*

		l.	*s.*	*d*
7	Drs { *Foreign Linnen,* for 12 Pieces of Holland (N° 1) of 25 Yards each, in all 300 Yards received, at 4 *s* per Yard. —	60	00	0
1	*Cash* received —— ——	44	00	00
		104	00	00

| | 104 | 00 | 00 |

May 11

——————————— *May* 11. ———————————

7
2 *Salmons Debtor* to *Raisins*, for 12 Barrels of Salmons (N 1)
at 2 *l.* 5 *s.* per Barrel, cured with *Spanish* Salt, received in
Barter with *Robert White*, for 15 Barrels of Raisins
(N°. 1.) delivered at 1 *l.* 16 *s.* ————   27 | 00 | 00

———————————————————————————

6
7 *Accepted Bills* payable to me, *Debtor* to *Foreign Linnen*, for
4 Pieces of Holland (N°. 1) 25 Yards each, is 100 Yards
Sold and delivered to *Abraham Fairholm* at 5 *s.* 3 *d* per
Yard, payable by him in 5 Months is. ————   ————   26 | 5 | 00

——————————— 14 ———————————

7 *Salmons Debtor* to *Sundry Accounts*, for 8 Lasts (N°. 1) cured
with *Spanish* Salt. Bought and received of Mr *James*
Montgomery, at 2 *l.* 5 *s* per Barrel is 216 *l* viz

		l.	*s.*	*d*
1	Caſh paid. ————	60	00	00
3	Crs { Mr. *Andrew Cochran*, by my Bill ——	40	00	00
7	*Ja. Montgomery*, payable on Demand.	116	00	00

                                              216 00 00 | 216 | 00 | 00

———————————————————————————

1
2 *Caſh Debtor* to *Tobacco*, for 3 Hogſheads at 4 *l.* 14 *s* per
Hogſhead, is. ————   ——   ——   14 | 2 | 00

——————————— 20 ———————————

2 *Sundry Accounts Debtors* to *Tobacco*, for 2 Hogſheads 9 *l* 12 *s*
viz.

		l	*s*	*d*
1	Caſh received. ——— —— ———	2	00	00
6	Drs { *Jo Houſton*, for 4 Barrels of Figs received in Barter of the Tobacco, and ſold to him at 1 *l* 18 *s* per Barrel payable on demand, is ——— —— —	7	12	00

                                                9 12 00 | 9 | 12 | 00

Obſerve The Figs may be entered Both as received, and as
diſpoſed of But there being no Account of Figs yet in
the Leger, this is a more Convenient way, and to the
ſame Purpoſe for the State of the Accounts.

——————— *May* 20. ———————

7 | *Scotch Linnen Debtor* to *Sundry Accounts,* for 750 Yards (N° 1) at 16 *d per* Yard, is 50 *l.* received in Barter with *Ninian Nicholson.* For, *viz*

                                  l.   *s.*   *d.*

6   ⎧ *Iron,* (N°. 1) 200 Stone, delivered at
Crs ⎨   3 *s.* 6 *d per* Stone. ——— ——— 35 00 00
1   ⎩ *Cash.* ——— ——— ——— 15 00 00

                                           50 00 00 | 50 00 00

——————— 24 ———————

4 | *James Trustwell Debtor* to *Cash,* paid him in part. —— —— | 40 00 00
1

1 | *Cash Debtor* to *Daniel Trader,* paid me in part. —— —— | 20 00 00
5

——————— 28 ———————

6 | *Alexander Black Debtor* to *Sundry Accounts,* 15 *l* 2 *s.* 8 *d.* Having received a Bill on him from *Jo. Paton,* for 15 *l.* payable on demand Which he has taken up towards Payment of Part of my Debt to him, which is not payable till 8 *Aug viz.*

                                   l   *s*   *d*

5   ⎧ *Jo. Paton,* for the Contents of the Bill. - 15 00 00
Crs ⎨
8   ⎩ *Profit* and *Loss,* for discount till 8 *Aug* - 00 2 8

                                         15 2 8 | 15 2 8

——————— 30. ———————

8 | *Figs Debtor* to *Cash,* for 16 Barrels (N°. 1) Bought and received for ready Money, at 2 *l* 4 *s. per* Barrel, is —— —— | 35 4 00
1

1 | *Cash Debtor* to *Iron,* for 300 Stone (N°. 1) Sold and delivered for ready Money, at 4 *s. per* Stone. —— —— | 60 00 00
6

7 | *James Montgomery, Debtor* to *Sundry Accounts,* 116 *l* paid him what I owed for Salmons, *viz.*

                                   l.   *s.*   *d.*

1   ⎧ *Cash.* ——— ——— ——— —— 108 8 00
Crs. ⎨
6   ⎩ *Jo. Houston,* by my Bill —— —— 7 12 00

                                         116 00 00 | 116 00 00

June 3.

	l.	*s.*	*d.*

——————— *June* 3. ———————

6 | *Iron* Debtor to *Sundry Accounts,* for 300 Stone (N°. 2) at 3 s. 4 d. per Stone, is 50 l. Bought and received from *Daniel Trader,* viz.

		l	*s.*	*d*
1	Crs. { *Cash* paid. —— —— —— ——	32	10	00
5	{ *Dan. Trader.* —— —— ——	17	10	00
		50	00	00

50 | 00 | 00

8 | *Delivery Account* of *Buying,* Debtor to *Sundry Accounts,* for 24 Barrels of Raisins, at 1 l. 10 s. per Barrel, is 36 l. Bought upon Forehand Bargain, from Mr *Andrew Cochran,* to be delivered the 1st of *July* next, viz.

		l.	*s*	*d.*
1	Crs. { *Cash* advanced. —— ——	16	00	00
3	{ *Andrew Cochran,* payable on delivery -	20	00	00
		36	00	00

36 | 00 | 00

——————— 6. ———————

4 | *David Johnston,* Debtor to *Sundry Accounts,* for 120 l which I have paid him thus, viz.

		l	*s*	*d*
1	Crs { *Cash* paid —— —— ——	117	00	00
8	{ *Profit* and *Loss,* discounted to me ——	3	00	00
		120	00	00

120 | 00 | 00

——————— 7 ———————

5/4 | *John Paton,* Debtor to *Paper,* for 10 Bales (N°. 1) Sold and delivered to him, at 4 l. 18 s per Bale, payable in 10 Months.

49 | 00 | 00

9 | *Sundry Accounts,* Debtors to *Delivery Account* of *Selling,* for 13 Barrels of Raisins, at 1 l. 15 s. 8 d per Barrel, is 23 l. 3 s. 8 d. Sold upon Forehand Bargain, to *John Houston,* to be delivered the 10th of *July* next, viz

		l	*s*	*d*
1	{ *Cash,* received. —— ——	13	3	8
6	Drs. { *John Houston,* payable 20 days after delivery. —— —— ——	10	00	00
		23	3	8

23 | 3 | 8

June 7.

			l.	s.	d.

— *June* 7. —

1/6   *Cash Debtor to Account* of *Bills*-payable to me, received from *John Hutchison.* —   6 | 00 | 00

— 10. —

5   *Peter Chapman,* Debtor to *Sundry Accounts,* for Payment I have made him, *viz.*

		l.	s.	d.
c	Broad Cloth { 2 Pieces (N°. 1.) 20 Yd. each, at 18 s. is —	36	00	00
2	{ 2 Pieces (N°. 2.) 18 Yd. each, at 15 s. is —	27	00	00
		63	00	00
1	Crs. { Cash. —	9	00	00
		72	00	00

72 | 00 | 00

— 12. —

8   *Delivery Account* of *Buying,* Debtor to *Sundry Accounts,* for 20 Bales of Paper, at 3 l. 16 s. per Bale, is 76 l. Bought upon Forehand Bargain, from Mr. *William Wallace,* to be delivered the 1st of *Aug.* next, *viz.*

		l.	s.	d.
7	Crs. { Foreign Linnen, for 4 Pieces of Holland (N°. 1.) 25 Yards each, is 100 Yards, given of Advance, at 4 s. per Yard. -	20	00	00
2	{ W. Wallace, payable at *Martinmas* next.	56	00	00
		76	00	00

76 | 00 | 00

4   *Sundry Accounts Debtors* to *William Smith,* 31 l. 10 s. Having paid what he owes me, *viz.*

		l.	s.	d.
8	Drs { Figs, for 8 Barrels (N°. 2.) at 2 l. 10 s. is —	20	00	00
1	{ Cash. —	11	10	00
		31	10	00

31 | 10 | 00

June 15.

		l.	s	d.

—————— *June* 15. ——————

9 | *Sundry Accounts, Debtors* to *Delivery Account* of *Selling*, for 8 Bales of Paper, at 4*l.* per Bale, is 32*l.* Sold upon Fore-hand Bargain, to *William Smith*, to be delivered the 5th of *Aug.* next, *viz.*

		l.	s	d
5	Drs. { *Daniel Trader, per* Bill on him, on demand. ——— ———	18	00	00
4	{ *Will Smith*, payable upon delivery. -	14	00	00
		32	00	00

32 00 00

8 | *Sundry Accounts Debtors* to *Figs*, for 18 Barrels, *viz.* 16 of (N°. 1) and 2 of (N°. 2) at 2*l.* 17*s.* per Barrel, is 51*l* 6*s.* Sold and delivered to *Peter Chapman, viz.*

		l.	s	d
1	Drs. { *Cash* received. —— —— —	15	00	00
4	{ Mr. *James Trustwell, per* Bill on him, payable on demand —— —	20	00	00
5	{ *Peter Chapman*, payable in 20 days. —	16	6	00
		51	6	00

51 6 00

—————— 18. ——————

3 | *Andrew Hunter, Debtor* to *Sundry Accounts*, for principal Sum lent him upon his Bond of this date, with the Interest due at the Term of Payment, *viz.*

		l	s.	d.
1	Crs { *Cash*, principle Sum lent, payable at *Martinmas* next. —— ——	100	00	00
8	{ *Profit* and *Loss*, for the Interest due at the Term of Payment, at 6 *per* Cent. — —— ——	2	11	5
		102	11	5

102 11 5

9 | *Voyage* to *London* in the *Hind* of *Aberdeen, J. M. Master, Debtor* to *Sundry Accounts*, for the following Goods and Charges, shipped for my Account in the said Ship, to be consigned to *John Blackwood*, Factor there, *viz.*

S   Crs.

		l.	s.	d.	l.	s.	d.

5   *Brandy,* for 56 Casks (N°. 1. and 2.)   156   00   00

Crs {

1   *Cash,* for Charges ———   l.   s.   d.   2   16   00

Advanced Freight. ——   9   00   00   23   01   00

Insurance, in the Hands

of *A. Trusty,* at 7½.-   11   5   00

                                179   1   00   179   1   00

——————— *June* 21. ———————

4   Mr. *David Johnston,* Debtor to *Sundry Accounts,* 34 *l* for two *Butts* of *Sack,* which I this Day bought of *Richard Duke* for ready Money, and sold to *Ditto Johnston.* Who received the same from *R. D viz.*

                                                l   s.   d.

1   Crs { *Cash* paid for the Sack.   ——— ———   30   00   00

8   *Profit* and *Loss*   Gained by the Sale. -   4   00   00

                                                34   00   00   34   00   00

9   *Voyage* to *Rochel,* in the *Swan* of *Peter-Head,* D F *Master* Debtor to *Sundry Accounts,* for the following Goods, shipped for my Account in the said Ship, to be consigned to *Daniel Stratton,* Factor there, *viz.*

                                                l.   s.   d.

7   *Salmons,* for 8 Last (N°. 1.) Cost - -   216   00   00

1   Crs { *Cash,* paid for 240 Yards *Plaidin,* to *Alex. Brigs,* with Charges on the whole ——— ———   11   16   8

7   *James Montgomery,* for 40 Barrels of Beef, this Day received of him, payable in 1 Month. ——— ———   60   00   00

                                                287   16   8   287   16   8

——————— 22. ———————

9   *Bottomree Account,* Debtor to *Sundry Accounts,* for 74 *l* the Principal and Interest lent to *Thomas Speedwell,* on *Bottomree* of his Ship the *Mary* of *Stone-Hyve,* to be paid at her safe Arrival at *Lisbon,* to *Cornelius Mandole,* my Factor there, *viz.*

                                                                Crs.

		l.	*s.*	*d.*	*l.*	*s*	*d.*

1	Crs. { *Caſh* lent. ——— ——— ——— ———	50	00	00			
8	{ *Profit* and *Loſs*, for the Intereſt. —— —	24	00	00			
		74	00	00	74	00	00

——————— *June* 22. ———————

9	*Wager's Account, Debtor* to *Caſh*, conſigned in the Hands of
1	*J. B.* upon a Wager againſt *John Ramſay*, that the *Britiſh*
	Parliament will not be adjourned before the 1ſt of *July*
	next. ——— ——— ——— ———				5	00	00

——————— 25. ———————

10 | *Account of Wooll, Debtor* to *Sundry Accounts*, for 4 Packs, Nᵒ.
and Prices following. Bought and received of Mr *James*
Truſtwell, viz.

Nᵒ.		Stone.	℔.
1	Contains	18	00
2	———	22	14
3	———	30	00
4	———	25	10
	Total	96	8	Groſs.
	Allowed for Tare.	3	00	
		93	08	Neat Weight.

Which at 10 *s.* 7 *d.* per Stone, is 49 *l* 9 *s* 6 *d.* $\frac{1}{4}$ *viz.*

		l	*s*	*d.*			
1	{ *Caſh* paid ——— ——— ———	19	9	6$\frac{1}{4}$			
8	Crs. { *Figs*, 6 Barrels (Nᵒ. 2) at 3 *l* per B.	18	00	00			
4	{ *Ja Truſtwell*, payable the 1ſt of *Aug.*	12	00	00			
		49	9	6$\frac{1}{4}$	49	9	6$\frac{1}{4}$

9 | *Bottomree Account, Debtor* to *Sundry Accounts*, for 50 *l* Prin-
cipal and Intereſt, lent to *Hercules Handy*, upon *Bottomree*
of his Ship, the *Owner's Goodwill* Bound for *Stockholm*,
to be paid to me at her ſafe return to *Aberdeen, viz*

		l	*s.*	*d.*			
1	{ *Caſh* lent ——— ——— ———	40	00	00			
8	Crs. { *Profit* and *Loſs*, for the Intereſt. ———	10	00	00			
		50	00	00	50	00	00

————————— *June 25.* —————————

		l.	s	d.

9/1 *Wager's Account, Debtor* to *Cash,* consigned in the Hands of Mr. *Matthew St Clare,* in a Wager against *Thomas Murray,* upon a private Affair, to be determined the 12*th* of *July* next. — ▪ — ▪ — ▪ — ▪

10 00 00

————————— 28. —————————

1/10 *Cash Debtor* to *Insurance Account,* for Præmium of Insurance of 300 *l* upon the *Grey-bound* of *Leith,* bound for *Virginia,* the Præmium at 15 *per Cent,* is ——— ———

45 00 00

10/1 *Sheep-Skins, Debtor* to *Cash,* for 20 Packs, at 2 *l.* 13 *s.* 4 *d* per Pack. Bought for ready Money, is ———

53 6 8

————————— *July 2.* —————————

2/8 *Raisins, Debtor* to *Delivery Account of Buying,* for 24 Barrels (Nº 2.) received from Mr. *Andrew Cochran,* in performance of a Forehand Bargain, at 1 *l* 10 *s per* Barrel. ———

36 00 00

3/1 Mr. *Andrew Cochran, Debtor* to *Cash,* paid him. ———

20 00 00

8/5 *Delivery Account of Buying, Debtor* to *Daniel Trader,* for 5 Pieces of Holland of 20 Yards each, is 100 Yards Bought of him at 5 *s. per* Yard, to be delivered the 20*th* of *July* next, under Penalty of 5 *l.* ——— ———

25 00 00

————————— 4. —————————

10 *Voyage to Bordeaux,* in the *Success* of *Aberdeen, J K Master, Debtor* to *Sundry Accounts,* for the following Goods shipped upon my Account, committed to the Care of Mr. *Quintin Malcolm* Supra-Cargo Bound first for *Bordeaux,* with a Power to carry them to any other Port of *France,* where he can make the best Market, *viz.*

		l.	s.	d.			
7	⌠ *Salmons,* for 12 Barrels (Nº. 1) at 2 *l.* 5 *s. per* Barrel, is ——— ———	27	00	00			
10	Crs ⎨ *Wooll,* 4 Packs, Neat Weight 93 Stone 8 ℔. at 10 *s.* 7 *d per* Stone. ———	49	9	6½			
10	⌡ *Cash,* for Charges at Shipping. ———	2	8	00			

		l.	s	d.
		78	17	6½

78 17 6½

July 4

		l.	*s.*	*d.*

——————— *July* 4. ———————

| 8/9 | *Profit* and *Loſs, Debtor* to *Bottomree Account,* for the Principal and Intereſt lent to *Hercules Handy* upon his Ship, the *Owner's-Goodwill.* Which is Loſt in her Voyage to *Stockholm.* ——— | 500 | 00 | 00 |

——————— 10. ———————

| 11 | *Voyage* to *Amſterdam* in the *Wild-Cat* of *Aberdeen,* G S *Maſter, Debtor* to *Sundry Accounts,* for the following Goods ſhipped upon my Account and Risk, to be conſigned to *Herman van Rymer,* viz. | | | |

		l	*s.*	*d.*
10	Crs. { *Sheep-Skins,* 20 Packs. ———	53	6	8
10	{ *Caſh,* for Charges. ———	3	00	00
		56	6	8

56 | 6 | 8

| 10/10 | *Caſh, Debtor* to *Inſurance Account,* for the Præmium of Inſuring 100 *l.* to *Archibal Cockburn,* upon the *Unicorn* of *Pitten-Weem* D L *Maſter* Bound for *Leghorn,* Præmium paid. ——— | 1 | 20 | 00 |

——————— 12. ———————

| 2 | *Sundry Accounts, Debtors* to *Raiſins,* for 19 Barrels (N° 2) delivered to *John Houſton,* at 1 *l.* 15 *s* 8 *d.* per Barrel, is 33 *l* 17 *s.* 8 *d* viz. | | | |

		l.	*s*	*d*
9	Drs { *Delivery Account of Selling,* for 13 Barrels formerly ſold ———	23	3	8
6	{ *Jo. Houſton,* for 6 Barrels now ſold, payable the 2d of *Aug.* ———	10	14	00
		33	17	8

33 | 17 | 8

| 8/9 | *Profit,* &c *Debtor* to *Wager's Account,* the Wager againſt *Thomas Murray* being loſt. ——— | 10 | 00 | 00 |

| 10/9 | *Caſh, Debtor* to *Wager's Account,* gained upon a Horſe-race —— | 15 | 00 | 00 |

| 11/9 | *John Blackwood* of *London* my *Account of Brandy, Debtor* to *Voyage* to *London,* &c. for 56 Casks of Brandy conſigned him, value ——— | 179 | 1 | 00 |

July 15.

		l.	*s.*	*d.*

──────────────── *July 15.* ────────────────

10 / 9 — Cʃh, *Debtor* to *Wager's Account*, received for the Wager gained of *John Ramʃey.* ——— ——— ——— | 10 | 00 | 00.

──────────────── 16. ────────────────

6 / 10 — *Accepted Bills due to me, Debtor* to *Inʃurance Account*, for Præmium of Inʃuring 600 *l.* upon the *Speedwell* of *Leith*, *Nicholas Armʃtrong, Maʃter*, bound for *Aleppo*, which at 15 *l* per *Cent*, is 90 *l* For which I have got an accepted Bill on *Jeremy Thomʃon*, payable in 3 Months. ——— ——— | 90 | 00 | 00

11 / 9 — *Cornelius Mandole* of *Lisbon*, my *Account Current, Debtor* to *Bottomree Account*, for 222 Milrees, which at 6 s 8 d per Milree, is 74 *l* received by him from *Thomas Speedwell* for my Account. ——— | 74 | 00 | 00

──────────────── 20. ────────────────

6 / 2 — *Accepted Bills due to me, Debtor* to *Broad Cloth*, for 2 Pieces (N° 2) contains 18 Yards each, ʃold and delivered to *James Stevenʃon*, at 16 s. per Yard, for which I have an accepted Bill on *Gideon Keith*, payable in 2 Months. ——— | 28 | 16 | 00

──────────────── 22. ────────────────

5 — *Daniel Trader, Debtor* to *Sundry Accounts*, for a 100 Yards of Holland, bought of him upon Forehand Bargain, which he has failed to deliver, *viz*

		l.	*s.*	*d*
8	Crs { *Delivery Account* of *Buying*, for the Value of the Holland. —— ———	25	00	00
8	{ *Profit*, &c for the Penalty. ——— ———	5	00	00

30 00 00 | 30 | 00 | 00

11 / 11 — *John Blackwood* of *London*, my *Account Current, Debtor* to Ditto my *Account of Brandy*, for 20 Casks ʃold for ready Money, the Neat Produce deducting Charges, being ——— ——— | 120 | 00 | 00

──────────────── 25 ────────────────

10 / 5 — *Caʃh Debtor* to *Peter Chapman*, received of him 18 Lewid'ors, for Payment of ——— ——— ——— ——— | 16 | 6 | 00

——————— *July 25.* ———————   *l.* | *s* | *d.*

9/11 | *Wager's Account, Debtor* to *Hazard Account,* for 6 *l.* engaged for upon Parole, in a Wager againſt *Simeon Wilfull,* that there will be no Peace between *Britain* and *Spain,* before the 10*th* of *Aug.* next ——————   6 | 00 | 00

——————— 28. ———————

10/8 | *Caſh Debtor* to *Profit,* &c gain'd by 18 Lewid'ors, which I took for 16 *l.* 6 *s* and have given away for 17 *l.* 11 *s* the Gain is ——————   1 | 5 | 00

——————— 30. ———————

10/10 | *Inſurance Account, Debtor* to *Caſh,* paid to *Archibald Cockburn,* 80 *l* for 100 *l* which I inſured to him upon the *Unicorn* of *Pitten-Weem,* now caſt away in her Voyage to *Leghorn.* ——————   80 | 00 | 00

——————— *Auguſt* 1. ———————

10/2 | *Caſh Debtor* to *Wine,* for 10 Hogſheads of Claret ſold, *viz* 2. of (N° 2.) at 10 *l. per* Hogſhead, and 8 of (N° 3) at 14 *l. per* Hogſhead.   Total ——————   132 | 00 | 00

2/10 | *Wine Debtor* to *Caſh,* for 4 Hogſheads of White-Wine, bought at 9 *l per* Hogſhead, is ——————   36 | 00 | 00

2/4 | *Broad Cloth Debtor* to *David Johnſton,* for 3 Pieces, bought and received of him, payable the 1ſt of *Octob.* next, *viz.* —

N°.   *l.*   *s.*   *d.*
1   Contains 25 Yards each, at 14 *s.* is -   17   10   00
2   ——————   30 Yards each, at 16 *s.* 8 *d.* -   25   00   00
3   ——————   18 Yards each, at 12 *s.* ——   10   16   00
                                           ————————
                                           53   6   00   53 | 6 | 00

——————— 3 ———————

4/8 | *Paper Debtor* to *Delivery Account* of *Buying,* for 20 Bales (N°. 2) received in Performance of Forehand Bargain from *William Wallace.* ——————   76 | 00 | 00

3/4 | *William Wallace, Debtor* to *William Smith, per* my Bill. -   6 | 00 | 00

Auguſt 3.

——————————— *August* 3. ———————————

9 | *Delivery Account* of *Selling, Debtor* to *Sundry Accounts,* for 8 Bales of Paper, formerly fold upon Forehand Bargain to *William Smith* ; whereof I have now delivered 6 Bales ; both being Content to paſs from the other **2** Bales, *viz.*

		l.	*s.*	*d.*
4	Crs {*Paper,* for 6 Bales (N°. 2.) delivered. -	24	00	00
4	{*William Smith,* 2 Bales retained. ——	8	00	00
		32	00	00

32 | **00** | **00**

11 | *Voyage* from *Bourdeaux* in the *Succeſs* of *Aberdeen, Debtor* to
10 | *Voyage* to *Bourdeaux,* &c for 7 Hogſheads of Claret-Wine, loaded for my Account, by *Quintin Malcolm* Supra-Cargo, in return of 12 Barrels of Salmons fold by him there, the neat Proceeds of which is 160 Crowns, at *56 d per* Crown. -

37 | **6** | **8**

——————————— 5. ———————————

10 | *Caſh Debtor* to *Sundry Accounts,* for a Bill drawn by me upon *John Blackwood,* my *Factor* at *London,* payable to *Chriſtopher Higgins* (or Order) upon Sight, preſently paid to me, *viz.*

		l.	*s.*	*d.*
11	Crs {*J. Blackwood,* my *Account Current,* for the Contents of the Bill. ———	100	00	00
8	{*Profit,* &c. for Exchange. —— —	2	00	00
		102	00	00

102 | **00** | **00**

——————————— 8. ———————————

10 | *Caſh Debtor* to *John Houſton,* for 20 Carolus's, received from
6 | him to Account, at 23 *s* a Piece, is —— —— ——

23 | **00** | **00**

10 | *Sundry Accounts Debtors* to *Caſh,* for 20 Carolus's, which I took for 23 *l.* and have again delivered to *Alexander Black,* for 22 *l.* 10 *s.* to Account betwixt us, *viz.*

		l.	*s.*	*d*
6	Drs. {*Alexander Black* —— —— —	22	10	00
8	{*Profit,* &c. Loſt by them. —— —— —	00	10	00
		23	00	00

23 | **00** | **00**

——————— *August* 8. ———————

		l.	s.	d.

$\frac{12}{11}$ *Herman van Rymer* of *Amsterdam*, my *Account* of *Sheep-Skins,*
Debtor to *Voyage* to *Amsterdam,* in the *Wild-Cat* of *Aberdeen,* for 18 Packs, consigned to him (the other 2 Packs shipped being lost at Sea) the Value of the whole 20 Packs being charged to the 18 is —— —— 56 6 8

$\frac{12}{12}$ *Herman van Rymer,* my *Account Current, Debtor to Ditto* my *Account* of *Sheep-Skins,* for 10 Packs sold for ready Money, neat Proceeds of which (deducting Charges and Freight in the whole) *per Account,* is 436$\frac{4}{7}$ Guilders, at 22 d. *per* Guilder, is ——— ——— —— 40 00 00

Observe That a Learner may better understand the Rules of this Art, I shall point out several other ways, that this Transaction may be entered.

1 *Profit, &c* May be *Debtor* for the 2 Packs lost, and my *Account* of *Skins* for the 18 *Voyage* being *Creditor.* The 10 Packs sold being entered as before. Or,

2 *Profit, &c. Debtor* for the 2 Packs lost, my *Account* of *Skins* for the 8 unsold, and my *Account Current* for the 10 sold. And *Voyage Creditor* for the whole. Or,

3 *Ditto* my *Account* of *Skins, Debtor* for 8 Packs, valuing them only as 8 Packs really cost, and my *Account Current Debtor* for 10 Packs as they are sold. Neglecting the 2 Packs lost.

——————— 10. ———————

$\frac{12}{9}$ *Daniel Stratton* of *Rochel,* my *Account* of *Goods per* the *Swan* of *Peterhead, Debtor* to *Voyage* to *Rochel,* &c. for the following Goods consigned to him, and which he has received, as *per* Advice, *viz.*

	l	s.	d
8 Last of Salmons. —— ——	216	00	00
40 Barrels of Beef —— —— ——	60	00	00
240 Yards of *Plaidin.* —— ——	7	00	00
Charges at Shipping. —— —— —	4	16	8
	287	16	8

287 16 8

T

August 10.

		l	*s.*	*d.*

—————————— *August* 10. ——————————

12 / 11 *Voyage* from *Lisbon* in the *Red-Lyon* of *Montross*, *Debtor* to *Cornelius Mandole* of *Lisbon*, my *Account Current*, for 50 Barrels of Raisins. Bought and shipped by him for my Account. Cost (with all Charges and his Provision) 222 Milrees, which at 6 *s.* 8 *d* is ——— ——— ——— **74 00 00**

——————————— 13. ———————————

9 / 11 *Wager's Account*, *Debtor* to *Hazard Account*, for 10 *l.* engaged upon Parole, in a Wager upon a private Affair against Mr *John Justice*, to be determined by Mr. *John Meen.* — **10 00 00**

9 *Bottomree Account*, *Debtor* to *Sundry Accounts*, lent to *Laurence Lovemoney*, upon *Bottomree* of his Ship, the *Faulcon* of *Aberdeen*, bound for *Genoa*, 60 *l.* to be repaid to me at his safe return, with 20 *l.* Interest for the Risk, *viz.*

                               l.   *s.*   *d*

10 Crs. { *Cash*, Principal. ——— ——— ——— 60 00 00
8   { *Profit*, &c. Interest. ——— ——— ——— 20 00 00

                                      80 00 00   **80 00 00**

——————————— 14 ———————————

7 *Sundry Accounts*, *Debtors* to *Foreign Linnen*, for 100 Yards (N° 1) at 3 *s.* 6 *d per* Yard is 18 *l.* 6 *s.* 8 *d* delivered to *James Trustwell*, *viz.*

                                 l.   *s*   *d.*

4 Drs { *Ja. Trustwell* ——— ——— ——— 12 00 00
10   { *Cash* received. ——— ——— ——— 6 6 8

                                    18 6 8   **18 6 8**

10 / 6 *Cash Debtor* to *Accepted Bills*, due to me, received from *Gideon Keith* ——— ——— ——— **28 16 00**

11 / 11 *John Blackwood* of *London*, my *Account Current*, *Debtor* to *John Blackwood*, my *Account of Brandy*, for 36 Casks, sold for ready Money. Neat Proceeds. ——— ——— **200 00 00**

August 15.

		l.	s	d.
	——————August 15.——————			
12	*Herman van Rymer* of *Amsterdam,* my *Account Current,* Debtor			
12	to *Herman van Rymer,* my *Account of Sheep-Skins,* for 8 Packs sold for ready Money. Neat Proceeds 400 Guilders, 22 d. ½ is ————— —————	37	10	00
10	*Cash* Debtor to *John Blackwood* of *London,* my *Account Current.* Received for a Bill upon him payable to *J. R.* which			
11	he has paid me. —————	20	00	00
	———— 16 ————			
12	*Hero Moy* of *Amsterdam,* his *Account of Goods per Leopard* of			
10	*Aberdeen,* Debtor to *Cash,* paid of Charges upon the following Goods consigned to me, to sell for his Account.			

Received   Charges paid

	l.	s	d.
8 Packs of *Flanders* Flax. Petty Customs.	2	10	00
40 Dozen of Wooll-Cards Shoar Dues — —	00	18	00
50 ℔ of Bohea-Tea. Carriage. ———	00	6	8
	3	14	8

		l.	s	d.
	Neat Charges	3	14	8
13	*Cash* Debtor to *Herman van Rymer,* my *Account Current,* for my Bill on him, payable to *J B.* (or Order) upon Sight.			
12	436 Guilders which at 22 d ½. is —————	40	8	5
	———— 19, ————			
9	*Sundry Accounts Debtors* to *Wager's Account,* for the Wager against *Simeon Wilfull* gained, there being no Peace yet concluded between *Britain* and *Spain, viz.*			

		l.	s.	d
11	Dis { *Hazard Account,* to Ballance the former Entry. ————— —————	6	00	00
13	{ *Cash* received. ——— —————	6	00	00
		12	00	00

		l.	s	d.
		12	00	00
11	*Hazard Account* Debtor to *Wager's Account,* the Wager			
9	against Mr. *John Justice* being decided —————	10	00	00
9	*Wager's Account,* Debtor to *Cash,* paid for this Wager lost	10	00	00
13				
	———— 20 ————			
13	*Cash* Debtor to *Hero Moy's Account of Goods,* for 8 Packs of			
12	Flax. Sold at 4 *l* per Pack, is ——— —————	32	00	00

T 2   *August* 20

		l.	s.	d.

——————— *August* 20. ———————

13	*Hero Moy,* his *Account Current, Debtor* to *Cash,* remitted to him in the Bill of *John Duncanson,* on *Maurice Moliere* at 10 days Sight 208 ¼ ⅔ Guilders, which at 23 *d.* is 20 *l.* paid by me. ———	20	00	00
13				

7	*Foreign Linnen, Debtor* to *Sundry Accounts,* for 6 Pieces of Fine Muslin, received this Day from aboard a Bark of *Inverness,* from *London;* sent me by *John Blackwood,* by Order, and in return of my Brandy sold by him, *viz.*			

		l.	s.	d.

11	Crs {	*Jo Blackwood,* my *Account Current,* for the Value of 6 Pieces of Muslin 40 Yards each: Prime Cost and Charges at *London* amounts to ———	123	10	00
13		*Cash,* for Freight and Charges paid here. ———	000	15	00

		124	5	00	124	5	00

——————— 22. ———————

13	*Daniel Stratton* of *Rochel,* my *Account of Sales, Debtor* to *Ditto Stratton,* my *Account* of *Goods,* &c for 8 Last of Salmons. Sold by him, one Time, to Sundry Persons. Neat Proceeds thereof, deducting all Charges, (with the Freight upon the whole Cargo cleared by him) is 1500 Crowns, at 4 *s. per* Crown. ——— ———	300	00	00
12				

8	*Delivery Account* of *Buying, Debtor* to *Sundry Accounts,* for 100 *Bolls* of Wheat, bought of *Thomas Dalziel,* at 1 *l* 10 *s per* Boll, to be delivered the 1*st* of *Nov.* next, *viz*			

		l.	s	d.

13	Crs {	*Cash* advanced. ——— ———	10	0	00
13		*Tho Dalziel,* payable at *Martinmas.* ———	140	00	00

		150	00	00	150	00	00

3	*Andrew Cochran, Debtor* to *Herman van Rymer* my *Account Current,* for 400 Guilders, at 22 *d.* ¼ is 37 *l.* 10 *s* drawn upon *Ditto Rymer,* payable at single Usance to *Ditto Cochran* (or Order) the Value to be paid to me in 1 Month. ———	37	10	
12				

August 23

		l	*s*	d.
——————— *August* 23. ———————				

		l	*s*	d.
3 / 12	*Peter Chapman, Debtor* to *Hero Moy* his *Account* of *Goods, &c.* for 40 Dozen of Wool-Cards, fold at 16 *s per* Dozen, payable in 20 Days. ———————	32	00	00
14 / 10	*Daniel Stratton* of *Rochel* my *Account* of *Wool, Debtor* to *Voyage* to *Bourdeaux,* &c. for 4 Packs configned to him, by *Quintin Malcolm,* my *Supra-Cargo* Value (Including a Proportion of all Charges). ———	55	9	6½
——————— 24. ———————				
8 / 12	*Profit, &c. Debtor* to *Voyage* from *Lisbon,* &c. for 50 Barrels of Raifins loft. Value ——— ——— ——	74	00	00
——————— 26. ———————				
14 / 13	*Charles Chareu* of *Bourdeaux,* our *Account* of *Exchange* in *Company, Debtor* to *Cafh,* paid for a Bill remitted to him for 400 Crowns, which at 56 *d. per* Crown, is 93 *l* 6 *s.* 8 *d* the Draught of *Peter Stuart* upon *Elias Morgan,* paid by me. ——— ——— ——— ———	93	6	8
14 / 14	*Houfe* in *Caftle-Street, Debtor* to *John Campbel* 300 *l* 15 *s.* *viz.* 300 *l.* the Price of the faid *Houfe* bought of him, payable in 1 Year. And 15 *s* the 1ft Quarter of an Annuity of 3 *l.* payable Quarterly to him as part of the Price of the faid *Houfe* during the Life of his Mother, and for her Behoof. Total ——— ——— ———	300	15	00
14 / 14	*William Davidfon, Debtor* to *Houfe* in *Caftle-Street,* for ½ Years Rent, from *Whit-Sunday* laft, payable at *Martinmas* next. ——— ——— ———	10	00	00
——————— 29 ———————				
14	*Houfe* in *Broad-Street, Debtor* to *Sundry Accounts,* for 230 *l* the Value of the faid *Houfe,* left me in Legacy, by *D. M.* my *Uncle,* with the Burden of the following Legacy, *viz.*			

Crs.

			l.	*s.*	*d*	*l.*	*s.*	*d.*
8	Crs { *Profit, &c.* free Gain to me. ———		200	00	00			
15	*Thomas Richman,* for a Legacy which I'm bound to pay him by Virtue of my said *Uncle's* Will. ———		30	00	00			
			230	00	00	230	00	00

————— *August* 29. —————

15								
13	*Ship* the *Dragon* of *Aberdeen,* Debtor to *Thomas Dalziel,* for ⅓ of the said Ship bought of him, payable at *Candlemas* next ——— ——— ———					100	00	00

————— 30. —————

15								
13	*Benjamin Barclay,* my *Account* with him in *Company,* Debtor to *Cash,* stocked with him for an Inland Trade to be managed by him. ——— ——— ———					20	00	00

6								
11	*Accepted Bills* due to me, Debtor to *John Blackwood,* my *Account Current,* 76 *l.* 10 *s.* remitted to me in his own Bill upon *Alexander Gordon,* Merchant in *Aberdeen,* payable in 1 Month. Accepted. ——— ———					76	10	00

————— *Sept.* 2 —————

13	*Hero Moy* of *Amsterdam,* his *Account Current,* Debtor to *Sundry Accounts,* for the following Goods bought by his Order, and for his *Account,* shipped aboard the *Rose* of *Kinghorn,* J. C. *Master,* for *Amsterdam, viz.*		*l*	*s.*	*d.*			
13	Crs { *Cash,* paid for 4 Packs of *Sheep-Skins,* with Charges at Buying and Shipping.		14	15	00			
8	*Profit, &c.* for my Commission. ———		00	15	00			
			15	10	00	15	10	00

3								
8	*Andrew Cochran,* Debtor to *Profit, &c.* for 50 *l.* left me in a Legacy by a Friend, payable by *Ditto Cochran,* Executor to the deceased ——— ———					50	00	00

8	*Sundry Accounts,* Debtors to *Profit, &c* for the Apprentice-Fee of *John Brown,* Son to *Adam Brown,* whom I have this Day taken for my Apprentice for 3 Years, *viz.*

Drs.

			l.	s.	d		l.	s.	d.

| 13 | Drs { Cash, paid me. —————— ——— | 20 | 00 | 00 | | | |
| 15 | Adam Brown, payable in 1 Year. — | 50 | 00 | 00 | | | |

| | | 70 | 00 | 00 | 70 | 00 | 00 |

———————————— Sept. 5. ————————————

13	Cash, Debtor to Charles Chareu, our *Account of Exchange* in
14	Company, for his Bill remitted to me the Draught of *Allan*
	Bruyere on *Andrew Dick*, 200 Crowns, at 58 d. is — — 48 6 8.

———————————— 6 ————————————

| 2 | Wine, Debtor to *Sundry Accounts*, for 7 Hogsheads of Claret
(N° 2) received from aboard the *Success* of *Aberdeen* from
Bourdeaux, viz. |

		l.	s	d
11	Voyage from *Bourdeaux*, for the prime			
	Crs { Cost of 7 Hogsheads in *France*. ———	37	6	8
13	Cash, for Duty and Charges here. ———	5	10	00

| | | 42 | 16 | 8 | 42 | 16 | 8 |

———————————— 7 ————————————

| 12 | Hero Moy his *Account of Goods*, &c Debtor to *Sundry Accounts*,
for the Charges and Commission due to me upon the whole,
which Goods are now all out of my Hands (his 50 ℔ of
Bohea Tea being this Day shipped for *London* by his Order,
as *per* Wast-Book) viz. |

		l.	s.	d
13	Crs { Cash, laid out ——— — ———	4	14	8
8	Profit, &c. for Commission — —	12	00	00

| | | 16 | 14 | 8 | 16 | 14 | 8 |

| 2 | Wine, Debtor to *Cash*, paid for 15 Gallons to fill up the 7 |
| 13 | Hogsheads of Claret, which came last from *Bourdeaux* —   3 00 00 |

| 15 | Christianus Marbach of *Rotterdam*, his *Account Current*, Debtor
to *Sundry Accounts*, 72 l. 8 s for the following Goods,
bought for his Account, to be sent him by the first Oc-
casion, viz. |

Cis.

		l.	*s.*	*d.*	*l.*	*s.*	*d.*
3	⎧ *Andrew Cochran,* for 200 pair of Stockings, payable in 4 Months ⎯ ⎯	50	00	00			
13	*Cash,* paid in Part of 700 Yards of *Plaidin* (with Charges on the whole). ⎯	8	8	00			
15	Crs ⎨ *Tho Richman,* for the Remainder of the *Plaidin,* payable in 2 Months. ⎯	10	00	00			
8	⎩ *Profit,* &c for my Commiſſion. ⎯ ⎯	4	00	00			
		72	8	00	72	8	00

──────────── *Sept* 10 ────────────

15	*Thomas Richman, Debtor* to *Charles Chareu,* our *Account* of *Exchange,* for 500 Crowns, at 57 *d.* is 119*l* 15*s* 10*d* drawn by me on *Ditto Chareu,* payable at ſingle Uſance to *Anthony van Helm* (or Order) to be paid me by *Ditto Richman* in 1 Month. ⎯ ⎯				119	15	10
14							

──────────────────────

15	*Daniel Stratton* of *Rochel,* my *Account Current, Debtor* to *Ditto,* my *Account of Sales,* for 1500 Crowns at 4 *s.* of out-ſtanding Debts received by him, is ⎯				300	00	00
13							

──────────── 11. ────────────

16	*Voyage* from *Amsterdam* in the *Lamb* of *Aberdeen, Debtor* to *Herman van Rymer,* my *Account Current,* for the following Goods, bought and ſhipped by him, by my Order *viz.*						
12							

		l.	*s.*	*d.*			
	100 ℔. Weight of Coffee. ⎯ ⎯	40	00	00			
	4 Packs of Flax, 18 Stone each. ⎯	37	00	00			
	Charges and Commiſſion. ⎯	8	16	9			
	Total is 981 Guilders, at 21 *d.* equal to	85	16	9	85	16	9

──────────── 13 ────────────

13	*Cash Debtor* to *Peter Chapman,* being for Payment of what he owed for *Hero Moy's Account of Goods.* ⎯ ⎯				32	00	00
5							
12	*Hero Moy's Account of Goods, Debtor* to his *Account Current,* for the neat Proceeds of his Goods, which are all diſpoſed of, and the Debts received ⎯ ⎯				43	10	8
13							

──────────────────────

15	*Christianus Marbach,* his *Account Current, Debtor* to *Cash,* paid of advanced Freight and other Charges upon his Goods bought the 7*th* of this Month: This day ſhipped aboard the *Mermaid, Magnus Black,* Maſter. ⎯ ⎯				6	00	00
13							

		l.	s.	d.

——————— *Sept.* 13. ———————

$\frac{9}{13}$ *Wager's Account*, Debtor to *Cash*, confined in the Hands of Mr *Gabriel Bowman* in a Wager againſt *Thomas Arrow-Smith*, that the *Crocodile* of *Aberdeen*, now at *Virginia*, will not be home before the 1ſt of *November* next. —— —— | 10 | 00 | 00

——————— 15. ———————

$\frac{4}{6}$ *David Johnſton*, Debtor to *Accepted Bills due to me*, for a Bill on him by Aſſignment from Mr. *Alexander Gordon*, payable on Demand, as *per* Waſt-Book. —— | 76 | 10 | 00

6 *Sundry Accounts Debtors* to *Iron*, for 500 Stone (N° 1.) at 3 *s. per* Stone, is 75 *l.* delivered to *James Montgomery*, for Payment of 60 *l* I owed him for 40 Barrels of Beef ; and I have received the Surplus in Caſh, *viz.*

		l.	s.	d.
$\frac{7}{13}$	Drs $\begin{cases} \textit{James Montgomery.} \\ \textit{Cash.} \end{cases}$ —— —— ——	60	00	00
		15	00	00
		75	00	00

75 | 00 | 00

——————— 18. ———————

$\frac{15}{6}$ *Benjamin Barclay*, my *Account with him in Company* ½, Debtor to *Alexander Black*, for 10 *l* payable in 2 Months, drawn upon me by *Ditto Barclay*, as part of my Share of certain Goods, bought by him for our Account, the Reſt being already in his Hands —— —— —— | 10 | 00 | 00

$\frac{15}{12}$ *Daniel Stratton* of *Rochel*, my *Account Current*, Debtor to *Ditto*, my *Account of Goods*, for 40 Barrels of Beef ſold for ready Money. Neat proceeds *per* Account 336 Crowns, at 57 *d. per* Crown. —— —— —— | 79 | 16 | 00

16 *Voyage* from *Rochel* to *Amſterdam*, Debtor to *Sundry Accounts*, for my 4 Packs of Wool formerly conſigned to *Daniel Stratton* at *Rochel*, ſhipped by him for *Amſterdam*, by my Order, *viz.*

		l.	s.	d.
14	Crs $\begin{cases} \textit{Dan Stratton}, \text{ my } \textit{Account of Wool} \text{ -- --} \end{cases}$	55	9	6½
15	$\begin{cases} \textit{Ditto} \text{ ——— my } \textit{Account Current}, \text{ for} \\ \text{his Proviſion and Charges, } 6 \\ \text{Crowns, at 57 } d. per \text{ Crown. ——} \end{cases}$	1	8	6
		56	18	00½

56 | 18 | 00½

U

		l.	*s*	*d.*

——————— *Sept.* 18. ———————

$\frac{13}{6}$ *Cash Debtor* to *John Houston*, paid by him what he owes me. - | 3 | 14 | 00 |

$\frac{14}{16}$ *Charles Charcu*, our *Account of Exchange*, Debtor to *Accepted Bills due by me*, 300 Crowns drawn on me, payable to Mr. *Robert Blackwood* at single Usance, is at 57 *d. per* Crown. ——— ——— ——— | 71 | 5 | 00 |

$\frac{16}{13}$ *Voyage* from *Amsterdam*, in the *Lamb* of *Aberdeen*, Debtor to *Cash*, 5 *l* paid Charges upon the Coffee, and Flax sent me by *Herman van Rymer*, this Day arrived. ——— | 5 | 00 | 00 |

16 *Sundry Accounts Debtors* to *Voyage* from *Amsterdam*, for the Coffee and Flax received, *viz.*

	l.	*s.*	*d*

16 ⎰ *Flax*, 4 Packs, 18 Stone each Pack, Value, prime Cost and Charges ——— 43 00 00

16 Drs.⎨ *Adam Brown*, for 100 ℔ of Coffee sold to, and received by him, payable in 6 Months. ——— ——— 60 00 00

103 00 00 | 103 | 00 | 00 |

Observe There are various other Ways of entering this Transaction As,

1 To Enter the *Flax* and *Coffee* each *Debtor* for what they Cost in *Holland*, for which the *Voyage* is before *Debtor*, and now to be made *Creditor*. Then to charge each *Debtor* to *Cash* for their Share of 5 *l* paid here : And lastly to enter the Sale of the *Coffee*

2 Make the *Voyage Debtor* for the 5 *l* as before Then Enter the *Flax* and *Coffee* each *Debtor* for the Value, Including the 5 *l*, and lastly Enter the Sale of the *Coffee*.

——————— 25. ———————

$\frac{12}{15}$ *Herman van Rymer*, my *Account Current*, Debtor to *Daniel Stratton*, my *Account Current*; for a Bill drawn by *Ditto Rymer*, on *Ditto Stratton* for my Account, 180 Crowns, which at 56 *d.* is Equal to 458 ⅚ Guilders, at 22 *d. per* Guilder. ——— ——— ——— | 42 | 00 | 00 |

					l.	*s*	*d.*

─────────── Sept. 25. ───────────

15	*Sundry Accounts,* *Debtors* to *Daniel Stratton,* my *Account Current,* for 100 Crowns drawn upon him, at 57 *d* payable at Sight to *D. B* (or Order) for which I have received of *David Broomfield, viz.*		

				l.	*s*	*d.*
2	Drs. { *Broad Cloth,* (N°. 1.) 2 Pieces, 16 Yards each, at 10 *s.* is ─ ─ ─	16	00	00
13	*Cash.* ───────	7	13	4

			23	13	4	23	13	4

─────────── 28 ───────────

15	*Sundry Accounts,* *Debtors* to *Benjamin Barclay,* my *Account with him in Company,* received of him for my Share of our Goods in Partnership. Sold by him, *viz.*		

			l	*s*	*d.*
13	Drs { *Cash.* ───────	25	00	00
6	*Iron,* 100 Stone, at 3 *s.* ───	15	00	00

			40	00	00	40	00	00

13 / 16	*Hero Moy,* his *Account Current,* Debtor to *Accepted Bills,* due by me; for his Bill payable to Mr. *Robert Clark,* at single Usance. ───────	8	00	8

─────────── Octob. 5. ───────────

15	*Sundry Accounts,* *Debtors* to *Christianus Marbach* of *Rotterdam,* his *Account Current,* for the following Goods and Bill remitted me by him, for Payment of what he owes by his *Account Current, viz*		

			l	*s.*	*d.*
7	Drs.{ *Foreign Linnen,* 4 Pieces of Holland, 30 Yards each, cost with Charges. ──	20	00	00
16	*Flax,* for 4 Packs, 18 Stone each. ──	36	00	00
6	*Accepted Bills, due to me,* for a Bill on *George Gordon,* payable in 2 Months.	22	8	00

			78	8	00	78	8	00

13	*Sundry Accounts,* *Debtors* to *Cash,* paid of Charges upon those Goods here, *viz.*

			l.	s.	d.	l.	s.	d.
7	Drs. {	*Foreign Linnen.* ——— ———	1	13	00			
16		*Flax.* ——— ———	2	19	00			
			4	12	00	4	12	00

6 | *Sundry Accounts, Debtors* to *Accepted Bills, due to me,* for the Payment made me by *Abraham Fairholm, viz.*

			l.	s.	d.			
13	Drs. {	*Cash* received. ——— ———	24	00	00			
8		*Profit* and *Loss,* discounted to him. —	2	5	00			
			26	5	00	26	5	00

——— 7. ———

8 | *Profit* and *Loss, Debtor* to *Sundry Accounts,* for the following Articles paid, and owing, of the Expences of Trade and Living, *viz.*

				l.	s.	d			
13	Crs. {	*Cash paid.* {	(By Book of Charges of Trade, 20 *l.* — — By Book of Expence of Living, 30 *l.* — —)	50	00	00			
16		*Account of outstanding Charges.* {	(By Book of Expences, 15 *l* —— Owing to *J. S.* at Martinmas, 2 *l.*)	17	00	00			
				67	00	00	67	0	00

LEGER

LEGER-BOOK.

Number 1.

Of me *A. M.* Merchant in *Aberdeen:*

From the Firſt of *May,* 1729.

		DEBTOR.	*l.*	*s.*	*d.*

STOCK.

1729						
May	1	To Mr. *David Johnston.*	4	1200	00	00
		Mr. *James Truftwell.*	4	600	00	00
				1800	00	00
Oct.	8	To *Ballance,* for my prefent Free Eftate.	172	547	2	5½
		Sum		2727	2	5½

CASH.

1729						
May	1	To *Stock.*	—	800	00	00
	2	To *Wine.*	2	48	00	00
	6	To *Paper.*	4	100	00	00
	8	To *Raifins*	2	8	00	00
	11	To *Broad Cloth.*	2	44	00	00
	14	To *Tobacco.*	2	14	2	00
	20	To *Tobacco.*	2	2	00	00
	24	To *Daniel Trader.*	5	20	00	00
	30	To *Iron.*	6	60	00	00
June	7	To *Delivery Account* of Selling.	9	13	3	8
		To *Accepted Bills.* payable to me.	6	6	00	00
	12	To *William Smith.*	4	11	10	00
	15	To *Figs.*	8	15	00	00
	28	To *Infurance Account.*	10	45	00	00
		Transferred to	10	1096	15	8
		Fol. 1				

CREDITOR. | *l.* | *s* | *d.*

STOCK.

1729				*l.*	*s*	*d.*
May	1	By *Cash.*		800	00	00
		Wine —— 20 Hogsheads of Claret.	2	213	00	00
		Tobacco —— 18 Hogsheads of *Virginia.*	2	200	14	00
		Raisins —— 30 Barrels	2	48	00	00
		Broad Cloth —— 14 Pieces.	2	203	12	00
		Mr. *William Wallice.*	3	103	5	00
		Andrew Hunter.	3	80	00	00
		Andrew Cochran.	3	140	00	00
		Moveables and Houshold Furniture.	3	200	00	00
				1988	11	00
Oct.	8	By *Profit* and *Loss,* gained since *May* 1	17	738	11	5 ½
		Sum.		2727	2	5 ½

CASH.

1729				*l.*	*s*	*d.*
May	6	By *Brandy.*	5	16	60	00
	8	By *Brandy.*	5	60	00	00
	14	By *Salmons*	7	60	00	00
	20	By *Scotch Linnen,*	7	15	00	00
	24	By *James Trustwell*	4	40	00	00
	30	By *Figs*	8	35	4	00
		By *James Montgomery*	7	108	8	00
June	3	By *Iron.*	6	32	10	00
		By *Delivery Account of Buying.*	8	16	00	00
	6	By *David Johnston.*	4	117	00	00
	10	By *Peter Chapman*	5	9	00	00
	18	By *Andrew Hunter.*	3	100	00	00
		By *Voyage* to London, &c.	9	23	1	00
	21	By *David Johnston.*	4	30	00	00
		By *Voyage* to Rochel, &c.	9	11	16	8
	22	By *Bottomree Account.*	9	50	00	00
		By *Wager's Account.*	9	5	00	00
	25	By *Wool.*	10	19	9	6 ½
		By *Bottomree Account.*	9	40	00	00
		By *Wager's Account.*	9	10	00	00
	28	By *Sheep-Skins*	10	53	6	8
July	2	By *Andrew Cochran.*	3	20	00	00
		Transferred to	10	871	15	10 ½
		Fol. 2.				

DEBTOR   *l.*   *s.*   *d.*

WINE.

	White Hds	Claret Hds		*l.*	*s.*	*d.*
1729 *May* 1 — To *Stock*, N°. 1. 6 Hogsheads, N°. 2. 4 Hogsheads, N°. 3. 10 Hogsheads. Total.		20	1	213	00	00
Aug. 1 — To *Cash*, N° 1 at 9 *l.* per Hogshead. —	4		10	36	00	00
Sept. 6 — To *Voyage* from *Bourdeaux, &c* prime Cost. — } N°. 4		7	11	37	6	8
To *Cash*, for Duty and Charges, here — }			13	5	10	00
7 — To *Cash*, for 15 Gallons to fill up the last 7 Hogsheads. —			13	3	00	00
Oct. 8 — To *Profit* and *Loss* —			16	36	10	00
Sum	4	27		331	6	8

TOBACCO

	Hds.		*l.*	*s.*	*d.*
1729 *May* 1 — To *Stock*, neat Weight, 600 ℔ each Hogshead, at 11 *l* 3 *s*. —	18	1	200	14	00

RAISINS.

	N°. 1 Barrels	N°. 2 Barrels		*l.*	*s.*	*d.*
1729 *May* 1 — To *Stock*, at 1 *l.* 12 *s.* per Barrel. —	30		1	48	00	00
July 2 — To *Delivery Account* of *Buying*, at 1 *l.* 10 *s* per Barrel. —		24	8	36	00	00
Oct. 8 — To *Profit* and *Loss*. —			16	12	7	8
Sum.	30	24		96	7	8

BROAD CLOTH

	Pieces		*l.*	*s.*	*d.*
1729 *May* 1 — To *Stock*, N° 1. 8 Pieces, N°. 2. 6 Pieces. Total. —	14	1	203	12	00
Aug. 1 — To *David Johnston*, N°. 1, 2, 3. each 1 Piece. —	3	4	53	6	00
Sept. 25 — To *Daniel Stratton*, my *Account Current*, N°. 4 16 Yards a Piece. —	2	16	16	00	00
Oct. 8 — To *Profit* and *Loss*. —		16	23	14	00
Sum.	19		296	12	00

CREDITOR.

		WINE.	White Hds.	Claret Hds.		l.	s	d.
1729 *May*	2	By *Cash*...Of N° 1. at 12 *l. per* Hogshead.		4	1	48	00	00
	7	By *Daniel Trader*...*per* Bill on him, N° 1 1 Hogshead, N°. 2. 2 Hogsheads. —		3	5	37	10	00
Aug.	1	By *Cash*. .For 2 Hogsheads, N°. 2. at 10 *l* and 8 of N°. 3 at 14 *l per* Hogshead		10	10	132	00	00
Oct.	8	By *Ballance* .. Of Claret 1 Hogshead N° 1 7 N°. 4. 2 N°. 3. *White* 4 Hogsheads	4	10	17	113	16	8
		Sum.	4	27		331	6	8

		TOBACCO.	Hds.		l.	s	d.
1729 *May*	14	By *Cash*. .... At 4 *l.* 14 *s. per* Hogshead.	3	1	14	2	00
	20	By *Cash* . . . . } . At 4 *l* 16 *s. per* Hogshead.		1	2	00	00
		By *John Houston* }	2	6	7	12	00
Oct.	8	By *Ballance.* — — —	13	17	144	19	00
		By *Profit* and *Loss.* — — —		16	32	1	00
		Sum.	18		200	14	00

		RAISINS.	N° 1 Barrels	N°. 2 Barrels		l.	s	d.
1729 *May*	8	By *Cash.* — — —			1	8	00	00
		By *John Houston.* } N°. 1. at 2 *l. per* Barrel.	10		6	6	00	00
		By *Accepted Bills.* }			6	6	00	00
	11	By *Salmons.* .... At 1 *l.* 16 *s. per* Barrel	15		7	27	00	00
July	12	By *Delivery Account* of *Selling*. . To *John Houston* — — —		13	9	23	3	8
		By *John Houston.* ..... At 1 *l.* 15 *s.* 8 *d.*		6	6	10	14	00
Oct.	8	By *Ballance.* — — —	5	5	17	15	10	00
		Sum.	30	24		96	7	8

		BROAD CLOTH.	Pieces		l.	s	d.
1729 *May*	2	By *William Smith* ... Each Piece 18 Yards, at 17 *s.* 6 *d.* N° 2. — — —	2	4	31	10	00
	11	By *Foreign Linnen* } 20 Yards each Piece, at 17 *s.* 4 *d.* N° 1. —	6	7	60	00	00
		By *Cash.* . . . . . }		1	44	00	00
June	10	By *Peter Chapman*. N°. 1 and 2. 2 Pieces each	4	5	63	00	00
July	20	By *Accepted Bills*, &c .. N° 2. 18 Yards each, at 16 *s. per* Yard. — — —	2	6	28	16	00
Oct.	8	By *Ballance*. ... N°. 1, 2, 3. each 1 Piece, and N°. 4. 2 Pieces. — — —	5	17	69	6	00
		Sum.	19		296	12	00

			DEBTOR		l.	s	d.

WILLIAM WALLACE

1729							
May	1	To *Stock*..... By Bond, Principal and Interest payable at *Martinmas* next. ———	1	103	5	00
Aug.	3	To *William Smith*. .... For my Bill. ———	4	6	00	00
		Sum		109	5	00

ANDREW HUNTER.

1729							
May	1	To *Stock* ..... *Per* Account. ———	1	80	00	00
June	18	To *Cash*. Lent by Bond, payable at *Martinmas* next.	1	100	00	00
		To *Profit, &c*. .For Interest to the Term of Payment	8	2	11	5
		Sum.		182	11	5

ANDREW COCHRAN.

1729							
May	1	To *Stock*. . .....*Per* Account. ——— ———	1	140	00	00
July	2	To *Cash*. . . .Paid the Remainder of the *Raisins* Delivered. ——— ———	1	20	00	00
Aug.	22	To *Herman van Rymer, my Account Current.* ———	12	37	10	00
Sept	2	To *Profit* and *Loss*. . . For a Legacy payable by him.	8	50	00	00
		Sum.		247	10	00

MOVEABLES, &c.

1729							
May	1	To *Stock*. .... *Per* particular Inventory thereof	1	200	00	00

WILLIAM

					CREDITOR.	*l.*	*s.*	*d.*

WILLIAM WALLACE

1729									
June	12	By *Delivery Account* of *Buying*. . . . . Payable at Martinmas next.		8	56	00	00
Octo	8	By *Ballance*.		17	53	5	00
				Sum.	109	5	00

ANDREW HUNTER

1729									
May	6	By *Brandy*. . . . . . *Per* my Bill on him to *D. Watson*.	5	80	00	00
Octo	8	By *Ballance*. . . . . . Owing upon Bond.	17	102	11	5
				Sum	182	11	5

ANDREW COCHRAN

1729									
May	8	By *Iron* . . . . . . *Per* my Bill on him.	6	100	00	00
	14	By *Salmons*. . . . *Per* my Bill on him	7	40	00	00
June	3	By *Delivery Account* of *Buying*. . . . Payable upon Delivery	8	20	00	00
Sept	7	By *Christianus Marbach, his Account Current*.	15	50	00	00
Octo.	8	By *Ballance*.	17	37	10	00
				Sum	247	10	00

MOVEABLES, &c.

1729									
Octo.	8	By *Ballance*.	17	200	00	00

		DEBTOR.		*l.*	*s.*	*d.*

DAVID JOHNSTON.

1729						
June	6	To *Cash* . . . . . Paid.	1	117	00	00
		To *Profit* and *Loss* . . . . Discounted.	8	3	00	00
	21	To *Cash* . . . . ⎫ . For Sack paid; and sold to him.	1	30	00	00
		To *Profit &c.* ⎭	8	4	00	00
Sept	15	To *Accepted Bills* . . . For Bill of *Alexander Gorden,* payable on demand	6	76	10	00
		Sum.		230	10	00

JAMES TRUSTWELL.

1729						
May	24	To *Cash.*	1	40	00	00
June	15	To *Figs* . . . . . . Per *P. C'.*s Bill, payable on demand.	8	20	00	00
Aug.	14	To *Foreign Linnen.*	7	12	00	00
		Sum.		72	00	00

WILLIAM SMITH.

1729						
May	2	To *Broad Cloth.* . . . . Payable in 2 Months.	2	31	10	00
June	15	To *Delivery Account* of *Selling.* . Payable on delivery.	9	14	00	00
		Sum.		45	10	00

PAPER.

			N° 1 Bales.	N° 2. Bales.		*l.*	*s.*	*d.*
1729								
May	4	To *Peter Chapman.* . . At 4 *l. per* Bale	18		5	72	00	00
Aug	3	To *Delivery Account* of *Buying.* . . . . From *William Wallace.*		20	8	76	00	00
Oct.	8	To *Profit* and *Loss.*			16	15	4	00
		Sum.	18	20		163	4	00

DAVID

			CREDITOR		*l.*	*s.*	*d.*

DAVID JOHNSTON.

1729					*l.*	*s.*	*d.*
May	1	By *Stock* .... Payable the 1ſt of *Nov* next. —	1	120	00	00
Aug	1	By *Broad Cloth* .... Payable the 1ſt of *Oct.* next	2	53	6	00
Oct.	8	By *Ballance.* —	17	57	4	00
			Sum.		230	10	00

JAMES TRUSTWELL.

1729							
May	1	By *Stock.* ...... Payable on demand. —	1	60	00	00
June	25	By *Wooll.* .. .... Payable the 1ſt of *Aug.* —	10	12	00	00
			Sum.		72	00	00

WILLIAM SMITH.

1729							
June	12	By *Figs* } —	8	20	00	00
		By *Caſh.* } —	1	11	10	00
Aug.	3	By *William Wallace.* .... By my Bill. —	3	6	00	00
		By *Delivery Account* of *Selling.* —	9	8	00	00
			Sum.		45	10	00

PAPER.

1729				N°. 1. Bales.	N°. 2. Bales		*l.*	*s.*	*d.*
May	6	By *Caſh* .... } At 5 *l* per Bale. —			1	10	00	00
		By *John Paton.* }		5	5	15	00	00
June	7	By *John Paton.* ... At 4 *l* 18 *s.* per Bale	10	5	49	00	00
Aug.	3	By *Delivery Account* of *Selling.* .... To *William Smith.* —		6	9	24	0	00
Oct.	8	By *Ballance.* —	3	14	17	65	4	00
		Sum	18	20		163	4	00

		DEBTOR		*l.*	*s.*	*d.*

PETER CHAPMAN.

1729						
June	10	To *Broad Cloth.* ⎱ For Payment made to him. ——	2	63	00	00
		To *Cash* . . . ⎰	1	9	00	00
	15	To *Figs.* . . . . Payable in 20 days. ——	8	16	6	00
Aug	23	To *Hero May's Account* of *Goods*. . . Payable in 20 days	12	32	00	00
		Sum		120	6	00

JOHN PATON.

1729						
May	6	To *Paper.* . . . Payable in 20 days ——	4	15	00	00
June	7	To *Paper* . . . . . Payable in 10 Months ——	4	49	00	00
		Sum.		64	00	00

BRANDY.

1729				Casks				
May	6	To *Cash* . . . . . . ⎱ N° 1. 3 *l.* ⎱		1	16	00	00
		To *Andrew Hunter*. . *Per* my Bill. ⎰ *per* Cask. ⎰	32	3	80	00	00
	8	To *Cash.* . . . N° 2. at 2 *l.* 10 *s. per* Cask. —	24	1	60	00	00
		Sum.	56		156	00	00

DANIEL TRADER.

1729						
May	7	To *Wine* . *Per* E *Freeman's* Bill, payable on Demand.	2	37	10	00
June	15	To *Delivery Account* of *Selling* . . . . *Per* D. *T*'s Bill on Demand.	9	18	00	00
July	22	To *Delivery Account* of *Buying* . . *For* a 100 Yards of *Holland*, not delivered. ——	8	25	00	00
		To *Profit* and *Loss.* . . . . . For the Penalty, for Non-performance. —— ——	8	5	00	00
		Sum.		85	10	00

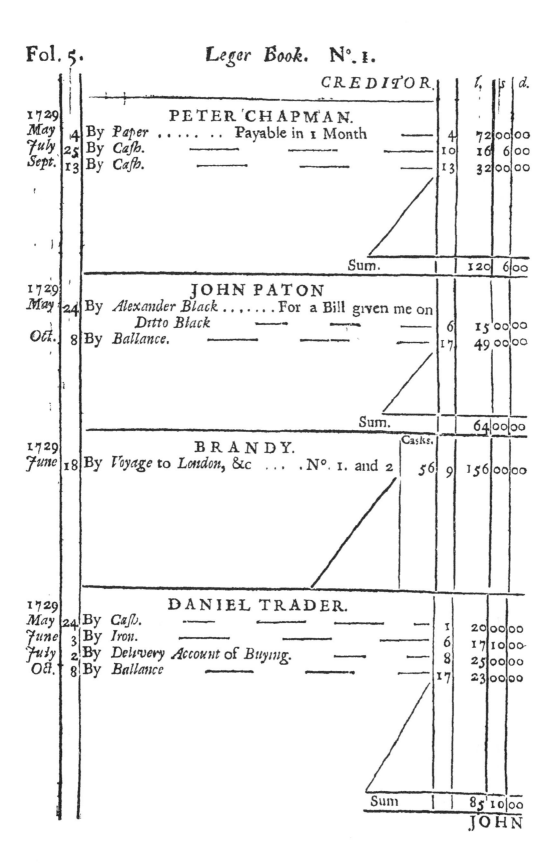

CREDITOR.   *l.*   *s*   *d.*

PETER CHAPMAN.

1729					*l.*	*s*	*d.*
May	4	By *Paper* .... Payable in 1 Month ———	4	72	00	00
July	25	By *Cash.* ——— ——— ——— ———	10	16	6	00
Sept.	13	By *Cash.* ——— ——— ———	13	32	00	00
			Sum.		120	6	00

JOHN PATON

1729					*l.*	*s*	*d.*
May	24	By *Alexander Black* ....For a Bill given me on *Ditto Black* ——— ——— ———	6	15	00	00
Oct.	8	By *Ballance.* ——— ——— ———	17	49	00	00
			Sum.		64	00	00

BRANDY.

1729				Casks.		*l.*	*s*	*d.*
June	18	By *Voyage* to *London*, &c ... .N°. 1. and 2	56	9	156	00	00

DANIEL TRADER.

1729					*l.*	*s*	*d.*
May	24	By *Cash.* ——— ——— ———	1	20	00	00
June	3	By *Iron.* ——— ——— ———	6	17	10	00
July	2	By *Delivery Account* of *Buying.* ——— ———	8	25	00	00
Oct.	8	By *Ballance* ——— ——— ———	17	23	00	00
			Sum		85	10	00

JOHN

		DEBTOR.	*l.*	*s.*	*d.*

JOHN HOUSTON.

1729					
May	8	To *Raisins.* ...... Payable in 2 Months. ——— 2	6	00	00
	20	To *Tobacco.* ... . Given for *Figs* sold to him ; payable on Demand. ——— ——— 2	7	12	00
June	7	To *Delivery Account* of *Selling* ... Payable in 20 days after Delivery. ——— ——— 9	10	00	00
July	12	To *Raisins.* .. . .. Payable the 2d of *Aug* next. 2	10	14	00
		Sum.	34	6	00

ACCEPTED BILLS, *due to me,*

1729					
May	8	1. To *Raisins.* .... Due by *Jo Hutchison, per J. H's* Bill in 10 Days. 2	6	00	00
	11	2. To *Foreign Linnen.* . Due by *Abraham Fairholm,* in 5 Months ——— ——— 7	26	5	00
July	16	3. To *Insurance Account.* . By *Jeremy Thomson,* in 3 Months ——— 10	90	00	00
	20	4. To *Broad Cloth* ..By *Gideon Keith,* in 2 Months 2	28	16	00
Aug.	30	5. To *John Blackwood,* my *Account Current.* ...By *Alexander Gordon,* in 1 Month. ——— ——— 11	76	10	00
Oct.	5	6. To *Christianus Marbach, his Account Current.* By *George Gordon,* in 2 Months. ——— ——— 15	22	8	00
		Sum	249	19	00

IRON.

1729			Stone.			
May	8	To *Alexander Black* ...... · } N°. 1. at 3 s 1000	—	50	00	00
		To *Andrew Cochran, per my* Bill. }	3	100	00	00
June	3	To *Cash* .. · } N°. 2. at 3 s. 4 d per Stone 300	1	32	10	00
		To *Daniel Trader.* }	5	17	10	00
Sept.	28	To *Benjamin Barclay my Account with him.* N°. 1. at 3 s. ——— ——— 100	15	15	00	00
Oct	8	To *Profit* and *Loss* ——— ———	16	20	00	00
		Sum. 1400		235	00	00

ALEXANDER BLACK

1729					
May	28	To *John Paton.* ..... Per Bill. } ——— 5	15	00	00
		To *Profit* and *Loss.* . For discount. } ——— ——— 8		2	8
Aug	8	To *Cash.* ——— 10	22	10	00
Oct.	8	To *Ballance.* ——— 17	22	7	4
		Sum.	60	00	00

JOHN

		CREDITOR.		l.	s	d.

JOHN HOUSTON.

1729				l.	s	d.
May	30	By *James Montgomery.*	7	7	12	00
Aug.	8	By *Cash.*	10	23	00	00
Sept.	18	By *Cash.*	13	3	14	00
		Sum.		34	6	00

ACCEPTED BILLS, *due to me,*

1729							
June	7	1	By *Cash* .... From *John Hutchison.*	1	6	00	00
Aug	14	4	By *Cash.* .... From *Gideon Keith*	10	28	16	00
Sept	15	5	By *David Johnston.* .. For Payment of *Alexander Gordon.*	4	76	10	00
Oct.	7	2	By *Cash* .... Received } From *A. Fairholm*	13	24	00	00
			By *Profit* and *Loss.* Discounted }	8	2	5	00
Oct.	8		By *Ballance.* .... N°. 3. and 6.	17	112	8	00
			Sum		249	19	00

IRON

				Stone		l.	s	d.
1729								
May	20	By *Scotch Linnen* ... At 3 s. 6 d. per Stone, N°. 1.	200	7	35	00	00
	30	By *Cash* .... At 4 s. per Stone N°. 1. —	300	1	60	00	00
Sept.	15	By *James Montgomery.* } At 3 s per Stone, N° 1.	500		60	00	00
		By *Cash.* .... }			15	00	00
Oct.	8	By *Ballance.* ...... N°. 1. 100 St. N°. 2 300 St.	400	17	65	00	00
		Sum.	14 00		235	00	00

ALEXANDER BLACK.

1729						
May	8	By *Iron.* ..... Payable in 3 Months		50	00	00
Sept.	18	By *Benjamin Barclay, my Account in Company* .... Payable in 2 Months.	15	10	00	00
		Sum		60	00	00

Y

FORLIGN

DEBTOR.

1729				Holld Pieces.	Musln Pieces.	l.	s.	d.
			FOREIGN LINNEN.					
May	11	To	*Broad Cloth.* . . . 25 Yards Each Piece, at 4 s. . . . N°. 1	12	2	60	00	00
Aug.	20	To	*John Blackwood, my Account Current* — 40 Yards each Piece.	6	11	128	10	00
		To	*Cash* . . . . . . For Charges here.		13		15	
Oct.	5	To	*Christianus Marbach,* &c. . . . . N°. 1. 30 Yards each	4	15	20	00	00
		To	*Cash.*		13	1	13	00
Oct.	8	To	*Profit and Loss.* — —		16	4	11	8
			Sum.	16	6	210	9	8

1729					Barrels	l.	s.	d.
			SALMONS.					
May	11	To	*Raisins* . . . At 2 l. 5 s. per Barrel . N°. 1.	12	2	27	00	00
	14	To	*Cash.* . . . . At 2 l. 5 s. per Barrel		1	60	00	00
		To	*Andrew Cochran.* . . . . . . N°. 1. —	96	3	40	00	00
		To	*James Montgomery* — — —			116	00	00
			Sum.		108	243	00	00

1730						l.	s.	d.
			JAMES MONTGOMERY.					
May	30	To	*Cash* . . . . . . For Payment of the Salmons.		1	108	8	00
		To	*John Houston.*		6	7	12	00
Sept	15	To	*Iron* . . . . Given for Payment of the Beef.		6	60	00	00
			Sum			176	00	00

1729				Yards.		l.	s.	d.
			SCOTCH LINNEN.					
May	20	To	*Cash* . . . . At 16 d. per Yard. . . . . N°. 1	750	1	15	00	00
		To	*Iron*		6	35	00	00
			Sum.	750		50	00	00

FOREIGN

FOREIGN LINNEN.

1729			Hhd Pieces	Musl. Pieces	l.	s.	d.
May	11	By *Accepted Bills due to me.* —— —— .... At 5 s. 3 d. per Yard.... Nº. 1.	4	6	26	5	00
June	12	By *Delivery Account of Buying*....: At 4 s. per Yard.... Nº. 1 ——	4	8	20	00	00
Aug.	14	By *James Trustwell* } At 3 s. 6 d. ... Nº. 1	4	4	12	00	00
		By *Cash* ..... }		10	6	6	8
Oct.	8	By *Ballance*........ Muslin Nº. 1. —	4 6	17	145	18	00
		Sum.	16	6	210	9	8

SALMONS.

1729			Barrels		l.	s.	d.
June	21	By *Voyage to Rochel, &c.* ...... Nº. 1. —	96	9	216	00	00
July	4	To *Voyage to Bourdeaux, &c.* ..... Nº. 1. —	12	10	27	00	00
		Sum.	108		243	00	00

JAMES MONTGOMERY.

1729					l.	s.	d.
May	14	By *Salmons*...... Payable on Demand — —			116	00	00
June	21	By *Voyage to Rochel, &c.* ..... For 40 Barrels of *Beef*..... Payable in 1 Month. —		9	60	00	00
		Sum			176	00	00

SCOTCH LINNEN.

1729			Yards.		l.	s.	d.
Oct.	8	By *Ballance*........... Nº. 1. —	750	17	50	00	00

PROFIT

			DEBTOR.		*l.*	*s.*	*d.*
1729			**PROFIT** *and* **LOSS.**				
July	4	To *Bottomree Account.*		9	50	00	00
	12	To *Wager's Account.*		9	10	00	00
Aug	8	To *Cash.*		10	1	0	00
	24	To *Voyage* from *Lisbon,* &c.		12	74	00	00
Oct	7	To *Accepted Bills due to me.*		6	2	5	00
		To *Cash.*		13	50	00	00
		To *Account* of *out-standing Charges.*		16	17	00	00
			Transferred to fol	16	203	15	00

				Barrels		*l.*	*s.*	*d.*
1729			**FIGS**					
May	30	To *Cash* .... At 2 *l.* 4 *s.* per Barrel. N°. 1.		16	1	35	4	00
June	12	To *William Smith* .... At 2 *l* 10 *s* per						
		Barrel. .... N°. 2.		8	4	20	00	00
Oct.	8	To *Profit* and *Loss.*		16		14	2	00
			Sum	24		69	6	00

					l.	*s.*	*d.*
1729		**DELIVERY ACCOUNT** *of* **BUYING**					
June	3	To *Cash* ...... ⎱ 24 Barrels of Raisins, to be ⎰		1	16	00	00
		To *Andrew Cochran.* ⎰ delivered 1 *July* next. - -⎱		3	20	00	00
	12	To *Foreign Linnen.* . ⎱ 20 Bales of Paper, to be⎰		7	2	00	00
		To *William Wallace.* ⎰ delivered 1 *Aug* next - -⎱		3	56	00	00
July	2	To *Daniel Trader* .... 5 Pieces of Holland ..					
		... the 20*th* of *July*		5	25	00	00
Aug.	22	To *Thomas Dalziel.* ⎱ 100 Bolls of Wheat. . . ⎰		13	140	00	00
		To *Cash.* .. ... . ⎰ the 1*st* of *Nov.* next. ⎱		13	10	00	00
			Sum		287	00	00

PROFIT

			CREDITOR.		*l.*	*s.*	*d.*

PROFIT *and* LOSS.

1729							
May	28	By *Alexander Black.*		6		2	8
June	6	By *David Johnston.*		4	3	00	00
	18	By *Andrew Hunter.*		3	2	11	5
	21	By *David Johnston.*		4	4	00	00
	22	By *Bottomree Account.*		9	24	00	00
	25	By *Bottomree Account.*		9	10	00	00
July	22	By *Daniel Trader.*		5	5	00	00
	28	By *Cash.*		10	1	5	00
Aug.	5	By *Cash.*		10	2	00	00
	13	By *Bottomree Account.*		9	20	00	00
	29	By *House* in *Broad Street.*		14	200	00	00
Sept.	2	By *Hero Moy's Account Current.*		13		15	00
		By *Andrew Cochran.*		3	50	00	00
		By *Cash*		13	20	00	00
		By *Adam Brown*		15	50	00	00
	6	By *Hero Moy's Account of Goods, &c.*		12	12	00	00
	7	By *Christianus Marbach, his Account Current*		15	4	00	00
			Transferred to fol	16	408	14	1

FIGS.

				Barrels			
1729							
June	15	By *Cash* ...... } 2 Barrels N° 2 16 }			1	15	00	00
		By *James Trustwell.* } N° 1. . At 2 *l* }	18	4	20	00	00
		By *Peter Chapman* : } 17 *s.* }		5	16	6	00
	25	By *Wool* ...... N°. 2 ..... At 3 *l.* per Barrel	6	10	18	00	00
			Sum	24	69	6	00

DELIVERY ACCOUNT *of* BUYING

1729							
July	2	By *Raisins.* ..... Received 24 Barrels from *Andrew Cochran.*		2	36	00	00
	22	By *Daniel Trader* .... For 5 Pieces of Holland, not delivered.		5	25	00	00
Aug.	3	By *Paper.* .. ... 20 Bales from *William Wallace* -		4	76	00	00
Oct.	8	By *Ballance.* .... For 100 Bolls of Wheat, *&c.*		17	150	00	00
			Sum		287	00	00

DELIVERY

			DEBTOR.		l.	s.	d.
			DELIVERY ACCOUNT of SELLING.				
1729							
July	12	To Raisins..... 13 Barrels.....Delivered to John Houston.		2	23	3	8
Aug	3	To Paper........ 6 Bales to William Smith.		4	24	00	00
		To William Smith..... 2 Bales not delivered.		4	8	00	00
			Sum.		55	3	8
			VOYAGE to LONDON in the HIND of ABERDEEN　J. M. Master.				
1729							
June	18	To Brandy..... 56 Casks Nº 1, 2.		5	156	00	00
		To Cash...... For Charges and Insurance, &c.		1	23	1	00
			Sum.		179	1	00
			VOYAGE to ROCHEL in the SWAN of PETER-HEAD D F. Master.				
1729							
June	21	To Salmons.....8 Last Nº. 1.		7	216	00	00
		To James Montgomery. .... For 40 Barrels.		7	60	00	00
		To Cash..... Paid for 240 Yards of Plaiden, with Charges on the whole.		1	11	16	8
			Sum		287	16	8
			BOTTOMREE ACCOUNT.				
1729							
June	22	To Cash ..... Lent Thomas Speedwell.		1	50	00	00
		To Profit and Loss ..... For the Interest.		8	24	00	00
	25	To Cash .... Lent Hercules Handy.		1	40	00	00
		To Profit and Loss. .... For the Interest.		8	10	00	00
Aug	13	To Cash..... Lent Laurance Lovemoney		10	60	00	00
		To Profit and Loss...... For the Interest.		8	20	00	00
			Sum.		204	0	00
			WAGER's ACCOUNT.				
1729							
June	22	To Cash........ Against John Ramsey.		1	5	00	00
	25	To Cash .... Against Thomas Murray.		1	10	00	00
July	25	To Hazard Account...... Against Simeon Wilfull		11	6	00	00
Aug.	13	To Hazard Account ... Against Mr. John Justice		11	10	00	00
	19	To Cash..... Lost against Mr. John Justice.		13	10	00	00
Sept.	13	To Cash...... Against Thomas Arrowsmith.		13	10	00	00
Oct.	8	To Profit and Loss...... For Closing this Account.		16	16	00	00
			Sum.		67	00	00

		CREDITOR.		*l.*	*s.*	*d.*
1729		**DELIVERY ACCOUNT** *of* **SELLING**				
June	7	By *Cash*.......⎱13 Barrels of Raisins, to be⎱	1	13	3	8
		By *John Houston*.⎰ delivered the 10th of *July* next.⎰	6	10	00	00
	15	By *Daniel Trader*.⎱8 Bales of Paper, to be de-⎱	5	18	00	00
		By *William Smith*.⎰ livered the 5th of *Aug.* next.⎰	4	14	00	00
		Sum.		55	3	8
1729		**VOYAGE** *to* **LONDON** *in the* **HIND** *of* **ABERDEEN.** J. M. *Master.*				
July	12	By *John Blackwood*, *my Account of Brandy*....... 56 Casks.	11	179	1	00
1729		**VOYAGE** *to* **ROCHEL** *in the* **SWAN** *of* **PETER-HEAD.** D. F. *Master.*				
Aug.	10	By *Daniel Stratton*, *my Account* of Goods, &c. .... The whole received.	12	287	16	8
1729		**BOTTOMREE ACCOUNT.**				
July	4	By *Profit and Loss*......... Hercules Handy's Ship being Lost.	8	50	00	00
	16	By *Cornelius Mandole*, *my Account Current*......... Received from *Thomas Speedwell*	11	74	00	00
Oct.	8	By *Ballance*...... Upon *Laurance Lovemoney's* Ship.	17	80	00	00
		Sum.		204	00	00
1729		**WAGER's ACCOUNT.**				
July	12	By *Profit and Loss*.... Lost, against *Thomas Murray.*	8	10	00	00
		By *Cash*..... Gained upon a Horse-Race.	10	15	00	00
	15	By *Cash*...... Gained (with my own Stake) against *John Ramsey.*	10	10	00	00
Aug.	19	By *Hazard Account*....... To Ballance the Wager against *Simeon Wilfull.*	11	6	00	00
		By *Cash*...... Gained and received of this Wager	13	6	00	00
		By *Hazard Account*....... To Ballance the Article against Mr. *John Justice.*	11	10	00	00
Oct.	8	By *Ballance*...... For the Wager against *Thomas Arrowsmith*, undecided.	17	10	00	00
		Sum.		67	00	00

					Packs	l.	s.	d.
			DEBTOR.					
1729		**W O O L L**						
June	25	To Cash........ } Nº. 1, 2, 3, 4.		4	1	19	9	6½
		To Figs........			8	18	00	00
		To James Trustwell.			4	12	00	00
			Sum	4		49	9	6½
1729		**I N S U R A N C E A C C O U N T.**						
July	30	To Cash ...... Lost upon the Unicorn of Pitten-Weem				80	00	00
Oct.	8	To Profit and Loss.			16	67	00	00
			Sum.			147	00	00
1729		**S H E E P - S K I N S.**		Packs.				
June	28	To Cash..... ...At 2 l. 13 s. 4 d. per Pack.		20	1	53	6	8
1729		**VOYAGE to BOURDEAUX, in the SUC-CESS of ABERDEEN.　J. K. Master.**						
July	4	To Salmons...... 12 Barrels. Nº. 1.			7	27	00	00
		To Wooll .. .... 4 Packs.				49	9	6½
		To Cash .. . For Charges				2	18	00
Oct.	8	To Profit and Loss..... .. upon the Salmons.			17	13	18	8
			Sum.			92	16	2½
1729		**C A S H.**						
		Transferred	from fol	1	1096	15	8
July	10	To Insurance Account.				120	00	
	12	To Wager's Account.			9	15	00	00
	15	To Wager's Account.			9	10	00	00
	25	To Peter Chapman.			5	16	6	00
	28	To Profit and Loss.			8	1	15	00
Aug	1	To Wine.			2	132	00	00
	5	To John Blackwood, my Account Current			11	100	00	00
		To Profit and Loss.			8	20	00	00
	8	To John Houston			6	23	00	00
	14	To Foreign Linnen.			7	6	6	8
		To Accepted Bills due to me.			6	28	16	00
	15	To John Blackwood, my Account Current.			11	20	00	00
	16	To Herman van Rymer, my Account Current.			12	40	8	5
			Transferred to fol. 14			1503	17	9

					l.	*s.*	*d.*
			CREDITOR.				
1729		W O O L.		Packs			
July	2	By *Voyage* to *Bourdeaux*, &c. — —		4	49	9	6½
1729		I N S U R A N C E A C C O U N T.					
June	28	By *Cash* ...... For Insurance on the *Greyhound* of *Leith.*		1	45	00	00
July	10	By *Cash* .... For Insurance on the *Unicorn* of *Pitten-Weem.*			12	00	00
	16	By *Accepted Bills*, &c. ...... For Insurance on the *Speedwell* of *Leith.*		6	90	00	00
			Sum.		147	00	00
1729		S H E E P - S K I N S.		Packs.			
July	10	By *Voyage* to *Amsterdam*, &c. —		20 11	53	6	8
1729		V O Y A G E *to* B O U R D E A U X, *in the* SUC-CESS *of* A B E R D E E N. J K. *Master*					
Aug.	3	By *Voyage* from *Bourdeaux*, &c. .... For 12 Barrels of Salmons. —		11	37	6	8
	23	By *Daniel Stratton*, my *Account of Wool*. .... For 4 Packs of Wool. —		14	55	9	6½
			Sum.		9:	16	2½
1729		C A S H.					
		Transferred — — from fol		1	871	15	10½
July	2	By *Voyage* to *Bourdeaux*, &c			2	8	00
	10	By *Voyage* to *Amsterdam*, &c.		11	3	00	00
	30	By *Insurance Account.*			80	00	00
Aug.	1	By *Wine.*		2	36	00	00
	8	By *Alexander Black* }		6	22	10	00
		By *Profit* and *Loss* }		8		10	00
	13	By *Bottomree Account.*		9	60	00	00
	16	By *Hero Moy's Account of Goods.*		12	3	14	8
		Transferred to fol.		13	1079	18	6½

				DEBTOR.		*l.*	*s.*	*d.*

1729		VOYAGE *to* AMSTERDAM *in the* WILD-CAT *of* ABERDEEN. G. S. *Master.*						
July	10	To *Sheep-Skins.* . . . . . . 20 Packs shipped.	—	10		53	6	8
		To *Cash.* . . . . . . For Charges.	—	10		3	00	00
				Sum.		56	6	8

					Casks.			
1729		JOHN BLACKWOOD *of* LONDON, *my* ACCOUNT *of* BRANDY.						
July	12	To *Voyage* to London, &c. . . . . . Nº. 1, 2.	—	56	9	179	1	00
Oct.	8	To *Profit* and *Loss.*	—		17	140	19	00
				Sum.	56	320	00	00

					Milrees			
1729		CORNELIUS MANDOLE *of* LIS-BON, *my* ACCOUNT CURRENT						
July	16	To *Bottomree Account.* . . . . . . At 6 *s.* 8 *d.* per Milree.	—	222	9	74	00	00

1729		JOHN BLACKWOOD *of* LONDON, *my* ACCOUNT CURRENT.						
July	22	To *John Blackwood, my Account of Brandy.*	—			120	00	00
Aug	14	To *John Blackwood, my Account of Brandy.*	—			200	00	00
				Sum.		320	00	00

1729		HAZARD ACCOUNT.						
Aug	19	To *Wager's Account* . . . . . . To Ballance the Article against *Simeon Wilful.*	—		9	6	00	00
		To *Wager's Account* . . . . . . To ballance the Article against Mr. *John Justice.*	—		9	10	00	00
				Sum.		16	00	00

1729		VOYAGE *from* BOURDEAUX *in the* SUCCESS *of* ABERDEEN.						
Aug.	3	To *Voyage* to Bourdeaux, &c. . . For 7 Hogsheads of Claret.	—	10		37	6	8

						CREDITOR		*l.*	*s.*	*d.*

VOYAGE to AMSTERDAM in the WILD-CAT of ABERDEEN G. S Mafter

1729										
Aug.	8	By *Herman van Rymer, my Account* of Sheep-Skins ... For 18 Packs; the other 2 Packs loft at Sea					12	56	6	8

JOHN BLACKWOOD of LONDON, *my* ACCOUNT of BRANDY. Casks.

1729										
July	22	By *John Blackwood, my Account Current.*			20		120	00	00	
Aug.	14	By *John Blackwood, my Account Current.*			36		200	00	00	
		Sum			56		320	00	00	

CORNELIUS MANDOLE of LIS-BON, *my* ACCOUNT CURRENT. Milrees

1729										
Aug.	10	By *Voyage* from *Lisbon,* &c. .... 50 Barrels of Raifins.				222	12	74	00	00

JOHN BLACKWOOD of LONDON, *my* ACCOUNT CURRENT.

1729										
Aug.	5	By *Cafh* ...... Received for a Bill upon him.				10	100	00	00	
	15	By *Cafh* ...... For a Bill upon him.				10	20	00	00	
	20	By *Foreign Linnen.*				7	123	10	00	
	30	By *Accepted Bills,* due to me..... Remitted to me.				6	76	10	00	
		Sum.					320	00	00	

HAZARD ACCOUNT

1729										
July	25	By *Wager's Account.* .... Againft *Simeon Wilful*				9	6	00	00	
Aug	13	By *Wager's Account.* .... Againft Mr. *John Juftice*				9	10	00	00	
		Sum					16	00	00	

VOYAGE from BOURDEAUX in the SUCCESS of ABERDEEN.

1729										
Sept.	6	By *Wine* ...... For 7 Hogfheads of Claret.				2	37	6	8	

HERMAN

				DEBTOR.		*l.*	*s.*	*d.*
1729		HERMAN van RYMER *of* AMSTERDAM, *my* ACCOUNT *of* SHEEP-SKINS.			Packs.			
Aug.	8	To *Voyage* to *Amsterdam,* &c. ————			18 11	56	6	8
Oct.	8	To *Profit* and *Lofs.* ————			17	21	3	4
				Sum.	18	77	10	00
1729		DANIEL STRATTON *of* ROCHEL, *my* ACCOUNT *of* GOODS. *per* SWAN *of* PETERHEAD.						
Aug.	10	To *Voyage* to *Rochel* . . . . For 8 Laft of Salmons, 40 Barrels of Beef, and 240 Yards of *Plaiden* . . . . Total Charge.			9	287	16	8
Oct.	8	To *Profit* and *Lofs* . . . . . Gained on the Salmons and Beef.			17	100	19	4
				Sum.		388	16	00
1729		VOYAGE *from* LISBON *in the* RED LYON *of* MONTROSE.						
Aug	10	To *Cornelius Mandole, my Account Current* . . . . For 50 Barrels of Raifins. ————			11	74	00	00
1729		HERMAN van RYMER *of* AMSTERDAM, *my* ACCOUNT CURRENT.			Guild.			
Aug	8	To *Herman van Rymer, my Account of Sheep-Skins* . . . . . At 22 *d.* per Guilder. ————		436,⁴		40	00	00
	15	To *Herman van Rymer, my Account of Sheep-Skins* . . . . . At 22 *d* ————		400		37	10	00
Sept.	25	To *Daniel Stratton, my Account Current* . . . At 22 *d* ————		458⁷	15	42	00	00
Oct.	8	To *Ballance* . . . . . . At 22 *d.* ————		522⁴	17	47	19	3½
				Sum.	1817	167	9	3½
1729		HERO MOY *of* AMSTERDAM, *his* ACCOUNT *of* GOODS *per* LEOPARD *of* ABERDEEN.	Tea. Pound	Cards. Dozen	Flax. Packs			
Aug.	16	To *Cafh* For Charges upon Receipt of	50	40	8 10	3	14	8
Sept.	6	To *Cafh.* . . . . . Paid more Charges			13	4	14	8
		To *Profit* and *Lofs.* . . . . For my Commiffion. ————			8	12	00	00
	13	To *Ditto, his Account Current* . . . . For neat Proceeds. ————			13	43	10	8
			Sum.	50	40	8	64	00	00

				CREDITOR.	Packs	*l*	*s.*	*d.*
1729			HERMAN van RYMER *of* AMSTERDAM, *my* ACCOUNT *of* SHEEP-SKINS.					
Aug	8	By *Herman van Rymer, my Account Current.* ..... Sold.			10	40	00	00
	15	By *Herman van Rymer, my Account Current.* ..... Sold.			8	37	10	00
			Sum.		18	77	10	00

			CREDITOR.		*l*	*s.*	*d.*
1729		DANIEL STRATTON *of* ROCHEL, *my* ACCOUNT *of* GOODS. *per* SWAN *of* PETERHEAD.					
Aug.	22	By *Daniel Stratton, my Account of Sales* ..... For 8 Laft of Salmons.	13	300	00	00	
Sept,	18	By *Daniel Stratton, my Account Current.* ..... For 40 Barrels of Beef.	15	79	16	00	
Oct.	8	By *Ballance* ...... For 240 Yards of *Plaiden.*	17	9	00	00	
			Sum	388	16	00	

				l	*s.*	*d.*
1729		VOYAGE *from* LISBON *in the* RED LYON *of* MONTROSE.				
Aug.	24	By *Profit* and *Lofs.* ..... The Ship being caft away	8	74	00	00

			CREDITOR.	Guild		*l*	*s.*	*d.*
1729		HERMAN van RYMER *of* AMSTERDAM, *my* ACCOUNT CURRENT					
Aug.	16	By *Cafh.* ...... For my Bill upon him. . At 22 *d* ¼ per Guilder.	436	13	40	8	5
	22	By *Andrew Cochran.* .. .. At 22 *d* ½	400	3	37	10	00
Sept	11	By *Voyage form Amfterdam,* &c At 21 *d*	981	16	85	16	0
Oct.	8	By *Profit* and *Lofs.*		17	3	14	1
			Sum	1817		167	9	1

				Tea Pound.	Cards Dozen.	Flax. Packs.	*l*	*s.*	*d.*
1729		HERO MOY *of* AMSTERDAM, *his* ACCOUNT *of* GOODS. *per* LEOPARD *of* ABERDEEN.							
Aug	20	By *Cafh* . ... For			8	13	3200	00
	23	By *Peter Chapman.*		40	3	3200	00	
		N. B. Sent by Order to *London*	50					
		Sum.	50	40	8	64	00	00

				DEBTOR.		*l.*	*s.*	*d.*
1729				C A S H.				
			Transferred ——— ———	from fol. 10	1503	17	9
Aug.	19	To	*Wager's Account.* ——— ———	9	6	00	00
	20	To	*Hero Moy's Account of Goods,* &c. ———	12	32	00	00
Sept.	2	To	*Profit and Loss.* ——— ———	8	20	00	00
	5	To	*Charles Charcu, our Account of Exchange.* ——	14	48	6	8
	13	To	*Peter Chapman.* ——— ———	5	32	00	00
	15	To	*Iron.* ——— ———	6	15	00	00
	18	To	*John Houston* ——— ———	6	3	14	00
	25	To	*Daniel Stratton, my Account Current* ———	15	7	13	4
	28	To	*Benjamin Barclay, my Account with him.* ——	15	25	00	00
Oct.	7	To	*Accepted Bills due to me.* —— ——	6	24	00	00
				Sum.		1717	11	9
1729			HERO MOY *of* AMSTERDAM, *his* ACCOUNT CURRENT.				
Aug.	20	To	*Cash* ... .. Remitted to him 208 $\frac{14}{23}$ Guilders, at 23 *d. per* Guilder, is ———		20	00	00
Sept.	2	To	*Cash* .... Paid for 4 Packs of Sheep-Skins, for his Account. ——— ———		14	15	00
		To	*Profit and Loss*........ For my Commission. —	8		15	00
	28	To	*Accepted Bills due by me.* .... To Robert Clark.	16	8	00	8
				Sum		43	10	8
1729			DANIEL STRATTON *of* ROCHEL, *my* ACCOUNT *of* SALES	Crown			
Aug.	22	To	*Daniel Stratton, my Account of Goods,* &c. .... At 4 *s. per* Crown ——— ——	1500 12	300	00	00
1729			THOMAS DALZIEL.				
Oct.	8	To	*Ballance.* —— —— ——	17	240	00	00

				l.	*s.*	*d.*
		CREDITOR.				
1729		**CASH.**				
		Transferred — — from fol. 10		1079	18	6½
Aug.	19	By *Wager's Account.*	9	100	00	00
	20	By *Hero Moy's Account Current.*		200	00	00
		By *Foreign Linnen.*	7		15	00
	22	By *Delivery Account of Buying.*	8	100	00	00
	26	By *Charles Chareu, our Account of Exchange.*	14	93	6	8
	30	By *Benjamin Barclay, my Account with him in Company.*	15	200	00	00
Sept.	2	By *Hero Moy's Account Current.*		14	15	00
	6	By *Wine*	2	5	10	00
	7	By *Hero Moy's Account of Goods, &c*	12	4	14	8
		By *Wine.*	2	300	00	00
		By *Christianus Marbach, his Account Current.*	15	8	8	00
	13	By *Christianus Marbach, his Account Current.*	15	600	00	00
		By *Wager's Account*	9	100	00	00
	18	By *Voyage* from *Amsterdam, &c.*	16	500	00	00
Oct.	5	By *Foreign Linnen* ..... And By *Flax.* (7	16	4	12	00
	7	By *Profit and Loss.*	8	500	00	00
	8	By *Ballance.*	17	371	11	10½
		Sum.		1717	11	9
1729		**HERO MOY of AMSTERDAM,** **his ACCOUNT CURRENT**				
Sept.	13	By *Ditto, his Account of Goods... For neat Proceeds.*	12	43	10	8
1729		**DANIEL STRATTON of ROCHEL,** Crown **my ACCOUNT of SALES**				
Sept.	13	By *Daniel Stratton, my Account Current* ... The Debts being paid	1500 15	300	00	00
1729		**THOMAS DALZILL.**				
Aug.	22	By *Delivery Account of Buying .. ...Payable at Martinmas next.*	8	140	0	00
	29	By *Ship Dragon of Aberdeen. ..... . Payable at Candlemas next.*	15	100	00	00
		Sum		240	00	00

			DEBTOR.		*l.*	*s.*	*d.*

1729

DANIEL STRATTON *of* ROCHEL, *my* ACCOUNT *of* WOOL

| *Aug* | 23 | To *Voyage* to *Bourdeaux,* &c. . . . . . 4 Packs. | — | 10 | 55 | 9 | 6½ |

1729

CHARLES CHAREU *of* BOUR-DEAUX, *our* ACCOUNT *of* EX-CHANGE *in* COMPANY.

				Crown			
Aug.	26	To *Cash* . . . . . . Remitted to him, at 56 *d.*	400		93	6	8
Sept	18	To *Accepted Bills due by me* . . . . Drawn on me, at 57 *d.*	300	16	71	5	00
Oct	8	To *His Account Current.*	—		1	15	5
		To *Profit* and *Loss.*	—	17	1	15	5
		Sum.	700		168	2	6

1729

CHARLES CHAREU, *his* ACCOUNT CURRENT.

| *Oct* | 8 | To *Ballance.* | — | 17 | 1 | 15 | 5 |

1729

HOUSE *in* CASTLE-STREET.

Aug	26	To *John Campbel.*	—		300	15	00
Oct.	8	To *Profit* and *Loss.*	—	17	10	00	00
		Sum			310	15	00

1729

JOHN CAMPBEL.

| *Oct.* | 8 | To *Ballance.* | — | 17 | 300 | 15 | 00 |

1729

WILLIAM DAVIDSON.

| *Aug.* | 26 | To *House* in *Castle-Street* . . . . . For ¼ Years Rent payable at *Martimnas* next. | — | | 10 | 00 | 00 |

1729

HOUSE *in* BROAD-STREET.

Aug.	29	To *Profit* and *Loss* . . .	—	8	200	00	00
		To *Thomas Richman*	—	15	30	00	00
		Sum			230	00	00

		CREDITOR.		l,	s	d

DANIEL STRATTON of ROCHEL,
my ACCOUNT of WOOL

1729							
Sept.	18	By *Voyage* from *Rochel* to *Amsterdam* . . . . Shipped 4 Packs. ——	16	55	9	6½

Crown

CHARLES CHAREU of BOUR-
DEAUX, our ACCOUNT of EX-
CHANGE in COMPANY.

1729							
Sept.	5	By *Cash* . . . . Remitted to me at 58 d. —	200	13	48	6	8
	7	By *Thomas Richman* . . . . Drawn by me, at 57 d. ——	500	15	119	15	10
		Sum	700		168	2	6

CHARLES CHAREU, his ACCOUNT
CURRENT.

1729							
Oct.	8	By *Ditto, our Account of Exchange in Company.* —			1	13	5

HOUSE in CASTLE-STREET.

1729							
Aug.	26	By *William Davidson.* . . . . ½ Years Rent from *Whitsunday* Last. ——		10	00	00
Oct.	8	By *Ballance.* ——	17	300	15	00
		Sum.		310	15	00

JOHN CAMPBEL.

1729							
Aug	26	By *House* in *Castle-Street* . . . . . { 300 l payable 1 Year hence 15 s. ¼ of a Year hence. }	300	15	00

WILLIAM DAVIDSON.

1729							
Oct.	8	By *Ballance.* ——	17	1000	00

HOUSE in BROAD-STREET.

1729							
Oct.	8	By *Ballance.* ——	17	230	00	00

A a　　　　　　　　　　　THOMAS

			DEBTOR.		*l.*	*s.*	*d.*

THOMAS RICHMAN.

1729							
Sept.	10	To *Charles Chareu, our Account of Exchange in Company.* .... Payable in 1 Month. ———	14	119	15	10

SHIP *the* DRAGON *of* ABERDEEN, *my* ¼.

1729							
Aug.	29	To *Thomas Dalziel.* ——— ——— ———	13	100	00	00

BENJAMIN BARCLAY, *my* ACCOUNT
with him in COMPANY. ½

Aug	30	To *Cash.* .. .... Stocked with him. ———	13	20	00	00
Sept.	18	To *Alexander Black* .... For Bill payable to *Ditto Black.* ——— ——— ———	6	10	00	00
Oct.	8	To *Profit* and *Loss.* ——— ——— ———	17	10	00	00
		Sum.		40	00	00

ADAM BROWN.

1729							
Sept.	2	To *Profit* and *Loss.* .. .. For the Remainder of his Sons Prentice Fee payable in 1 Year. ———	8	50	00	00
	18	To *Voyage* from *Amsterdam.* .... For 100 ℔ of Coffee, payable in 6 Months. ———	16	60	00	00
		Sum.		110	00	00

CHRISTIANUS MARBACH *of* ROTTERDAM,
his ACCOUNT CURRENT.

1729							
Sept.	7	To *Andrew Cochran.* .... For 200 Pair of Stockings.	3	50	00	00
		To *Cash.* .. .... For Part of 750 Yards of *Plaiden,* with Charges on the whole. ———	13	8	8	00
		To *Thomas Richman* . For the Rest of the *Plaiden*		10	00	00
		To *Profit* and *Loss* ... . For my Commission. ———	8	4	00	00
	13	To *Cash* ...... Paid at Shipping the above Goods.	13	6	00	00
		Sum.		78	8	00

DANIEL STRATTON *of* ROCHEL,
_my_ ACCOUNT CURRENT.

1729			Crown				
Sept.	10	To *Ditto, my Account of Sales.* ... . At 4 *s.* ———	1500	13	300	00	00
	18	To *Ditto, my Account of Goods.* ... At 4 *s.* 9 *d.*	336	12	79	16	00
Oct.	8	To *Profit* and *Loss.* ——— - ———		17	48	19	2
		Sum.	1836		428	15	2

		CREDITOR.		*l.*	*s.*	*d.*
1729		**THOMAS RICHMAN.**				
Aug.	29	By *House* in *Broad-Street.*	14	30	00	00
Sept.	7	By *Christianus Marbach,* his *Account Current.*		10	00	00
Oct.	8	By *Ballance.*	17	79	15	10
		Sum.		119	15	10
1729		**SHIP** *the* **DRAGON** *of* **ABERDEEN,** *my ¼.*				
Oct.	8	By *Ballance.*	17	100	00	00
1729		**BENJAMIN BARCLAY,** *my* **ACCOUNT** *with him in* **COMPANY. ½**				
Sept.	28	By *Cash.* } For clearing my Concerns with him.	13	25	00	00
		By *Iron.* }	6	15	00	00
		Sum		40	00	00
1729		**ADAM BROWN.**				
Oct.	8	By *Ballance.*	17	110	00	00
1729		**CHRISTIANUS MARBACH** *of* **ROTTERDAM,** *his* **ACCOUNT CURRENT.**				
Oct.	5	By *Foreign Linnen......* 4 Pieces of Holland. }	7	20	00	00
		By *Flax......* 4 Packs. }	16	36	00	00
		By *Accepted Bills due to me...* By *G. Gordon.* }	6	22	8	00
		Sum.		78	8	00

		DANIEL STRATTON *of* **ROCHEL,** *my* **ACCOUNT CURRENT.**	Crown	*l.*	*s.*	*d.*
1729						
Sept.	18	By *Voyage* from *Rochel* to *Amsterdam* For Charges upon my Wool shipped for *Amsterdam.*	6	16	1	8	6
	25	By *Herman van Rymer,* my *Account Current .. ..* At *56 d.*	180	12	42	00	00
		By *Broad Cloth.* } For my Bill on him at *57 d.*	100	2	16	00	00
		By *Cash.....* }		13	7	13	4
Oct.	8	By *Ballance.*	1550	17	361	13	4
		Sum.	1836		428	15	2

		DEBTOR.		l.	s.	d.
1729		**VOYAGE *from* AMSTERDAM *in the*** **LAMB *of* ABERDEEN.**				
Sept.	11	To *Herman van Rymer, my Account Current*.... For 100 ℔ of Coffee, and 74 ℔ of Cinnamon.	12	85	16	9
	18	To *Cash* .. .Paid Charges and Duty upon Receipt of these Goods.	13	5	00	00
Oct.	8	To *Profit and Loss.*	17	12	3	3
		Sum.		103	00	00
1729		**VOYAGE *from* ROCHEL *to* AMSTERDAM.**				
Sept	18	To *Daniel Stratton, my Account of Wool* .. 4 Packs	14	55	9	6½
		To *Ditto, my Account Current.*	15	1	8	6
		Sum		56	18	00½
1729		**ACCEPTED BILLS *due by me.***				
Oct.	8	To *Ballance* ......Nᵒ. 1, 2.	17	79	5	8

		FLAX.	Packs.			
1729						
Sept.	18	To *Voyage* from *Amsterdam, &c* ....Nᵒ. 1. 18 Stone each Pack.	4	43	00	00
Oct.	5	To *Christianus Markach, &c.* Nᵒ. 2 18 Stone	15 / 4	36	00	00
		To *Cash* ..... For Charges each Pack,	13 / 4	2	19	00
		Sum	8	81	19	00

		ACCOUNT *of* OUTSTANDING CHARGES.				
1729						
Oct.	8	To *Ballance*	17	1	00	00

		PROFIT *and* LOSS.				
1729		Transferred from fol.	8	203	15	00
Oct	8	To *Tobacco.*	2	62	1	00
		To *Herman van Rymer, my Account Current.*	12	3	14	1½
		Transferred to fol	17	239	10	1½

		CREDITOR.		*l.*	*s.*	*d.*
1729		**VOYAGE** *from* **AMSTERDAM** *in the* **LAMB** *of* **ABERDEEN.**				
Sept. 18	By *Flax* . . . . . . For 4 Packs. ——— ———			43	00	00
	By *Adam Brown* . . . . . . For 100 ℔. of Coffee. ——	15	60	00	00
			Sum	103	00	00
1729		**VOYAGE** *from* **ROCHEL** *to* **AMSTERDAM.**				
Oct. 8	By *Ballance.* ——— ——— ———		17	56	18	00½
1729		**ACCEPTED BILLS** *due by me.*				
Sept. 18	1. By *Charles Chareu,* our *Account of Exchange,* &c. . . To Mr *Robert Blackwood,* at single Usance.	14	71	5	00
28	2. By *Hero Moy,* his *Account Current* . . . . To *Robert Clark* at single Usance. ——— ———	13	8	00	8
			Sum.	79	5	8
1729		**F L A X.**	Packs.			
Oct. 8	By *Ballance.* ——— ——— ———	8 17	81	19	00
1729		**ACCOUNT** *of* **OUTSTANDING CHARGES**				
Oct. 7	By *Profit* and *Loss.* . . Due to sundry Persons, *per Book* of *Expences* of *Trade* and *Living.* ——	8	17	00	00
1729		**P R O F I T** *and* **L O S S.**				
	Transferred ——— ——— *from fol*	8	408	14	1
Oct. 8	By *Wine* ——— ——— ———	2	36	10	00
	By *Raisins* ——— ——— ———	2	12	7	8
	By *Broad Cloth* . . ——— ———	2	23	14	00
	By *Paper* ——— ——— ———	4	15	4	00
	By *Iron.* ——— ——— ———	6	20	00	00
	By *Foreign Linnen* ——— ———	7	4	11	8
	By *Figs.* ——— ——— ———	8	14	2	00
	By *Wager's Account.* ——— ———	9	16	00	00
	By *Insurance Account.* ——— ———	10	67	00	00
			Transferred to fol	17	618	3	5

				DEBTOR		*l.*	*s.*	*d.*

PROFIT *and* LOSS.

1725			Transferred ——— ——— ———	from fol.	16	239	10	1½
Oʒ.	8	To *Stock*........ Neat Gain since *May* the 1ſt. ———		1	738	11	5½

				Sum.		978	1	7

BALLANCE.

1725							
Oʒ.	8	To *Caſh.* ———————	13	371	11	10½
		To *Wine.*...... 10 Hogſheads of Claret, and 4 Hogſheads of White.	2	113	16	8
		To *Tobacco.*........ 13 Hogſheads. ———	2	144	19	00
		To *Raiſins.*........ 10 Barrels. ———	2	15	10	00
		To *Broad Cloth.*........ 5 Pieces. ———	2	69	0	00
		To *William Wallace.* ——— ———	3	53	5	00
		To *Andrew Hunter.* ——— ———	3	102	11	5
		To *Andrew Cochran.* ——— ———	3	37	10	00
		To *Moveables, &c.* ——— ———	3	200	00	00
		To *David Johnſton.* ——— ———	4	57	4	00
		To *Paper.*........ 17 Bales. ———	4	65	4	00
		To *John Paton.* ——— ———	5	40	00	00
		To *Daniel Trader.* ——— ———	5	23	00	00
		To *Accepted Bills due to me.* ———	6	112	8	00
		To *Iron.*........ 400 Stone. ———	6	65	00	00
		To *Foreign Linnen.*........ 4 Pieces of Holland, 6 Pieces of Muſlin.	7	145	18	00
		To *Scotch Linnen.*........ 750 Yards. ———	7	50	00	00
		To *Delivery Account* of *Buying.* .. 100 Bolls of Wheat, *&c.*	8	150	00	00
		To *Bottomree Account.*...... By *Laurance Lovemoney.* ———	9	80	00	00
		To *Wager's Account.*...... Againſt *Thomas Arrowſmith.* ———	9	10	00	00
		To *Daniel Stratton, my Account* of *Goods, &c.* ...... 240 Yards of *Plaiden.* ———	12	6	00	00
		To *Houſe* in *Caſtle-Street.* ———	14	300	15	00
		To *William Davidſon.* ———	14	10	00	00
		To *Houſe* in *Broad-Street.* ———	14	230	00	00
		To *Thomas Richman.* ———	15	79	15	10
		To *Ship Dragon* of *Aberdeen.* ———	15	100	00	00
		To *Adam Brown.* ———	15	110	00	00
		To *Daniel Stratton, my Account Current* ..... 1550 Crowns.	15	361	13	4
		To *Voyage* from *Rochel* to *Amſterdam.* ..... 4 Packs of Wool.	16	56	18	00
		To *Flax.*........ 8 Packs. ———	16	81	19	00

				Sum.		3250	5	2

PROFIT

					l.	s.	d.
		CREDITOR.					
1729		PROFIT and LOSS.					
		Transferred —————— from fol.	16		618	3	5
Oct.	8	By *Voyage to Bourdeaux.* ———	10		13	18	8
		By *John Blackwood, my Account of Brandy.* ———	11		140	19	00
		By *Herman van Rymer, my Account of Sheep-Skins.* ———	12		21	3	4
		By *Daniel Stratton, my Account of Goods, &c.* ———	12		100	19	4
		By *Charles Chareu, our Account of Exchange in Company.* ———	14		1	15	5
		By *House in Castle-Street.* ———	14		100	00	00
		By *Benjamin Barclay, my Account with him in Company.* ———	15		100	00	00
		By *Daniel Stratton, my Account Current.* ———	15		48	19	2
		By *Voyage* from *Amsterdam.* ———	16		12	3	3
		Sum.			978	1	7
1729		BALLANCE.					
Oct.	8	By *Alexander Black.* ———	6		22	7	4
		By *Herman van Rymer, my Account Current.* . . . . 522 $\frac{5}{11}$ Guilders. ———	12		47	19	3$\frac{1}{2}$
		By *Thomas Dalziel.* ———	13		240	00	00
		By *Charles Chareu, his Account Current.* ———	14		1	15	5
		By *John Campbel.* ———	14		300	15	00
		By *Accepted Bills due by me.* ———	16		79	5	8
		By *Account of out-standing Charges.* ———	16		17	00	00
		By *Stock* . . . . My present *Free Estate.* ———	1		2547	2	5$\frac{1}{2}$
		Sum.			3256	5	2

INDEX to the LEGER, N°. 1.

A
B

	Fol.
Brandy.	5
Accepted Bills due to me.	6
Alexander Black.	6
Jo. Blackwood, my Acc. Brandy.	11
Bottomree Account.	9
Ja. Blackwood, my Account Curr.	11
Benj. Barclay, my Acc. with him.	15
Adam Brown	15
Accepted Bills due by me.	16
Ballance.	17

C

Cash.	2, 10, 13
Broad Cloth.	2
Andrew Cochran.	3
Peter Chapman.	5
Ch. Chareu, our Acc. of Excha.	14
Ch. Chareu, his Acc. Current.	14
John Campbel.	14

D

Delivery Account of Buying.	8
——— of Selling.	9
Thomas Dalziel.	13
William Davidson.	14

E
F

Figs.	8
Flax.	16

G
H

Andrew Hunter	3
John Houston	6
Hazard Account.	11
House in Castle-Street.	14
——— in Broad-Street.	14

I

David Johnston.	4
Iron.	6
Insurance Account.	10

K
L

Foreign Linnen.	7
Scotch Linnen.	7

M

	Fol.
Moveables, &c.	3
James Montgomery.	7
Corn. Mandole, my Acc. Curr.	11
Hero Moy's Acc. of Goods.	12
——— Acc. Current.	13
Chr. Marbach, his Acc. Curr.	15

N
O

Outstanding Charges.	16

P

John Paton.	5
Paper.	4
Profit and Loss.	8, 16, 17

Q
R

Raisins.	2
Her. van Rymer, my Acc. Skins.	12
——— my Acc. Current.	12
Thomas Richman.	15

S

Stock.	1
William Smith.	4
Salmons	7
Sheep-Skins.	10
D. Stratton, my Acc. of Goods, &c.	12
——— my Acc. of Sales.	13
——— my Acc. of Wool.	14
——— my Acc. Current.	15
Ship Dragon.	15

T

Tobacco.	2
James Trustwell.	4
Danel Trader.	5

W

Wine.	1
William Wallace.	5
Wool.	10
Wager's Account.	9

V

Voyage to London, &c.	6
——— to Amsterdam, &c.	11
——— to Rochel, &c.	9
——— to Bourdeaux.	10
——— from Lisbon.	1
——— from Bourdeaux.	11
——— from Rochel to Amsterdam.	16
——— from Amsterdam.	16

W A S T - B O O K.

Number 2.

Of me *A. M.* Merchant in *Aberdeen :*

From the Eighth of *October*, 1729.

In which the Debtors and Creditors are mark'd on the Margin ; according to the Second Method of a Journal, explained near the End of Chap. 1. *of the preceeding Treatise.*

WAST-BOOK, N°. 2.

			l.	*s.*	*d.*

<table>
<tr><td rowspan="30">
Sundry Accounts,
(viz The se-
veral Subjects
which make up
my Estate) are
Debtors
to
1 Stock.
</td></tr>
</table>

————— *Aberdeen* October 8, 1729. —————

Inventory of the Estate and Debts of me *A M* Merchant in *Aberdeen*, taken from the Ballance of the preceeding *Leger*, N° 1.

		l.	*s.*	*d.*
1	I have in *Cash.*	371	11	10½
2	I have of *Wine*, 14 Hogsheads, *viz.*			

Claret	N°	Hds.	*l.*	*s*	*d.*
	1	1	8	00	0
	2	7	45	16	8
	3	2	24	00	0
		10	77	16	8
White		4 Hds.	36	00	0
		14	113	16	8

		l.	*s.*	*d.*
		113	16	8
2	I have of *Tobacco*, 13 Hogsheads, at 11 *l.* 3 *s.* is	144	19	00
2	I have of *Raisins*, 5 Barrels, N°. 1. 8 *l.* also, 5 Barrels, N°. 2. 7 *l.* 10 *s* Total Value.	15	10	00
2	I have of *Broad Cloth*, 5 Pieces, *viz.*			

N°.	Ps	Cont. Yds.		*l.*	*s.*
1	1	—— 25	at 14 *s.* is.	17	10
2	1	—— 30	16 *s.* 8 *d.*	25	00
3	1	—— 18	12 *s.*	10	16
4	2	—— 16 each.	10 *s.*	16	00
	5			69	06

		l.	*s.*	*d.*
		69	6	00
2	I have of *Iron*, 400 Stone, N°. 1. 100 Stone 15 *l.* N° 2 300 Stone 50 *l.* ——	65	00	00
2	I have of *Linnen Cloth*, viz.			

		l.	*s*
Holland, 4 Pieces, 30 Yards each.		21	13
Muslin, 6 Pieces 40 Yards each.		124	5
Scotch Linnen, 750 Yards		50	00
		195	18

		l.	*s.*	*d.*
		195	18	00
2	I have of *Paper* 17 Bales, *viz* N°. 1. to 3. 12 *l.* N°. 2. to 14 53 *l.* 4 *s.* Total.	65	4	00
2	I have of *Flax*, 8 Packs, cont. 18 St. each. ——	81	19	00
3	I have 100 Bolls of Wheat, to be received of *Thomas Dalziel*, the 1st of *November* next	150	00	00
	Transferred	1273	4	6½

		l.	*s*	*d*
	Transferred ——— ——— ———	1273	4	6¼
3	I have a Houſe in *Caſtle-Street*, marked N°. 1.	300	15	00
	—— Another in *Broad-Street*, N°. 2. ——	230	00	00
3	I have ¼ of the Ship the *Dragon* of *Aberdeen*.	100	00	00
3	I have 240 Yards of *Plaiden*; in the Hands of *Daniel Stratton* Factor at *Rochel*. ——	9	00	00
3	I have on board the *Fortune*, upon her Voyage from *Rochel* to *Amſterdam*, 4 Packs of Wool	56	18	00 ½
3	I have conſigned in a Wager againſt *Thomas Arrowſmith*. ———	10	00	00
3	I have of *Moveables*, per particular *Inventory*	200	00	00
	There is due to me by the following Perſons, *viz.*			
3	By *William Wallace* ——— ———	53	5	00
4	*Andrew Hunter*; upon Bond, Principal and Intereſt ——— ——— ———	102	11	5
4	*Andrew Cochran*. ——— ———	37	10	00
4	*David Johnſton*. ——— ———	57	4	00
4	*John Paton*. ——— ———	49	0	00
4	*Daniel Trader*. ——— ———	23	00	00
4	*William Davidſon*. ——— ———	10	00	00
4	*Thomas Richman*. ——— ———	79	15	10
5	*Adam Brown*. ——— ———	110	00	00
5	*Daniel Stratton* of *Rochel*, 1550 Crowns. -	361	13	4
5	*Laurance Lovemoney*, upon Bottomree of his Ship, the *Faulcon*, upon her Voyage to *Genoa*. ——— ———	80	00	00
	{ *George Gordon*, payable the 5th of December. —— } By *Accepted* Bills.	22	8	00
5	{ *Jeremy Thompſon*, 16 Oct. }	90	00	00
	Sum.	3256	5	2

	I owe the following Debts, *viz.*			
5	To *Alexander Black*. ——— ———	22	7	4
5	*Herman van Rymer* of *Amſterdam* 522 Guilders. ———	47	19	3½
5	*Thomas Dalziel*. ——— ———	240	00	00
6	*Charles Charen* of *Bourdeaux*, for his Account Current. ——— ———	1	15	5
6	*John Campbel*. ——— ———	300	15	00
	{ *Robert Blackwood*, payable the 18th of Oct. —— —— } By *Accepted* Bills.	71	5	00
5	{ *Robert Clark*, 28 Oct. —— }	8	00	8
6	Sundry Perſons, *per* Book of Charges ——	17	00	00
	Sum.	709	2	8

{ *Stock is Debtor to Sundry Accounts, (viz. To the Perſons to whom I owe).* }

		l.	s.	d.		l.	s.	d.

———— *Oct.* 10. ————

2	Crs. { *Wine.* — —	70	00	00
2	{ *Raiſins.* ———	19	00	00
2	{ *Iron.* — —	80	00	00
1	Dr. *Caſh.* — —	169	00	00

Sold for Ready Money,
7 Hogſheads of Claret,
N°. 2. at 10 *l.* per Hogs-   *l.*
head, is   —   70
Alſo, 10 Barrels of
    Raiſins, at 1 *l.* 18 *s.*
    per Barrel, is   — 19
Alſo, 400 Stone of *Iron.* 80

        169   169 | 00 | 00

5	Dr. { *H. v. Rymer,*			
	{ *my Acc. Curr.*	70	00	00
3	Cr. *Voyage* from *Ro-chel.*			

I have advice from *Her-
man van Rymer* of *Amſterdam,* that he has received
from on Board the *Fortune,*
my 4 Packs of Wool ſhipped
at *Rochel;* and that he has
ſold the ſame for Ready
Money: The neat Proceeds
of which Amount to 800
Guilders, which at the preſent
Rate of Exchange at 1 *s* 9 *d* is   70 | 00 | 00

———— 12 ————

5	Crs. { *Accepted Bills.*	90	00	00
4	{ *Daniel Trader.*	23	00	00
4	{ *Dav. Johnſton.*	57	4	00
1	Dr. *Caſh.* — —	170	4	00

Received Payment of the
following Debts, in Caſh, *viz*
             l.   *s.*
Of Mr.   *Jeremy*
   Thompſon —   90   0
   Daniel Trader.   23   0
   David Johnſton.   57   4

        170   4   170 | 4 | 00

———— 16 ————

6	Drs { *C Ch his Acc*			
	{ *Current.* --	1	15	5
6	{ *Ditto our Acc*			
	{ *of Exchan.*	45	14	7
5	Cr. { *D. Stratton,*			
	{ *my Account*			
	{ *Current.* --	47	10	00

Remitted to *Charles Chareu*
of *Bourdeaux,* 200 Crowns,
at 57 *d* in my own Bill on
Daniel Stratton, Factor at
Rochel, payable at ſingle
Uſance.   —   —   47 | 10 | 00

                     N. B

		l.	s.	d.		l.	s.	d.

| | | | | | *N. B.* 1 l. 15 s. 5 d or 7 $\frac{5}{12}$ Crowns, is for Payment of what I owed him of Gain upon the laſt Account of Exchange And 45 l. 14 s. 7 d. or 192$\frac{3}{4}$ Crowns, is for a new Account of Exchange | | | |

3	Crs. { An. Cochran.	37	10	00	I have entered into an Equal Partnerſhip with Mr *Andrew Cochran*, for an Inland Trade , to be under his Direction and Management. In purſuance whereof he is to Employ 37 l. 10 s. which he owes me *per* Account And I have given him 2 l. 10 s. more which makes in all 40 l for my Stock, to be laid out in ſuch Goods as he ſhall think beſt			
5	Caſh — —	2	10	00				
4	Dr. { An. Cochran, my Account with him in Company. -	40	00	00		40	00	00

3	Crs. { Dan Stratton, my Account of Plaiden.	11	17	6	Received advice from *Daniel Stratton* of *Rochel*, that he hath ſold my 240 Yards of *Plaiden*, for ready Money Neat Proceeds 50 Crowns ; which at 57 d is 11 l. 17 s 6 d And for Payment of this, and what more he owed me, he has remitted 535 Crowns, at 57 d is 127 l. 1 s. 3 d in Bills of *Pierre Fontaine*, on Mr *Thomas Richman*, at 24 days ſight. Accepted. ——			
5	Ditto, my Acc. Current.	115	3	9				
4	Dr. *Tho. Richman*	127	1	3		127	1	3

—— 18 ——

| 6 | Dr. { Outſtanding Charges. | | | | I have paid to ſeveral Perſons, to whom I owed for Houſhold Expences ; as marked in the Book of Expences. —— | | | |
| 1 | Cr. Caſh. — — | 15 | 00 | 00 | | 15 | 00 | 00 |

Drawn

		l.	*s.*	*d.*		*l.*	*s.*	*d.*
					———— *Oct.* 18 ————			
1	Dr. *Caſh.* —— —	25	7	10	Drawn upon *Herman van Rymer* for my Account 277 Guilders; for Payment of 277 $\frac{2}{11}$ Guilders, at 1 *s.* 10 *d.* is 25 *l* 7 *s.* 10 *d.* payable to *Alexander Drummond,* or order, at 10 days ſight, which he has paid me in Caſh. ——			
5	Cr. { *Herman van Rymer, my Acc. Curr.*					25	7	10
					———— 19 ————			
6	Dr { *Hero Moy's Account of Spices.* —				This day received from on board the *Leopard* of *Aberdeen*, the following Goods conſigned to me by *Hero Moy* of *Amſterdam*, to ſell for his Account.			
1	Cr. *Caſh.* ——	2	6	00	Received. *Mace* 10 Barrels *Cloves* 8 Barrels. } Paid Charges	2	6	00
					———— 21 ————			
6	Drs. { *Wheat* ——	118	00	00	*Thomas Dalziel* has this day delivered me 80 Bolls of Wheat, which I accept in full of our Bargain for 100 Bolls, The 80 Bolls at the Price formerly charged, *viz.* 1 *l.* 10 *s.* is 120 *l*; whereof was formerly advanced 10 *l.* and I have cleared the Remainder, thus.			
5	{ *Tho. Dalziel*	32	00	00				
3	Cr. { *Delivery Account, &c.*	150	00	00				
					l			
5	Dr. *Tho. Dalziel.*				Paid in Caſh. —— 108			
1	Cr. *Caſh.* —— —	108	00	00	He has diſcounted me. —— —— 2			
					110			
					The 20 Bolls not delivered. —— 30			
					140	140	00	00
					Daniel			

			l.	*s.*	*d.*		*l.*	*s.*	*d.*
2	Crs.	Broad Cloth, &c —	69	6	00	——— Oct 21 ———			
1		Caſh. — —	141	18	00	*Daniel Trader* and I have agreed to Trade in Company,			
7		D T's Acc in Company -	105	12	00	He for ⅓ and I ⅔, to be under my Direction and Management, being allowed 3			
7	Dr.	Broad Cloth in Company. -	316	16	00	*per Cent* Commiſſion. For his Share, he has delivered me 8 Pieces of Broad Cloth, worth			
						105 *l.* 12 *s.* For my Share I put in 5 Pieces, which I have had ſome time, worth 69 *l.* And 9 Pieces now bought for Ready Money 141 *l.* 18 *s.* Total Stock. ———			
							316	16	00
1	Drs.	Caſh. — —	24	00	00	——— 22 ———			
4		D Johnſton. -	18	00	00	Sold for the Account of *Hero Moy* of *Amſterdam*, 6 Barrels of *Mace*,			
6	Cr.	H. Moy's Acc. of Spices. --	42	00	00	at 4 *l* per Barrel, for Ready Money. ——— 24			
						Alſo to *David Johnſton*, 4 Barrels of *Cloves*, at 4 *l* 10 *s* payable in 3 Months, is ——— —— 18			
						42	42	00	00
7	Drs.	Goods in Company. ———	54	00	00	*David Johnſton, Alexander Black* and I, have entered into			
1		Caſh. — —	6	00	00	Partnerſhip, each for ⅓, to be under my Direction, for			
7	Cr.	D J's Acc. in Company.	60	00	00	which I am allowed Commiſſion			
5	Drs.	A. B's particular Acc.	22	7	4	In purſuance of this Contract, I have received of *David Johnſton* 6			
1		Caſh. — —	37	12	8	Hogſheads of *Claret*, value 54 *l* and in Caſh			
7	Cr.	A. B's Acc. in Company.	60	00	00	6 *l* Sum ——— — 60			
						Of *Alexander Black* 37 *l*. 12 *s*. 8 *d* And being in his Debt 22 *l*. 7 *s*. 4 *d*. I am to lay out that for him. Sum —— 60			
							120	120	00	00
						For my Share I am to lay out --- —— — 60			

		l.	s.	d.		l.	s.	d.
7	Cr { Broad Cloth in Company				—— Oct. 23. —— Sold for the Account of *Daniel Trader* and me, 10 Pieces of *Broad Cloth* for Ready Money —— ——	160	00	00
1	Dr. Caſh. — —	160	00	00				
7	Dr. { Goods in Company. —				Bought for the Account of *David Johnſton* and *Company*, 40 Packs of *Sheep-Skins*; which with Charges, paid all in Ready Money, is 126 *l.* Equal to the Money received by me from the Partners, and my own Share. —— ——			
1	Cr Caſh.	126	00	00		126	00	00
4	Dr *W. Davidſon*				—— 26 —— I have ſold for the Account of *David Johnſton* and *Company*, 4 Hogſheads of *Claret*, at 12 *l.* per Hogſhead, to *William Davidſon*, payable in 4 Months. —— —— ——			
7	Cr { Goods in Company —	48	00	00		48	00	00
1	Drs { Caſh — —	118	15	00	Sold for Account of *Daniel Trader* and me, to Mr *Robert Blackwood*, 12 Pieces of *Broad Cloth*, value 190 *l.* whereof received in Caſh 118 *l.* 15 *s.* The Remainder I owe him upon Account of *Accepted Bills*, and make good to my Partner. —— —— ——			
5	{ Accepted Bills	71	5	00				
7	Cr. { Broad Cloth in Company	190	00	00		190	00	00
	Crs. { Caſh — —	1	10	00	—— 27. —— All the *Broad Cloth* in Company with *Daniel Trader* being diſpoſed of; I find due to me for Petty Charges paid 1 *l.* 10 *s.* and for Commiſſion 8 *l.* 16 *s.* Total ——	10	6	00
	{ D *T*'s Acc. in Company. -	7	12	8				
	{ Profit and Loſs	24	1	4				
	Dr { Broad Cloth in Company	33	4	00	There is gained on the Account —— ——	22	18	00
	Dr { D. *T*'s Acc. in Company. -				Paid *Daniel Trader*, ½ of the neat Product in Caſh. ——			
	Cr Caſh. — —	113	4	8		113	4	8

The

		l.	s.	d.		l	s.	d.
					———— 28.————			

| 1 8 | Drs. { Caſh. — — H. Moy's Acc. Current. -- | 56 24 | 00 00 | 00 00 | The *Faulçon* of *Aberdeen* being arrived from *Genoa.* I have received of *Laurance Lovemoney,* payment of the Money lent him on Bottomree, with Intereſt. | | | |
| 5 | Cr. Bottomree Acc. | 80 | 00 | 00 | | | | |

In *Caſh.* —— —— 56

A Bill upon *Hero Moy* of *Amſter.* 170 10/11 Guilders, at 22 *d.* which I have ſent indorſed to himſelf for his Account   24

—— 80   80 | 00 | 00

| 8 3 | Dr. *Profit* and *Loſs.* Cr. *Wager's* Acc. | 10 | 00 | 00 | The *Wager* againſt *Thomas Arrowſmith* is gone againſt me: The *Crocodil* being arrived. —— | 10 | 00 | 00 |

———— 30.————

| 8 1 4 7 | Dr. { Linnen in Company. Cr Caſh. — — Dr. { Dan. Trader's particular Ac. Cr. { His Account in Company | 60 20 | 00 00 | 00 00 | Bought for Account betwixt *Daniel Trader* and me; 400 Yards of *Linnen,* at 3 *s.* for Ready Money, is —— | 60 | 00 | 00 |

———— *Nov.* 2.————

| 1 7 | Dr. Caſh. — — Cr. { Goods in Company. —— | 40 | 00 | 00 | Sold for Account of *David Johnſton* and *Company,* 10 Packs of *Sheep-Skins,* at 4 *l* per Pack, for Ready Money, is | 40 | 00 | 00 |

			l.	*s.*	*d.*		*l.*	*s.*	*d.*
						———— *Nov.* 2 ————			
1	Crs. {	*Caſh.* —— ——	40	00	00	Bought for Account of the			
3		*W. Wallace* -	80	00	00	ſaid *Company,* 20 Packs of			
7	Dr. {	*Goods in Com-*				*Wool,* 120 *l* from *William*			
		pany. ——	120	00	00	*Wallace* : whereof			

Paid by *Caſh* of the   *l.*
Company's.   ——   40
The Remainder pay-
able in 1 Month.   80
————
120   120 | 00 | 00

			l.	*s.*	*d.*
4'5	Drs. {	*Each Part-*			
7		*ners parti-*			
		cular Acc			
		to his Acc.			
		inCompany	40	00	00
7	Drs. {	*Each Acc. in*			
		Company, to			
		their parti-			
		cular Acc.	13	6	8

Obſerve. As I have made the *Debtors* and *Creditors* here: The Partners have Credit upon their *Accounts in Company,* for their Shares of what is now bought, and their *particular Accounts* are *Debtors.* Notwithſtanding a Part is Paid by their own *Caſh* ; and ſo it might ſtand, without any further Entry ; Becauſe at rendering the Accounts, it will eaſily be found that a Part of this Debt is already cleared by their own *Caſh.* But it makes all eaſier at laſt, If, as is here done, I diſcharge my ſelf of this Money, by making their *Accounts in Company* Debtors for the Shares of it ; and Diſcharge then ſo much of the Debt now charged to their *Particular Accounts,* by making theſe *Creditors.*

			l.	*s.*	*d.*		*l.*	*s.*	*d.*
						———— 4. ————			
5	Dr.	*Accepted Bills.*	35	6	3	Remitted to me by *Charles*			
		Char. Charcu,				*Charcu,* for *our Account of*			
6	Cr. {	*our Acc. of*				*Exchange,* 150 Crowns, at			
		Exchange				56½, in the Bills of *Alexander*			
		in Company.				*Black,* upon *David Liſet,* in			
						10 days. Accepted. ——	35	6	3

		l.	s.	d.		l.	s.	d.
					—— *Nov.* 4 ——			
4	⎰ A. C's parti-				Mr. *Andrew Cochran* has			
	⎱ cular *Acc.*	30	00	00	Drawn upon me 60 *l*; the			
6	Drs.⎰ My *Acc.* with				Total Value of certain Goods,			
	⎱ him *in Com-*				bought by him for our Ac-			
	pany. ——	30	00	00	count in *Company*: Which I			
					have paid in *Caſh.* —— I	60	00	00
1	Cr. *Caſh.* ——	60	00	00				
					—— 5 ——			
4	⎰ D. T's parti-				Sold for the Account of			
	⎱ cular *Acc.*	13	13	4	*Daniel Trader* and me 100			
7	Drs.⎰ His *Acc. in*				Yards of *Linnen*, at 4 *s* for			
	⎱ *Company.* -	6	6	8	which I have received a Bill			
8	Cr. ⎰ *Linnen in*				on *Ditto Trader*, payable on			
	⎱ *Company.*	20	00	00	demand. ——	20	00	00
8	Dr. ⎰ *Linnen in*							
	⎱ *Company.*				Brought for the Account of			
4	Cr. *An Hunter.* --	35	00	00	*Daniel Trader* and me, 200			
4	Dr. ⎰ D. T's parti-				Yards of *Linnen*, at 3 s. 6 *d.*			
	⎱ cular *Acc.*				from *Andrew Hunter*, pay-			
7	Cr ⎰ His *Acc. in*				able in 20 days. —— ——	35	00	00
	⎱ *Company.* -	11	13	4				
					—— 8. ——			
7	⎰ Goods *in Com-*				Shipp'd on Board the			
	Crs.⎰ *pany.* ——	120	00	00	*Speedwell*, for *Amſterdam*;			
1	⎱ *Caſh.* ——	22	14	00	consigned to *Hero Moy*; for			
					Account of *David Johnſton*			
8	Dr. *Voyage*, &c. --	142	14	00	and *Company*; 20 Packs of			
					Wool; and have paid Charges			
					and Inſurance, *viz.*			
						l.	s.	
4.5	⎰ *Each Part-*				20 Packs of *Wool*,			
	⎱ *ner's parti-*				worth. —— ——	120	00	
	Drs.⎰ cular *Acc.*				Charges paid in			
7	Crs.⎰ *Their Accounts*	7	11	4	*Caſh.* —— ——	2	14	
	⎱ *in Company.*				Inſurance made on			
					the whole, in			
					the Hands of			
					John Thompſon.			
					Præmium at 10			
					per Cent paid. -	12	00	
					Freight advanced.	8	00	
						142	14	
						142	14	00

		l.	s.	d.		l.	s.	d.
					——— Nov. 8. ———			
1	Dr. Caſh. — —	85	00	00	Sold for Account of David Johnſton and Company, 20 Packs of Sheep-Skins, at 4 l. 5 s. per Pack; for ready Money. — ' — —			
7	Cr. { Goods in Company —					85	00	00
					—— 11 ——			
7	Drs { D. J's Acc in Company	28	6	8	Paid to David Johnſton, and Alexander Black, for their Accounts in Company, in Caſh, to each 28 l. 6 s. 8 d. Total. — —			
7	{ A. B's Acc in Company	28	6	8				
1	Cr Caſh. — —	56	13	4		56	13	4
4	Dr W. Davidſon. -	27	00	00	Sold for Account of David Johnſton, and Company, 2 Hogſheads of Wine, to William Davidſon, payable the 26th of April next. — —			
7	Cr. { Goods in Company. —					27	00	00
					—— 12. ——			
6	Dr. { C Chareu, our Account of Exchange in Company.				Remitted to Charles Chareu of Bourdeaux, for our Account of Exchange, 200 Crowns, at 56 d; in Bills of A G. on J. F. which I have paid in Caſh, is			
1	Cr. Caſh. — —	46	13	4		46	13	4
					—— 15. ——			
3	Dr. W Wallace. --	57	10	00	Sold for Account of Daniel Trader and me, 300 Yards of Linnen, at 3 s. 10 d. to William Wallace, payable on demand, is — —			
8	Cr. { Linnen in Company. —					57	10	00
1	Dr Caſh — —	35	6	3	Received Payment of the Bill remitted by Charles Chareu, on David Liſet. —			
	Cr. Accepted Bills					35	6	3
1	Dr. Caſh. — —	100	00	00	Sold for ready Money, 8 Packs of Flax. — — —			
2	Cr Flax — —					100	00	00
1	Dr. Caſh. — —	2	11	5	Received of Andrew Hunter, the Intereſt due on his Bond at Martinmaſs. — —			
4	Cr. An. Hunter --					2	11	5
					Sold			

		l.	s.	d.		l.	s	d.
					---------*Nov.* 19---------			
					Sold for Account of *David Johnſton*, and *Company* ; 10 Packs of *Sheep-Skins*, at 4 *l.* 10 *s* per Pack : For which I have got an Aſſignment on *Alexander Black*, payable on			
5	Drs. { A. B's particular Acc	30	00	00	demand, is — —	45	00	00
7	His Acc in Company. -	15	00	00	*Alexander Black* has Accepted the Aſſignment, and taken a Receipt for his ½ ——	15	00	00
7	Cr. { Goods in Company. ——	45	00	00	Promiſing to pay the Reſt in a few Days — — —	30	00	00
					——— 20. ———			
1	Dr. *Caſh.* ——	50	00	00	*James Ballantine*, and I have entered into an equal			
9	Cr. { *Ja.* B's Acc. in Company				Partnerſhip ; to be under my Direction , at 2½ *per Cent* Commiſſion : In purſuance of which he has given me *50 l* to be laid out (with as much of mine) upon ſuch Goods as are fit for *London.* — —	50	00	00
					——— 22. ———			
1	Drs { *Caſh.* — —	17	10	00	Received of *David Johnſton*, Payment of what he owed			
6	H. Moy's Acc. of Spices. -		10	00	for *Hero Moy's* Account of *Goods,* viz.			
						l	s	
					In *Caſh* — — 17 10			
4	Cr. D. *Johnſton.* --	18	00	00	Abated for 2 Months advance. 10			
					18 00	18	00	00
8	Dr { H Moy's Acc Current --				Remitted to *Hero Moy* for his Account, 15 *l.* 4 *s* which			
1	Cr. *Caſh.* — —	15	4	00	at 23 *d per* Guilder, is 177½ Guilders in the Bill of *Andrew Cochran*, on *J R.* payable on Sight. Paid me in *Caſh.* —	15	4	00
					Paid			

		l.	s.	d.		l.	s.	d.
					———*Nov 23.*———			
6	Dr. *Jo. Campbell.* –	300	15	00	Paid in *Caſh* to Mr. *John Campbell*, the Price of my Houſe in *Caſtle-Street*, bought of him ; together with the 1ſt Quarter of the Annuity due to his Mother. Total. –	300	15	00
1	Cr. *Caſh.* — —							
4	Crs {*W. Davidſon.*	10	00	00	I have bought off the Annuity upon my Houſe in *Caſtle-Street* for 50 l. whereof			
1	{*Caſh.* — —	40	00	00				
					l.			
3	Dr *Acc. of Houſes.*	50	00	00	Paid in *Caſh* — — 40			
					By an Aſſignment on			
					William Davidſon. - 10			
					50	50	00	00
					—— 25. ——			
2	Crs. {*Linnen Cloth.*	50	00	00	This Day ſhipped for *London* on Board the *Succeſs.* C. D. *Maſter* : Conſigned to *John Blackwood*, to ſell for my Account, 750 Yards l. s.			
1	{*Caſh.* — —	1	15	00				
9	Dr. *Voyage, &c.* —	51	15	00	of *Linnen*, Value. — 50 00			
					Paid Charges, at			
					Shipping. — 1 15			
					51 15	51	15	00
					—— 28. ——			
9	Dr {*H. Moy, our*				Received advice from *Hero Moy* of *Amſterdam*, that he has received from on Board the *Speedwell* ; 20 Packs of *Wool*, ſhipped for the Account of *David Johnſton* and *Company* ; Alſo that he has ſold the ſame for Ready Money, neat Proceeds 2496 Guilders ; which at 20 *d.* is — —			
	{ *Acc. Curr*	208	00	00				
8	Cr. *Voyage, &c.* —					208	00	00
					Bought			

		l.	*s.*	*d.*	— — — *Decem.* 2. — — —	*l.*	*s.*	*d.*
1	Crs. { *Caſh* — —	133	10	00	Bought with Ready Money for the Account of *James Ballantine*, and me, each ½, the following Goods ; which I have alſo this Day ſhipped on Board our Ship the *Dragon* (whereof belongs to him ⅔, and to me ⅓) for *London*, conſigned to *John Blackwood*.			
9	{ *J. B's Acc. in Company.* -	15	00	00				
3	{ *Ship the Dragon.* —	15	00	00				
9	Dr. *Voyage, &c.* -	163	10	00				
9	Dr. { *J. B's particular Acc*							
9	Cr { *His Acc. in Company* -	16	5	00	*l.* *s.* Coarſe Linnen 1000 Yards — — 50 00 *Brandy*, 5 Hogsheads — — 80 00 Charges Paid. — 3 10			
					133 10	133	10	00
3	Drs. { *Ship the Dragon* —	12	00	00	I have advanced for the Ship's Out-ſet and Men's Wages. — — —			
9	{ *J. B's particular Acc.*	8	00	00		20	00	00
F	Cr. *Caſh.* — —	20	00	00	*Obſerve* Becauſe we are Equal in the *Trade*, but unequal in the Ship ; we have agreed to make the *Freight* of this Voyage 30 *l.* — —			
9	Dr. { *J B's particular Acc*					30	00	00
3	Cr. { *Ship the Dragon.* —	3	00	00				

Obſerve alſo That I keep Accounts only for my Partner's Share of the *Trade*, but not for his Share of the Ship And keep ſeparate Accounts for my own Share of the Ship, ſo as I may know my *Gain* or *Loſs* by the Ship, and by the *Trade* ſeparately, which being conſidered will explain the Reaſon of the *Debtors* and *Creditors*, to which the Laſt two Articles are placed

Remitted

		l.	s.	d.		l.	s	d.
					------ Decem. 5.------			
1	Dr. *Caſh* — —				Remitted to me by *Charles*			
6	Cr { C. *Chareu, our* *Account* of *Exchange.*	32	13	4	*Chareu of Bourdeaux*, for our *Account* of *Exchange,* 140 *Crowns,* at 57½ *d.* in the Bills of *J. L.* on *Archibal Stuart,* payable on Sight, which I have received — — —	32	13	4
					------ 9. ------			
4	Crs. { A. *C's Parti-* *cular Acc* - My *Account* *with* *him* *in Company*	30	00	00	Received of Mr. *Andrew Cochran* 70 *l* viz. 30 *l.* which I formerly paid for him ; and 40 *l.* for my Share of the Sales of certain *Goods* in *Company* betwixt us ; under his Ma- nagement. — —			
6		40	00	00				
1	Dr. *Caſh* — —	70	00	00		70	00	00
1	Drs { *Caſh* — — *Profit and Loſs* *in Company*	73	00	00	Received Payment of *Wil- liam Davidſon,* what he owed for *Goods* in *Company,* with *David Johnſton,* viz.			
9		2	00	00				
4	Cr. *W. Davidſon.* -	75	00	00	*l.* In *Caſh.* — — 73 Abated him for Ad- vance. — — 2 ——— 75	75	00	00
					---- 16 ----			
7	Crs { D. *T's Acc.* *in Company* *His Particu-* *lar Account*	20	16	8	Bought for Account of *Daniel Trader,* and me, 500 Yards of *Linnen,* at 2 s. 6 d. per Yard of D. K. for which I have drawn on *Daniel Trader,* payable on demand.			
4		41	13	4				
8	Dr. { *Linnen* in *Company.*	62	10	00		62	10	00
					---- 20 ----			
7	Dr. { D. *J's Acc.* *in Company.*				*David Johnſton* has recei- ved of *Alexander Black,* 15 *l.* his Share of a Sale of the *Company's Goods,* owing by *Ditto Black* upon Bill. —			
5	Cr. { A. *B's Parti-* *cular Acc.*	15	00	00		15	00	00
					Aſſigned			

		l.	s.	d.		l.	s	d
7	Dr. { D. T's Acc. in Company.				—— Decem. 22. —— Aſſigned to *Daniel Trader*, for Account of his Concerns with me, on *William Wallace* for 19 l. 3 s. 4 d His ⅓ of the Debt owing by *Ditto Wallace*			
3	Cr. *W. Wallace.* --	19	3	4		19	3	4
1	Dr. *Caſh.* — —	212	00	00	—— 24. —— Drawn upon *Hero Moy* for the Account of *David Johnſton* and Company, 2496 Guilders, payable to *A. M* or order, at 10 days Sight, for which I have received in *Caſh.* — — —			
9	Cr. { H. Moy, our Acc. Curr.					212	00	00
3	Dr. *W. Wallace.* --	80	00	00	—— 25. ——			
1	Cr. *Caſh.* — —				Paid *William Wallace* for the Account of *David Johnſton* and Company, out of the Company's Money. — —			
4:5	Crs. { Each Partner's particular Acc By his Acc in Company.	26	13	4		80	00	00
7								
9	Dr. { J. B our Acc. Current. --	200	00	00	I have advice from *John Blackwood* of *London*, that he has received from on Board the *Succeſs*, the *Linnen* and *Brandy* ſhipped for Account of *James Ballantine*, and me; and that he has ſold the ſame for Ready Money. Neat Proceeds *per* Account. — —			
9	Cr. *Voyage, &c.* --					200	00	00
9	Crs. { J. B our Acc Current --	80	00	00	Drawn on *John Blackwood* of *London*, for the Account of *James Ballantine*, and me, 80 l. payable to *A. D* or order, upon Sight. For which I have received in *Caſh.* — — —			
9	J. B's Acc. in Company	1	5	00				
8	Profit and Loſs	1	5	00				
1	Dr. *Caſh.* — —	82	10	00		82	10	00
1	Dr. *Caſh.* — —	40	00	00	—— 26. —— Sold for Ready Money 4 Hogſhead of *White Wine*, at 10 l per Hogſhead, is —			
2	Cr. *Wine.* — —				D d Received	40	00	00

		l.	s.	d.		l.	s.	d.
					—— Decem 26. ——			
1	Dr. *Caſh.* — —	22	8	00	Received Payment of the Bill on *George Gordon,* in *Caſh.* ——	22	8	00
5	Cr. *Accepted Bills.*							
6	Drs. { *Outſtanding Charges.*	2	00	00	Paid to *J. S* the ½ Years Cellar *Rent,* charged in the laſt *General Ballance.* ——	2	00	00
1	Cr. *Caſh.* — —							
8	Dr *Profit* and *Loſs*	20	00	00	Paid of Houſhold Expences ſince laſt Ballancing. —— —	20	00	00
1	Cr. *Caſh* ——							
					—— 28 ——			
8	Crs. { *Profit* and *Loſs*	13	6	00	This day *David Johnſton, Alexander Black,* and I, have ballanced our Accounts, the State of which is thus, *viz.*			
1	{ *Caſh.* — —	3	00	00				
9	Dr. { *Profit* and *Loſs*	16	6	00	After charging 3 *l* due to me for petty Charges, (not			
	{ *in Company.*				yet ſtated) and 13 *l.* 6 *s.* for			
7	{ *Goods in Company.* —	65	00	00	my Commiſſion, which is in all. —— —	16	6	00
8	Drs. { *Voyage to Amſterdam.* --	65	6	00	I find the following Articles of Gain.			
9	{ *H. Moy,* our *Acc. Curr.*	4	00	00	Upon the *Account* of *Goods* (which are all diſpos'd of) *l s.*			
9	Cr. { *Profit* and *Loſs*	134	6	00	there is — — 65 0			
	{ *in Company.*				Upon the *Voyage* to			
7	{ *D. J's Acc in Company*	38	13	4	*Amſterdam.* —— 65 6 Upon *Hero Moy* our			
7	Crs. { *A. B's Acc. in Company*	38	13	4	*Account Current* (by *Exchange*). 4 0			
8	{ *Profit* and *Loſs*	38	13	4	134 6	134	6	00
9	Dr. { *Profit* and *Loſs*	116	00	00	The Ballance of the Account of *Profit* and *Loſs* in *Company,* is — — —	116	00	00
	{ *in Company.*							
								I

		l.	s.	d.		l.	s.	d.
					——— *Decem.* 28. ———			
1	Crs. { Caſh. — —	55	6	8	I have cleared with the aforeſaid Partners, and Payment of their Ready Money in my Hands, thus,			
4	D. *J*'s particular Acc.	7	11	4				
7	Dr. { D. *J*'s Acc in Company.	62	18	00		l.	s.	d.
					To *David Johnſton* in *Caſh.* -	55	6	8
					He owes me by his *Particular Account.* —	7	11	4
					Sum 62 18 0	62	18	00
1	Crs. { Caſh. — —	40	6	8	To *Alex Black*, in *Caſh.* ——	40	6	8
5	A. B's particular Acc.	22	11	4	He owes me by his particular Account. —	22	11	4
7	Dr. { A. B's Acc. in Company.	62	18	00				
					Sum. 62 18 0	62	18	00
					——— 30. ———			
1	Crs. { Caſh. — —	1	10	00	There is due to me upon the Account of *Linnen* in *Company* with *Daniel Trader*, viz.			
7	D. *T*'s Acc in Company.	2	19	8				
8	Profit and Loſs	13	00	4		l.	s.	
8	Dr { Linnen in Company.	17	10	00	Of Petty Charges — 1 10			
					My Commiſſion. --- 7 1			
					8 11	8	11	00
					The Neat Gain upon what is Sold. —	8	19	00
8	Crs. { Profit and Loſs	19	18	4	There is due to me, by the Account with *James Ballantine*, for Commiſſion — —	3	6	8
9	*J*. B's Acc. in Company.	16	11	8				
9	Dr. *Voyage, &c.* --	36	10	00	After this, the Neat Gain on the *Voyage* to *London*, is --	33	3	4
					D d 2 Having			

		l.	*s.*	*d.*
	Having clofed and ballanced the *Leger* of this *Waft-Book*: The State of the Account of *Ballance* is, Thus, *viz*			
9	Dr. *Ballance* for — —	2984	17	11½
1	Crs. *Cafh*. — —	491	13	8½
2	*Wine*.... .3 Hogfheads of *Claret*. —	32	00	00
2	*Tobacco*......13 Hogfheads. — —	144	19	00
2	*Linnen Cloth*.... 4 Pieces of *Holland*; and 6 Pieces of *Muflin*. — — —	145	18	00
2	*Paper*. ...17 Bales. — —	65	4	00
3	*Account of Houfes*..... N°. 1, 2. —	580	15	00
3	*Ship the Dragon*. — —	100	00	00
3	*Moveables*. — —	200	00	00
3	*William Wallace*. — —	91	11	8
4	*Andrew Hunter*. — —	100	00	00
4	*John Paton*. — —	49	00	00
4	*Daniel Trader*. — —	3	13	4
4	*Thomas Richman*. — —	206	17	3
5	*Adam Brown*. — —	110	00	00
5	*Daniel Stratton*, my *Account Current*. —	194	12	6
6	*Charles Charen*, his *Account Current*. —	23	13	8
6	*Andrew Cochran*, my *Account with him in Company*. —	30	00	00
6	*Wheat*........80 Bolls. — —	118	00	00
9	*Linnen in Company with Daniel Trader*. —	97	10	00
9	*Voyage to London*.......750 Yards of *Linnen*. — —	51	15	00
9	*James Ballantin's particular Account*. —	27	15	00
9	*John Blackwood, our Account Current for Company with David Johnfton*, &c. —	120	00	00
9	Cr. *Ballance*. — — —	2984	17	11½
4	Drs. *Andrew Hunter*. — —	35	00	00
5	*Thomas Dalziel*. — —	100	00	00
5	*Accepted Bills*. — —	8	00	8
7	*Daniel Trader's Account in Company*. —	29	19	8
9	*James Ballantin's Account in Company*. —	99	11	8½
1	*Stock* (my prefent free Eftate) — —	2712	5	11

Lege-

LEGER. N°.2.

Of me *A. M.* Merchant in *Aberdeen :*

From the Eighth of *October,* 1729.

Obſerve. *In this Leger : When an* Account *is Debtor to, or Creditor by one Other, the two Numbers Written after the Name of that Other, are, the Firſt for the Number of that* Account *(all the* Accounts *being numbered in Order, from the Beginning), and the Other for the* Folio *where it Stands. And where an* Account *is Debtor to, or Creditor by* Sundry, *there you'll find the Letters* N°. *and after it the Numbers of the* Accounts : *Then the Letters* Fol. *and after it the Numbers of the* Folios *where thoſe* Accounts *ſtand ; in Order, as the Numbers of the* Accounts *are taken.*

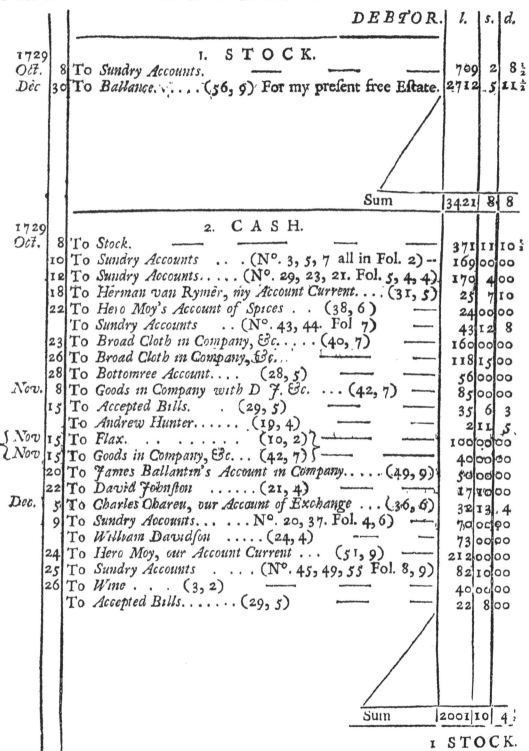

		DEBTOR.	l.	s.	d.

1. S T O C K.

1729					
Oct.	8	To *Sundry Accounts.*	709	2	8½
Dec	30	To *Ballance.* . . . . (56, 9) For my present free Estate.	2712	5	11½
		Sum	3421	8	8

2. C A S H.

1729					
Oct.	8	To *Stock.*	371	11	10½
	10	To *Sundry Accounts* . . . (Nº. 3, 5, 7 all in Fol. 2) —	169	00	00
	12	To *Sundry Accounts* . . . . (Nº. 29, 23, 21. Fol. 5, 4, 4)	170	4	00
	18	To *Herman van Rymer, my Account Current.* . . . (31, 5)	25	7	10
	22	To *Hero Moy's Account of Spices* . . (38, 6)	24	00	00
		To *Sundry Accounts* . . (Nº. 43, 44. Fol 7) —	43	12	8
	23	To *Broad Cloth in Company, &c.* . . . . (40, 7)	160	00	00
	26	To *Broad Cloth in Company, &c.* . .	118	15	00
	28	To *Bottomree Account.* . . . (28, 5) —	56	00	00
Nov.	8	To *Goods in Company with D J. &c.* . . . (42, 7)	85	00	00
	15	To *Accepted Bills.* . (29, 5)	35	6	3
		To *Andrew Hunter.* . . . . . . (19, 4)	2	11	5
{Nov	15	To *Flax* . . . . (10, 2)}	100	00	00
{Nov	15	To *Goods in Company, &c.* . . . (42, 7)}	40	00	00
	20	To *James Ballantin's Account in Company.* . . . . . (49, 9)	50	00	00
	22	To *David Johnston* . . . . . . (21, 4)	17	10	00
Dec.	5	To *Charles Obareu, our Account of Exchange* . . . (36, 6)	32	13	4
	9	To *Sundry Accounts* . . . . . . Nº. 20, 37. Fol. 4, 6) —	70	00	00
		To *William Davidson* . . . . . (24, 4) —	73	00	00
	24	To *Hero Moy, our Account Current* . . . (51, 9)	212	00	00
	25	To *Sundry Accounts* . . . . (Nº. 45, 49, 55 Fol. 8, 9)	82	10	00
	26	To *Wine* . . . (3, 2) —	40	00	00
		To *Accepted Bills.* . . . . . . (29, 5) —	22	8	00
		Sum	2001	10	4

1 STOCK.

CREDITOR. | *l.* | *s.* | *d.*

1. S T O C K.

					l.	*s.*	*d.*
1729							
Oct.	8	By *Sundry Accounts.*	— —	— —	3256	5	2
Dec.	30	By *Profit* and *Lofs* ...... (45, 8)	— —	— —	165	3	6
		Sum			3421	8	8

2. C A S H.

				l.	*s.*	*d.*
1729						
Oct.	16	By *Andrew Cochran, my Account with him in Company* . (37, 6)		2	10	00
	18	By *Account of Outftanding Charges* .. . (35, 6)	—	15	00	00
	19	By *Hero Moy's Account of Spices*... .. (38, 6)	—	2	6	00
	21	By *Thomas Dalziel* .... (32, 5)	—	108	00	00
		By *Brodd Cloth in Company with D. T.* .. . . . (40, 7)	141	18	00
	23	By *Goods in Company with D. J. &c* ..... (42, 7)	—	126	00	00
	27	By *Sundry Accounts* .... (N°. 40, 41. Fol 7)	—	114	14	8
	30	By *Linnen in Company with D. T.* ..... (47, 8)	—	60	00	00
Nov.	2	By *Goods in Company with D. J.* ...... (42, 7)	—	40	00	00
	4	By *Sundry Accounts* ..... (N°. 20, 37. Fol. 4, 6)	--	60	00	00
	8	By *Voyage to Amfterdam, &c.* ...... (48, 8)	—	22	14	00
	11	By *Sundry Accounts* .... (N°. 43, 44 Fol. 7)	—	56	13	4
		By *Charles Chareu, our Account of Exchange.* . (36, 6)	46	13	4
	22	By *Hero Moy's Account Current* ..... (46, 8)	—	15	4	00
	23	By *Sundry Accounts* .... (N°. 34, 12. Fol. 6, 3)	—	340	15	00
	25	By *Voyage to London, &c.* .... (50, 9)	—	1	15	00
Dec.	2	By *Sundry Accounts* ...... (N°. 52, 53 Fol 9)	—	153	10	00
	25	By *William Wallace* ...... (18, 3)	—	80	00	00
	28	By *Profit* and *Lofs* ...... (45, 8)	—	20	00	00
	30	By *Linnen in Company with D T.* ..... (47, 8)	—	1	10	00
		By *Sundry Accounts* .... (N° 43, 44, 54 Fol. 7, 9)	98	13	4
		By *Outftanding Charges* ...... (35, 6)	—	2	00	00
	30	By *Ballance* .... .. (56, 9)	—	491	13	8 ½
		Sum		2001	10	4 ½

3 WINE.

DEBTOR. *l.* *s.* *d.*

1729			3. W I N E.	Claret. Hds.	White. Hds.			
Oct.	8	To *Stock* . . . . . (*Claret*, Nº. 1, 2, 3) ———	10	4	113	16	8
Dec.	30	To *Profit* and *Loss* . . . . . . (45, 8) ———			28	3	4
		Sum.	10	4	142	00	00

1729			4 T O B A C C O.		Hds.			
Oct.	8	To *Stock*. ———		13	144	19	00

1729			5 R A I S I N S.		Barrels			
Oct	8	To *Stock* . . . . Of Nº 1, 2. ———		10	15	10	00
Dec	30	To *Profit* and *Loss* . . . . . . (45, 8) ———			3	10	00
		Sum.		10	19	00	00

1729			6. B R O A D C L O T H.		Pieces.			
Oct.	8	To *Stock* . . . . . . (Nº. 1, 2, 3, 4) ———		5	69	6	00

1729			7. I R O N.		Stone.			
Oct.	8	To *Stock* . . . . Of Nº. 1, 2 ———		400	65	00	00
Dec.	30	To *Profit* and *Loss* . . . . . . (45, 8) ———			15	00	00
		Sum.		400	80	00	00

1729			8. L I N N E N C L O T H.	Scotch Linnen Yards	Holld Pieces	Muflin Pieces			
Oct.	8	To *Stock*. ———	750	4	6	195	18	00

1729			9. P A P E R.			Bales.			
Oct.	8	To *Stock* . . . . Of Nº. 1, 2. ———			17	65	4	00

1729			10 F L A X.			Packs			
Oct.	8	To *Stock* ———			8	81	19	00
Dec.	30	To *Profit* and *Loss* . . . . (45, 8) ———				18	1	00
		Sum.			8	100	00	00

			CREDITOR	Claret Hds.	White Hds.	l	s.	d.
3. WINE.								
1729								
Oct.	10	By *Cash.* (2, 1) ...... N°. 2.	——	7		70	00	00
Dec.	6	By *Cash.*			4	40	00	00
	30	By *Ballance.* (56, 9) ...... N°. 1, 3.	——	3		32	00	00
			Sum	10	4	142	00	00

					Hds	l	s.	d.
4. TOBACCO.								
1729								
Dec.	30	By *Ballance* ..... (56, 9)	——		13	144	19	00

					Barrel	l	s.	d.
5. RAISINS.								
1729								
Oct.	10	By *Cash* ...... (2, 1) —— (N°. 1, 2)			10	19	00	00

					Pieces.	l	s.	d.
6. BROADCLOTH.								
1729								
Oct.	21	By *Broad Cloth in Company with D. T.*	——		5	69	6	00

					Stone	l	s.	d.
7. IRON.								
1729								
Oct.	10	By *Cash* .... (2, 1)	——		400	80	00	00

				Scorch Linnen Yards	Holld Pieces.	Muslin Pieces	l	s.	d.
8. LINNENCLOTH.									
1729									
Nov.	25	By *Voyage to London, &c.* .... (50, 9)	750			50	00	00
Dec.	30	By *Ballance.* ...... (56, 9)	——	4	6	145	18	00
			Sum	750	4	6	195	18	00

					Bales	l	s.	d.
9. PAPER.								
1729								
Dec.	30	By *Ballance* .... (56, 9)	——		17	65	4	00

					Packs	l	s.	d.
10. FLAX.								
1729								
Nov.	15	By *Cash.*	——		8	100	00	00

E e   11 DELIVERY

			DEBTOR.	*l.*	*s.*	*d.*

1729			11. DELIVERY ACCOUNT *of* BUYING.			
Oct.	8	To *Stock.* . . . . .100 Bolls of Wheat, by *Thomas* *Dalziel,* 1ft *Nov.* next.	150	00	00

1729			12. ACCOUNT *of* HOUSES.			
Oct.	8	To *Stock* . . . . . Nº. 1 worth 300 *l* 15 *s.* Nº. 2. 230 *l.*	530	15	00
Nov	23	To *Sundry Accounts.* . . . .(Nº. 2, 24. Fol. 1, 4) for Nº. 1.	50	00	00
		Sum.	580	15	00

1729			13. SHIP *the* DRAGON *of* ABERDEEN, ⅓.			
Oct.	8	To *Stock*	100	00	00
Dec.	2	To *Cash.* . . . (2, 1)	12	00	00
	30	To *Profit* and *Lofs.* . .(45, 8)	6	00	00
		Sum.	118	00	00

				Yards			
1729			14. DANIEL STRATTON, *my* AC-COUNT *of* PLAIDEN				
Oct	8	To *Stock.*	240	9	00	00
Dec.	30	To *Profit* and *Lofs.* . . . . . . (45, 8)		2	17	6
		Sum	240	11	17	6

1729			15. VOYAGE *from* ROCHEL *to* AMSTERDAM			
Oct.	8	To *Stock.* . . . . . . For 4 Packs of *Wool.*	56	18	00½
Dec.	30	To *Profit* and *Lofs.* . . . . . . (45, 8)	13	1	11½
		Sum.	70	00	00

1729			16. WAGER's ACCOUNT.			
Oct.	8	To *Stock.* . . . . . . Againft *Thomas Arrowfmith.*	10	00	00

1729			17. MOVEABLES.			
Oct.	8	To *Stock.*	200	00	00

1729			18. WILLIAM WALLACE.			
Oct.	8	To *Stock.*	53	5	00
Nov	15	To *Linnen in Company, &c.* (47, 8)	57	10	00
Dec.	25	To *Cash.* . . . . . . (2, 1)	80	00	00
		Sum.	190	15	00

			l.	*s.*	*d.*
		CREDITOR.			
1729		11. DELIVERY ACCOUNT *of* BUYING.			
Oct.	21	By *Sundry Accounts* . . . . (N°. 38, 32. Fol. 6, 5) 80 Bolls delivered, 20 Bolls not delivered. ——	150	00	00
1729		12. ACCOUNT *of* HOUSES.			
Dec.	30	By *Ballance* . . . . (56, 9) —— —— ——	580	15	00
1729		13. SHIP *the* DRAGON *of* ABERDEEN, ⅓.			
Dec.	2	By *Sundry Accounts* . . . . (N°. 52, 53. Fol. 9) —	18	00	00
	30	By *Ballance* . . . . . . (56, 9) —— ——	100	00	00
		Sum.	118	00	00

			Yards.	*l.*	*s.*	*d.*
1729		14. DANIEL STRATTON, *my* AC- COUNT *of* PLAIDEN.				
Oct.	16	By *Thomas Richman.* —— ——	240	11	17	6

			l.	*s.*	*d.*
1729		15. VOYAGE *from* ROCHEL *to* AMSTERDAM.			
Oct.	12	By *Herman van Rymer, my Account Current* . . . . 31, 5. For 4 Packs of *Wool*.	70	00	00
1729		16. WAGER's ACCOUNT.			
Oct.	28	By *Profit* and *Loss* . . . . (45, 8) Lost with *Thomas* *Arrowsmith*.	10	00	00
1729		17. MOVEABLES.			
Dec.	30	By *Ballance.* . . . . . . (56, 9) —— ——	200	00	00
1729		18. WILLIAM WALLACE.			
Nov.	2	By *Goods in Company with D. J. &c.* . . . . . (42, 7) —	80	00	00
Dec.	22	By *Daniel Trader's Account in Company* . . . . (41, 7)	19	3	4
	30	By *Ballance* . . . . . . (56, 9) —— ——	91	11	8
		Sum	190	15	00

19. ANDREW

		DEBTOR.	l.	s.	d.
		19. A N D R E W H U N T E R.			
1729 Oct	8	To *Stock*..... By Bond 100 l. Principal. 2 l. 11 s. 5 d. Interest, due at *Martinmass* next.	102	11	5
Dec.	30	To *Ballance*. . . . . . . (56, 9)	35	00	00
		Sum.	137	11	5
		20. A N D R E W C O C H R A N.			
1729 Oct	8	To *Stock.*	37	10	00
Nov	4	To *Cash*. . . . . . (2, 1)	30	00	00
		Sum.	67	10	00
		21. D A V I D J O H N S T O N.			
1729 Oct.	8	To *Stock.*	57	4	00
	22	To *Hero Muy's Account of Spices*. . . . . (38, 6) payable in 3 Months.	18	00	00
Nov.	2	To *His Account in Company*. . . . . . (43, 7)	40	00	00
	8	To *His Account in Company.*	7	11	4
		Sum.	122	15	4
		22. J O H N P A T O N.			
1729 Oct.	8	To *Stock.*	49	00	00
		23. D A N I E L T R A D E R.			
1729 Oct.	8	To *Stock.*	23	00	00
	30	To *His Account in Company*. . . . . (41, 7)	20	00	00
Nov.	5	To *Linnen in Company*. . . . . (47, 8)	13	13	4
		To *His Account in Company*. . . . . (41, 7)	11	13	4
		Sum.	68	6	8
		24. W I L L I A M D A V I D S O N.			
1729 Oct.	8	To *Stock.*	10	00	00
	25	To *Goods in Company with D J. &c.* . . . . . . (42, 7) Payable in 6 Months.	48	00	00
Nov.	11	To *Goods in Company with D. J. &c.* . . . . . Payable the 26th of *April* next.	27	00	00
		Sum.	85	00	00
		25. T H O M A S R I C H M A N.			
1729 Oct	8	To *Stock.*	79	15	10
	16	To *Sundry Accounts*. . . . . (N°. 14, 27. Fol 3, 5)	127	1	3
		Sum.	206	17	1

19. ANDREW

		CREDITOR.	l.	s.	d.
19. ANDREW HUNTER.					
1729 Nov.	5	By Linnen in Company, &c. ...... payable in 20 days.	35	00	00
	15	By Cash .. ... (2, 1) ——— ———	2	11	5
Dec	30	By Ballance ...... (56, 9)	100	00	00
		Sum.	137	11	5
20. ANDREW COCHRAN					
1729 Oct.	16	By Andrew Cochran, my Account with him in Company.			
		...... (37, 6) ——— ———	37	10	00
Dec.	9	By Cash... .. (2, 1) ——— ———	30	00	00
		Sum.	67	10	00
21. DAVID JOHNSTON.					
1729 Oct	12	By Cash. ..... (2, 1)	57	4	00
Nov.	2	By His Account in Company. ...... (43, 7) —	13	6	8
	22	By Sundry Accounts. ...... (N°. 2, 38. Fol. 1, 6) —	18	00	00
Dec.	25	By His Account in Company. .... (43, 7) — —	26	13	4
	28	By His Account in Company.	7	11	4
		Sum.	122	15	4
22. JOHN PATON.					
1729 Dec.	30	By Ballance. .... (56, 9) —	49	00	00
23. DANIEL TRADER.					
1729 Oct.	10	By Cash. ...... (2, 1) — — —	23	00	00
Dec.	16	By Linnen in Company ...... (47, 8) — —	41	13	4
	30	By Ballance. ...... (56, 9) — —	3	13	4
		Sum.	68	6	8
24. WILLIAM DAVIDSON.					
1729 Nov	23	By Account of Houses, &c. ..... (12, 3) —	10	00	00
Dec.	9	By Sundry Accounts. .... (N°. 2, 53. Fol 1, 9) —	75	00	00
		Sum.	85	00	00
25. THOMAS RICHMAN.					
1729 Dec.	30	By Ballance. ...... (56, 9) ——— ———	206	17	1

26. ADAM

DEBTOR. | l | s. | d.

26. ADAM BROWN.

1729						
Oct.	8	To *Stock.*		110	00	00

27. DANIEL STRATTON *my* ACCOUNT CURRENT.

			Crown			
1729						
Oct.	8	To *Stock.*	1550	361	13	4

28. BOTTOMREE ACCOUNT.

1729						
Oct	8	To *Stock.* . . . . Due by *Laurence Lovemony.*		80	00	00

29. ACCEPTED BILLS.

				Due to me			Due by me.		
				l.	s.	d			
1729									
Oct.	8	1. To *Stock.* Due By *George Gordon* . . . Payable *Dec. 5.*		22	8	00			
		2 . . . . By *Jeremy Thompson.* 16 Oct		90	00	00			
	26	1 To *Broad Cloth in Company, &c.* . . (40, 7) To *Robert Blackwood.*					71	5	00
Nov.	4	3 To *Charles Chareu, our Account of Exchange.* . . (35, 6) By *Daniel Liset.*		35	6	3			
Dec.	30	2 To *Ballance.* . . . . . . (56, 9)					8	00	8
		Sum.		147	14	3	79	5	8

30. ALEXANDER BLACK.

1729						
Oct	22	To *His Account in Company* . . . (44, 7)		22	7	4
Nov	2	To *His Account in Company.*		40	00	00
	8	To *His Account in Company.*		7	11	4
	19	To *Goods in Company.* . . . . . (42, 7)		30	00	00
		Sum.		99	18	8

31. HERMAN van RYMER, *my* ACCOUNT CURRENT.

			Guild.			
1729						
Oct.	12	To *Voyage from Rochel, &c.* . . . . (15, 3)	800	70	00	00
Dec.	30	To *Profit* and *Loss* . . . . . . (45, 8)		3	7	1½
		Sum	800	73	7	1½

32. THOMAS DALZIEL.

1729						
Oct.	21	To *Sundry Accounts.* . . . (N°. 11, 2 Fol 3, 1)		140	00	00
	30	To *Ballance.* . . . (56, 9)		100	00	00
		Sum.		240	00	00

26. ADAM

		CREDITOR	*l.*	*s.*	*d*

26. ADAM BROWN.

1729						
Dec.	30	By *Ballance* . . . . . . (56, 9)	110	00	00

27. DANIEL STRATTON, *my* **ACCOUNT CURRENT.**

1729				Crown			
Oct.	16	By *Sundry Accounts* . . . . . (N° 33, 36 Fol 6)	200	47	10	00
		By *Thomas Richman* . . . . . . (25, 4)	485	115	3	9
Dec.	30	By *Ballance* . . . . . (56, 9)	865	194	12	6
		By *Profit* and *Lofs* . . . . . . (45, 8)		4	7	1
		Sum.	1550	361	13	4

28 BOTTOMREE ACCOUNT.

1729						
Oct.	28	By *Sundry Accounts* . . . . . . (N°. 2, 46 Fol. 1, 8) From *Laurance Lovemony*		80	00	00

29. ACCEPTED BILLS.

1729				Due to me *l.* *s.* *d.*			Due by me.		
Oct.	8	1	By *Stock.* Due { To Robert Blackwood . . Payable 18 Oct.				71	5	00
		2 . . . . { To Robert Clark . . . 28 Oct				8	00	8
	12	2.	By *Cafh* . . . . (2, 1) By *Jeremy Thompfon.*	90	00	00			
Nov.	15		By *Cafh* . . . . . . By *Daniel Lifet.*	35	6	3			
Dec.	25		By *Cafh* . . . . . By George Gordon.	22	8	00			
			Sum	147	14	3	79	5	8

30. ALEXANDER BLACK.

1729						
Oct.	8	By *Stock.*	22	7	4
Nov.	2	By *His Account in Company* . . . . . (44, 7)	13	6	8
Dec.	20	By *David Johnfton's Account in Company* . . . (43, 7)	15	00	00
	25	By *His Account in Company* . . . . . . (44, 7)	26	13	4
	28	By *His Account in Company.*	22	11	4
		Sum	99	18	8

31. HERMAN van RYMER, *my* **ACCOUNT CURRENT.**

1729				Guild.			
Oct.	8	By *Stock*	522,	47	19	3
		By *Cafh* . . . . . . (2, 1)	277,	25	7	10
		Sum.	800	73	7	1

32. THOMAS DALZIEL.

1729						
Oct.	8	By *Stock.*	240	00	00

33 CHARLES

		DEBTOR.	l.	s.	d.

33 CHARLES CHAREU, his ACCOUNT CURRENT.

1729			l.	s.	d.
Oct.	16	To Daniel Stratton, my Account Current......(27, 5)	1	15	5
Dec.	30	To Ditto, our Account of Exchange.......(36, 6) —	23	13	8
		Sum.	25	9	1

34. JOHN CAMPBEL.

1729					
Nov.	23	To Cash.........(2, 1) ———	300	15 00	00

35 ACCOUNT of OUTSTANDING CHARGES.

1729					
Oct.	18	To Cash........(2, 1) Paid sundry Persons, per Book of Charges ———	15 00	00	
Dec.	26	To Cash....Paid J S. ———	2 00	00	
		Sum.	17 00	00	

36. CHARLES CHAREU, our ACCOUNT of EXCHANGE.

1729			Crown	l.	s.	d.
Oct.	16	To Daniel Stratton, my Account Current...(27, 5)	192	45	14	7
Nov.	11	To Cash......(2, 1) ———	200	46	13	4
		Sum.	392	92	7	11

37. ANDREW COCHRAN, my ACCOUNT with him in COMPANY.

1729					
Oct.	16	To Sundry Accounts.......(N°. 20, 2. Fol. 4, 1) —	40 00	00	
Nov.	4	To Cash......(2, 1)	30 00	00	
		Sum.	70 00	00	

38. HERO MOY's ACCOUNT of SPICES.

1729			Mace, Barrels	Cloves Barrels	l.	s.	d.
Oct.	19	To Cash......(2, 1) ———	10	8	2	6	00
Nov.	22	To David Johnston.......(21, 4) Discounted to him. ———				10	00
Dec.	30	To His Account Current......(46, 8) —			39	4	00
		Sum.	10	8	42 00	00	

39. WHEAT.

1729			Bolls.	l.	s.	d.
Oct.	21	To Delivery Account of Buying ...(11, 3) —	80	118 00	00	

33. CHARLES

					CREDITOR		*l.*	*s.*	*d.*

1729   33. CHARLES CHAREU, *his* ACCOUNT CURRENT.

				l.	*s.*	*d.*
Oct.	8	By *Stock.*		1	15	5
		By *Ballance* ...... (56, 9)		23	13	8
			Sum	25	9	1

1729   34. JOHN CAMPBEL.

				l.	*s.*	*d.*
Oct.	8	By *Stock.*		300	15	00

1729   35. ACCOUNT *of* OUTSTANDING CHARGES.

				l.	*s.*	*d.*
Oct.	8	By *Stock* ...... Due to sundry Persons, *per* Book of Charges		17	00	00

1729   36 CHARLES CHAREU, *our* ACCOUNT *of* EXCHANGE.

				Crown	*l.*	*s.*	*d.*
Nov.	4	By *Accepted Bills* ...... (29, 5)		150	35	6	3
Dec.	5	By *Cash* ...... (2, 1)		140	32	13	4
	30	By *His Account Current* ...... (33, 6)		102	22	19	00
		By *Sundry Accounts* ..... (N° 33, 45 Fol 6,8) For the Loss.			1	9	4
			Sum.	392	92	7	11

1729   37. ANDREW COCHRAN, *my* ACCOUNT *with him in* COMPANY.

				l.	*s.*	*d.*
Dec.	9	By *Cash* ...... (2, 1)		40	00	00
	30	By *Ballance* ...... (56, 9)		30	00	00
			Sum	70	00	00

1729   38. HERO MOY's ACCOUNT *of* SPICES.

				Mace Barrels	Coves Barrels	*l.*	*s.*	*d.*
Oct.	22	By *Sundry Accounts* ... (N°. 21, 2. Fol. 4, 1)		6	4	42	00	00
		Undisposed of		4	4			
			Sum	10	8	42	00	00

1729   39. WHEAT.

				Bolls.	*l.*	*s.*	*d.*
Dec.	30	By *Ballance* .. (56, 9)		80	118	00	0

F f

     BROAD

			DEBTOR.	l.	s.	d.
1729	**40**	**BROAD CLOTH** *in* **COMPANY** *with* **D. T.** Pieces				
Oct.	21	To *Sundry Accounts*... (N°. 6, 2, 41. Fol 2, 1, 7)	22	316	16	00
	27	To *Sundry Accounts* .. (N°. 2, 41, 45. Fol. 1, 7, 8)		33	4	00
		Sum	22	350	00	00
1729		**41. DANIEL TRADER's ACCOUNT** *in* **COMPANY** ⅓.				
Oct.	27	To *Cash* .(2, 1)		113	4	8
Nov.	5	To *Linnen in Company* ...(47, 8)		6	6	8
Dec.	22	To *William Wallace* . ...(18, 3)		19	3	4
	30	To *Ballance*... .(56, 9)		29	19	8
		Sum.		168	14	4
1729		**42. GOODS** *in* **COMPANY** *with* **DAVID JOHN-STON** *and* **ALEXANDER BLACK.**				
Oct.	22	To *D J's Account in Company* ...(43, 7) For 6 Hogsheads of Claret Wine		54	00	00
	23	To *Cash* ...(2, 1) For 40 Packs of Sheep-Skins.		126	00	00
Nov	2	To *Sundry Accounts*.. (N° 2, 18. Fol. 1, 3) For 20 Packs of Wool.		120	00	00
Dec.	28	To *Profit* and *Loss in Company*.....(54, 9)		65	00	00
		Sum.		365	00	00
1729	**43**	**DAVID JOHNSTON's ACCOUNT** *in* **COMPANY** ⅓.				
Nov	2	To *His particular Account* . ...(21, 4)		13	6	8
	11	To *Cash* . ...(2, 1)		28	6	8
Dec.	20	To *Alexander Black's particular Account*.....(53, 9)		15	00	00
	25	To *His particular Account*. ...(43, 7)		26	13	4
	28	To *Sundry Accounts* ... .(N° 2, 21 Fol 1, 4) For clearing this Account.		62	18	00
		Sum		146	4	8
1729	**44**	**ALEXANDER BLACK's ACCOUNT** *in* **COMPANY**				
Nov.	2	To *His particular Account*....(30, 5)		13	6	8
	11	To *Cash* .....(2, 1)		28	6	8
	19	To *Goods in Company*. ... .(42, 7)		15	00	00
Dec.	25	To *His particular Account* . (30, 5)		26	13	4
	28	To *Sundry Accounts*... . .(N°. 2, 30 Fol 1, 5) For clearing this Account		62	18	00
		Sum.		146	4	8

		CREDITOR	Pieces.	l.	s.	d.
1729		40 BROAD CLOTH *in* COMPANY *with* D T.				
Oct.	23	By *Cash* ...... (2, 1) ———— ————	10	160	00	00
	26	By *Sundry Accounts* ...... (Nº. 2, 29 Fol 1, 5)	12	190	00	00
		Sum	22	350	00	00

			l.	s.	d.
1729		41. DANIEL TRADER's ACCOUNT *in* COMPANY ⅓.			
Oct.	21	By *Broad Cloth in Company* . ..For 8 Pieces stocked by him. (40, 7) ———— ————	105	12	00
	27	By *Broad Cloth in Company*..... For his Share of Gain	7	12	8
	30	By *His parti Acc* . (23, 4) For his Share of 400 Yds. *Lin*.	20	00	00
Nov.	5	By *His particular Account* ... ..(23, 4) ————	11	13	4
Dec.	16	By *Linnen in Company*. .. ... (47, 8)	20	16	8
	30	By *Linnen in Company*. ———— ————	2	19	8
		Sum.	168	14	4

			l.	s.	d.
1729		42. GOODS *in* COMPANY *with* DAVID JOHN-STON *and* ALEXANDER BLACK.			
Oct.	23	By *William Davidson*... (24, 4) For 4 Hds. of Claret	48	00	00
Nov.	2	By *Cash* . ... (2, 1) For 10 Packs of Sheep-Skins	40	00	00
	8	By *Voyage to Amsterdam*, &c.. ..... (48, 8) For 20 Packs of Wool. ———— ————	120	00	00
		By *Cash*..... (2, 1) For 20 Packs of Sheep-Skins —	85	00	00
	11	By *William Davidson*....(24, 4) For 2 Hds. of Claret	27	00	00
	19	By *Sundry Accounts*...... (Nº. 30, 44 Fol. 5, 7) For 10 Packs of Sheep-Skins. ———— ————	45	00	00
		Sum.	365	00	00

			l.	s.	d.
1729		43. DAVID JOHNSTON's ACCOUNT *in* COMPANY ⅓.			
Oct.	22	By *Sundry Acc*. . (Nº 42, 2 Fol 7, 1) Stocked by him.	60	00	00
Nov	2	By *His particular Account* ...... (21, 4) For his Share of 20 Packs of Wool.	40	00	00
	8	By *His parti Acc.* For Charges at shipping the Wool	7	11	4
Dec	28	By *Profit and Loss in Company* ... .(54, 9) For his Share of Gain. ———— ————	38	13	4
		Sum	146	4	8

			l.	s.	d.
1729		44. ALEXANDER BLACK's ACCOUNT *in* COMPANY ⅓.			
Oct.	22	By *Sundry Acc* (Nº 30, 2 Fol 5, 1) Stocked by him.	60	00	00
Nov.	2	By *His particular Account* . ... (30, 5) For his Share of 20 Packs of Wool.	40	00	00
	8	By *His particular Account*....... .. . For his Share of Charges at shipping the Wool ———— ————	7	11	4
Dec.	28	By *Profit and Loss, in Company*..... (54, 9)	38	13	4
		Sum	146	4	8

			DEBTOR.	l.	s	d.
		45 P R O F I T *and* L O S S.				
1729						
Oct.	28	To *Wager's Account* . . . . . (16, 3)	—	100	00	00
Dec.	28	To *Cash* . . . . . . (2, 1)	—	20	00	00
	30	To *Daniel Stratton, my Account Current.*	—	4	7	1
		To *Charles Chateu, our Account of Exchange.*	—		14	8
		To *Stock* . . . . . Gained since the 8*th* of *October.*	—	165	3	6.
		Sum.		200	5	3
		46. HERO MOY's ACCOUNT CURRENT.				
1729						
Oct.	28	To *Bottomree Account* . . . . (28, 5)	—	24	00	00
Nov.	22	To *Cash* . . . . . (2, 1)	—	15	4	00
		Sum.		39	4	00

			Yards.	l.	s	d.
		47 LINNEN *in* COMPANY *with* D T				
1729						
Oct.	31	To *Cash* . . . . . (2, 1) At 3 *s.* per Yard, N°. 1.	400	60	00	00
Nov	5	To *Andrew Hunter* . . . . (19, 4) At 3 *s.* 6 *d.*				
		N° 2	200	35	00	00
Dec	16	To *Sundry Accounts* . . . . (N°. 23, 41. Fol 4, 7)				
		At 2 *s* 6 *d* N°. 3	500	62	10	00
	30	To *Sundry Accounts.* . . . . (N°. 2, 45. Fol 1, 8)				
		For Charges	—	17	10	00
		Sum.	1100	175	00	00

			l.	s	d.
		48. VOYAGE *to* AMSTERDAM *for the* COMPANY *with* D J. &*c.*			
1729					
Nov.	8	To *Sundry Accounts.* . . . . (N°. 42, 2 Fol. 7, 1)			
		For 20 Packs of Wool	—	142	14	00
Dec.	28	To *Profit and Loss, in Company.* . . . (54, 9)	—	65	6	00
		Sum.		208	00	00

45. PROFIT

			CREDITOR.	l	s.	d.
			45 P R O F I T *and* L O S S.			
1729						
Oct.	27	By	*Broad Cloth in Company with D. T.* . . . . . . (40, 7)	24	1	4
Dec.	25	By	*Cash* . . . . (2, 1)	1	5	00
	28	By	*Profit and Loss, in Company with D. J. &c.*			
			(54, 9)	51	19	4
	30	By	*Linnen in Company with D T.* . . . (47, 8)	13	00	4
		By	*Voyage to London in Company with J. B.* . . . . (52, 9)	19	18	4
		By	*Wine* . . . . (3, 2)	28	3	4
		By	*Raisins*	3	10	00
		By	*Iron.*	15	00	00
		By	*Flax.*	18	1	00
		By	*Ship the Dragon.*	6	00	00
		By	*Daniel Stratton, my Account Current.*	2	17	6
		By	*Voyage from Rochel, &c*	13	1	11½
		By	*Herman van Rymer, my Account Current.*	3	7	1½
			Sum.	200	5	3
1729			46. HERO MOY's ACCOUNT CURRENT.			
Dec.	30	By	*His Account of Spices* . . . . (38, 6)	39	4	00

			47. LINNEN *in* COMPANY *with* D T	Yards.			
1729							
Nov.	5	By	*Sundry Accounts* . . . . . . (Nº 23, 41. Fol 4, 7)				
			At 4 s. per Yard, Nº 1.	100	20	00	00
	15	By	*William Wallace* . . . . . . (18, 3) At 3 s. 10 d				
			Nº 1.	300	57	10	00
D c.	30	By	*Ballance* . . . . . . (56, 9) Nº. 2, 3.	700	97	10	00
			Sum.	1100	175	00	00

			48 VOYAGE *to* AMSTERDAM, *for the* COMPANY *with* D. J *&c*			
1729						
Nov.	28	By	*Hero Moy, our Account Current* . . . . . . (51, 9) For 20 Packs of Wool.	208	00	00

			DEBTOR.	*l.*	*s.*	*d.*
1729		49　JAMES BALANTINE's ACCOUNT *in* COMPANY ½.				
Dec.	30	To *Ballance* .... (56, 9) —————— —————		99	11	8
1729		50.　VOYAGE *to* LONDON *in the* SUCCESS, &c.				
Nov.	25	To *Sundry Accounts* .... (N°.8, 2. Fol. 2, 1) For 750 Yards of Linnen. ————		51	15	00
1729		51.　HERO MQY *of* AMSTERDAM, *our* ACCOUNT CURRENT *for* COMPANY *with* D. J. &c.	Guild.			
Nov.	28	To *Voyage to Amsterdam*, &c.. ... (48, 8) —	2496	208	00	00
Dec.	28	To *Profit* and *Loss, in Company* ... (54, 9) —		4	00	00
		Sum	2496	212	00	00
1729		52.　VOYAGE *to* LONDON *in the* DRAGON, *for* COMPANY *with* JAMES BALANTINE.				
Dec.	2	To *Sundry Accounts* .... (N° 2, 49, 13. Fol. 1, 9, 3) 1000 Yards of Linnen; 5 Hogsheads of Claret. -		163	10	00
	30	To *Sundry Acc*... (N°. 45, 49. Fol 8, 9) For Gain, &c.		36	10	00
		Sum.		200	00	00
1729		53.　JAMES BALANTINE's *particular* ACCOUNT				
Dec	2	To *Sundry Accounts* .... (N° 49, 2, 13. Fol. 9, 1, 3)		27	15	00
1729		54.　PROFIT *and* LOSS *in* COMPANY *with* D J. &c.				
Dec.	9	To *William Davidson*.. .. .. (24, 4) For Discount		2	00	00
	28	To *Sundry Accounts* .. ..(N°. 2, 45 Fol. 1, 8) For Charges, and my Commission. ———		16	6	00
		To *Sundry Accounts*. ... (N°. 43, 44, 45 Fol. 7, 8) For Neat Gain. ———— ———		116	00	00
		Sum		134	6	00
1729		55　JOHN BLACKWOOD *of* LONDON, *our* ACCOUNT CURRENT *with* JAMES BALANTINE.				
Dec	25	To *Voyage to London in Company*, &c. ———— ———		200	00	00
1729		56　BALLANCE.				
Dec	30	To *Sundry Accounts* ... The Total of my Gross Estate.		2984	17	11

		CREDITOR.	l.	s.	d.
1729	49. JAMES BALANTINE's ACCOUNT *in* COMPANY ½.				
Nov. 20	By *Cash* .... (2, 1) Stocked by him.		5000	00	00
Dec 2	By *Sundry Accounts* ...... (Nº. 52, 53. Fol 9)		31	15	00
25	By *Cash* .... (2, 1)		1	5	00
30	By *Voyage to London, in Company, &c.* ..... (52, 9)		16	11	8
		Sum	99	11	8
1729	50 VOYAGE *to* LONDON *in the* SUCCESS, &c.				
Dec. 30	By *Ballance* .. .. (56, 9)		51	15	00
1729	51. HERO MOY *of* AMSTERDAM, our ACCOUNT CURRENT *for* COMPANY *with* D. J. &c.	Guild.			
Dec. 24	By *Cash* .. .... (2, 1)	2496	212	00	00
1729	52. VOYAGE *to* LONDON *in the* DRAGON, *for* COMPANY *with* JAMES BALANTINE.				
Dec. 25	By *John Blackwood, our Account Current.* ..... (55, 9) All received and sold.		200	00	00
1729	53 JAMES BALANTINE's *particular* ACCOUNT.				
Dec. 30	By *Ballance* . . . .. (56, 9)		27	15	00
1729	54. PROFIT *and* LOSS *in* COMPANY, *with* D. J. &c				
Dec. 28	By *Sundry Accounts* ... (Nº. 42, 48, 51. Fol. 7, 8, 9) Gained upon the Accounts.		134	6	00
1729	55. JOHN BLACKWOOD *of* LONDON, *our* ACCOUNT CURRENT *with* JAMES BALANTINE.				
Dec. 25	By *Cash* ... (2, 1)		80	00	00
	By *Ballance* (56, 9)		120	00	00
		Sum.	200	00	00
1729	56. B A L L A N C E.				
Dec. 30	By *Sundry Accounts*. . . . . . The Total of my Debts.		272	12	00
	By *Stock* . . . . My present Free Estate.		2712	5	11
		Sum	2984	17	11

INDEX of the Preceeding LEGER. N°. 2.

Fol.

B
Adam Brown ——— ——— 5
Bottomree Account. ——— 5
Accepted Bills. ——— 5
Alexander Black's parti. Acc. — 5
Alexander Black's Acc. in Comp. 7
James Ballantine's Acc. in Comp. 9
Ja. Ballantine's particular Acc. 9
Jo. Blackwood, our Account Curr. 9
Ballance. 9

C
Cash. ——— 1
Broad Cloth. ——— 2
Andrew Cochran. ——— 4
Ch. Chareu, his Acc Current. — 6
John Campbel ——— 6
Outstanding Charges. ——— 6
Ch. Chareu, our Acc. of Excha. — 6
Andr. Cochran, my Acc. with him. 6
Broad Cloth in Comp. with D. T. 7

D
Delivery Account of Buying. — 3
William Davidson. ——— 4
Thomas Dalziel. ——— 5

F
Flax. ——— 2

G
Goods in Comp. with D. J. &c. 7

H
Account of Houses. ——— 3
Andrew Hunter ——— 4

I
Iron. ——— 2
David Johnston's particular Acc. 4
David Johnston's Acc. in Company. 7

Fol.

L
Linnen. ——— 2
Linnen in Company, &c. — 8

M
Moveables. ——— 3
Hero Moy's Acc. Current. ——— 8
Hero Moy's Acc. of Spices. ——— 6
H Moy, our Acc. Curr &c. — 9

P
Paper. ——— 2
John Paton. ——— 4
Profit and Loss. ——— 8
Profit, &c. in Company, &c. 9

R
Raisins. ——— 2
Thomas Richman. ——— 4
Her. van Rymer, my Acc Curr. 5

S
Stock. ——— 1
Ship Dragon. ——— 3
D. Stratton, my Acc. of Plaiden. 3
D. Stratton, my Acc. Current. — 5

T
Tobacco. ——— 2
Daniel Trader's particular Acc. 4
D. Trader's Acc in Company. — 7

V
Voyage from Rochel, &c. — 3
——— to Amsterdam, &c. — 8
——— to London. ——— 9
——— to London in Company. — 9

W
Wine. ——— 2
William Wallace ——— 3
Wager's Account. ——— 3
Wheat. 6

A TABLE

OF ALL THE

VARIETY of CASES or EXAMPLES,

That are Contain'd in the Preceeding

WASTE-BOOKS.

Digested under distinct HEADS, with their DATES, *by which you may find them, in Order to their being compared with the JOURNAL and LEGER. The First WASTE-BOOK Ends with* October 8. *Therefore what you find dated after that, must be sought for in the Second WASTE-BOOK*

Cases.	PROPER DOMESTICK TRADE; *and First, of Buying and Selling.*
1	GOODS bought, and paid in Cash, *May* 8.
2	Goods bought on Time, *May* 4.
3	Goods bought, and Part paid in Cash, and Part owing, *May* 6.
4	Goods bought, and paid in Cash, and Bills, *May* 8.
5	Goods bought, and Part paid in Money and Bills, and Part owing, *May* 14
6	Goods bought, and Part paid in Money, the Rest to discompt what the Seller owes me, *June* 3. Or you may call this receiving Payment of Debt, and giving the Surplus.
7	Bought part of a Ship, *Aug.* 29.
8	Goods bought for Cash, but immediately sold to another, who receives them, *June* 21.
9	Goods sold for Cash, *May* 2.
10	Goods sold on Time, *May* 2.
11	Goods sold, Part paid, Part owing, *May* 6
12	Goods sold, and received a Bill for Payment, *May* 7.
13	Goods sold, and received Part in Money and Bills, Part owing, *May* 8.

G g

Goods

14| Goods sold, and received part in Cash, the Rest I owed the Seller, which is paying a Debt with Goods, and receiving the Surplus, *Aug.* 14.

15| Goods *bartered* for other Goods, *May* 11. Surplus received, the Goods received, immediately disposed of, *May* 20

Paid Overplus, *May* 20. Owing the Overplus, *June* 25

16| Goods bought, to be delivered at a certain Time, and Part of the Value advanced. *See June* 3, 12 *July* 2.

17| Received the Goods formerly bought on *Forehand-Bargain, July* 17. *Aug.* 3. By Consent there is less received than was agreed, for, *Oct.* 21.

18| Goods sold, to be delivered, and Part received *per* Advance, *June* 7, 15.

19| Delivered the Goods sold on *Forehand-Bargain, July* 17. When Part is retained by Consent. *See Aug.* 13.

20| Protested against the Seller for not delivering the Goods bought on *Forehand-Bargain,* and have charged him for the Value and Penalty, *July* 22.

21| Bought a House with the Burden of an Annuity, and am assigned to some Rent owing by the present Possessor, *Aug.* 26

22| Bought off the Annuity, *Nov.* 23

PAYING *of* DEBTS.

23| Paid a Debt with Cash, *May* 24 With Cash and Bills, *May* 30. Abatement allowed, *June* 6 *See Case* 15. With foreign Coin upon which I have lost, *Aug.* 8

24| Paid a Debt due for Household Expences, *Oct* 18.

25| Received Payment of Debt in Cash, *May* 24. *See also Nov.* 15. In a Bill payable on Demand, which is accepted to discompt what I owe that Person on whom the Bill is, but my Debt not being yet payable to him, I charge him with the Interest, *May* 28. In Money and Goods, *June* 12. Discount allowed, *Oct.* 5.

BORROWING *or* LENDING MONEY *on* BOND *or* BOTTOMREE, *and what relates thereto.*

26| Money lent on Bond, *June* 18. Interest due paid to me, and the next Terms Interest placed to Accompt, *Nov.* 15.

27| Money lent on Bottomree, *June* 22, 25. *Aug.* 13. Ship lost, *July* 4. The Money paid to my Factor, *July* 16. *See Case* 58. Received Payment myself by Bill and Cash, *Oct.* 8.

INSURANCE.

28| Insured Goods to another, and received Payment, *June* 28. *July* 10. The Præmium owing, 16

29| Paid for Goods lost, which I had insured, *July* 10.

WAGERING.

30| Consigned Money upon a Wager, *June* 22.

31| Wagered upon Parole, *July* 25.

32| Gained a Wager formerly consigned upon, *July* 15, which was on Parole, and now paid, *Aug.* 19.

33| Money gained upon a Wager immediately decided, *July* 2.

Lost

34 Loft a Wager configned upon, *July* 12; which was upon Parôle, and now paid, *Aug.* 19.

A few fingular C A S E S.

35 A Houfe left me in Legacy, and am burdened with the Payment of fome Money, *Aug.* 29.

36 Got a Legacy due by the Exe-cutor, *Sept.* 2.

37 Taken an Apprentice, and re-ceived Money in Part, *Sept.* 2

38 Brought a total Sum of Charges of Merchandize paid, from the Book of Charges, into the Grand Books, *Oct.* 7

39 Gained upon fome foreign Coin which I have fold, *July* 28.

40 Brought a total Sum of Houfhold Expences, Part paid, and Part ow-ing, into the Grand Books, *Oct.* 7.

P R O P E R   F O R E I G N   T R A D E.

41 Ship'd Goods which were entered in my Books, with Charges and Infurance. *See June* 18. *July* 4, 10 The Goods not entred into their proper Accompt, *June* 21.

42 Advifed, that my Factor has received my Goods configned to him, but not difpofed of, *July* 12. *Aug.* 10.

43 Advifed, that my Factor has fold my Goods, lying in his Hands for ready Money, *July* 22 On Time, *Aug.* 22.

44 Advifed by my Super Cargo, that he has configned my Goods to a Factor, being himfelf ready to fail homewards, *Aug.* 23.

45 Advifed by my Super Cargo, of his being fafe at his Port, felling my Goods for ready Money, and loading the Value in Return, *Aug.* 3

46 Advifed, that my Factor has received Goods of mine configned to him (part of the Cargo being loft at Sea) and fold Part thereof for ready Money, *Oct.* 12.

47 Advifed, that my Factor has bought and fhipped Goods for my Accompt, *Aug* 10. *Sept* 11.

48 Advifed of the Lofs of Cargo at Sea, *Aug.* 24.

49 Advifed, that my Factor has received Payment of Debts owing for my Goods fold by him, *Sept.* 10

50 Advifed of the Sale of my Goods formerly received, and the Value remitted, with more alfo for the Payment of a former Debt, *Oct.* 16

51 Received Goods formerly ad-vifed to have been fhipped by my Factor, or Super Cargo, *Sept.* 6. and part immediately fold, *Sept.* 22.

52 Received Goods fent by my Factor with the firft Advice con-cerning them, *Aug.* 20.

53 Received Advice that fome of my Factors has fhipped off Goods of mine to another Factor, *Sept.* 18.

54 Advifed, that one of my Factors has drawn on another for my Ac-compt, *Sept.* 25.

55 Drawn by me on my Factor for my Accompt, the Contents received in Cafh, *Aug.* 5, 15, in Goods and Money, *Sept* 25. The Contents owing, *Aug.* 23.

56 Remitted to me a Bill by my Factor for my Accompt, accepted at Ufance, *Aug.* 30.

57 Advifed by my Factor that he has received Money of mine, which was lent on Bottomree, *July* 26. *See Cafe* 26.

F A C T O-

FACTORAGE, *and what relates thereto.*

58　Received Goods to fell in Commiffion, and Charges paid at Receipt, *Aug* 16.

59　Sold the Goods for Cafh, *Aug.* 20. On Time, *Aug.* 23

60　Ship'd off the Goods by Order, and have ftated my Charges to Accompt, *Sept.* 7.

61　Received Payment of my Employers out-ftanding Debts, *Sept.* 13. And have clofed the Accompt of Goods, which are all fold, *Sept.* 13. Abatement made to the Buyer. *Nov.* 22.

62　Remitted to my Employer for his Accompt, the Contents inftantly paid, *Aug* 20.

63　Drawn upon me by my Employer at Ufance, *Sept.* 28.

64　Bought, and fhipped Goods, with Charges and Provifion, *Sept* 2.

65　Bought and received Goods for my Employers Accompt, to be fent away by the firft Occafion, Coft and Provifion ftated, *Sept.* 7. Paid more Charges at Shipping them, *Sept.* 13.

66　Received Goods fent me by my Employer, in Return for what he owes me, alfo a Bill for Part, *Oct.* 5.

EXCHANGE *in* PARTNERSHIP.

67　Drawn by me for our Accompt of Exchange, *Sept.* 10

68　Remitted to me for our Accompt, *Sept* 7.

69　Drawn on me for our Accompt, *Sept.* 22.

70　Remitted to me for our Accompt, *Sept.* 26.

COMPANY TRADE, *when my Partner is Manager.*

71　Given Money for my Share of Stock, *Aug.* 30.

72　Allowed the Manager for my Stock, to take what he owes me, *Oct.* 16.

73　Drawn on me for my Share of the Goods bought for the Company, *Sept.* 18. Drawn for more than my Share, *Nov.* 4.

74　Received Goods and Cafh in Payment of my Share of the Stock and Gain in Partnerfhip, *Sept.* 28.

75　Received of my Partner Payment of a former Debt, alfo more on Accompt of my Concerns, *Dec.* 9.

COMPANY TRADE, *when I am Manager, and keep Accompts in my own Books.*

76　Entered into Partnerfhip, and received Goods of my Partner, to which I added of my own, *Oct.* 27. Received Goods and Money from my Partner, *Oct.* 22. *Nov.* 20

77　Sold Company Wares for Cafh, *Oct.* 23. On Time, *Oct.* 26. For Money and a Debt I owe the Buyer, *Oct.* 26. Received a Bill for the Price, on my Partner, *Nov.* 5. My Partner has taken a Receipt for his own Share of the Bill, *Nov.* 19.

78　Bought Goods for the Company, with Money received of the Partners, for that Effect, *Oct.* 23.

With

With my own Cash, *Oct.* 30 Paid Part with the Company's Cash, and Part owing, *Nov.* 2 The whole owing, *Nov.* 5. Drawn on my Partner for all

79 Bought Goods for Company, and have ship'd them on board a Ship belonging to the Company, the Partners being unequal in the Ship, and equal in the Cargo, and have laid out Money for my Part-

80 ner, *Dec.* 2.

Ship'd the Company's Goods,

81 paying Charges, *Nov.* 8.

Paid my Partners for their Accompt in Cash, *Nov.* 11. By Assign-

82 ment, *Dec.* 22.

Received Payment of a Debt

83 owing to the Company, *Dec.* 9.

One Partner receives of Another his Share of Debt owing for the Company's Goods by this Partner.

Paid a Debt owing for the Company with their own Money, *December* 25.

84 Advised, that our Factor has received our Goods, and sold them for Cash, *Nov.* 28.

85 Drawn on our Factor, and received the Contents, *Dec.* 24.

86 Drawn on our Factor for Company Accompt, and have received Payment with Gain by Exchange, *Dec* 25

87 Adjusted Accompts with my Partners, and have paid their Shares, *Oct.* 27 *Dec.* 28.

88 Examined the State of Accompts of Company, and have placed to Accompt several Charges, and Provision owing, also collected the Gain, and made a Dividend thereof, in order to bring my Books to a Close.

APPENDIX,

APPENDIX,

CONTAINING,

INSTRUCTIONS *for the* APPLICATION *of the preceeding* ART, *to the Bufinefs of* RETAILERS, *and* PRIVATE CONCERNS; *more efpecially for Gentlemen of* LAND ESTATES, *and their* STEWARDS *or* FACTORS

INTRODUCTION.

WHEN any Art depends upon few, and thofe general Principles, whereby it is applicable to a Variety of 'Things, which, tho' different among themfelves, have yet a common Nature that makes them equally fubject to the fame general Rules, It is very reafonably judged to be fufficient, that fome particular Branch of the Application be clearly explained. That Branch indeed, ought to be fuch, as, by it the Nature, Defign and Tendency of the Art may beft appear: For where the greateft Variety of Circumftances occur, there we learn beft, the Senfe of general Rules, and what ought to be allowed for, in different Circumftances, fo as to obtain the End. Accordingly I have in the preceeding Treatife laid before you the Defign of this artificial *Book-keeping*, with the general Rules and Notions thereof, and have explained and illuftrated the fame in a particular Application to *Merchants Accompts*, ftrictly taken. You have feen how a regular *Accompt* is begun, carried on, and finifhed: And to the Induftrious, who have carefully read and impreffed the *general Notions*, and alfo diligently confidered and compared the Precepts and Examples given, it will be no difficulty to make fuch an Application to any other Subject of Accompts as may anfwer any reafonable defign or demand concerning the fame. For it is impoffible that any Body who is once apprized of the Defign and Reafon of any Method in General, and together with this has feen a proper Application of Particulars, fhould not have the Ufe of their Judgment fo let in, as to be able to

reafon

reason from the Design of the Method, and the Matter they apply it to, for what ought to be done : In a Word, there is nothing here but general Rules, and the Application depends upon a judicious Reflection and Recollection of the Truth and Juſtice of firſt Principles, and a prudent Foreſight of Conſe- quences, which is learnt by Practice, either of fictitious or real Caſes, (for they have the ſame Effect, if the Firſt be well choſen) after the Principles upon which that Practice depends are duly unfolded. Conſidering this with myſelf, I could ſee no great Neceſſity of inſiſting further upon the Application of this Method, and at moſt, there can be no more required but general Hints of what is to be, or may be done, upon any other Subject, to open a Tract for the Application : Nor is it neceſſary to mention every Subject ; a Genius that needs this, ſeems but ill affected to this kind of Knowledge. Sup- poſing therefore, any Body to underſtand the preceeding general Principles, and the Application already made, I ſhall but touch upon ſome other Things which I referred to this Place ; and particularly I ſhall do what farther can be reaſonably expected, to make obvious the Application to the Matter of ſome *private Accompts*, eſpecially to the Concerns of Gentlemen of Land Eſtates.

In order to what I deſign in this Place there is one general Reflection to be made, *viz.* That the Conveniency or Inconveniency of any Method, depends upon the Nature of one's Eſtate or Dealings, and this ought to be conſulted in the firſt Place. For ſuch ways of Accompting, as in great and diffuſed Trade prevent Confuſion, by an artfull and regular diſpoſing of Things, if applied to mean and narrow Dealings, will create Confuſion, at leaſt, will give more Work to do than is needful : For a few Things ſhew themſelves readily, and are examined by meer Inſpection ; ſuppoſing no other Method but a *Waſte-Book* Record ; every Corner whereof, (in very ſmall Dealings) the Accomptant's Eye is acquainted with, ſo as he can readily turn to what he wants, But this in larger Accompts is impoſſible, which makes Order, the ſtricteſt Form, and much Writing abſolutely neceſſary. Yet this one Rule muſt be indiſpenſibly obſerved in all Caſes, *viz.* That a true and exact Memorial of every Thing belonging to the *Accompt* be made, juſt as Things occur ; and if Buſineſs increaſes, ſo that a nearer Approach to the Perfection of Accompt- ing be neceſſary, then this will ſerve as a Ground-work upon which you may raiſe the Accompt to what Form you pleaſe. In ſhort, the leaſt you can do will be ſome part of the Method already explained : For all Methods what- ever are a Part of this, (which comprehends the greateſt Simplicity in its *Waſte-Book*, and Art in the *Leger*) and as far as they come ſhort of it, want ſo much of deſirable Perfection ; making Allowance for ſuch Caſes as not only admit but require an Abatement of the Rigour of Art.

I s h a l l therefore begin the Applications deſigned here with ſuch Subjects as do not require, and ſcarcely admit, the utmoſt Pitch of this Art ; and gradually proceed to others which do.

§ I. *For more* PRIVATE PERSONS.

(1.) I SHALL firſt conſider a Perſon in a *ſingle State* ; who has no Buſineſs, but the Receiving at certain Times in a Year a Sum of Money, which he lays out again for his private and perſonal Expences ; If this Perſon writes Things in a *Pocket-Book* as they fall out, he can without any other Form, very eaſily ſatisfy himſelf how his ſmall Affairs ſtand , eſpecially, if he writes down his Receipts in one Place, and his Payments in another , for what elſe may Occur, its no great Matter where it ſtand, ſo it be there. And becauſe he may have a daily Expending, therefore to make eaſy Work, he may put a Sum of Money once a Week in his Pocket, or lay it by it ſelf, and take it out daily as he needs, and at the Weeks End write what is Spent that Week. And if he would come nearer the Art, he may monthly or quarterly make a Digeſt of the Articles of Caſh given out and received, collecting them under proper Denominations, as *Clothing*, (which may be alſo ſubdivided) *Neceſ-ſary Charges of Diet, incidental Expences, Coals and Candles, Waſhing, Houſe-Rent*, &c and what other Things happen, he may methodiſe accord-ing to his fancy

(2) I F we conſider one in a *married State* : But whoſe Fortune conſiſts alſo of Money as before *This Perſon*, as he has a greater Variety of Ex-pences ; muſt be very careful to keep an exact Accompt of all the Caſh he receives and pays. And to make this Accompt more diſtinct and orderly, it will be beſt to keep the Particulars of the Payments, in a ſeparate Book, and to bring them into the Caſh-Book (or Accompt) once a Week, in Totals, digeſted under ſuch different Denominations as he thinks fit, as *Fiſh, Fleſh, Coals, Candles, Bread or Meal, Ale or Malt, Cloaths*, &c *and for Houſe-Rents. Accompts* paid to *Shopkeepers* and *Tradeſmen*, as they are paid all at once, they come in Groſs into the Caſh Accompt of which he may make other Subdiviſions as he thinks proper to repreſent the State of his Expences more particularly. For Example, Things which are digeſted under proper Heads, and ſo brought into the Caſh Accompt, may be again drawn into an Abſtract, ſhewing the Total of each Kind of Expences for every Month, by dividing a Page into twelve Columns, with the Names of the twelve Months, *January, Fe-bruary*, &c and then in ſo many Articles upon the Margin, ſet the Names of the ſeveral Heads of Expences, and againſt each, under the reſpective Month, the Sum of that Kind of Expences in that Month , then will the Sum of the Money in the Columns under each Month be the Total Expence of that Month, and the Aggregate of theſe Sums will be the Years Expences But you may have another Proſpect of the Years Expences, by adding the Expences of a particular Kind, for every Month, and ſetting the Sum in a ſeparate Column, and the Sum of that Column will alſo be the whole years Expences. For other Things as *Furniture* intruſted with a *Houſe-keeper*, there ought to be an *Inventory* ; and it is the Truſtees Buſineſs to keep an

Exact

Exact Accompt how it is difposed of, for which a fhort *Memorandum* made from Time to Time will ferve

AGAIN, as a *Wife* or *Houfe-keeper* has the laying out of the moft Part of the Common and daily Expences of a Family. If thefe, as they ought, keep an Accompt of all they receive and lay out ; The Mafter of the Family will have no more to do, fo far as thofe Accompts go, but to digeft and bring them in Totals, into the *Cafh-Book.*: And if the Perfon, who is intrufted with the Disburfments, is taught to make the Digefts, or Collection of the Articles, under proper Heads (as may very eafily be done) the Other will have Little to do.

FOR the *Furniture* of a *Houfe*, there ought to be an exact *Inventory* of it taken in the Beginning of the Year ; or when you begin your Accompts ; and an Account of all the Reparations and Additions made to it.

THE PERSONS now under Confideration have no great Neceffity for any other than the *Cafh Accompt.* But if he will give his Accompts a more Artificial Form ; Then he may begin them by an Inventory of all his Effects and Furniture : And the Money, and Debts payable to him, as the Fund of his Living, for the following Year , Enter thefe upon a *Stock Accompt* ; and keep particular Accompts for the *Perfons*, and the *Subjects* by which his Money is payable ; and an Accompt of *Furniture* for that Article. , Then thefe Accompts are to be difcharged as they pay or are difpofed of. If he borrows or lends Money, let the Lender or Borrower have an Accompt : And the *Profit* and *Lofs Accompt* will Ballance againft the *Cafh-Accompt* for all the Articles that are Expences.

§ II. *For Working* TRADESMEN, *or* HANDYCRAFTS-MEN.

THESE may keep Accompts of their Expences of Living the fame Way as before : But it will alfo be neceffary to make a diftinct Accompt of the *Charges* and *Profit* of their Bufinefs, which may eafily be done ; by an exact Accompt of all they Pay or Owe for the Materials and Inftruments of their Work, with Servants Wages, and Taxes upon their Trade ; and of all they Receive or is due for their Work. Their Accompts ought to begin with an exact *Inventory* of all the *Furniture* belonging to the Family, and to their Bufinefs And they may conveniently keep Accompts for the Materials of their Work, to fatisfy them of the Difpofal thereof (which will be a Check upon Servants, who have Accefs to thofe Things) and they muft keep Accompts for the Perfons they deal with, both in Buying and Selling If thefe know any Thing of the Principles of Book-keeping, they will eafily apply them : So that I fhall fay no more.

§ III. *For* PETTY-TRADERS *and* RETAILERS.

(1.) FOR PETTY TRADERS. Who deal in fome hundreds of Trifling Wares, and make Sales to the Value of a Farthing or Half-penny,

thefe

thefe cannot pretend to keep orderly Accompts: The beft they can do, is to be careful that Servants do not wrong them; for they have no Accompt of Goods; and if you ask what of any Kind remains with them, they muft go look, failing their Memory Thefe muft have a *Cafh-Accompt*, which they Charge once a Week with the Money received, and difcharge for what they give out; it is not Convenient that they fhould touch the *Cafh-Box* or *Till*, oftner than once a Week, when it is Compleat; but if they do, they muft keep a feparate Accompt of what they take out, to know what was received Befides which, they will have a kind of *Leger*, for the Perfons with whom they deal upon Credit, in which they give every *Debtor* or *Creditor* an Accompt, with *Debt* and *Credit* both on one Side, either with a double Money Column, or conftant Deductions, as the *Debts* and *Credits* fucceed one another, but if many Articles of *Debt* and *Credit* come after one another, they are not fummed till an Article of the oppofite Kind occur, and then the Accompt is ballanced till that Time, and the prefent Receipt or Payment ftated; and this Book may have an *Index* to find every Accompt readily They may alfo for the fake of Thofe, have a *Memorandum*, by way of *Day-Book*, wherein all Things of this Nature are writ down, and then carry'd into the other.

(2.) THERE is another Kind of *Retailers* (or *Shop-keepers*) that are more Confiderable; who commonly deal in a few different Species of Goods, as *Linnen-Drapers*, *Woollen-Drapers*, *Mercers*, &c. Thefe may keep better formed Accompts; tho' there is a common Deficiency here; they keep a *Leger for Perfons and Wares* diftinct, without any formal Connection or Reference of the Accompts, in their feveral Articles; whereby there can no regular Ballance be made of fuch Accompts. In the Accompts of *Perfons*, they ufe the Formality of a *Debtor* and *Creditor* Stile, which is meer fhew, without the real Value of a regular Accompt; there being no oppofite Correfpondent *Debtors* and *Creditors* to be found. For their *Leger of Wares*, as they call it, contains nothing of This, and is but an imperfect Contrivance, which they fatisfy themfelves with, to know how much remains: But the Worft is, that in allotting fpaces for the Accompts of Wares, I know them who give no more than they fuppofe may ferve for the Retail of the Quantity firft entred on that Space; and when it is difpofed of, they take a new Space for a new Parcel; which in a quick Trade will be very troublefome, and confufed too, if there be any of the old Parcels remaining, unlefs they carry it to the new Accompt But for the more confiderable *Retailers*, I fee no neceffity for them to come fhort of the utmoft Pitch of Art. What if they deal in fifty different kinds of Goods? And befides, retail to the Value of a Shilling, or even Sixpence, they may purfue the *Method* in its Perfection with no great trouble; at leaft there is no reafon to grudge the Labour of their Servants, who poffibly have more time lying upon their Hands, than would do the Bufinefs. Befides all this, they have frequently ways of their own that are more troublefome. It is no difficulty to find out what they ought to do. For any *By-Books* to ferve particular Views of their own, I leave them

to

to their Fancy : But I would at leaft keep three *Grand-Books*, a *Wafte*, *Journal*, *and Leger*, or two at leaft, joining the Firft two into one. Let the *Wafte-Book* contain every Thing that is done in the Shop, both the Sales on Truft, and for Cafh ; which is the only Thing ordinarily neglected ; I would not have a Groats worth omitted : And to make Things eafy for carrying forward out of this *Book*, you may put all the Sales in a Part of the Book by themfelves, and even put Sales upon *Truft*, and for *Cafh*, feparate ; a very narrow Page will ferve, and becaufe there may be other Tranfactions that will require more Room, make your Book of an ordinary Size, but what is affigned for thefe Sales, may be divided into two or more Columns, for a few Words will ferve every Article. Your *Wafte-Book* being daily filled up, in this Manner, you may carry it forward once a Week, and Place every Thing to its proper Accompt. You may make your *Wafte and Journal* in one, by marking the *Debtors* and *Creditors* on the Margin, againft every fingle Tranfaction of Value : And for thofe Accompts, where the only Trouble appears to be, fuppofing them many and fmall, it will be eafily got over, by this Weekly transfering, for now you muft make a Digeft of thefe Articles : *That is*, having firft read them over, to find what Accompts they belong to, and having prepared Columns for the Purpofe, under the Name of each diftinct Species, write the Quantity and Value of that Kind difpofed of that Week ; let all the Articles belonging to *the Sales for Cafh*, be firft fet down and fummed, and then the Articles on *Truft* with the *Debtors* Name after it, and Sum the Whole, and fo Matters are prepared for the *Leger*. The Total Sum of Each muft be carried to the *Creditor* Side of the Accompt in the *Leger*.—— *By Sundry Accompts*, the Sum belonging to *Cafh* is carried to its *Debtor-Side*, and what is due by every *Perfon*, *To his Accompt*, and, to make the *Leger* Shorter, take the Total *Cafh* received that Week, in one Sum *To Sundry Accompts* ; and you may do the like for Perfons Accompts. Thefe Digefts ought to be put into the *Wafte-Book*, immediate'y after what they belong to, with this *Title*.——*Digeft of this Weeks Sales* ; with the Name of each Parcel of Goods write *Creditor*, and againft the Sum of the *Cafh* Write *Cafh Debtor*, and fo againft every *Perfons* Name who was trufted, and it will be as good as a *Journal* And becaufe it is very Convenient to have a *Cafh-Accompt*, fet a part another Place of the Book, in which, by a double Money Column, write all other Receipts and Payments the Sums of which are to be carried as oft as you pleafe into the *Legar Accompt of Cafh*, and to the *Perfons Accompts* who paid or received, or the *Accompt of Goods* for which you paid Cafh. Thefe, and every Tranfaction of the *Wafte*, being truly transferred into the *Leger*, you have a true State of your Affairs as oft as you pleafe, at the Coft only of a little *Pen*, *Ink*, *Paper*, and fuch Pains as will turn at laft into Pleafure, when you Experience the Benefit of it You may make other Divifions in your *Wafte-Book*, as you think fit, but that it may be all as one Book, containing the Number of Pages through the whole Leaves.

N o w

Now for the *Retailers Leger-Book*, becaufe there are commonly many Articles of *Debt* to one of *Credit*, upon *Mens Accompts* with whom they deal, and many Articles of *Credit* for one of *Debt*, upon *Accompt of Wares*, they may keep the *Debt* and *Credit* both on one Side by double Money Columns, in the one of which let the *Debt*, and in the other the *Credit* be fet   And as to *Accompts of Wares*, becaufe it will be too much to have a double Column of Money and Goods both; efpecially if there happen to be more than one Species under a general Denomination, therefore the Quantities received and delivered may go into one Column, conveniently enough, providing you make a Ballance, upon every new Receipt, *i. e* having drawn a Line under the Quantity firft entered, all given out fuccced in the fame Column, and where a new Parcel is received, fum up the former Quantities difpofed of, and Subftract the Sum from the preceeding Quantity on Hand, and after the Remainder is Written down, enter the new Parcel   The *Gain* or *Lofs* may be calculated and ftated at this Time, and placed in the proper Money Column, *Debtor* Column, if *Gain*, and *Creditor*, if *Lofs*; and after This the Value of the remaining Part drawn out againft it.   But this may be done as feldom as you pleafe; and even delay'd till you come to make a general Ballance of Accompts   The Spaces affigned to every *Accompt of Wares*, may be fo large as to ferve a Years Trade; and it will be no very great *Leger*, confidering you transfer the *Sales* by the Total of the whole Week's Tranfactions, and perhaps more.   Of one diftinct Kind there may be many Species, even more than can be well brought into one Accompt   For Example, *A Retailer* has forty Pieces of *Broad Cloth*, differing in Colour oi Finenefs, which are too many for one Accompt, if you would give each a diftinct Column, but tho' this were done, I forefee a Difficulty, for peihaps befoie all this is difpofed of, more is purchafed which will require new Columns, and the only and common Way to diftinguifh fuch Differences, is by numbeiing the Pieces. Now, if as many of the old Pieces aie difpofed of, as of new come in, then the fame Columns may ferve, by affigning the fame Numbers to the New, which the Old had   But if the Columns are too many, make two or more Accompts, and diftinguifh them by Affoitments affigning fiom fuch to fuch a Number, to the Firft, Second, &c Affortment.   Of which Artifice I have fpoken in the preceeding Tieatife   And then when new Pieces come in, let them be enteied upon thofe Accompts wheie the Quantity upon fome Number is all difpofed of, that fo eveiy Quantity in the fame Column may have always the fame Number   By this Means you'll have the Accompts ieafonably diftinct, and when this cannot be done, make a new Accompt, but after this Method the *Gain* oi *Lofs* will only appeai in General upon the whole Accompt, and not upon every Piece, if thofe of different Value fuccced upon the fame Number, unlefs, at eveiy new Receipt, the *Gain* oi *Lofs* maie upon the Piece difpofed of, be placed to the Accompt   In fhort, when much of one's Trade lies upon few Things, it will be neceffary by fome fuch Artifice, to keep many Accompts for feveral Species of the fame Thing, to prevent the Confufion of too general an Accompt, othciwife, cne Accompt may

ieive

ferve for all, and with one fingle Colum for the total Quantity of all the Pieces, which you may enter thus, *Debtor to Cafh, or A. B.* &c. for feven Pieces, from N° 1 to 7 containing in all —— Yards (to be put in the inner Column) and the Total drawn out: When any is difpofed of, narrate of what Number it is, and at the weekly Transfer mark the Numbers to which the Quantities difpofed of belonged ; and when new Parcels come in, give them new Numbers. By this way, neither the Quantity remaining, nor Gain upon the Part fold, of any particular Number, will appear ; but you'll find it, by the Date in the *Wafte-Book* ; where particular Quantities and Prices are written at large ; but the *Leger Accompt* will give the total *Gain or Lofs*, and Quantity of all the Pieces remaining ; and to diftinguifh the Species in Order to the Transferring the Accompt into a New Space, *the Wafte-Book* muft be confulted, and the Particulars received compared with what are dif-pofed of.

P E R H A P S, you may find it Convenient to confider the Colours of the Pieces, and to make the Diftinction that way ; all that are of one fimple Colour, as *Red, Black, Blew,* &c. may poffefs diftinct Accompts ; and for mixed Colours, it will be no great difficulty to diftinguifh them according to the prevailing Colour, and bring all that are upon one under the fame Affortment, and into the fame Accompt ; and thus you need but one inner Column for the total Quantities, but be fure to refer to the Numbers marked on the Pieces. From what I have faid here, you'll eafily contrive proper Ways for other Things

OBSERVE, Dealers in a lower Value than what I have laft fuppofed, may follow the fame Method, if they'll take the Trouble to keep an exact *Day-Book,* and write down the fmalleft Sale they make. And for their *Leger,* they may have Accompts of Wares, however triffling they are, by the fame Method of making Affortments. Let the more valuable Things have diftinct Accompts ; and for petty Wares, fuppofe they deal in five hundred of them, fifty Accompts will do their Bufinefs. Thus, let every Affortment have ten Species, and to every Affortment an Accompt, with ten inner Columns, mark'd with the Names of the feveral Wares And the Diftinctions of thofe which have Species under them, muft be here neglected ; except, in fo far as a Reference to the *Day-Book* may clear it ; and that will be done by the Date, at the Pofting of the *Accompt of Sales,* whereby you'll find all the Particulars of that Total together ; and confequently with a little Pains, the Species of Each ; which ought to be mentioned in the *Day-Book,* and particularly in the *Digeft.*

A s I have Written this Appendix for the Benefit of fuch as are fuppofed to have read, and underftood the preceeding Treatife, only for a Hint of Things, therefore I fee no neceffity to give more particular Examples.

§ IV. *For* Gentlemen *of* Land-Estates; *And their* Stewards, *or* Factors.

I Shall not use many Arguments to recommend regular Accompting, to Perfons who vifibly have fo great Occafion for it If there is little to do, they have the lefs Excufe, and if there is much, they have the more need of fuch an Art, as may enable them to know readily the diftinct State and Pofture of their Affairs: Unlefs they are willing to be cheated without Controul, as wou'd be no great Difficulty, nor is it very Rare with cunning and difhoneft Servants, who take all advantages of their Mafters Ignorance or Negligence; and if nothing of this Kind were to be feared Is it no Pleafure for a Gentleman to know whether his Affairs profper or go back? To know what Part of his Fortune yields beft, and what Part of his Expences is greateft? That he may add or retrench as he fees moft Convenient · And in a Word, fo to regulate his Affairs, as to make the beft he can of his Fortune, and the beft Ufe of what he Receives

I do not propofe to be very particular; yet I fhall endeavour to Chalk out fuch a Method, as will be enough for one who has but the leaft Talent at Thinking; and has examined the preceeding Treatife, with reafonable Care. And to execute my Defign with the beft Advantage, I take for Example, a Gentleman of a plentiful Fortune, whom I fhall fuppofe willing to beftow Time and Pains in keeping regular Accompts of his Concerns, upon the Profpect both of Pleafure and Profit, from his Labour The Subject Matter of the Accompts to be kept is, in general, the Product of his Eftate, and the Difpofal thereof. But there are many accomptable Branches here, fo that a meer Cafh Accompt of Receipts and Expences will not ferve For I fhall fuppofe a Gentleman is concerned with Rents, which he either collects him-felf, or by his Factors, Stewards, or Bailiffs, who are accountable to him : With the Management of his Lands : With Intereft Money received, or paid, or both : With Houfe-keeping, which he ought to take accompt of. With the ordinary and extraordinary Expences of his Retinue, Pleafures, &c. Now there are many neceffary Demands to be made concerning thefe Branches of his Bufinefs: For it is fit he fhould know at all Times (or have it in his Power with a little Pains to know) what his Tenants owe: How his Factor or Stewards Accompts ftand: How it is with his Farms and Stock in Hand: What his Expences of every Kind are, &c. all which may be refolved by an orderly Method; fo that he may know when he pleafes, how it is with the Total of his Affairs; whether his Eftate advances, or goes back. And the chief Encouragement to this Work is, that by a regular Accompt, where every Thing is carefully Recorded, a Gentleman may difcover what is the Occafion of his Lofs; what Branch has failed; and confequently he will forefee the Way to help fuch Misfortune, for the Time to come, if the Fault was his own; and if not, it is at leaft a Pleafure to be confcious of this: Next for the Method of a Gentleman's Accompts. And this I fhall explain, by laying down, firſt a more general Method, unconfined to the Stricter Rules of Art ; and then ſhew how to bring all Things to the Stricteſt Forms of *Debtor* and *Creditor.*

I. *For a more General Method.*

Th e *Books* neceſſary to be kept are :

(1) A *Great Waſte-Book* containing a plain Narrative of all Things as they occur, as Receipts and Payments ; every Thing given and received ; and, in ſhort, whatever is done in a Gentleman's Buſineſs, relating to any Thing or Perſon he is concerned with, out of which the following *Books* are made up

(2) A *Caſh-Book,* containing in a plain Narrative Stile, upon the *Debtor-Side,* all Receipts of Money, and upon the *Creditor,* all Payments ; and tho' there are ſeveral Articles received or paid together, belonging to the ſame Accompt, which are entered particularly in the *Waſte,* yet they may be ſet down here in a Total Sum : For Example, there is paid for divers Pieces of *Houſhold Furniture,* all particularly mentioned in the *Waſte-Book,* yet, in the *Caſh-Book,* there needs no more than ſay, *paid for Houſhold Furniture,* &c. This is a very neceſſary Book, becauſe much of a Gentleman's Concerns runs thro' his Caſh ; and this Book ought to be filled up daily ; and it will ſhew the State of Caſh better, if inſtead of carrying the Sums of the old Pages into the New, you make a *Ballance,* and carry over the Difference to the *Creditor-Side* of the new Pages, which will ſhew how much was in *Caſh* at that Time, and when any Article is thus transferred into the *Caſh-Book,* make ſome Mark upon it in the *Waſte-Book,* to ſignifie this In a ſmall Concern, this Book might be ſufficient for all, becauſe it will be no great Trouble, at any time to caſt ones Eye over a few Particulars, which are diſtinguiſhed by the Months wherein they occurred ; which a good Memory will make very uſeful, and may ſtill be made more uſeful, by making monthly Digeſts or Abſtracts thereof, bringing every Article under proper Denominations, and that this may be the more eaſily done, you may after every Article, as it is ſet down, write immediately before the Money Column, ſome Letter of the Alphabet, and it will be beſt to take them in order Set $\overline{A}$ to the firſt Article, and obſerve to ſet the ſame Letter to every ſucceeding Article of that Kind, in that Month, and a new Letter to Articles of another Nature, taking the Letter $\overline{B}$ to the firſt Article of another Kind, and ſo on : This being done, both on the *Debtor* and *Creditor Side,* when you come to make your Digeſt, it will be very eaſy : For going through the Diſburſements of that Month, you'll find, by the different Letters, how many accomptable Branches there are, whoſe Denominations write down, as *Houſhold-Expences, Apparel, Servants-Wages, Intereſt, Books,* &c. and having collected on a looſe Paper, all the Sums belonging to each, as you know them by the Letter, ſet the Total againſt its proper Title, and if all theſe accomptable

Titles,

Titles, be written down succeffively under one another, and the Page divided into twelve Columns, titled upon the Top with the twelve Months, then this will ferve for the whole Year's Abftract; and muft therefore be put in fome feparate Place of the Book; an Abftract of the Receipts may be made the fame Way, tho' there will not be here fo many Branches; there will be *Land-Rents, Intereft, Cattle fold, Corn fold,* &c. And obferve, that, as it is in your Choice, how many Things you bring under one Title, fo you may make more or lefs, according as it will be ufeful for making Things diftinct: But this Choice muft be determined in filling up the *Cafh-Book.*

(3.) There muft be a *Book of Accompts with Tenants,* where, in diftinct Places, every one's Charge and Difcharge may be plainly and fairly written, without any great Formality of Stile; and if you give it a Show of *Debtor* and *Creditor-Side* (there is another *Leger,* of which afterwards) it will be fo much the more Diftinct; and when any Accompts have been ftated with them, it is fit to carry the Ballance to a new Space; or having clofed, or drawn Lines under, enter the Ballance properly in the fame Space, and carry it on while that can hold any Thing: The great Advantage of having Accompts thus clofed, at every Adjuftment made between Parties, is, that you have no further back to go than the laft Reckoning, when you come next to accompt with them; and this makes fuch fimple Men as you have to do with very eafie, who are unwilling to go any further back.

(4.) A Book of petty Accompts with Servants and Workmen, &c.

(5) A Book of *Real Accompts*; containing an Accompt of *Cattle, Corn,* and other *Stock or Furniture*; to know at all Times, what you have, and how it is difpofed of.

OBSERVE. If a Gentleman advance no nearer to the artificial Part of Accompting, he muft keep an Accompt with every Perfon, with whom he has Dealings; and thefe may be kept in the fame Book with his Tenants Accompts; and indeed both the laft two Books may go in one; and you may allot diftinct Parts for them; the laft will take no great Room compared with the other. Thefe Books of Accompts muft have Indexes.

(6) But, I fuppofe a Gentleman willing to go farther. I fhall therefore next, more particularly fhow how he may open and begin his Accompts, in a regular Manner, in order to their being carried on and clofed according to Art.

II. *For a more particular and artificial Method.*

(1) It is indifpenfably neceffary, that a Gentleman have always a clear Rent-Roll of his Eftate; and, becaufe Rents rife and fall fometimes, it will require that fuch a Roll be fiequently made, that the prefent State of the Rents may always appear; there is no Difficulty in making a diftinct and clear Rental-Book; you may do it thus, the Page being divided into Columns,

for

for the following Ufes: Let the Names of the *Grounds and Farms*, be firft upon the left Hand, in the next fet the Names of the *Tenants* ; then, in fo many diftinct Columns, every kind of Rent which is paid, as *Oats, Barley, Poultry*, &c. and *Money* in the laft Place: The Columns being infcribed with thefe Names, fet them under the Quantities payable ; and it is fit you confider all the Variety that is payable out of the whole Lands ; that a Column may be made for each, through all the Pages of the *Rental-Book* ; for tho' the fame Farms pay not of every Kind, yet there may be a Mixture ; and then having Columns for each in every Page, you can the more eafily find the Sum of every Kind, by carrying the Sum of every Page over to the Head of the next And if the Lands are divided into Mannors, (or Baronies) then place the Name of each Mannor next the Lands belonging to it ; and if you pleafe you may fum each Mannor by it felf; and in this Cafe, to make your Columns, you need not confider more than the Variety payable out of that Mannor And at laft, make an Abftract of the whole, for the Totals of each Mannor ; the Sum of this Abftract is the Total Year's Rent. If you pleafe to make another Money Column, in it you may fet the yearly Rent, according to the Valuation, by which publick Taxes are paid, and this you may call the Parifh Value.

In fuch Eftates where there are *Oats, Barley*, &c. paid in the Rent, the Total Yearly Rent is not known by the *Rental-Book*, in Money Value, becaufe the Price of thofe Changes But the true Defign of a *Rental-Book*, is no more than to know the yearly Rent, of every Species ; yet if you'll fet an arbitary Value on every Part of the Rent, which you may only do for the Totals, then you'll have the whole in Money, which reckoning at twenty (or as many as you pleafe) Years Purchafe, the Sum is your *Real Eftate*, in Diftinction from what is called your *Perfonal Eftate*, confifting of *Moveable Effects*, as *Money, Cattle, Houfe-Furniture, Arrears of Rents*, &c.

If the Tithes payable out of the Lands, be included in the *Rent-Roll*, thefe muft be deducted from the Sum, the Remainder is the neat Rent belonging to the Mafter ; but if you put that in the *Rental*, it is beft to fet it down in a feparate Article ; and in fumming up the Columns, keep the Rents and Tithes diftinct

(2) To open your *Wafte-Book* in Form, there muft be a full and exact *Inventory* made of all your *Perfonal Eftate*, viz. *Ready Money, Jewels* and *Plate* ; and all Manner of *Houfhold Furniture, Books* and *Pictures*, &c. Stock of *Corn* and *Cattle* upon the Grounds in Hand ; *Corn, Meal*, &c. in the *Granaries*, and other Kinds of *Moveable Effects* ; the *Seed* in the Ground, alfo the *Stores* of *Provifion* of all Sorts, which are then in the Houfe, *Money* out upon Intereft ; and *Arrears* of *Rents*, due by the Tenants, &c.

If your Rent is all Money (or putting an arbitary Value upon it) you may bring an Article for your *Real Eftate*, into the *Inventory* ; but this is needlefs.

Of all thefe Things you make particular *Inventories*, which muft be carefully preferved, and enter the Totals into the general *Inventories* of your *Wafte-Book*,

Book; as *per particular Inventory thereof*; at least those which have numerous *Items*, as *House-Furniture*, *Books*, &c.

THERE must also be made an exact List of your Debts.

YOUR *Waste-Book* being thus opened, you continue from Time to Time, to write in it whatever occurs in your Affairs, and out of it be sure daily to fill up your *Cash-Book*, as before described.

THE *Book of Accompts* with the Tenants, must be begun as soon as the *Waste-Book*; because from this the Article of Arrears in the Inventory comes; which is brought there in one Total: Those Arrears are first entered on the Accompt, and then the current Year's Rent upon the *Debtor-Side*; and on the *Creditor*, the Payments, tho' in a plain Stile.

BEFORE we proceed further, let us consider what is the best Time for beginning the Accompts. If the Rent is all Money, the Beginning of the Year, or of *January*, will do well, and the Accompt of Arrears will be what's due preceeding *Martinmas* last, for Estates in *Scotland*, and *Christmas* for *England*. But when there is *Oats*, *Barley*, &c. which is commonly payable betwixt *Christmas* and *Candlemas*, it will be best to begin the Accompts on the First of *March*, that there may be as little Arrears as possible; besides, what is due of *Corn*, &c. can now be charged in Money, because the Term of Delivery is past; and before this Time, there is commonly a publick Rate set upon *Farm Corns*, &c. at which Rate the Tenants are obliged to pay to their Masters what they fail to deliver In each *Tenant's Accompt*, let there be as many Columns, as there are Species of Rents, payable by that Tenant, with the Money Columns last: Set down the Arrears of every Kind in their respective Columns, all in a Line; having written before it, *Arrears due at Christmas or Candlemas last*; or suppose it is *March* 1729, say, *Preceeding, and for the Crop* 1728. And in the *Money Column*, set both the Arrears of *Money-Rent*, and the Value of the other Parts, or if you please to make two Lines, set the Arrears of *Money-Rent*, in one, and against the other Things, the Sum of their Values; and it will be fit to mark, at what Rate, every Thing is stated; but this done at the Beginning, is sufficient. Then to enter the current Year's Rent, you must make a Line for every Species payable, that the Value in Money may be orderly drawn out in case the *Corn*, &c. happen to be sold, or not be delivered in due time, tho' it will do if all are placed in a Line: Yet because the Rents will probably be paid at divers Times, which must be entered on the *Creditor-Side* of the Accompt, in distinct Articles, each with their Dates (for with these simple People, you cannot be too plain and particular) therefore there is no loss, to place them in distinct Articles, on the *Debtor-Side*; only, take Notice, that *Capons*, *Weathers*, and all of that Kind, may go in one Line, because ordinarly, there is a Value agreed upon by Master and Tenant, in Case of Non-Delivery. Now the Arrears, being all charged in Money, come in one gross Article of Money to the *Inventory* thus, *Total of the Arrears due by the Tenants preceeding, and for the Crop* 1728, as per *the Book of Accompts with the Tenants.*

TH

T H E current Year's Rent is not to be taken into the *Inventory*; but according as it is paid, fo will it be entered in the Books.

(3) T H E *Book of Petty Accompts*, I fuppofe to be carefully kept as above directed. Alfo the *Book of Real Accompts*; whereby you may readily know how every Thing is difpofed of But if you fhould think it too great a trouble, to enter every Thing into the *Wafte-Book*, and alfo into thefe *Digeft-Books*, as I may call them, which are made up Daily, or Weekly, out of the *Wafte*, you may put all in one great Book, which having numbred in Pages, in a continued Series, from one End to the Other, fubdivide it, and affign a Part of this Book for a *Cafh-Book*, another for your *Petty Accompts*, and a Third, for the *Real Accompts*, (but the Book of Accompts with the Tenants, will do as well by its felf, tho' it may be included here; and then it will be more eafy to turn to the Place of this Book, where Things are to be found.) The Book begins with the *Inventory*, and the firft Part will contain every other Thing that belongs not to the Parts now defcribed; but this does not hinder that fome Articles muft be entered in more than one of thefe Books, (or rather Divifions of the great Book.) For Example, I receive *Cafh* from the Tenants, I muft place it both in the *Cafh-Book*, and that of the *Tenants*. To have done, if the Concerns are fmall, fewer Books will ferve; tho' the whole in this Cafe will be no great Trouble, and in Concerns of great Extent, there ought no Pains to be fpared The Advantage of thefe *Digeft-Books* is manifeft, and a *general Memorial or Wafte-Book* is very ufeful, becaufe we can find in it, the whole Tranfactions of every Week, Month, &c. by themfelves, but efpecially becaufe Things are eafily Written down here in a plain Manner, as they occur, and fometimes in hafte, and then the Accomptant is eafy, and can take his Time for filling up the other Books, with more care and exactnefs.

(4.) To draw the whole Matter into a perfect Form, fo as we may be able to have a general Profpect of the Total, and Ballance Accompts in a regular Manner, there muft be added an univerfal *Leger* of the whole, and if you'll add a *Journal* too, it is nothing worfe for that; but the Inftructions for the *Journal* being only what Titles of Accompts we are to ufe for *Debtors* and *Creditors*, we fhall have thofe contained in the Inftructions for the *Leger*, which I fhall difpatch very foon, by fhewing what Accompts erected in the *Leger*, will comprehend a Gentleman's Bufinefs. Which are as follows.

(1.) *ACCOMPT* of the *Perfonal Eftate*, which muft contain on the *Debtor-Side*, all that is owing by the Proprietor, at making up the *Inventory*; and on the *Creditor-Side*, all the Effects, which at prefent belong to him by the *Inventory* The correfponding *Creditors* and *Debtors*, are to be found in the following Accompts

(2) *CASH* is *Debtor* for all received, and *Creditor* for all that is given out. But the *Cafh-Book* relieves this Accompt, and makes it very Short; becaufe, according to former Inftructions, the *Cafh-Book* is to be digefted once a Month, or Quarter, &c as you pleafe, and the Total only brought to the

Cafh-

Cash-Accompt in the *Leger.* —— To, *and,* By *Sundry Accompts,* as per *Cash-Book*; and the several Accompts, that have furnished, or received that *Cash,* are to be made *Creditors,* and *Debtors* in their own *Accompts* at this Time. This Accompt is clos'd with *Ballance,* being the *Cash* in Hand.

(3) *ACCOMPT* of *Houshold-Furniture, Books,* &c. it is *Debtor* for the Total, as per *Inventory* of all Manner of *Furniture, Jewels, Books,* &c. and for all afterwards purchased It is *Creditor* for what is lost, destroyed, or any way disposed of, and is closed with *Ballance* for the Value remaining

(4) *ACCOMPT* of *House-keeping.* Make it *Debtor* for all the Utensils of *Kitchen, Dairy, Brew-House,* &c. and for the Store of *Provisions* at present in the House, as per *Inventory,* and for what's afterwards purchased, also, for all the Expences of *House-keeping,* as *Money* expended, *Corn and Cattle,* &c. brought in for the Use of the House, *Wages* paid to Servants, belonging properly to the *House-keeping.* It is *Creditor* for what is due to the Servants for Wages, at making up the *Inventory*; and afterwards for all the *Waste* which happens to be sold, of that which was formerly brought in, and charged to that Accompt.

OBSERVE. A particular *Book of House-Expences* being kept, would relieve this Accompt, by bringing in the Total Monthly, but the *Cash-Book* performs this for all *Cash* immediately expended, and therefore you'll need only a *Memorial-Book* for other Things, as *Cattle, Corn,* &c. furnished from your own Stock; and these kind of Articles, may be digested the same Way, as the *Cash-Book,* and brought to the Accompts Monthly This Accompt is closed, *Creditor,* By *Ballance,* for the Value of the Utensils and Provisions remaining, and *Debtor,* To *Ballance,* for what is unpaid of the Servants Wages, for which it was at the Beginning made *Debtor*; after this it is closed with *Profit* and *Loss,* for the Difference, which is the neat Expences of *House-keeping,* within the Time of the Duration of this Accompt.

(5) *ACCOMPT* of the *Equipages.* This is an useful Accompt with very many, it is *Debtor* for the *Horses, Coaches, Furniture,* &c which are at making up the *Inventory,* and for all that is afterwards purchased, also, for all Expences, which belong properly to the *Retinue, Parade,* or *Sport.* It is *Creditor* for what Wages are due at making up the *Inventory,* to the Servants of the *Parade,* as *Groom, Coachman,* &c and for what Effects happen to be disposed of which were on the *Debtor-Side* of the Accompt. It will be closed with *Ballance, Profit* and *Loss,* as the last Accompt

(6.) IN great *House-keeping,* there will be Servants intrusted with considerable Managements, and for that Effect, a *Cash-Accompt* running in their Hands, which they receive, and lay out again, such as the *House-Keeper* For this, erect an Accompt of *Cash* in the *House-Keeper's Hands, Debtor* for all he or she receives, and *Creditor* for what, by their Accompt stated, is given out. And the like for any other Servant, who is in this manner intrusted, intrufted ; fuch as a *Steward*, who receives Rents from Tenants, and other Sums for his Mafter's behoof, and lays the fame out again upon his Accompt. Such Truftees make the *Leger Accompts* very eafy, becaufe their Accompts being called for, and ftated once a Month, or Quarter, the State of them is to be copied into the *Wafte-Book*, and then carried to the *Leger*, and *Journal*, in Sums under the feveral diftinct accomptable Titles : But take Notice that thefe Articles of *Cafh* given by your felf to the *Steward* or *Houfe-Keeper*, were, at giving them, placed in the *Cafh-Book*, and carried to the *Cafh-Accompt*, at transferring the *Cafh-Book* ; but if this State is made before that carrying forward, then charge *Cafh in Steward's Hands, Debtor* for all his Receipts , particularly to *Cafh*, for what you gave, and then at transferring the *Cafh-Book* , you muft remember that this is already done ; or omit it at entering the *Steward's Accompt*, and it will be entred at transferring the *Cafh-Book*.

OBSERVE. Thefe Accompts, as they are given in, will probably be rude enough, but you are to Methodize them, by placing every Article under proper Denominations, to make a diftinct State ; in which there is no need to write every Article ; but being fatisfied about them, you may join in one Sum feveral minute Things, to be placed in the *Wafte-Book* (or if you pleafe, you may make a feparate Book for thefe ftated Accompts) which muft not be crouded with every *Item* ; but *Items* paid, or received for the fame kind of Things, which cannot be fubdivided, put in one Sum ; and to make all more clear, you may put next each other, all fuch as belong to the fame Accompt in the *Leger*, and for Diftinctnefs, write over them what may exprefs the general Nature of every Sort : For Example, The *Steward* gives in his Accompt for one Month, wherein I find feveral Sums which he has received from the Tenants, thefe go together in diftinct Articles, and over them thefe Words, *received from divers Tenants*. Alfo, I find he has received Money for *Wool, Lambs, Butter, Cheefe and Hay* fold , thefe go in diftinct Articles, and over them is to be written, *received for feveral Things belonging to the Grazing*, and tho' there happen to be feveral *Items* in his Accompt upon each, yet, I take all the *Items* in a Total which belong to *Wool*, or to *Lambs*, &c. and fo of every Thing which has no Subdivifion. Thus the Matter will be prepared for another Form , and be ready to fettle more diftinctly in the proper Accompts of the *Leger*, (See the Accompt of *Grazing* below) In making this State, you may be lefs or more particular, as you pleafe, with the Subdivifions, but it is not good either to be too tedious, or too fhort, the one will be confufed, and the other obfcure.

THUS the monthly or quarterly Accompts of thefe Truftees or Managers, will come eafily into the Books in Totals, upon the feveral accomptable Titles ; and you'll be faved the Trouble of a Book of *Houfe-Expences*, becaufe whatever is fpent that way, is to be found in thefe ftated Accompts, and will at laft fettle in the Accompts that furnifh'd the feveral Articles ,

and

and in the Accompts of *House-Keeping*, which is *Debtor* for the whole; and remember that thefe Accompts be all called in, and ftated immediately before you Ballance and clofe your Books: But where there are no fuch Servants intrufted with the whole Disburfment, the Accompt muft be exactly kept by the Mafter himfelf, in a feparate Book, and transferred Quarterly; which will coft him the Trouble conftantly of enquiring how the Money was beftowed, and what other Things were made ufe of; unlefs he will fatisfy himfelf with a grofs Reckoning, as to the Money given out, but for other Things, he muft know them particularly for the fake of the Accompts to which they belong.

(7.) *ACCOMPT of the Husbandry*; it is *Debtor* for all the *Seed* in the *Ground*, *Utenfils* and *Cattle* of the *Plough*; which, at making the *Inventory*, belong to the Lands that are kept in Hand for the Service of the Family; as moft Gentlemen do keep more or lefs about their Seat, and afterwards for whatever is purchafed and brought in of that Kind for the Ufe of the *Husbandry*; alfo for Wages paid to Servants employed about this, and all other Expences of the *Husbandry*. It is *Creditor* for all the *Profits* made by *Corn* fold; alfo, for what is taken for the *Houfe-keeping*; and is clofed with *Ballance*, and *Profit* and *Lofs*, for the remaining Stock, and the neat *Gain* or *Lofs*.

OBSERVE. The *Corn* reaped off the Ground, ought to be placed to the *Credit* of this Accompt; but it cannot be well done, till it is threfhed out, and the Product diftinctly known; and therefore it is beft that a *Memorandum* only be made, in the Book of *Real Accompts*, of what *Corn* is reaped, until it is Threfhed; and then let the Quantity be entred in the fame Book, under the Title of, *Corn belonging to the Grounds about the Seat*, mentioning at fuch a Time fo much Threfhed out and Meafured. And as thefe are difpofed of, let the Value be fet on the *Creditor-Side* of the forefaid Accompt; which may be done in Totals, given out within a certain Time; and for what is taken for the Ufe of the Houfe, put an arbitrary Value upon it. And when you come to a general *Ballance*, you muft put an arbitrary Value on the remaining Stock of *Corn*, Threfhed, or not, and make this Accompt *Creditor* for the fame, (the *Debtor* you'll find below) then will the Accompt clofe regularly.

(8) *ACCOMPT of Grazing*: This is a Branch of what belongs to the *Grounds* in Hand; make it *Debtor* for the Value of all the *Pafture-Stock of Cattle*, which are upon the *Ground*, at making the *Inventory*, as *per Eftimate*; (and it may have inner Columns for the Species,) and afterwards for what more is purchafed and brought to increafe the Stock; alfo, for all Charges about the fame, as Servants Wages particularly employed in this, it is to be made *Creditor* for all that is difpofed of, either fold, loft, or made Ufe
of

of in the House, and particularly the *Profit* made by the *Lambs*, and other *Young* increased, as they are disposed of, and the *Wool*.

OBSERVE. (1) THE *Dairy Profits*, as *Butter* and *Cheese* sold, or made use of, properly belong to this *Accompt*; and for the *Milk* used in the House, you may put any Value on it you please, and place it to this *Accompt*, that the *Profits* may more distinctly appear; but you must also make the *Accompt* *Debtor* for all Charges of the *Dairy*, particularly the *Utensils* and *Vessels*

(2) FOR the *Corn*, *Straw* and *Hay*, consumed by the Cattle of the Pasture and Plough, they need not be stated; but what's taken to the Use of the Horses belonging to the Parade, or consumed any other way, ought to be placed to *Accompt*. And as to the *Hay*, which is thus used, or sold, place it either to this, or the former *Accompt*, no matter which: You may also Subdivide this *Accompt*, if you have a mind to it, and keep one for different Cattle. This *Accompt* closes with *Ballance*, *Profit* and *Loss*, as the former. But observe, that what increase of *Young* remain undisposed of, be first set on the *Debtor-Side*, To *Profit* and *Loss*, and then they come in to the *Ballance*, as part of the Stock in Hand.

(9.) THE *Granary Accompt*; which may have inner Columns for the several Species. Let this be charged *Debtor* for all the *Corn*, &c. that is in the *Granary*, at making the *Inventory*; and all afterwards received; particularly from the Tenants; also, for Expences belonging thereto: And *Creditor* for what's disposed of.

OBSERVE. When it is received, the Quantities are entred in the *Book of Real Accompts*; and also in the Tenants Accompts who delivers it, but no Value set upon it till disposed of, or when we come to a general *Ballance*, that the Quantity remaining must be valued And remember when any of the *Corn* belonging to the Grounds in Hand, are turned into the *Granary*, the *Accompt of Husbandry* must then be made *Creditor* for it; but the Value may stand unfilled up, until all is disposed of, or you make a Ballance.

THIS *Accompt* is closed with *Ballance*, for the Value remaining, *Profit* and *Loss*, for what's *Gain'd* or *Lost*, i. e what is received more or less than it was formerly valued at in the *Accompt*. See the Observations First and Fifth upon the next *Accompt*.

(10.) *ACCOMPT of the Land-Rents*. This is a general *Accompt* which serves in the *Leger*, for the whole Farms or Tenants, whose Book of Accompts, contains all the State of Affairs with them in a plain and particular Manner; such as will satisfy you both at all Times: But that the *Leger* may be compleat in its *Ballance*, and that you may have in it a perfect View of the whole Year's Income and Expences, and consequently of the Increase or

Decrease

Decreaſe of the Perſonal Eſtate, this Accompt muſt be uſed; which will very conveniently and compendiouſly bring in the Subſtance of the Tenants Accompts. Thus, it is *Debtor* for the Arrears due at making up the laſt *Inventory*, and afterwards for all Taxes and Repairs paid or allowed to the Tenants. It is *Creditor* for all that is paid by the Tenants of their Rent, or otherwiſe received by the Farms, ſuch as *Fines* or *Money* advanced for *Leaſes*.

OBSERVE. (1.) When any Thing is received of the Tenants, the ſame is placed in their *Book of Accompts*, and alſo in the *Caſh-Book*, and *Book of Real Accompts*, for the Articles belonging to thoſe. How the *Digeſts* of the *Caſh-Book* are made, I have already ſhewn, ſo that the Money received for Rents, comes in ſlowly, and in few Articles to this Accompt of Rents: And for the *Corn*, &c. it will come in perhaps ſlower, for the Receipts are entred both in the Book of Accompts with the Tenants, and in the Book of *Real Accompts*, but for this I would only carry it into the *Leger*, [Upon the *Granary-Accompt*, which is *Debtor* to *Land-Rents*] quarterly for what is diſpoſed of, and then enter it at the Value for which it was ſold, and what was taken for your own Uſe, ſtate at any Value you pleaſe. At the ſame time the *Granary-Accompt* muſt be made *Creditor*, for the ſame Quantity, at the ſame Value, becauſe it is diſpoſed of, the *Debtor* will be obvious, and if they are many, make it *Creditor* —— By *Sundry Accompts*. But for the *Perſonal Debtors*, it is fit they be charged in their Accompts, whenever they have bought and received it, but what goes to other Accompts comes in groſs Reckonings.

(2.) *TAXES* and *Repairs* allowed to Tenants, are to be charged in the *Caſh-Book* as *Caſh received*; and ſo it will be carry'd to the *Creditor-Side* of the *Accompt of Rents*, and immediately ſet on the *Creditor-Side*, as *Caſh* given out, and then *Accompt of Land-Rents*, will become *Debtor* for it; and thus the Ballance is exactly preſerved without any new Accompt.

(3) IF the Proprietor pays the Tithes, and takes up the ſame for the Tenants, as is practiſed in ſome Places, then theſe Tithes come into that Tenants Accompt as a Charge upon him, and when the Proprietor pays them, the *Accompt of Rents* muſt be made *Debtor*.

(4.) IF the Tenants owe you any other Articles beſides Rent, as if they buy *Corn* or *Cattle* from you, it is placed to their *Accompt*, and in the Book of *Real-Accompts*; and at transferring, the *Accompt of Land-Rents*, may Perſonate the *Debtor*, and will be alſo *Creditor* when they are paid.

(5) WHEN you come to a General *Ballance*, you muſt examine the Book of *Real Accompts*, and transfer what remains undone, and for the Quantities undiſpoſed of, charge them at the *Current*, or any Price you pleaſe, for which the *Granary Accompt* is *Debtor* to *Land-Rents*, then will both theſe Accompts cloſe. Of the one I have ſpoken already, and for the

K k

Land-Rents, clofe it *Creditor* by *Ballance* for the total *Arrears of Rent*, and other *Debts* owing by the Tenants, which you muft find by making an Abftract of the Accompts in their Books, and make *Land-Rents, Debtor*, to the *perfonal Eftate*, for the Sum of *Rent-Arrears*, before you make the Ballance; and for what other Debts they owe, it is *Debtor* to fome other Accompt, as the *Granary*, or *Accompt of Grazing*, for *Corn*, or *Cattle* bought, but probably this was ftated in fome former grofs reckoning from the Book of *Real-Accompts*, if not, it muft be done now   After this the Accompt is clofed with *Profit* and *Lofs*, which is the neat Income during the Time of this Accompt.   To find the total Arrears eafily, and in beft order, you muft make an Abftract of them in the Book of *Real-Accompts*, Thus, take as many Pages as will ferve, and having divided them into Columns for the following Ufes, fill them up from the Ballance of the *Tenants Accompts*; In the firft Column on the left Hand, fet the Perfons Names, and after it the Word, *For*, which will correfpond with the Name of the Ground he poffeffes, to be put in the next Column. Then in the next, fet the Total of the *Debtor-Side* of his Accompt, in Money Value (which muft now be put on every Thing due) both the Arrears due at commencing the Accompt, and the Year's Rent run fince; (or if you pleafe, give one Column for the laft Arrears, and another for the faid Year's Rent, and draw both into a Total, in another Column.) In the next, Place the Sum of the Difcharge.   Or divide this into feveral; in one place the Sum of the Money and other Things delivered, according as they are valued; in another, the Taxes allowed, and in another, the Repairs allowed, and then draw all thefe into a Total, in another Column.   After which follows the Remainder or Arrears due.

(11) There muft be an Accompt erected for every other Perfon with whom you deal, *Debtor* for what they owe you, and *Creditor* for what you owe them, this efpecially when your concern with them is confiderable; as when Money is borrowed or lent upon Intereft, or when Annuities or Penfions are owing, or when a great Quantity of *Corn* or *Cattle* is fold on Truft.

But there are feveral Accompts which may be conftantly running in fmall Articles with Tradefmen and Retailers; it is enough if thefe are kept in the Book of *petty Accompts*, and as the Payments are made, they are placed, both here, and in the *Cafh-Book*, and from this transferred into the *Leger*, but at making a general Ballance, this Book muft be examined, and an Abftract made of what remains due, and carried in a Total to the *Leger*, for which make the *Perfonal Eftate, Debtor to Accompt of fundry Perfons*, for feveral fmall Debts owing, as *per* Book of *petty Accompts*   It will be too much Trouble to digeft the Articles, and carry them to the feveral Accompts, for which they are owing, it is well enough for the purpose of ballancing the Book, to charge the *Perfonal Eftate* for the whole; but it would be better if all thefe Accompts were called for, and paid immediately before the clofing your Accompts.

(12.) *ACCOMPT* of *Profit* and *Lofs*. The Nature of the Charge and Difcharge of this Accompt is obvious, I have occafionally fpoken of it, in fhewing how the preceeding Accompts are clofed, what other Things in the Courfe of the Accompts belong to it, will be eafily known when they occur; fuch, as Intereft of Money received or paid, and all manner of incidental or uncertain Charges and Profits. But you may alfo fubdivide this Accompt, and bring nothing into it, till a general Ballance; when all will come into it in Totals. Thus, (1) Erect an *Accompt of Intereft*, *Debtor* for all you pay, and *Creditor* for what you receive, but the beft way is; to place to this *Accompt, the Intereft*, at the Term when due; and place the fame alfo to the Perfon's Accompts to, or by whom, due; and when paid, charge or difcharge them, but at making up the general Ballance, it will be fit to calculate, and ftate what's incurred to that Time, (whether it is a Term of Payment or not) that the Ballance may give a compleat View of the prefent State of Affairs After this clofe the Accompt with *Profit* and *Lofs*. (2) *Accompt of Incidents*; which make *Debtor* for all Charges of this Kind, as Gifts, Charity, Loffes at Game, Expences of Travelling, ordinary and extraordinary pocket Expence, &c. and *Creditor* for what's gain'd. The Accompt clofes with *Profit* and *Lofs*. It is fit the Accomptant keep a particular Accompt of thefe Things in a *Pocket-Book Memorandum*, at leaft he ought to know the Totals, which will eafily be done, by writing down every Sum of Money he puts in his Pocket, and expends this way, and what is disburfted by Servants will come in with their Accompts. But leaft there be too many Articles of Debt againft one of Credit, he may bring in here fome other Articles, which he may defire fhould, as a Fund, fupply thefe Expences; fuch as feveral contingent *Profits*, which may occur, as *Fines*, &c However, the Accompt will not be tedious, becaufe it need be filled up only every Month or Quarter.

OBSERVE The Expence of *Apparel*, and for *Education of Children*, may be placed to the Accompt of *Houfe-keeping*. To which alfo may be brought the Expence of *Orchards, and Gardens*, and to the *Creditor-Side*, the Profits of what's fold out of them, and thefe Accompts the *Gardiner* will keep and render Quarterly, &c. unlefs you would have a particular Accompt for this, which make *Debtor* for all Charges, and *Creditor* for the Profits; and in this Cafe it will be fit to fet a Value on what's furnifhed into the Houfe, and make *Houfe-keeping Debtor* for it, fo will this new Accompt be clofe with *Profit* and *Lofs*, for the neat *Gain* or *Lofs* If there be any Reafon for a feparate Accompt, it is becaufe there may be feveral

Expences

Expences about *Gardens*, which yield no Profit, but mere Pleasure, and which the Accompt of *House-keeping* has nothing to do with.

(13) T H E laft is the *Accompt of Ballances*, into which all the remaining Stock, Effects and Arrears of every Kind is brought to the *Debtor-Side*, and on the *Creditor*, all your *Debts*, It is therefore an Abftract of the total State of your Affairs, and fhews the State and Circumftances of the *Perfonal Eftate* at the time, (excepting always the current Years Rent, which is not yet due) and affords you the grofs Articles of a new *Inventory*, for another *Wafte-Book* Let this *Accompt of Ballance*, and *Profit and Lofs* be clofed with the *Accompt of the Perfonal Eftate*, and then this Accompt is ballanced, if all the Work be rightly performed, and every thing duly transferred from the *Subfervient-Books*, as I have all along directed

O B S E R V E I N making up your new Books, the particular *Inventories* muft be renewed, becaufe there may fome Alterations have happened to them, which are eafily found by the Books

Conclufion and Defence of the preceeding Inftructicns of this
S E C T I O N.

Y o u will poffibly complain of the Tedioufnefs of the Method here prefcribed , becaufe there muft be fo many Books kept ; but this Objection is foon removed, if you'll confider that the *Wafte-Book* is the leaft any prudent Man can do; the *Digefts* made out of it, are apparently the greateft Trouble , and yet you fee by the Nature and Ufe of them, how neceffary they would be , and I have propofed how the *Wafte-Book* may be abridg'd, tho' the Pains I think will be but ill faved Then for the *Leger*, its manifeft by the Defcription I have given of the Accompts, how eafie and compendious it will be ; becaufe moft of thofe Things which have many Articles, are brought here in Totals , fo that this Book is chiefly defigned for giving a neat, clean, and diftinct Abftract of the whole Bufinefs, when the Owner pleafes to call for it , but that there may not be too much to do, when this Demand comes, this Book is begun in Form, and gradually (tho' but flowly) filled up; and the clofing of the Accompts according to Art, anfwers the Demand perfectly ; and will give great Satisfaction to the Party interefted.   And if Gentlemen cannot do all the Drudgery of this Work with their own Hands, they may commit it to qualified Servants, who may do it by their Direction, and under their frequent Infpection and Examination.   But perhaps you'll fay, there is nothing faved by bringing in Things in Totals, into the *Leger*, becaufe they

are

are at large in other Books And you may therefore think, that one *Great Leger*, containing all Particulars, may be less Trouble. The Answer is plain, a *Leger-Book* kept according to Art must contain every Thing, but there's no absolute Necessity that it contain them particularly, for it's still a *Leger-Book*, if Articles are brought into an Accompt in Totals, and how particular we must be, depends upon our own Choice, which ought to be regulated by the Nature and Circumstances of the Thing, and in the present Case, besides, that a Gentleman is only accomptable to himself, and therefore may do beyond or under the Strictness of the Art as he pleases, the Matter will not so well bear it, because, (1.) You have to do with a simple Kind of People, who will require very particular and distinct Accompts, and every Thing said in the plainest Manner, therefore a separate Book with the Tenants is necessary, where their Charge and Discharge is to be set down very plain and particular (2) Most of the Accompts above mentioned, having many small *Items*, would not only swell the *Leger* too much, but make it confused, whereas by separate Accompts of Particulars, and those brought in Totals into the *Leger*, the State of Affairs becomes gradually more distinct, as they are brought into lesser Room ; and the Articles of a more diffused Accompt, being once adjusted, and the Matter reduced into a narrower Compass, as it is upon the Accompts of the *Leger*, before explained, a Gentleman needs not to be sollicitous to preserve the Rest, for that Book alone will satisfy him at any Time hereafter, how his Affairs stood at making up that Accompt, and even shew him, at least, in gross Reckonings, upon the several Accompts, by what Steps it came to that State, which the *Ballance Accompt* shows it was in ; and this Book transmitted to Posterity, will sufficiently recommend the prudent Conduct of the Owner, and be an Example of Vertue and Industry to his Successors I don't suppose however, that he may immediately throw away the other Books, because Things that are brought into the *Ballance Accompt* in gross, being to be found at large in these, they must be preserved, at least, till these Accompts are cleared, or till the State of the Accompt be adjusted betwixt Parties, in case it be necessary to produce the Particulars, but by degrees they lose their Use, and may at last be destroyed

The next (and perhaps it will be the First) Complaint, is, that I have given no Examples, I own the Imagination would be favoured by this, but I designed the Instructions of this Chapter, not for the Lazy and Indifferent, but for such as would oblige me, and themselves too, by a careful perusal of the former Treatise, and to them, I'm confident I have spoken very Plain and Intelligibly ; for whoever has any Notion of an Accompt, will easily conceive the Application from what is explained, and add or alter according to their Fancy, or as different Circumstances require For it was not to be expected, that I should mention every Thing, an apt

Genius having catched the Notion of a regular and artificial Accompt, and feen the Application in any one Inftance, will, with a little Pains, Tutor Himfelf through all the Reft. And it muft be acknowledged, that every one will take his own Choice, in the Application of general Rules, and have fome particular Ways, which perhaps may be beft for him, and it is but fit, that he who is to gain or lofe, be the Comptroller of his own Accompts, and therefore it were in vain to pretend, by numerous Applications, to foreftal their Choice; efpecially, becaufe an unforefeen Circumftance, may oblige them to take a different Way; and this I fay, not only with refpect to the Accompts of Gentlemens Concerns, but alfo to whatever elfe may require a perfect and regular Accompt.

INSTRUCTIONS *for* FACTORS, *or* STEWARDS *upon* LAND-ESTATES.

THERE is a kind of *Stewards*, who are not *Domeftick Servants* [and in *Scotland*, we call them rather *Chamberlains or Factors*] to whofe care is committed the collecting of *Rents*. They have a *Rent-Roll* of what they are to receive, which they charge themfelves with, and their Difcharge is compofed of all they have given to their Employer, or for his Accompt, or what has been given by the Tenants to their Mafter, or taken to the Houfe, alfo, whatever *Taxes or Repairs* are paid or allowed to the Tenants, Lands Wafte, or in Hand (if thefe laft are in their *Rent-Roll*) Arrears due by the Tenants, and *Corn* in the *Granaries*, and every other Thing that ought to be allowed: I'm ready to believe Thefe will draw out of the preceeding Work, fufficient Inftructions for keeping their Accompts; fo as to be able to clear with their Employers, to both their Satisfactions, and therefore I fhall give but a very general Hint of what I would have them do.

(1) A GENERAL *Wafte-Book* will be very neceffary, to contain all Matters tranfacted, relating to their *Mafter's Concerns*, under their Management.

(2.) OUT of this, let them make a *Cafh-Book*, in the Manner formerly directed; alfo, a Book of *Real Accompts*, that they may know what real Effects, befides Money, they have taken the Charge of, and how it is difpofed of, particularly the *Corn-Rents*, which have been delivered by the Tenants, and put in the *Granaries* under their Charge, to be difpofed and given out according to order. And, *Obferve*, if any of the *Farm-Corn* is fold before delivered, as it may happen, in this Cafe, Precepts are iffued to the Tenants, ordering them to deliver to the Buyer; the Tenants fhould be ordered to take a Receipt, and produce it immediately upon the

Delivery,

Delivery, and then let it be placed to their Accompt; place it also in the Book of *Real-Accompts*, both on the *Debtor-Side*, because it is delivered by the Tenants, and on the *Creditor-Side*, because it is also disposed of, and then the Digest of this Accompt will be the more distinctly made; If the Steward receives the Money for these Sales immediately, then he enters it also in the *Cash-Book*

(3) THEY must keep an exact Accompt with the Tenants in the Manner already directed, and with other Persons also, if the Business committed to them requires it

(4) IN these (to which let them add other subsidiary Books as they please, and find need) may their whole Business be comprehended, and they will be able upon a short Warning, to make a fair Accompt to their Employer, which is commonly done once a Year   Thus, let them go thro' the *Cash-Book*, and make a Digest of it, under proper Denominations, for their Master's Satisfaction at least, who will desire to know distinctly what furnished that *Cash*, and the distinct Accompts for which it was expended.   But in making up your Accompt, the first Article of Charge against you is the Accompt of Arrears, and current Year's Rent, when you entered upon the Management, therefore no more of the *Cash* received goes into your Charge, but what you received upon other Accompts, than *Money-Rent*   The Rest being in the Charge of the *Rent-Roll*, and all expended belongs to your Discharge, into which are reckoned the *Taxes* and *Repairs* paid or allowed to the Tenants   (2) The Book of *Real-Accompts* must be examined, to know what's in the *Granaries*, undisposed of, and how the Rest was disposed of, in order to your Discharge, which, for this Part of the Charge in the *Rent-Roll*, is made up of the Arrears undelivered by the Tenants, the Quantities in the *Granaries*, and the Total of what's disposed of; which you ought to digest, to shew how it was disposed of, and in the Discharge, bring it in in such a Manner as this, *viz. Sold to Sundry Persons out of the Granaries*, so much: *Given in for the House*, so much   *Received* (by such and such Persons) *from the Tenants by Precepts*, &c.   For the Money received by your Lord, for any of the Sales, you are not concerned with it, he takes the Quantity sold in your Discharge, and for what is paid in to you, the Quantity being placed on the Side of the Discharge, against so much of what is on the Side of the Charge, the Money you received for it is brought as a new Article of Charge against you from the *Cash-Book*, and if any Person to whom you sold your Lord's *Farm-Corn*, remains in Debt, which you'll know by their Accompt, make a List of such Debts, and place the Total as part of your Charge, and place it also in the Discharge, but if you only are accomptable to him for those, the Charge stands against you, and the Debtors fall in your Hand.   It is the same Case in all the Steps, when you buy the *Corn* from your Lord, to dispose of again, for your own Accompt.   (3) You must for

for your Lord's Satisfaction, make an Abstract of the Tenant's Accompts in the Manner above directed; that he may see distinctly how the Article of Arrears is made up; of the Arrears of *Corn-Rent*, I have said already. The Arrears of *Money-Rent* must also be brought to the Discharge, in a distinct Article, and the Rents of *Lands Waste*, and upon *Hand*, (when these are put in the Charge) your Year's Salary makes up the last Article of your Discharge.

Your Accompt of *Charge* and *Discharge* being thus made up, and the proper Vouchers of each Article produced, which are your Books and Papers, the *Ballance* shews what you have expended in your *Lord's Service* more than you received.

But if you would gradually prepare your self for this 'Compt and Reckoning, besides all that's formerly directed, you must have a *Leger*, in which a few general Accompts being kept, into them the Articles of your *Charge* and *Discharge* may be brought in Monthly or Quarterly Totals, from the other Books, and then they will be easily drawn into one Accompt, containing the whole State of *Charge* and *Discharge*. To perform this, let your *Leger* contain these Accompts, *viz.* (1.) *An Accompt for your Lord*, which will require a great Space, because this is the Accompt where all will terminate at last. Make it *Creditor* at your Entry, for the Arrears and current Year's Rent to be received, and afterwards for all such Articles, which, as you have seen above, belong to your *Charge*. Make it *Debtor* for what belongs to your *Discharge* Observe. This Accompt will require several inner Columns, for the Species of *Rents*, when they are many. (2.) *An Accompt of Rents belonging to*, &c. it is *Debtor*, for the Arrears, and current Year's Rent, at your Entrance; and *Creditor*, for the Rents paid by the Tenants, and every Thing allowed to them, and must have inner Columns. (3) A general *Cash-Accompt* (4.) A *Granary-Accompt*, *Debtor*, for all received, and *Creditor*, for what's given out. (5) *Accompts* for those Persons, to whom you sell your Lord's *Effects*, the *Debts* being under your Care to call in, but you may comprehend them in a general Accompt If you consider carefully the Use of these Accompts, you'll easily see how to connect the *Debtors* and *Creditors*, for the Articles which you enter, but most of them, will be the Totals of *Sundry Accompts*, and therefore in the transferring these Totals out of the several Books, (as the *Cash-Book*, and Book of *Real-Accompts*,) you must be careful to consider the Use of the Accompts here described, that you may make your Digest right, in Order to the said carrying Forwards When all is transferred, close your *Leger-Accompts* thus; carry the *Ballance* of all the Rest into the First, and then it will be ballanced · The *Creditor-Side* will shew the Total of the *Charge* against you, and the *Debtor-Side* your *Discharge*, but remember that the *Ballance* of the *Cash-Accompt*, which goes to the *Debtors-Side* of your *Lord's Accompt*, supposes you pay

him

him that immediately, otherwise you remain so much in his Debt: Or rather do this; make an *Accompt proper*, to present your self, which, make *Debtor*, for what you buy, or take, for your own Accompt, of your Lord's Effects; and make it *Creditor* by him for your Salary; and at ballancing, carry the *Ballance* of *Cash* into this Accompt, and carry the Ballance of this into your Lord's Accompt, which will itself then be ballanced; and the Article brought from your *proper Accompt*, is a Debt betwixt you and him; the other Articles of your *Discharge* being accepted. But after all, you may perhaps find this *Leger* only serviceable to your own Curiosity, for your Lord may be better Satisfied with a plain Charge and Discharge, according to the first Direction.

Some Directions for a MASTER, who Employs such STEWARDS.

FOR the *Master* who has such *Stewards*, as I have been now speaking to, he will be saved much Trouble in keeping Accompts with his Tenants, and the Thing he has to do is this, when he commits a *Charge* to his *Factor* or *Steward*, give him an Accompt in the *Leger*, and make him *Debtor* to the *Land-Rents*, for the Arrears (which being *Debtor* to the *Personal Estate* for the same, will be at last ballanced, for that Article) whatever afterwards he receives from his Factor, he must give him Credit for it; also, for whatever he receives for *Corn*, &c. sold, or any Thing brought into the House from the Tenants; and these may be filled up in Totals, in the *Leger*, from the particular Accompts kept of the same, as the *Cash-Book*, &c. and then when the *Steward* renders his Accompt, charge it with the Total of what (per *his Accompt given in*) he has received, which was not charged at the Beginning. And what besides the Things mentioned, he gives up in his Discharge, place to the *Credit* of his *Accompt*, and the *Debit* of the corresponding *Accompts*, as *Land-Rents* for the Arrears, and Salary (or *Profit* and *Loss*, for this last) the *Granary Accompt* for what remains there, &c. and then, if there is any Ballance upon his Accompt, he either clears it, or it will stand upon the Accompt. If his Commission is continued, Ballance his Accompt thus, make a new Accompt for him, and charge it *Debtor* to the old, for what he owes, or *Creditor*, if you owe him. Also, make it *Debtor* to the *Land-Rents* and *Granary-Accompt*, for the Arrears and Remains, which are to continue under his Management, in which Case, when you close the Accompts of your own Book, these Articles will come into the *Ballance* from your *Stewards Accompt*, and not from the Accompt of *Land-Rents* and *Granary*.

BUT because I suppose it most convenient for a Gentleman, who loves Regularity, to call his Servants to an *Audit* of their Accompts, immediately before he is to Ballance his own *Leger*, therefore I would let the old

L l

Accompt

Accompt of the *Steward* stand, and let the Ballance betwixt you (his *Charge* and *Discharge* being stated as directed) go into the *Accompt of Ballances*; then will the *Accompt of Land-Rents*, and *Granary*, be closed in the Manner already said, *i. e* the Arrears and Remains will come into the *Ballance-Accompt*, from these; the Quantity whereof you know, because those Accompts are made *Debtor* to the Factor for them; and then *Profit* and *Loss* takes the remaining Difference of the Accompt. So that your new Books will be opened with the same *Accompts* as the Former were; and when the *Inventory* is written into the *Waste-Book*, the first Thing you do, is that such a Factor's Commission is continued, under whose Charge is put such Arrears, &c. and in this new Book, make him *Debtor* to *Land-Rents* as before. The Method is the same, supposing a new Factor to be employed.

I F the Master pleases, he may demand and preserve a Copy of the Factor's Books, whereby he vouched the particulars of his Charge and Discharge; especially of the Book of Accompts with the Tenants, which may be useful afterwards, in case that Factor should be dismissed the Service.

F I N I S.

E R R A T A.

Page 15. Exam. 3^d. Line 4. for *Creditor*, read *Debtor*. At the Bottom of p. 23. dele *SECT* N. B. On the Top of the Page immediately following p. 96. r 97, instead of 87 and so on to the End of the Waste-Book N° 1. Page 124. Line 6 after *for*, instead of *we*, r. *which I.* Line 12 for *account of*, r. *accepted*. and in the Margent, for 5 r 6. Line 15. in the Margent (on the left Hand) for 5. r. 6. Page 128. Line 3. for *account of*, r. *accepted*. Page 135. in Lines, 24, 25, 26. after *yards*, dele *each*. Page 139 Line 5. after *Guilders*, r *at*. In Leger N°. 1 Fol. 7 on the Creditor-Side of S A L M O N S, for *To*, r. *By*. In Waste-Book, N° 2. p. 11 Article 3. Line 1. for *Brought*, r. *Bought*. and p. 13. Lin. ult. after *paid*, r. *by*. and p. 19. lin. 4. after *and*, r. *made*.

BOOKS Printed for, and Sold by J. Osborn *and* T. Longman, *at the* Ship *in* Pater-noster-Row; *and* F. Fayram, *and* E. Symon, *at the* Royal Exchange.

A New Syſtem of Arithmetick, Theorical and Practical. Wherein the Science of Numbers is Demonſtrated in a regular Courſe from its Firſt Principles, thro' all the Parts and Branches thereof; either known to the Ancients, or owing to the Improvements of the Moderns. The Practice and Application to the Affairs of Life and Commerce being alſo fully Explained: So as to make the Whole a Compleat Syſtem of Theory, for the Purpoſes of Men of Science, and of Practice, for Men of Buſineſs. By *Alexander Malcolm*, A. M. Teacher of the Mathematicks at *Aberdeen*.

A Treatiſe of Muſick, Speculative, Practical and Hiſtorical. Containing an Explanation of the Philoſophical and Rational Grounds and Principles thereof, The Nature and Office of the Scale of Muſick: The whole Art of Writing Notes ..And the general Rules of Compoſition. With a particular Account of the Antient Muſick, and a Compariſon thereof with the Modern. By *Alexander Malcolm*, A. M.

The Merchants Map of Commerce Wherein the Univerſal Manner and Matter relating to Trade and Merchandizes, are fully treated of, the Standards and current Coins of moſt Princes and Republicks obſerv'd. The real and imaginary Coins of Accounts and Exchanges expreſs'd The natural Products and artificial Commodities and Manufactures for Tranſportation declared. The Weights and Meaſures of all eminent Cities and Towns of Traffick in the Univerſe, collected one in another, and all reduc'd to the Meridian of Commerce practis'd in the famous City of *London*. By *Lewis Roberts*, Merchant. Uſeful for all Perſons who ſhall be employ'd in publick Affairs of Princes in foreign Parts, for Gentlemen and others travelling Abroad, and for all Merchants and their Factors, who negotiate in any Part of the World. The Fourth Edition, carefully corrected, and enlarg'd. To which is annexed, Advice concerning Bills of Exchange; wherein all Matters relating to Bills of Exchange, both Foreign and Domeſtick, is fully treated of. Together with that moſt perfect Treatiſe of Trade, entitled, *England*'s Benefit and Advantage by foreign Trade demonſtrated: By *Tho. Mun*, of *London*, Merchant.

Youth's Introduction to Trade and Buſineſs · Containing, 1ſt. Tables of the moſt uſeful Clerk like Contractions of Words · A Collection of the more uſeful *Engliſh* Words that are alike in Sound, but different in Signification; with proper Directions how to addreſs to Perſons of elevated Rank, and thoſe in Office. 2dly. Acquittances and Promiſſory Notes diverſify'd and adapted to ſuch Circumſtances as occur in real Buſineſs. 3dly. Variety of Bills of Parcels and Bills on Book Debts, to enter the Learner in the Manner and Method of Commerce. 4thly. Bills of Exchange with Directions neceſſary for the right Underſtanding and Management of Remittances. Several Orders for Goods, Letters of Credit, Invoyces, and other Merchant-like Examples. 5thly. Authentic Forms of ſuch Law Precedents as are moſt frequently to be met with in the Courſe of Traffick. 6thly A Collection of Queſtions to exerciſe the Learner in the Common Rules of Arithmetic, and to bring him acquainted with the Uſes, the Properties and Excellency of Numbers. Done upon the Plan of the late Colonel *Ayres*'s Eſſay. By *M. Clare*, Maſter of the Academy in Soho Square, *London*.

The

The History of the Revolutions that happen'd in the Government of the Roman Republick. Written in *French* by the Abbot *de Vertot*, of the Royal Academy of Inscriptions, &c. The Third Edition, English'd by Mr. *Ozell* from the Original newly reprinted at *Paris*, with Amendments and Additions by the Author himself, in almost every Page. In Two Volumes. To which is prefixt, a Translation of a Memorial sent from *London* by the late Earl *Stanhope* to the Abbot *de Vertot* at *Paris*; containing divers Questions relating to the Constitution of the *Roman* State. With the Abbot's Answer.

The Experienc'd Farrier, or, Farring Compleated: Containing every thing that belongs to a compleat Horseman, Groom, Farrier or Horseleach, with the Office of the Breeder, Keeper, Rider, Feeder, Buyer and Farrier: Shewing the Marks of Beauty, Goodness, Faults and Imperfections of Horses; with the best Method of Buying Dieting Shoeing, and otherwise managing of Horses for all Uses. Also plain Directions in the Knowledge of all Distempers and Accidents incident to Horses, &c. with the best Receipts and Methods used in their Cure, never published before. In two Parts Physical and Chyrurgical.

Philosophical Principles of Medicine. In Three Parts. Containing, 1. A Demonstration of the general Laws of Gravity, with their Effects upon Animal Bodys. 2. The more particular Laws which obtain in the Motion and Secretion of the vital Fluids, applied to the principal Diseases and Irregularities of the Animal Machine. 3. The primary and chief Intentions of Medicine in the Cure of Diseases, problematically propos'd and mechanically resolv'd. By *Tho. Morgan*, M. D. The Second Edition, with large Additions relating to the Nature and Manner of Animal Secretions in general, with a particular regard to the Urinary Evacuations; in which the *Bellinian* Hypothesis of Secretion is shewn to be false and absurd, as inconsistent with the Appearances of Nature, and all the Laws of Animal Motion.

An Analytick Treatise of Conick Sections, and their Use for resolving of Equations in determinate Problems; being the Posthumous Works of the Marquis *de L'Hospital*, Honorary Fellow of the Academy Royal of Sciences. Made English by *E. Stone*, F. R. S. 4to.

Mathematical Elements of Natural Philosophy, confirmed by Experiments: Or, an Introduction to Sir *Isaac Newton's* Philosophy. Written in Latin by *William James's Gravesende*, Doctor of Laws, and Philosophy, Professor of Mathematicks, and Astronomy, at *Leydon*. Translated into English by Dr. *Desaguliers*, in Two Volumes 8vo. The Second Edition corrected.

An Essay on Perspective, by the same Author. Translated into English, 8vo.

Physico Mechanical Experiments on various Subjects, containing an Account of several surprizing Phenomenas, touching Light and Electricity, producible on the Attrition of Bodies; with many other remarkable Appearances not before observ'd; together with the Explanations of all the Machines (the Figures of which are curiously Engrav'd on Copper) and other apparatus used in making the Experiments. To which is added, a Supplement containing several new Experiments, not in the former Edition. The Second Edition. By *F. Hawksbee*, F. R. S. 8vo.

Universal Arithmetick: Or, a Treatise of Arithmetical Compositions, and Resolution. By Sir *Isaac Newton*: to which is added, Dr. *Hally's* Method of finding the Roots of Equation Arithmetically. Translated from the Latin, by the late Mr. *Raphson*, and Revised and Corrected by Mr. *Cunn*, 8vo.

Introduction to Natural Philosophy: Or, Philosophical Lectures read in the University of *Oxford*, *Anno Dom.* 1700. To which are added, the Demonstrations of Monsieur *Huygens* Theorems, concerning the Centrifugal Force and Circular Motion. By *John Keil*, M. D. Savilian Professor of Astronomy, F. R. S. Translated from the last Edition of the Latin, 8vo.

For Product Safety Concerns and Information please contact our EU
representative GPSR@taylorandfrancis.com Taylor & Francis Verlag GmbH,
Kaufingerstraße 24, 80331 München, Germany

Printed and bound by CPI Group (UK) Ltd, Croydon, CR0 4YY
08/05/2025
01864370-0020